Europe United

A VOLUME IN THE SERIES

Cornell Studies in Security Affairs
edited by Robert J. Art, Robert Jervis, and Stephen M. Walt

A list of titles in this series is available at www.cornellpress.cornell.edu.

Europe United

*Power Politics and the Making of
the European Community*

Sebastian Rosato

CORNELL UNIVERSITY PRESS
ITHACA AND LONDON

Cornell University Press gratefully acknowledges receipt of a
grant in support of this publication from the Institute for Scholarship in the Liberal Arts, College of Arts and Letters, University
of Notre Dame.

First published 2011 by Cornell University Press

Printed in the United States of America

Library of Congress Cataloging-in-Publication Data

Rosato, Sebastian, 1972–
    Europe united : power politics and the making of the
European Community / Sebastian Rosato.
        p.   cm.—(Cornell studies in security affairs)
    Includes bibliographical references and index.
    ISBN 978-0-8014-4935-2 (cloth : alk. paper)
    1. European cooperation.   2. Europe—Foreign
relations—1945–   3. Europe—Economic integration.
4. Europe—Military relations.   5. Balance of power.
I. Title.   II. Series: Cornell studies in security affairs.

    JZ1570.A5R67 2011
    341.24'2—dc22
                                    2010025714

Cloth printing   10 9 8 7 6 5 4 3 2 1

To my parents

Contents

Tables

Acknowledgments

A wise man once told me that I could not survive in this business unless I surrounded myself with a lot of smart and supportive people. I have had the good fortune to come across both over the years, and it is a pleasure to acknowledge them here.

I owe my greatest intellectual debt to John Mearsheimer, who taught me everything I know about being a scholar. He has been a formidable critic, an unfailing supporter, and a good friend. Robert Pape was a constant source of ideas and had more faith in my abilities than I did. I am grateful for his insights and enthusiasm. Carles Boix and Duncan Snidal helped sharpen my arguments and provided encouragement every step of the way.

I am profoundly grateful to Michael Creswell, John Deak, Michael Desch, Alex Downes, Mark Gilbert, Michael Horowitz, Keir Lieber, Piers Ludlow, Michelle Murray, John Schuessler, Dominic Tierney, and my two reviewers, one of whom turned out to be Robert Art, for reading and commenting on the entire manuscript and on parts of it more than once. This book is immeasurably better for all of their efforts.

For comments and conversations that had a significant effect on my thinking as I worked on the project, I thank Nick Biziouras, Olivier Brighenti, Jasen Castillo, Maria Fanis, Frank Gavin, Charles Glaser, Seth Jones, Jenna Jordan, Dong Sun Lee, Charles Lipson, James McAllister, Timothy McKeown, Kathleen McNamara, John Owen, Craig Parsons, Mark Sheetz, Paul Staniland, Milan Svolik, Robert Trager, Lora Viola, Stephen Walt, Alexander Wendt, Joel Westra, Mark Wilson, and especially Marc Trachtenberg. My thanks also to Kathy Anderson, Cheri Gray, Susan Lynch, and Ann Townes for looking after me along the way. I am very grateful to Roger Haydon for shepherding me through the entire process at Cornell University Press, Ange Romeo-Hall for patiently guiding me through editing and production, and Mary McGovern for superb last-minute editing. My apologies to anyone I forgot.

I have had the good fortune to be invited to present my ideas at the Program on International Security Policy and the Program on International Politics, Economics, and Security at the University of Chicago, the Belfer Center for Science and International Affairs and the John M. Olin Institute for Strategic Studies at Harvard University, the European Union Center of Excellence at the University of Pittsburgh, the Security Studies Program at the Massachusetts Institute of Technology, the Burkle Seminar on Global Affairs at the University of California, Los Angeles, the Triangle Institute for Security Studies, and the Lone Star National Security Forum. I am grateful to all the participants at these workshops and seminars for their excellent questions and suggestions.

For invaluable research assistance, I am indebted to Andrew Bertoli, Mark Bond, Robert Brathwaite, Carol Hendrickson, Nicholas Houpt, Jacqueline Kallberg, Colleen Noonan, Maria Petnuch, Charles Ramsey, Michael Rowley, and Colleen Walter. Thanks are also due to the students who took my classes at the University of Chicago, the University of Notre Dame, and in Rome for debating many of the issues in this book with me before my own views were fully formed.

Despite these many intellectual debts, I alone am responsible for any remaining errors in the book.

I could not have written this book without the generous financial and logistical support I received from the Program on International Security Policy at the University of Chicago, the John M. Olin Institute for Strategic Studies and the Belfer Center for Science and International Affairs at Harvard University, and the Nanovic Institute for European Studies, the Institute for Scholarship in the Liberal Arts, and the Joan B. Kroc Institute for International Peace Studies at the University of Notre Dame. I am very grateful to everyone associated with these wonderful institutions, and especially Agustín Fuentes, A. James McAdams, Steven Miller, Daniel Philpott, Stephen Rosen, and Monica Duffy Toft.

I dedicate this book to my parents, Pasquale and Judith, who have been a constant source of love, support, and advice. I aspire to be the kind of parent that they have been to me. I would also be remiss if I did not thank my brothers, William and Michael, for keeping things in perspective.

Last but by no means least, I thank my girls. My daughters, Anna and Olivia, serve as a much-needed reminder that there is a lot more to life than my work. They are my pride and joy. Most of all, though, I thank my wife, Susan, without whom none of this would have been possible. She is my inspiration and my best friend. The next one is for her.

Abbreviations

ACC	Allied Control Council
AHC	Allied High Commission
ASEAN	Association of Southeast Asian Nations
BDI	Federation of German Industries
BOT	Board of Trade (UK)
BTO	Brussels Treaty Organization
CACM	Central American Common Market
CDU	Christian Democratic Union (FRG)
CEEC	Committee on European Economic Cooperation
CFM	Conference of Foreign Ministers
CFSP	Common Foreign and Security Policy
CNPF	National Council of French Employers
EC	European Community
ECA	Economic Cooperation Administration (US)
ECB	European Central Bank
ECSC	European Coal and Steel Community
ECUSG	European Customs Union Study Group
EDC	European Defense Community
EEC	European Economic Community
EERA	European Exchange Rate Agreement
EMA	European Monetary Agreement
EMS	European Monetary System
EMU	Economic and Monetary Union

EP	European Parliament
EPC	European Political Community
ESDP	European Security and Defense Policy
EU	European Union
Euratom	European Atomic Energy Community
FDP	Free Democratic Party (FRG)
FNSEA	National Federation of Farmers' Unions (France)
FRG	Federal Republic of Germany
FTA	Free Trade Area
GDP/GNP	Gross Domestic / National Product
IAR	International Authority for the Ruhr
JCS	Joint Chiefs of Staff (US)
MAC	Mutual Aid Committee (UK)
MAD	Mutual Aid Department (UK)
MRP	Popular Republican Movement (France)
MSB	Military Security Board
NAC	North Atlantic Council
NAFTA	North American Free Trade Agreement
NATO	North Atlantic Treaty Organization
NSC	National Security Council (US)
OEEC	Organization for European Economic Cooperation
OFD	Overseas Finance Division (UK)
OMGUS	Office of Military Government, United States
OSS	Office of Strategic Services (US)
PCF	French Communist Party
PPS	Policy Planning Staff (US)
RPF	Rally of the French People
RRF	Rapid Reaction Force
SACEUR	Supreme Allied Commander, Europe
SEA	Single European Act
SFIO	French Socialist Party
SPD	Social Democratic Party (FRG)
UEF	Union of European Federalists
WEU	Western European Union

1. Introduction

Western Europe, observed Winston Churchill less than two years after World War II, was "a rubble-heap, a charnel-house, a breeding-ground of pestilence and hate." Like many of his contemporaries, the former prime minister attributed the continent's misery to the nation-state system. A region divided into sovereign states animated by "ancient nationalistic feuds" could not remain reliably at peace. Indeed, his great fear was that the continent would never recover its past glories because the Europeans would "go on harrying and tormenting one another by war and vengeance" and "squander the first fruits of their toil upon the erection of new barriers, military fortifications and tariff walls."

Churchill's diagnosis of the situation prompted him to call for a "United Europe" based on Franco-German reconciliation. "If the people of Europe resolve to come together and work together for mutual advantage," he told his listeners, "they still have it in their power to sweep away the horrors and miseries which surround them, and to allow the streams of freedom, happiness and abundance to begin again their healing flow." Western Europe had a "supreme opportunity, and if it be cast away, no one can predict that it will ever return or what the resulting catastrophe will be."[1]

With the benefit of hindsight, most observers would argue that the Europeans have seized Churchill's "supreme opportunity" and built a "United Europe." Once distinct and competing nation-states are now members of a supranational community that has no parallel in modern times. That this should have happened in the very region that gave birth to the nation-state system makes the achievement all the more remarkable. How,

1. Winston Churchill, *Never Give In! The Best of Winston Churchill's Speeches*, ed. Winston S. Churchill (New York: Hyperion, 2003), 437–38.

then, are we to explain this extraordinary political development? More specifically, how can we account for the construction of the European Community (EC)?[2]

The Argument

My central argument is that the making of the European Community is best understood as an attempt by the major west European states, and especially France and Germany, to balance against the Soviet Union and one another.

In the first instance, the Europeans were driven together by their collective fear of Soviet domination. When the guns fell silent on May 8, 1945, the Soviet Union was by far the most powerful state in Europe. None of the former great powers in the western half of the continent could hope to balance its power on their own. Moreover, they worried that the Americans, who had stepped in to defend them from the USSR after the war, might withdraw their forces in the not-too-distant future. This being the case, their only option if they wanted to provide for their own security, especially over the longer term, was the construction of some kind of west European coalition. Vladislav Zubok puts the point well: "In a sense, the Cold War polarization was the 'midwife' of the European Community."[3]

The sheer magnitude of the Soviet threat convinced the west Europeans that they must surrender their sovereignty and construct a military-economic coalition governed by a central authority. There was general agreement that a traditional alliance of the major states in the western half of Europe would be no match for the Soviet Union. Although a regular coalition of their national armies might approximate the Red Army in terms of size, it would not be nearly as effective as the single military force at Moscow's disposal. Similarly, as long as they retained separate national economies, they would not benefit from the economies of scale and technological advances that were accruing—and would continue to accrue—to the USSR by virtue of its vast single economic space. In order to compete effectively with the Soviets without U.S. help, the Europeans would have to establish a single military and economy of their own, a task that would, in turn, entail the creation of a central governing authority. This was not a welcome prospect since it required them to surrender their sovereignty over key policy areas. But the Europeans believed they had little choice. If

2. With the signature of the Treaty on European Union on February 7, 1992, the EC came to be known as the European Union (EU). Because this book is concerned mainly with events prior to 1992, I refer to the European Community, the Community, or the EC throughout.

3. Vladislav Zubok, "The Soviet Union and European Integration from Stalin to Gorbachev," *Journal of European Integration History* 2, no. 1 (1996): 85.

they were to avoid domination by the Soviet Union, then centralization was the only option. As Tony Judt notes, "For nations reared within living memory on grandeur and glory, 'Europe' would always be an uncomfortable transition: a compromise, not a choice."[4]

France and West Germany were fairly evenly matched and therefore agreed to share control of the emerging centralized coalition, an arrangement that has come to be known as integration. In power terms, there was little difference between France and the Federal Republic in the 1950s, and consequently both Paris and Bonn understood that they could not seize control of the coalition. They therefore settled for the more modest goal of preserving the roughly even balance of power between them. The best way to do that, they concluded, was to control the group jointly. If control was shared, they would have an equal say in policymaking, and the policies reached through the joint decision-making process would be applied uniformly to both of them.

In short, integration was at root a response to balance of power considerations. The decision to surrender sovereignty and establish a centrally governed coalition was driven by fear of the overwhelming power of the Soviet Union. No group of European states had faced such a mighty adversary since the advent of the nation-state system. Even as they came together in this unprecedented way, however, the French and the West Germans eyed one another warily and worried about the distribution of power within the coalition. It was this concern that led them to conclude that they had to share control of the group: to integrate and establish a community. Integration was the only formula that could conceivably maintain the existing, relatively even, balance of power between them.

Major Events

This kind of reasoning played out twice in the 1950s and in doing so established the core of today's EC. The European Coal and Steel Community (ECSC) was clearly the product of balance of power considerations. The French proposed the heavy-industry pool on May 9, 1950, believing that a centrally governed and jointly managed community of this kind would simultaneously establish a bulwark against Soviet expansion and maintain an even balance of power between France and the newly established Federal Republic. The Germans shared this view. Chancellor Konrad Adenauer, for example, was convinced of the need to construct a substantial counterweight to Soviet power in the western half of the continent and understood that the most Germany could hope for was joint control of the emerging entity. Given such a coincidence of views, it was only a matter of time before the two sides ironed out the details. France, Germany, Italy, and the Benelux states (Belgium, the Netherlands, and Luxembourg)—the

4. Tony Judt, *Postwar: A History of Europe since 1945* (New York: Penguin, 2005), 769.

Six—signed the Treaty of Paris establishing the ECSC on April 18, 1951, and the coal and steel pool began operations on July 23, 1952.

In the mid-1950s, the west Europeans went a step further and created the European Economic Community (EEC), again based on balance of power thinking. Although there had been talk of a full-blown economic community for some time, the process that ultimately led to the creation of the EEC began on June 3, 1955, when the Six declared their intention to establish common economic institutions, progressively fuse their national economies, and create a common market. The French and German decisions to commit to the process were based on pure balance of power calculations: a jointly controlled, regionwide economic community would produce enough power to deter Soviet aggression in the event of an American withdrawal from the continent and maintain a rough balance of power within western Europe. It took some time to negotiate the details of the agreement, but the decision had been made. On March 25, 1957, the Six signed the Treaty of Rome establishing the EEC.

The Europeans took it for granted that their economic community had to be buttressed by a fixed exchange rate system in order to survive.[5] The general view, notes Sima Lieberman, was that currency fluctuations "led to trade wars, increased protectionism and a general fall in national income." As Francesco Giavazzi and Alberto Giovannini observe, this meant that the Europeans had a "pronounced . . . distaste for exchange rate volatility."[6]

Early on, the stability they were looking for was provided by their common membership in the Bretton Woods fixed exchange rate system. "It should be borne in mind," states Jacques van Ypersele, "that the creation of the European Economic Community took place in the context of international monetary stability. The Bretton Woods system . . . was at the time not in dispute. Therefore it was nearly unthinkable to set up in the EEC an independent monetary system."[7] Horst Ungerer makes essentially the

5. On this point, see Emmanuel Apel, *European Monetary Integration, 1958–2002* (London: Routledge, 1998), 29; Barry Eichengreen, *The European Economy since 1945: Coordinated Capitalism and Beyond* (Princeton: Princeton University Press, 2007), 189, 246; Francesco Giavazzi and Alberto Giovannini, *Limiting Exchange Rate Flexibility: The European Monetary System* (Cambridge: MIT Press, 1989), 1–7; and Horst Ungerer, *A Concise History of European Monetary Integration: From EPU to EMU* (Westport, Conn.: Quorum, 1997), 55, 63, 97, 128, 137. I follow Jeffry A. Frieden in treating arrangements that require states to keep their currencies within narrow exchange rate target zones as equivalent to fixed rate systems ("Real Sources of European Currency Policy: Sectoral Interests and European Monetary Integration," *International Organization* 56, no. 4 [2002]: 834, n. 3).

6. Sima Lieberman, *The Long Road to a European Monetary Union* (Lanham, Md.: University Press of America, 1992), 6; and Giavazzi and Giovannini, *Limiting*, 6.

7. Jacques van Ypersele, *The European Monetary System: Operation and Outlook* (Cambridge, Mass.: Woodhead Faulkner, 1985), 34. On Bretton Woods, see Michael D. Bordo, "The Bretton Woods International Monetary System: A Historical Overview," in *A Retrospective on the Bretton Woods System: Lessons for International Monetary Reform,*

same point: "When the negotiations on the EEC Treaty started, there existed a global monetary framework . . . that did not seem to require, on a regional basis, specific obligations for the coordination of monetary and exchange rate policies."[8]

Nevertheless, because they believed that the Bretton Woods rules allowed for an unacceptable degree of exchange rate fluctuation and that large swings might damage the community, the Europeans tailored the system to their own needs. The European Monetary Agreement (EMA), which entered into force on December 27, 1958, required participating states to limit exchange rate movements to three quarters of the spread allowed by Bretton Woods.[9]

By the late 1950s, then, balance of power considerations had pushed the Europeans to integrate their economies. Fearing they might be left to contain the Soviets without American help and cognizant that their long-term power rested on an economic base, they established a multistate economic coalition. This was no ordinary arrangement, however. Given the Soviet Union's overwhelming power advantage, the west Europeans understood that they would only be competitive if they built a single regional economy governed by a central authority. Thus, there is good evidence "pointing to Joseph Stalin as the true federator of Western Europe."[10] At the same time, none of the major players had the power to seize command of the emerging entity and none were willing to hand over the reins to their partners. They therefore agreed to a system of joint control. In doing so, they became the first group of states to establish an integrated economic community in modern times.

These economic successes were not replicated in the military realm. Although the Six signed a treaty establishing a European Defense Community (EDC) on May 27, 1952, the French National Assembly rejected it on August 30, 1954, thereby wrecking any chance that the Europeans would establish an integrated military force. Two months later, the Six and Britain agreed to form the Western European Union (WEU), a traditional military alliance that was itself embedded in the North Atlantic Treaty Organization (NATO).

The French decision, which is the key to understanding the whole affair, was clearly informed by balance of power calculations: NATO involved a commitment of U.S. power to the continent and would therefore

---

ed. Michael D. Bordo and Barry Eichengreen (Chicago: University of Chicago Press, 1993), 3–108. Note that the "full-blown" Bretton Woods system did not operate in Europe until December 1958 when the Six established current account convertibility.

8. Ungerer, *Concise*, 46.

9. For brief overviews of the EMA, see Apel, *European*, 24–25; and Ungerer, *Concise*, 29–30.

10. Josef Joffe, "Europe's American Pacifier," *Foreign Policy* no. 54 (1984): 69. Joffe disagrees with this assessment, arguing that integration was the result of the American presence in Europe during the cold war.

do more to offset Soviet and German capabilities than any purely European arrangement. Better still, France would not have to take the particularly undesirable step of surrendering military sovereignty to a supranational institution. Even with the United States agreeing to underwrite the NATO system, however, a problem remained: the Europeans continued to fear that the Americans might withdraw from the continent at a later date. This was where the WEU came in by providing the basis for a purely European military force in the event of American abandonment—it was, in effect, an embryonic defense community—and simultaneously ensuring that West Germany could not grow much more powerful than France.

The other notable "failure" was the United Kingdom's consistent refusal to engage in integration. This is not to say that the British opposed their continental allies' attempts to establish a community. In fact, they generally supported those efforts and wanted to be associated closely with whatever entity emerged from the discussions. But they would not consider integration for themselves, refusing to enter into the negotiations that would lead to the ECSC and EDC treaties, and quickly withdrawing from the EEC process. Their approach also reflected balance of power thinking. Like the French and the Germans, they were aware of the need to build a counterweight to Soviet power, hence their willingness to cooperate with the continent. At the same time, however, they understood that the luck of geography meant they were less immediately endangered than their allies, so they opted to buck-pass the integration burden to them. Britain would cooperate with the continental states for their common defense, but France and Germany would pay the sovereignty costs of forming a centralized balancing coalition that could contain the Soviet Union.

Focusing on the '50s

It should be clear by now that I seek to explain events in Europe prior to 1960. I do so because the early cold war was a time of revolutionary change in the construction of the EC, whereas the period since then is best described as one of incremental development. Joseph Weiler makes the point well: "The importance of developments in this early period cannot be overstated. They transcend anything that has happened since."[11]

The organization of western Europe underwent a seismic change in the 1950s. In 1945, European integration was inconceivable. Within a decade and a half, however, the Six had constructed an integrated economic community that still exists today, albeit in modified form. By signing on to the ECSC and EEC treaties and the EMA, they committed to establish a single trading and monetary entity in the western half of the continent. Much re-

---

11. Joseph H. H. Weiler, *The Constitution of Europe: "Do the New Clothes Have an Emperor?" and Other Essays on European Integration* (Cambridge: Cambridge University Press, 1999), 16.

mained to be done, of course. As far as trade was concerned, the common market envisaged by the Treaty of Rome was not completed until 1968. But the decision to integrate and its initial implementation happened in the previous decade. Nor were the results instantaneous in the monetary realm. Nevertheless, the conclusion that they had achieved monetary integration was commonplace by the early 1960s. As Loukas Tsoukalis notes, there was a "widespread belief" by then, "at least in the Community circles, that a *de facto* monetary union had already been achieved." It was "considered as something bordering on sacrilege," observed a senior European Commission official, "to throw doubt on the permanent stability of exchange rates within the Community."[12]

The EC evolved substantially but incrementally in the ensuing decades. There were no transformative developments such as political, military, or fiscal integration. Nor were there any revolutionary alterations to the trading and monetary arrangements worked out in the early cold war. The most consequential change in the area of trade was the Single European Act (SEA), which went into effect on July 1, 1987, and set the objective of turning the common market into a single market.[13] Although the Europeans had, for the most part, removed internal tariffs and quotas and completed the common market, the goal of a barrier-free single market in the movement of goods, services, labor, and capital envisaged by the EEC treaty had yet to be achieved in the mid-1980s. The SEA rectified matters by calling for the removal of all previously legal nontariff barriers to the free movement of goods and factors of production by 1992. This was an important decision to be sure, but it did not mark a radical departure in the integration process. The SEA signatories were members of an integrated trade bloc before and after they promulgated the act, even if the scope of that bloc increased after 1987. This claim is not that controversial. According to Emmanuel Apel, the SEA simply "*reinforced* the original provisions of the Treaty of Rome." Meanwhile, Michael Gehler describes an "*evolution* from customs union to internal market . . . that took decades."[14]

Nor were there any revolutionary changes in monetary affairs. The first revision to the monetary regime came after the collapse of the Bretton Woods system when the former EMA participants sought to establish an exclusively European fixed exchange rate arrangement to replace it.[15] Their efforts spawned two different agreements in the 1970s: the European

12. Loukas Tsoukalis, *The Politics and Economics of European Monetary Integration* (London: George Allen and Unwin, 1977), 61–62.

13. For a history of the single market, see Gilles Grin, *The Battle of the Single European Market: Achievements and Economics, 1945–2000* (London: Kegan Paul, 2003).

14. Apel, *European*, 81; and Michael Gehler, "From Paneurope to the Single Currency: Recent Studies on the History of European Integration," *Contemporary European History* 15, no. 2 (2006): 283. Emphases added.

15. There were some suggestions that the Six establish a purely European system prior to 1970. See Tsoukalis, *Politics*, 51–81.

Exchange Rate Agreement (EERA), or "Snake," which went into effect on April 24, 1972, and the European Monetary System (EMS), which began operations on March 13, 1979.[16] Both were fixed but adjustable exchange rate systems that basically replicated the Bretton Woods and EMA arrangements, and therefore neither can be regarded as transformational. Again, this is an uncontroversial claim. Barry Eichengreen, for example, views the Snake as an attempt to "recreate the Bretton Woods system on a regional basis." Meanwhile, Ungerer points out that "it often has been said that the EMS was not much more than an enlarged snake and a regional Bretton Woods system." Giavazzi and Giovannini describe it as "simply a recent step in the historical quest for exchange rate stability in Europe."[17]

In contrast to these earlier agreements, the Maastricht Treaty ushering in Economic and Monetary Union (EMU) is often described as a revolutionary development.[18] Signed on February 7, 1992, it listed a set of macroeconomic and fiscal preconditions for participation in an economic and monetary union and laid out a process culminating in the creation of a single currency, the euro, and an independent European Central Bank (ECB) committed to price stability. The ECB began operations on June 1, 1998, and participating states locked their currencies on January 1, 1999, prompting Richard Cooper to declare the inauguration of "one of the most momentous monetary experiments of all time."[19]

Although the introduction of the euro and the creation of the ECB were events of great consequence, neither can be considered a revolution in the integration process. Clearly the single currency is a stricter arrangement than the fixed rate systems that preceded it. Therefore there is no doubt that the west Europeans accepted tighter constraints on their sovereignty when they adopted the euro. But, as Jeffry Frieden argues, the difference between it and its predecessors is a matter of degree, not of kind.[20] France and Germany adopted a stricter fixed exchange rate system, and the importance of their decision is not to be underestimated, but they did not fundamentally alter their sovereign status. Had they transitioned from a floating system to a pegged one, then they would have exchanged a situation in which they were formally sovereign in monetary matters for one in which

16. For an overview of the Snake and EMS, see Daniel Gros and Niels Thygesen, *European Monetary Integration* (London: Longman, 1992), 15–24, 34–99.

17. Eichengreen, *European*, 247; Ungerer, *Concise*, 164; and Giavazzi and Giovannini, *Limiting*, 1.

18. On Maastricht, see Kenneth Dyson and Kevin Featherstone, *The Road to Maastricht: Negotiating Economic and Monetary Union* (Oxford: Oxford University Press, 1999).

19. Richard N. Cooper, "European Monetary Integration, 1958–2002," *Foreign Affairs* 78, no. 2 (1999): 141.

20. Jeffry A. Frieden, "Economic Liberalization and the Politics of European Monetary Integration," in *Liberalization and Foreign Policy*, ed. Miles Kahler (New York: Columbia University Press, 1997), 239.

they were not. But they did not make this move in 1999. Rather, they essentially traded one fixed exchange rate regime for another.

Nor was the creation of the central bank a transformative step in terms of monetary sovereignty. William Bernhard, J. Lawrence Broz and William Roberts Clark have argued convincingly that despite important differences between them, fixing exchange rates and establishing an independent central bank can be viewed as "alternative forms" of monetary policy delegation.[21] Both require states to surrender their monetary autonomy. This has two implications in the case at hand. First, the Europeans were giving up more sovereignty than they had done to that point when they established a central bank. Second, the more politically consequential act of surrendering sovereignty at all had been taken in the 1950s when they pegged their exchange rates for the first time in decades. In other words, the ECB was much like the inauguration of the euro—it involved the alteration of an existing system, not the inception of a new one. As Andrew Moravcsik explains, "The single market and currency increasingly appear . . . as the *finishing touches* to the construction of a European economic zone."[22]

Thus, by zeroing in on events in the 1950s, I account for a fundamental development: Europe's shift from sovereign state system to supranational community. Needless to say, this is not the only possible focus of inquiry. Analysts could seek to explain why the EC developed as it did after its formation, and there is, in fact, an extensive literature on the widening and deepening of the community. For scholars of international politics, however, the crucial task is figuring out why the states of western Europe took the virtually unprecedented step of giving up their sovereignty in the first place. Moravcsik puts the point well: "The most fundamental puzzle confronting those who seek to understand European integration [is] . . . to explain why sovereign governments . . . have chosen repeatedly to coordinate their core economic policies and surrender sovereign prerogatives within an international institution."[23]

Extensions

An understanding of balance of power politics can tell us a lot about international cooperation—certainly more than is generally assumed—and about the future of the EC.

Although I am interested mainly in explaining the construction of the EC, my argument applies to interstate cooperation more broadly. Specifically,

---

21. William Bernhard, J. Lawrence Broz, and William Roberts Clark, "The Political Economy of Monetary Institutions," *International Organization* 56, no. 4 (2002): 695.

22. Andrew Moravcsik, "Despotism in Brussels? Misreading the European Union," *Foreign Affairs* 80, no. 3 (2002): 121. Emphasis added.

23. Andrew Moravcsik, *The Choice for Europe: Social Purpose and State Power from Messina to Maastricht* (Ithaca: Cornell University Press, 1998), 1.

if we know how capabilities are distributed among a group of states and how the members of that group compare in power terms to a common adversary, then we can predict whether or not they will cooperate and, if they do, what form their cooperation will take. Indeed, balance of power considerations appear at least partially to explain the origins and shape of dozens of cooperative ventures, ranging from alliances and trade pacts at one end of the spectrum to national unifications at the other.

The key to understanding the Community's future is the collapse of the Soviet Union in 1991, which fundamentally altered the European balance of power. During the cold war, the Soviet threat gave the west Europeans a powerful incentive to integrate, and they responded by forming the EC. The Soviet Union's demise has removed that incentive. This being the case, France, Germany, and the others are unlikely to go down the road of political or military integration, and further economic integration is improbable. Indeed, as time passes, the economic community is likely to bear little resemblance to its current form.

Events since the end of the cold war support this pessimistic conclusion. Despite lofty rhetoric to the contrary, the Europeans have not considered, let alone attempted, political integration in the past two decades. Experts agree, for example, that even the much-hyped European Constitution was in no way a blueprint for political union. A similar story applies in the military realm. Although the Europeans have certainly cooperated in military affairs, they have not made any move toward establishing an integrated defense community. In other words, there has been no meaningful political or military integration since 1991. With no threat on the horizon that compares to the cold war Soviet Union, this will probably remain the case.

The economic community, meanwhile, is likely to unravel over time to the point where it becomes a shadow of its former self. Simply put, the collapse of the Soviet Union has shorn it of its fundamental purpose. Consequently, narrow national self-interest is likely to trump commitment to the Community, thereby condemning it to a slow demise. The effects of the end of the cold war have been felt for some time now. To be sure, prosperous economic conditions during the 1990s ensured that the EC survived the death of the USSR. But worsening conditions since the turn of the millennium have seen the reemergence of nationalism—member states, especially France and Germany, have consistently put national interests ahead of those of the Community, routinely violating the rules that underpin the single market and the single currency. With further economic woes on the horizon, this process of unraveling is likely to continue.

Debates

My account stands in stark contrast to the conventional wisdom. According to one popular current of thought, the EC is the product of a desire to transcend the nation-state system. By the late 1940s, so the story goes, the Europeans had concluded that competing national political units were the cause of war and must be eliminated if the continent was to remain at peace. As members of a supranational community rather than separate nation-states, France and Germany would be less likely to compete and more likely to cooperate. "Determined that they would never again take up arms against one another," argues Jeremy Rifkin in a prominent statement of this view, "the nations of Europe searched for a political mechanism that could bring them together and move them beyond their ancient rivalries." Their solution was the EC. Jean-Baptiste Duroselle makes broadly the same argument in his European Commission–sanctioned history of Europe: "Many Europeans felt that the sheer scale of Europe's devastation obliged them to start afresh. What they must do was heal past wounds and mend rifts—bring about, in fact, a profound and historic reform by uniting, in whatever fashion, the different European states."[24]

The claim that European integration is best understood in terms of the enlightened pursuit of economic self-interest may be even more influential. Alan Milward offers a trenchant statement of this argument, asserting that the "true origins of the European Community are economic and social," and that the only arrangements "with any chance of success were those which found the point of intersection with the successful pursuit of the national economic and social advantage of all parties." John Gillingham concurs in his magisterial account of the integration process, claiming that most European statesmen were committed from the outset to a "recovery process that would eventually restore a Europe wrecked by two world wars to economic conditions like those that had obtained in the nineteenth century . . . a place where re-knit commercial and financial ties between nations would create essential networks of prosperity and so prevent war." This is also the view of T. R. Reid, who believes that the initial impulse toward union was a desire "to produce, once and for all, an end to war on the continent, and an end to poverty." To his mind, the EC is the culmination of a "plan for profits and for peace at the same time."[25]

Although proponents of these schools of thought disagree, sometimes vehemently, about the origins of the EC, virtually all of them would reject my claim that the drive to integration was a product of balance of power thinking. The view was neatly summed up by German foreign minister Joschka Fischer in a speech at Humboldt University at the turn of the

24. Jeremy Rifkin, *The European Dream: How Europe's Vision of the Future Is Quietly Eclipsing the American Dream* (Cambridge: Polity, 2005), 200; and Jean-Baptiste Duroselle, *Europe: A History of Its Peoples*, trans. Richard Mayne (London: Viking, 1990), 383.

25. Alan S. Milward, *The European Rescue of the Nation-State* (London: Routledge, 1992), xi; John Gillingham, *European Integration, 1950–2003: Superstate or New Market Economy?* (Cambridge: Cambridge University Press, 2003), 3; and T. R. Reid, *The United States of Europe: The New Superpower and the End of American Supremacy* (New York: Penguin, 2005), 25, 42.

millennium: "European integration was the response to centuries of a precarious balance of powers on this continent which again and again resulted in terrible hegemonic wars. . . . The core of the concept of Europe after 1945 was, and still is, a rejection of the European balance-of-power principle . . . a rejection which took the form of closer meshing of vital interests and the transfer of nation-state sovereign rights to supranational European institutions."[26] In other words, the consensus view is that the origins of the EC lie in the rejection of balance of power politics, not its application.

The argument presented here is also likely to be controversial within the academy. Much like the public debate, the conventional scholarly wisdom holds that the EC is best understood as a product of economic self-interest or dissatisfaction with the nation-state system. Moravcsik focuses on the first of these motivations in *The Choice for Europe*, probably the most important book on this subject by a political scientist. He begins with the claim that powerful producers in France and West Germany stood to benefit from commercial liberalization and therefore called for interstate cooperation in the removal of barriers to intra-European trade. Their governments duly carried out these demands, and because the benefits of cooperating were especially high, they sought to lock them in by establishing powerful supranational institutions. Moravcsik finds substantial support for his claims, concluding that integration has been driven by "pressures to coordinate policy responses to rising opportunities for profitable economic exchange" and the desire of west European governments to commit "one another to cooperate . . . where joint gains were large."[27]

The most influential statement of the view that the EC is the result of an attempt to transcend the nation-state system appears in Craig Parsons' *A Certain Idea of Europe*. The Great Depression, World War II, and the onset of the cold war, he argues, unsettled old assumptions about how to organize western Europe. Although most members of the political elite determined that only slight changes were in order, a small group came to a more radical conclusion. In order to guarantee their future security and prosperity, the Europeans were going to have to eliminate the nation-state system and replace it with a supranational arrangement. When members of this "pro-community" group came to power, and they did so consistently in the 1950s, they acted on their beliefs and built the EC. "Only because certain leaders repeatedly chose 'community' projects," Parsons declares, "did the EU gradually arise."[28]

26. Joschka Fischer, "From Confederacy to Federation: Thoughts on the Finality of European Integration," speech delivered at Humboldt University, Berlin, May 12, 2000, http://www.centers.law.nyu.edu/jeanmonnet/papers/00/symp.html.

27. Moravcsik, *Choice*, 4, 6.

28. Craig Parsons, *A Certain Idea of Europe* (Ithaca: Cornell University Press, 2003), 1.

Regardless of where they stand in this debate, most scholars dismiss balance of power explanations for the formation of the EC.[29] Moravcsik examines four "geopolitical" accounts of the sources of state preferences for integration and finds them all wanting. The little supportive evidence that he does find validates "liberal constructivist" variants of the argument, rather than "Realist power-balancing" ones. "Threats from the Soviet Union and Germany," he asserts, did not "generate overwhelming pressure for integration." Parsons, meanwhile, argues that policymakers who engage in balance of power thinking prefer not to establish supranational institutions. Had such individuals dominated the policymaking process, Europe would resemble the "thinly institutionalized rule" instead of "standing out as exceptional in international politics."[30]

Indeed, it is generally agreed that realists, who privilege the balance of power in their analyses, cannot account for the origins of the community. "The dominant theory of International Relations," asserts Simon Collard-Wexler in a typical statement of this view, "gives a poor account of one of the most important processes of contemporary world politics in a historically volatile region." Terrence Hopmann concurs: "French-German cooperation in the aftermath of more than a century of intense conflict and their integration with other European states within the European Union" is the "most significant post-World War II anomaly that seems to challenge the fundamental premises of realism."[31]

One of my chief goals in writing this book is to overturn this consensus by proposing a balance of power theory of integration and demonstrating that it has greater explanatory power than the two accounts that currently dominate the debate. That enterprise involves two tasks. First, I construct a balance of power theory of interstate cooperation. My basic argument is that states cooperate in a centralized or decentralized fashion depending on the power of their common adversary, and that if they opt for centralization, they unify or integrate depending on the distribution of capabilities among them. For comparative purposes, I describe the interest group and

29. The most common balance of power explanation holds that the United States acted as western Europe's pacifier, thereby allowing the Europeans to cooperate for mutual gain. A slightly different version of this argument maintains that the United States acted both as a pacifier and a booster of European cooperation. For examples of these arguments, see Joffe, "Europe's"; and Geir Lundestad, *Empire by Integration: The United States and European Integration, 1945–1997* (Oxford: Oxford University Press, 1998). Both arguments suffer from the same problems. American hegemony may have provided the Europeans with an opportunity to cooperate, but it did not give them a motive for doing so, and it certainly did not push them to engage in the kind of centralized cooperation exemplified by the EC.

30. Moravcsik, *Choice*, 478; and Parsons, *Certain*, 2.

31. Simon Collard-Wexler, "Integration under Anarchy: Neorealism and the European Union," *European Journal of International Relations* 12, no. 3 (2006): 399; and Terrence Hopmann, "Adapting International Relations Theory to the End of the Cold War," *Journal of Cold War Studies* 5, no. 3 (2003): 98.

ideational entrepreneurship arguments as well. Second, I evaluate how well the three theories account for the key events that shaped the EC. Then, as a further check, I determine whether they can explain why integration has been such a rare phenomenon, and whether they can account for historical cases that resemble the postwar west European experience.

My analysis allows me to cut to the heart of more fundamental debates between the three major approaches to explaining international politics—realism, liberalism, and constructivism—about the determinants of interstate cooperation and the rise and fall of international institutions. European integration is one of the most surprising examples of cooperation in modern times. Having fought three major wars in seventy-five years, France and Germany were unlikely candidates for reconciliation. In the late 1940s, few would have predicted the last six decades of tight, extensive, and sustained cooperation. Just as striking is the fact that the Franco-German relationship has involved unprecedented institutionalization. "No other region of the world," argues one observer, "has institutions as extensive and as well-developed as those in Europe."[32] Moreover, only the Europeans have built institutions that require member states to surrender a large portion of their sovereignty. This means that, in explaining the construction of the EC, we are furthering our understanding of interstate cooperation and institutions.

My particular contribution to these broader debates is twofold. First, I develop an explicitly realist theory when it is generally agreed that realists have the least to offer on these subjects.[33] As Robert Jervis explains, most observers "believe that realists argue that international politics is characterized by great conflict and that institutions play only a small role."[34] Second, by casting doubt on the arguments of Moravcsik and Parsons, I challenge the equally prevalent assumption that the liberal and constructivist approaches they represent are better placed to explain instances of interstate cooperation and the formation of international institutions.

Definitions, Cases, Methods

In order to construct and then test my theory against its competitors, I must first be clear about what it is that I am trying to explain and how I plan to evaluate the power of my argument. Accordingly, this section is devoted to

32. John J. Mearsheimer, "The False Promise of International Institutions," *International Security* 19, no. 3 (1994): 6.

33. On the hallmarks of a realist theory, see John J. Mearsheimer, *The Tragedy of Great Power Politics* (New York: W. W. Norton, 2001), 17–18.

34. Robert Jervis, "Realism, Liberalism, and Cooperation: Understanding the Debate," *International Security* 24, no. 1 (1999): 42.

defining terms, clarifying the explanatory task, and describing the methods that I employ.

Definitions

I define integration as a form of centralized cooperation whereby states agree to joint control over their militaries or economies, or to cede authority over military or economic affairs to a supranational institution.

Several aspects of this definition bear elaboration. First, states cooperate and form coalitions when they pool their resources and coordinate their policies. As David Lake observes, cooperation occurs when "the resources and efforts of two or more polities . . . [are] brought together in some organized or coordinated fashion."[35]

Second, states can, in principle, cooperate in a centralized or decentralized fashion.[36] If they choose decentralized cooperation, they retain a high degree of authority over policymaking and form military alliances or trade pacts. Centralized cooperation, on the other hand, involves surrendering authority over policymaking to a single focal entity or central actor. States give up the right to make policy autonomously or, more simply, they relinquish sovereignty.

Third, centralization simply means that a central actor or single focal entity dictates policy for a group of states; it implies nothing about the identity of that actor. Therefore, I distinguish between two types of centralized cooperation. Unification occurs when a single state makes policy for the entire group. Integration occurs when the members make policy jointly or agree to abide by policies made by a supranational entity. Policymaking is still centralized—a single policy applies to the entire group—but rather than resting in any one state's hands it is determined by the member states acting together or by a supranational institution. I refer to the products of unification as "unions," and because they involve common policymaking, I refer to the products of integration as "communities."

Cases

In the pages that follow, I examine French, German, and British decision making regarding the coal and steel pool, the defense community, and the common market. I seek to answer the following questions:

35. David A. Lake, *Entangling Relations: American Foreign Policy in Its Century* (Princeton: Princeton University Press, 1999), 25. For a definition of cooperation that emphasizes policy coordination, see Robert O. Keohane, *After Hegemony: Cooperation and Discord in the World Political Economy* (Princeton: Princeton University Press, 1984), 51–52.

36. For a similar statement, see Katja Weber, *Hierarchy amidst Anarchy: Transaction Costs and Institutional Choice* (Albany: State University of New York Press, 2000), 4–6.

Industrial integration. Why did France propose a coal and steel pool with its erstwhile enemy so soon after World War II? Why did the Germans embrace the French proposal and join them in establishing the ECSC? And why did the British refuse to enter into the heavy-industry negotiations?

Military integration. Why did France agree to establish an integrated military force in 1952? Having signed the EDC treaty, why did the French subsequently refuse to ratify it and instead seek German membership in the WEU and NATO in 1954? Why did the Germans welcome the prospect of an integrated European army and sign and ratify the EDC treaty? And why did Britain refuse to become involved in the EDC negotiations from the outset?

Economic integration. Why did the Europeans not achieve economic integration prior to the mid-1950s? Why did the French agree to create a supranational common market and then carry through on their commitment? Why did Germany welcome the common market proposal in 1955 and make substantial concessions to France in order to establish the EEC? And why did the British initially join the discussions, quickly pull out, and then propose a competing industrial free trade area in October 1956, before finally seeking to associate with, but not join, the EEC?

Having established how well my theory and its competitors explain the construction of the EC, I then determine whether they travel beyond postwar Europe. Can they account for the fact that there have been no other examples of interstate integration since 1815? Do they offer an explanation for events similar to the creation of the Community, including the formation of various alliances and trade pacts, the nineteenth-century unifications of Italy and Germany, and the founding of the United States of America?

Methods

How should theories be tested? A theory is comprised of a hypothesis stipulating an association between an independent (or causal) variable and a dependent (or outcome) variable, and a causal logic that explains the connection between the two. To test a theory fully, then, we should determine whether there is support for the hypothesis, that is, whether there is a correlation between the independent and dependent variables, and whether there is a causal relationship between them.[37] Therefore, an evaluation of the theories of integration described in this book rests on answering two questions: Is there support for each theory's core hypothesis? Is there a compelling explanation for why this should be the case?

Determining whether the data support a given theory's hypothesis is a fairly straightforward matter. Take the French decision to establish the coal

---

37. On correlation versus causation, see David Dessler, "Beyond Correlations: Toward a Causal Theory of War," *International Studies Quarterly* 35, no. 3 (1991): 337–55.

and steel community. Simplifying somewhat, my hypothesis is that integration is associated with a particular distribution of power. Thus, we can have greater confidence in my theory if the French decision coincided with the power distribution that I claim leads to integration. Likewise, its competitors are strengthened to the extent that the French decision coincided with the conditions that they identify as being important. I use this procedure in each case study chapter and in my analysis of how well the three theories travel beyond postwar western Europe. However, this kind of test only confirms that the independent variable proposed by a theory and the outcome in question are correlated—it does not prove that the relationship is causal.

Therefore, the bulk of this book is devoted to establishing whether or not there is support for the causal logics underpinning each theory. A causal logic is a statement about how an independent variable exerts a causal effect on a dependent variable. It elaborates a specific chain (or several chains) of causal mechanisms that connects these variables and takes the following form: A, the independent variable, causes B, the dependent variable, because A causes x, which causes y, which causes B.[38] A streamlined version of my theory, for example, holds that states opt for integration for the following reasons: they fear a common and overwhelming adversary and conclude that they must build a counterweight to it in order to ensure their security; they determine that they must organize their coalition in a centralized fashion in order to produce power efficiently; and they calculate that, given the prevailing within-coalition balance of power, the best that they can do is to share control of that coalition with their partners.

Process tracing is an excellent tool for testing causal logics and involves two steps. First, the investigator lays out the theory's causal logic in detail: "The cause-effect link that connects independent variable and outcome is unwrapped and divided into smaller steps."[39] Second, the investigator examines the historical record for evidence that events unfolded as the logic suggests and that important actors behaved and spoke as it stipulates. Ideally, we must examine the sequence of events as well as actors' claims about why they acted as they did. Do the testimony and actions of important actors support the causal logic under investigation? Do the timing and sequence of events match the proposed logic?

This procedure has the virtue of enabling us to establish causality. If there is good evidence for all of the steps in the proposed causal chain and those steps are linked as the causal logic stipulates, then we can be confident that the independent variable causes the outcome rather than merely being correlated with it.

38. Jon Elster, *Nuts and Bolts for the Social Sciences* (Cambridge: Cambridge University Press, 1989), 3–10.

39. Stephen Van Evera, *Guide to Methods for Students of Political Science* (Ithaca: Cornell University Press, 1997), 64.

Moreover, process tracing can help determine the relative explanatory power of the theories under investigation. The causal logics make unique predictions about patterns of events and the testimony of key actors, allowing us to use the historical record to adjudicate between them. If there is good evidence for my causal logic and evidence that contradicts the competitor logics, for example, then my theory gains considerable credibility. It has, in essence, performed better than the existing state of knowledge. However, if there is evidence for two or all three of the causal logics, then my theory provides only a partial explanation of the case.

Good process tracing involves two tasks: laying out the causal logics in clear fashion and corroborating the steps that comprise them. We cannot be confident in the conclusions drawn from process tracing unless the logics are clearly elaborated. The multiple links in the causal chain must be described so that the logic is, at least in principle, diagrammable.[40] Having done this, the investigator must then determine whether there is evidence for each posited micro-mechanism, a task that requires a close reading of the primary and secondary historical record. Provided they are read with care, secondary works provide a great deal of evidence regarding timing, motives, and calculations that can be used to verify proposed causal mechanisms. The key is to be aware of the arguments that historians are trying to make and the debates in which they are engaged in order to identify biases, gaps, inconsistencies, and weaknesses in the evidence they present. More prosaically, secondary works are invaluable for establishing the sequence of events and identifying key meetings, decisions, and actors. Nevertheless, even a thorough evaluation of the secondary record is likely to leave many questions unanswered. Historians will have different interpretations of the same event or document and will focus on different events and actors. In cases such as these, there is no substitute for examining primary documents to get to the bottom of a historical issue.[41]

I therefore make extensive use of the primary record.[42] Several of my claims rest on published primary documents. For example, I rely heavily

40. John Gerring, *Case Study Research: Principles and Practices* (Cambridge: Cambridge University Press, 2007), 172–73, 181–82; James Mahoney, "Nominal, Ordinal, and Narrative Appraisal in Macrocausal Analysis," *American Journal of Sociology* 104, no. 4 (1999): 1164–69; and Van Evera, *Guide*, 64–67.

41. For guides to dealing with historical evidence, see Alexander L. George and Andrew Bennett, *Case Studies and Theory Development in the Social Sciences* (Cambridge: MIT Press, 2005), 94–97, 99–105; and Marc Trachtenberg, *The Craft of International History: A Guide to Method* (Princeton: Princeton University Press, 2006), 51–60, 140–62.

42. Moravcsik recognizes the importance of primary sources and claims to use them extensively (*Choice*, 10–13, 80–84). But others have pointed out that he makes only limited use of such sources. See Jeffrey T. Anderson, "Review of *The Choice for Europe: Social Purpose and State Power from Messina to Maastricht* by Andrew Moravcsik," *American Political Science Review* 94, no. 2 (2000): 515–17; and Robert H. Lieshout, Mathieu L. L. Segers, and Anna M. van der Vleuten, "De Gaulle, Moravcsik, and the Choice for Europe: Soft Sources, Weak Evidence," *Journal of Cold War Studies* 6, no. 4 (2004): 89–139.

on the State Department's *Foreign Relations of the United States* series, which provides hundreds of accounts by American officials of European motives and calculations as they related to integration. Further evidence is available in the various collections of diplomatic documents for each of the major protagonists, including the *Documents on British Policy Overseas*, the *Documents diplomatiques français*, and *Die Kabinettsprotokolle der Bundesregierung*; in collections that deal specifically with the question of integration such as the *Bundesrepublik Deutschland und Frankreich* and the *Documents on the History of European Integration* series; and in the memoirs of many of the major players. I also make use of the unpublished primary record, including the British Cabinet records and the State Department's central files on France and Germany. Finally, I have mined histories of the period for statements, private conversations, meeting minutes, and the like that appear in published and unpublished primary documents that I have not examined myself. In other words, I have treated these histories as further collections of primary documents.

In examining these documents, I have focused on a series of targeted questions: What does the state in question want? What policy is it pursuing? What kind of reasoning lies behind that policy? What does each state do and how do they react to what others are doing? The upshot of using these documents and asking these questions, I believe, is that we can have greater confidence in my conclusions than those of other theorists who have gone before me.[43]

Roadmap

The rest of this book proceeds as follows. Chapter 2 describes my theory and its competitors. In the next three chapters, I test the theories against the historical record. Specifically, I seek to determine whether they can account for French, German, and British attitudes toward the ECSC, EDC, and EEC. Chapter 6 extends the analysis by checking how well my theory and its competitors travel beyond the postwar west European case and using my theory to make predictions about the future of the European Community.

Parsons makes more extensive use of the primary record, but only in relation to French decisions.

43. These questions are based on Trachtenberg, *Craft*, 141.

2. Explaining International Cooperation

My central argument is that the balance of power largely determines whether and how states cooperate with one another. This chapter presents my balance of power theory of cooperation, paying particular attention to its assumptions and causal logics. I begin with a brief discussion of power—what it is, why states want it, and what strategies they can adopt to deal with stronger competitors. One of these strategies—balancing—involves cooperating with other relatively weak states against a common powerful rival. Therefore the following section outlines the conditions under which states can form balancing coalitions. Specifically, I argue that states facing a merely superior adversary always have the option of balancing, whereas those facing an overwhelming opponent can only come together and balance against it under a restrictive set of conditions. Next, I explain why states that hope to balance against an overwhelming competitor are typically driven to establish centralized rather than decentralized coalitions. Having done that, I then show that the within-coalition distribution of capabilities determines whether centralized coalitions end up being unified or integrated. Finally, I describe the role that institutions play in facilitating these cooperative endeavors.

At the end of the chapter, I lay out the two currently dominant explanations for integration in order to pit my argument against them in the chapters that follow.

Balance of Power Politics

Mine is a balance of power theory of cooperation. Accordingly, this section unpacks the concept in three parts. First, I explain why states are compelled to compete for power. Second, I define power. Specifically, I argue that it has both a quantitative and a qualitative component. States are concerned not only with increasing their resources but also with organizing themselves as effectively as possible relative to their competitors. Third, I outline the strategies available to states dealing with more powerful rivals: balancing, buck-passing, and bandwagoning.

Aware that there is no international authority capable of protecting them and that they cannot know the intentions of others, states fear one another and worry about how much power they have compared to their competitors. The reason they pay careful attention to the balance of power is obvious: in an anarchic system, more powerful states have the means and may have the motive to hurt weaker ones. This being the case, states that want to ensure their security compete for power. Specifically, they try to preserve the power they have and to increase it when they believe they have an opportunity to do so.[1]

Power refers to material resources and organizational effectiveness, which together determine a state's ability to deter or defend against potential rivals.[2] Material capabilities are an essential element of power. At any given moment, military capabilities matter the most. Simply put, states must have large militaries equipped with advanced weaponry if they are to remain secure.[3] The primacy of military assets notwithstanding, the size and sophistication of a state's economy are crucial as well, particularly over the longer term, because economic might is the basis of military might. And if they want to remain competitive well into the future, states must be blessed with abundant physical and human capital, and especially with a large population and natural resource base.[4]

Organizational quality is equally important because it determines how effectively states can muster and deploy their material assets against their adversaries. The way a state organizes its military—including the recruitment practices it adopts, the training techniques it employs, and the command structure it puts in place—can have important effects on the size and effectiveness of its fighting forces. It is well known, for example, that new "organizational methods brought [Napoleonic] France ten years of nearly

---

1. This is the basic argument of Kenneth N. Waltz, *Theory of International Politics* (New York: McGraw-Hill, 1979), 102–28; and John J. Mearsheimer, *The Tragedy of Great Power Politics* (New York: W. W. Norton, 2001), 29–36.

2. On deterrence and defense, see Robert J. Art, "To What Ends Military Power?" *International Security* 4, no. 4 (1980): 3–35.

3. For a comprehensive discussion of military power, see Mearsheimer, *Tragedy*, 83–137.

4. Works that stress the importance of economic power include Dale C. Copeland, *The Origins of Major War* (Ithaca: Cornell University Press, 2000); Robert Gilpin, *War and Change in World Politics* (Cambridge: Cambridge University Press, 1981); and Paul M. Kennedy, *The Rise and Fall of the Great Powers: Economic Change and Military Conflict from 1500 to 2000* (New York: Random House, 1987).

unbroken victory against unreconstructed adversaries."[5] The same is true in the economic realm. Organizational decisions have important implications for growth and innovation, thereby directly influencing the size and technological sophistication of a state's economy. As Douglass North and Robert Paul Thomas observe, it is primarily the "nature of existing economic institutions . . . [that] determines whether the aggregate result is to be economic growth, stagnation, or decay."[6] In sum, states understand that the surest path to security lies in the accumulation of power. This, in turn, leads them to work hard on enhancing what one scholar has called their "organizational core and resource base."[7]

When confronted by a more powerful competitor, states can balance, buck-pass, or bandwagon. Balancing involves opposing another state directly in order to prevent it from upsetting the balance of power.[8] Success in this endeavor rests on arraying enough material capability against a potential aggressor to deter it and, if deterrence fails, to defeat it in war. Thus, prospective balancers seek to increase the military and economic assets at their disposal and, because power has an important organizational component, they also try to make qualitative improvements in how they are organized.

States can increase the resources they have available for balancing in two ways. First, they can mobilize more of their own assets by increasing military spending, building more weapons, or introducing conscription.[9] Second, they can ally with others and commit to use their military and economic resources for a common purpose. As James Morrow observes, "nations form alliances to increase their security by massing their capabilities against a common enemy."[10] These approaches are different in form, but the basic logic is the same: both increase the material resources deployed against a powerful adversary.

Aspiring balancers also work to upgrade the organization of their militaries and economies relative to their competitors. In military matters,

5. Geoffrey L. Herrera and Thomas G. Mahnken, "Military Diffusion in Nineteenth-Century Europe: The Napoleonic and Prussian Military Systems," in *The Diffusion of Military Technology and Ideas*, ed. Emily O. Goldman and Leslie C. Eliason (Stanford: Stanford University Press, 2003), 209.

6. Douglass C. North and Robert Paul Thomas, "An Economic Theory of the Growth of the Western World," *Economic History Review* 23, no. 1 (1970): 5.

7. João Resende-Santos, *Neorealism, States, and the Modern Mass Army* (Cambridge: Cambridge University Press, 2007), 63.

8. On balancing, see Mearsheimer, *Tragedy*, 156–57; Stephen M. Walt, *The Origins of Alliances* (Ithaca: Cornell University Press, 1987), 17–19; and Waltz, *Theory*, 118.

9. On this point, see Mearsheimer, *Tragedy*, 157; and James D. Morrow, "Arms versus Allies: Trade-Offs in the Search for Security," *International Organization* 47, no. 2 (1993): 215.

10. James D. Morrow, "Alliances and Asymmetry: An Alternative to the Capability Aggregation Model of Alliances," *American Journal of Political Science* 35, no. 4 (1991): 904.

notes Barry Posen, "states that wish to remain autonomous" worry about the "size and effectiveness of their military organizations relative to their neighbors" and therefore strive to adopt "successful practices."[11] A similar logic applies in the economic realm. As John Ikenberry observes, military competition has always "provided incentives for states to attend to the efficient organization of their economy."[12] How do states go about trying to improve their relative organizational effectiveness? Either through innovation, in which case they invent new practices or recombine existing ones in new ways, or by imitation, which involves copying policies that have already proved to be effective.[13]

Buck-passing and bandwagoning are the other options states have for dealing with a powerful competitor. States buck-pass when they get others to balance against a common adversary while they sit on the sidelines. They recognize the need for balancing, but try to ensure that someone else does it.[14] In contrast to the other two strategies, bandwagoning involves aligning with, not against, a more powerful opponent. The weaker state joins the stronger one in the hope of avoiding an attack.[15] A closely related strategy—once again the state in question makes no effort to offset the power of the more powerful contender—is hiding, in which case the weaker state ignores the threat, retreats into isolation, or declares neutrality.[16]

The Balance of Power and Cooperation

States confronting a common powerful competitor have an incentive to cooperate and balance against it. Cooperation is always possible when an adversary is merely superior to them, though they may decide that its

11. Barry R. Posen, "Nationalism, the Mass Army, and Military Power," *International Security* 18, no. 2 (1993): 82.

12. G. John Ikenberry, "The International Spread of Privatization Policies: Inducements, Learning, and 'Policy Bandwagoning'," in *The Political Economy of Public Sector Reform and Privatization*, ed. Ezra N. Suleiman and John Waterbury (Boulder, Colo.: Westview, 1990), 101.

13. On innovation, see Mearsheimer, *Tragedy*, 166–67; and Barry R. Posen, *The Sources of Military Doctrine: France, Britain, and Germany between the World Wars* (Ithaca: Cornell University Press, 1984), 29–33, 54–57. On imitation, see Resende-Santos, *Neorealism*, 47–92; and Waltz, *Theory*, 124, 127–28.

14. On buck-passing, see Thomas J. Christensen and Jack Snyder, "Chain Gangs and Passed Bucks: Predicting Alliance Patterns in Multipolarity," *International Organization* 44, no. 2 (1990): 137–68; Mearsheimer, *Tragedy*, 157–59; Posen, *Sources*, 63–64; and Waltz, *Theory*, 164–65.

15. On bandwagoning, see Eric J. Labs, "Do Weak States Bandwagon?" *Security Studies* 1, no. 3 (1992): 383–416; Mearsheimer, *Tragedy*, 162–64; Walt, *Origins*, 19–23; and Waltz, *Theory*, 126.

16. The term was introduced by Paul Schroeder, "Historical Reality vs. Neo-realist Theory," *International Security* 19, no. 1 (1994): 117.

power advantage is so slim that they need not join forces at all. When they confront an overwhelming competitor, on the other hand, they can only consider balancing against it under a restricted set of conditions. Specifically, they must have enough combined capabilities to stand up to their stronger opponent effectively, and it must not be able to destroy them before they put their coalition into place. In other words, the prevailing distribution of power must afford them both the means and the opportunity to construct a viable coalition. If it does not, they are liable to bandwagon or hide.

Superior and Overwhelming Competitors

In order to identify different classes of competitors, I first categorize states as great or minor powers. The following are usually listed as great powers after 1815: Austria-Hungary (1816–1918); Britain (1816–1945); France (1816–1940); Prussia/Germany (1816–1945); Russia/the Soviet Union (1816–1990); Italy (1861–1943); Japan (1895–1945); and the United States (1898–present).[17] In the interest of simplicity, I designate all the other states in the international system as minor powers.

This distinction allows me to classify relatively powerful states as either superior or overwhelming competitors. Great powers can only confront superior rivals. It is generally agreed that Napoleonic France, Wilhelmine Germany, and the Third Reich were the most powerful states in Europe in their respective eras, and there is little question that they were superior to the other great powers. But even they did not have an overwhelming power advantage over their peers; they were not so powerful as to render resistance or opposition useless. This observation is, in fact, built into most well-known definitions of a great power. "At a minimum," argues Jack Levy, great powers have "relative self-sufficiency with respect to military security." Meanwhile, John Mearsheimer defines a great power as a state with enough assets to "put up a serious fight in an all-out conventional war against the most powerful state in the world."[18] The same logic applies

17. This list is based on Vesna Danilovic, *When Stakes Are High: Deterrence and Conflict among Major Powers* (Ann Arbor: University of Michigan Press, 2002), 46; Jack S. Levy, *War in the Modern Great Power System, 1495–1975* (Lexington: University Press of Kentucky, 1983), 47; Mearsheimer, *Tragedy*, 404; J. David Singer and Melvin Small, *The Wages of War, 1816–1965: A Statistical Handbook* (New York: Wiley, 1972), 381; and Waltz, *Theory*, 162. There is near unanimity on the list of great powers before 1945, although some of the entry and exit dates are disputed. After 1945, Danilovic, Levy, and Singer and Small label Britain, France, Germany, Japan, and China as great or major powers. However, they note that the United States and the Soviet Union were in a class apart and designate them as superpowers or global contenders. Therefore I count the United States and Soviet Union as great powers after World War II and the others as minor powers.

18. Levy, *War*, 16; and Mearsheimer, *Tragedy*, 5.

among minor powers: the disparities between them are not so large that some can easily conquer the others. A minor power confronting a great power, however, faces an overwhelming competitor. Simply put, its prospects for survival in the event of a conflict are slim.

Dealing with Superior Competitors

States confronting a superior opponent balance or buck-pass. Their choice depends on the power gap between themselves and the more powerful state. If the gap is small, they are likely to buck-pass. Because at least one of them is capable of containing the superior state, they maneuver to get one another to bear the burden while they look on from the sidelines. If the gap is large, however, they balance. They understand that they must join forces to prevent the superior state from upsetting the balance of power. Dale Copeland summarizes the logic well: "Coalitional tightness is likely to vary between the extremes of concerted effort when the potential hegemon appears particularly strong, to coalitional disunity when the threat to the system appears minimal."[19]

States that choose to balance against superior competitors form decentralized coalitions. Because each of them can, by definition, put up a good fight against the superior power on its own, a straightforward agreement to act together is enough to make their powerful adversary think twice about attacking them. Knowing this, and reluctant to surrender sovereignty unless they have to, they prefer a decentralized arrangement to a centralized one.

What do decentralized coalitions look like? In the military realm, they take the form of alliances. The partners agree to act jointly to enhance their security but retain the right to autonomous decision making. David Lake makes the point well: "In an alliance . . . polities pool resources in pursuit of some common security objective while retaining complete authority over all areas of decision making."[20] Alliances also have economic implications. By agreeing to act in concert, allies effectively agree to pool their economic as well as their military resources in order to compete more successfully with a third party. Sometimes they go further and complement their alliance with specific economic arrangements such as trade pacts in the expectation that doing so will increase the overall wealth and therefore power of the coalition.[21] These agreements likewise require no meaningful surrender of sovereignty.

19. Copeland, *Origins*, 23.

20. David A. Lake, *Entangling Relations: American Foreign Policy in Its Century* (Princeton: Princeton University Press, 1999), 27.

21. For the logic, see Joanne S. Gowa, *Allies, Adversaries, and International Trade* (Princeton: Princeton University Press, 1994), 38.

Dealing with Overwhelming Competitors

States confronted by an overwhelming competitor balance or bandwagon. Two considerations drive their decision: whether or not the putative coalition, once formed, will have enough combined capability to stand up to the great power, and whether or not that same great power can crush their combination even before it forms. In other words, do they have the means to establish a viable coalition and an opportunity to put it into place?

The Means to Balance

In deciding whether or not to build a coalition, minor powers confronting a great power carefully assess their combined capabilities. If their combination is likely to be on the wrong end of a gross mismatch in power, they bandwagon or hide, reasoning that even if they successfully construct an alliance it will be too weak to defend itself. Moreover, the very act of coalition building may antagonize the great power, while bandwagoning may bring its protection and gratitude. As Stephen Walt notes, weak states tend to bandwagon rather than balance because they "can do little to affect the outcome (and may suffer grievously in the process)."[22] Of course, bandwagoning is not attractive in that it involves putting oneself at the mercy of others, but it is preferable to being forcibly subjugated or destroyed.

If the minor powers do have sufficient combined resources to avoid a gross mismatch, they can consider balancing. They know that if they manage to establish a coalition the great power is likely to be deterred from attacking them and, even if it is not, that they stand a decent chance of defeating it in war. This is not to say that groups of states with the requisite combined capabilities always coalesce to form balancing coalitions. Prospective members may prefer to bandwagon with the great power, hide, or let others bear the brunt of the balancing burden. Nevertheless, balancing is a viable option for such groups in a way that it is not for others with limited resources.

A potential coalition is likely to consider itself on the wrong end of a gross mismatch if it is at more than a 3:1 power disadvantage to an adjacent great power. To my knowledge, no one has ventured an opinion regarding how much military and economic might a state must have relative to a rival in order to be secure. But military experts have long argued that an attacker must have a threefold local advantage in combat power to break through a defender's front.[23] Assuming that both sides are equally efficient at translating gross resources into combat power, and the attacker strikes with equal force along an entire front, the defender must be at less than a 3:1 disadvantage in aggregate military and economic might to defend itself

22. Walt, *Origins*, 29.
23. On this point, see John J. Mearsheimer, "Assessing the Conventional Balance: The 3:1 Rule and Its Critics," *International Security* 13, no. 4 (1989): 54–89.

effectively. These assumptions are admittedly open to question. But over the last two hundred years, states trying to determine whether they had the gross resources to defend themselves would have had no more information than this. It is therefore reasonable to think that they would have reached the same conclusion.

In sum, whether balancing is an option at all for minor powers in a standoff with a great power depends on a simple power calculation: Does the group have enough aggregate capability to compete with an adjacent great power? If it does, then balancing is an option. If it does not, then the group members are likely to bandwagon or hide. Joseph Parent sums up the logic well: "Threats need to be extremely intense to suggest unification, but threats that are too intense overwhelm balancing efforts and render them futile."[24]

The Opportunity to Balance

Even if they have the aggregate capability to form a viable coalition, minor powers must worry that the great power will strangle their combination in the cradle. Great powers that care about their security are unlikely to stand by idly as groups of weaker states set about eroding their supremacy. Moreover, they can derail any coalition-building efforts relatively easily by threatening potential members or picking them off in a series of lopsided one-on-one fights.

Therefore, minor powers can combine only if the great power is unable to project its power against them. There are four scenarios in which a great power may be unable to stymie the coalition-building efforts of a collection of weaker states. First, the great power may have recently been defeated or exhausted in war. Second, it may be going through an internal upheaval or revolution. In both of these cases, the great power will be weaker than usual, thereby giving neighboring minor powers a window of opportunity to build an effective balancing coalition.[25]

Third, the great power may be suffering from overstretch.[26] Even great powers have finite resources and must choose how to allocate them. Because they typically develop wide-ranging interests across the globe, there will be times when they cannot spare the assets to head off the creation of a minor power coalition.

Finally, a great power can find it hard to strangle an incipient countervailing combination that is protected by a competing great power sponsor. Although this protector may inhabit the same region of the world as its client, this is unlikely because sponsors must worry that their clients could

---

24. Joseph M. Parent, "E Pluribus Unum: Political Unification and Political Realism" (PhD diss., Columbia University, 2005), 5.

25. On the consequences of revolutions, see Stephen M. Walt, *Revolution and War* (Ithaca: Cornell University Press, 1996), 21–22.

26. On overstretch, see Gilpin, *War*, 156–85; and Kennedy, *Rise*, xxiii.

turn on them from a position of strength in the future. They fear that they may be creating the geopolitical equivalent of Frankenstein's monster. A more likely scenario is that the potential coalition is sponsored by an off-shore great power. Because an offshore balancer is least secure when an-other region is dominated by a single state, it wants as many competing power centers as possible in that region. Therefore, it is likely to welcome and promote the formation of any formidable minor power coalition.[27]

In sum, whether or not states balance against an overwhelming rival is a function of both means and opportunity. They must have the combined means to form a viable counterweight at a time when the great power lacks the capacity to stop them.

The Logic of Integration

Generally speaking, states with both the combined means and the oppor-tunity to balance against an overwhelming competitor conclude that they must establish a coalition with a central governing authority to compete with it effectively. Centralization in turn raises the question of control. Who makes the decisions that apply to all of the coalition members? This time the within-coalition balance of power is crucial. If a single state is con-siderably more powerful than its prospective partners, it can seize control of policymaking and unify the group. But if power is fairly evenly distrib-uted among the coalition members, they integrate and agree to take au-thoritative decisions jointly.

Centralization

A group of minor powers that opts to balance against an overwhelming competitor cannot, by definition, be on the wrong end of a gross mismatch, but it is nevertheless likely to be inferior to its rival. In theory, of course, the group could possess combined assets that dwarf those of the great power. If there were many states in the group and several were exceptionally strong minor powers, the coalition might overawe a neighboring great power. In fact, however, there have been no such cases in modern times. All the mi-nor power coalitions I have been able to identify were weaker than the great powers in their region of the world.[28]

Given their comparative weakness, aspiring minor power coalitions put a premium on organizing themselves as efficiently as possible. Their mem-bers are acutely aware that even a slight increment in the great power's

27. On offshore balancing, see Christopher Layne, "From Preponderance to Off-shore Balancing: America's Future Grand Strategy," *International Security* 22, no. 1 (1997): 112–19.

28. See chapter 6.

relative potential could leave them vulnerable to domination. Therefore all aspects of the power-generating process become matters of intense concern. And because they have already maximized their available assets by agreeing to join forces, they are likely to turn to improving their relative organizational effectiveness for fear that poor organization could be the difference between life and death. As Otto Hintze observed: "Throughout the ages, pressure from without has been a determining influence on internal structure."[29]

In their quest for efficiency, the minor powers are likely to organize their coalition in a centralized fashion. In principle, they can reach this decision as a result of calculation or imitation, though in practice both logics are probably at work simultaneously. Pure calculation suggests that a centralized military is more powerful than a comparably sized decentralized one. The installation of a central governing authority, for example, enhances military coordination at the tactical, operational, and strategic levels. Similarly, it is only by establishing a large single economy from disparate smaller ones that the coalition members can benefit from the economies of scale and technological innovations that accrue to large single markets.[30] Thus innovation—so called because their calculations lead coalition members to adopt an organizational form they did not have previously—leads to centralization.

The decision to centralize can also be the consequence of an imitation logic. In this case, the coalition's quest to be as powerful as possible leads it to imitate the organizational features of the most powerful actors in the system, that is, the great powers.[31] Although no two great powers are exactly alike, they all share one key feature by virtue of the fact that they are states—they are organized in a centralized fashion. "Most scholars agree," notes Michael Desch, "that the state is (1) a set of institutions, (2) placed in a geographically bounded territory, that (3) has a monopoly upon rule within

---

29. Otto Hintze, *The Historical Essays of Otto Hintze*, ed. Felix Gilbert (Oxford: Oxford University Press, 1975), 183. There is a vast literature about the role of external threats on the internal organization of states. See, for example, Michael C. Desch, "War and Strong States, Peace and Weak States?" *International Organization* 50, no. 2 (1996): 240–50; Peter Gourevitch, "The Second Image Reversed: The International Sources of Domestic Politics," *International Organization* 32, no. 4 (1978): 882–900; and Charles Tilly, *Coercion, Capital, and European States, AD 990–1990* (Cambridge, Mass.: Blackwell, 1990), 14–15. Here I apply the logic to coalitions of states.

30. On economies of scale, see Paul R. Krugman and Maurice Obstfeld, *International Economics: Theory and Policy*, 4th ed. (Reading, Mass.: Addison-Wesley, 1997), 121–58, and for the claim that large markets foster innovation, see Christopher Freeman, *The Economics of Industrial Innovation* (Cambridge: MIT Press, 1982); and Jacob Schmookler, "Economic Sources of Inventive Activity," *Journal of Economic History* 22, no. 1 (1962): 1–20.

31. For the argument that states imitate the practices of the most powerful among them, see Resende-Santos, *Neorealism*, 82; and Waltz, *Theory*, 127.

that area."[32] In other words, all states possess a central governing authority. As a result, minor power coalitions quickly conclude that they must centralize in order to compete effectively in a great power world.[33]

Although balance of power considerations point strongly to the need for centralization, weak powers confronted by an overwhelming competitor are extremely reluctant to pursue that path because it involves relinquishing sovereignty. By establishing a central governing authority, states give up formal decision-making autonomy and, specifically, the right to manage their internal and external affairs without interference from others. More simply, they surrender their sovereignty.[34] This is a deeply unattractive move for two reasons. First, states believe that survival in a self-help world depends upon their ability to make decisions in what they judge to be their best interests.[35] Second, sovereignty is inextricably linked with nationalism, an especially powerful political ideology that holds that a nation—a body of individuals with an explicit and peculiar character—should have its own independent state.[36] Consequently, centralization is never a first choice however necessary it may be.

Given the importance that they attach to sovereignty, states facing off against an overwhelming rival cast around for alternatives to centralization. Specifically, they seek to identify an arrangement that promises to establish a favorable balance of power—one that is as advantageous as the one that they could establish by building a centralized coalition—without requiring them to give up their autonomy. Their reasoning is straightforward: given the option, they would rather be secure and sovereign than just secure.

If they are unable to come up with an arrangement that is preferable to centralization on power and sovereignty grounds, however, the minor powers opt to centralize decision-making authority. Of course, centraliza-

---

32. Desch, "War," 240.

33. My two-pronged explanation for centralization has a great deal in common with arguments about the emergence of the sovereign state system. See, for example, Richard Bean, "War and the Birth of the Nation State," *Journal of Economic History* 33, no. 1 (1973): 203–21; James Kurth, "The Post-Modern State," *National Interest* no. 28 (1992): 26–35; Hendrik Spruyt, *The Sovereign State and Its Competitors* (Princeton: Princeton University Press, 1994); Tilly, *Coercion*, 14–15; and Aristide R. Zolberg, "Strategic Interactions and the Formation of Modern States: France and England," *International Social Science Journal* 32, no. 4 (1980): 687–716.

34. For this definition—he calls it Westphalian sovereignty—see Stephen D. Krasner, *Sovereignty: Organized Hypocrisy* (Princeton: Princeton University Press, 1999), 20–25.

35. See, for example, Joseph M. Grieco, "Understanding the Problem of International Cooperation: The Limits of Neoliberal Institutionalism and the Future of Realist Theory," in *Neorealism and Neoliberalism: The Contemporary Debate*, ed. David A. Baldwin (New York: Columbia University Press, 1993), 315.

36. This definition relies on Stephen Van Evera, "Hypotheses on Nationalism and War," *International Security* 18, no. 4 (1994): 6.

tion involves a loss of sovereignty. But the coalition members understand that if they fail to centralize they are unlikely to survive and they therefore agree grudgingly to a centralized setup.[37] In effect, they make the best of a bad situation by trading away sovereignty for security. Put somewhat differently, they choose "life" ahead of "liberty."[38]

In sum, absent an alternative arrangement that promises to establish a favorable distribution of capabilities at no cost to their sovereignty, balance of power thinking prompts weak states confronting overwhelming competitors to opt for centralized cooperation. Aware that they do not have the capability to deal with the great power alone and that, even if they join forces, effective organization is at a premium, they form centrally organized balancing coalitions.

Integration and Unification

Even as they come together, states seek to gain control of their new coalition. "Even with the greatest of external pressure," observes Kenneth Waltz, "the unity of alliances is far from complete. States or parties in wartime or in electoral alliance, even as they adjust to one another, continue to jockey for advantage."[39] The reason is that they cannot divine one another's intentions. This is not to say that they believe their allies have malign intentions toward them. Indeed, the existence of a common and overwhelming adversary means that they can be reasonably confident that their partners are committed to cooperating with them in the short term. But they cannot know their intentions, and especially their future intentions, for sure. As Robert Jervis notes, "Minds can be changed, new leaders can come to power, values can shift, new opportunities and dangers can arise."[40] This uncertainty means that they pay careful attention to how their cooperative efforts might affect the balance of power among them. And this concern, in turn, means that they are reluctant to allow another state to control the coalition for fear that it might then have an opportunity to structure military or economic realities in its favor and dominate its partners.

37. For the claim that security or survival is more important than any other goals that states may have, see Waltz, *Theory*, 126.

38. Alexander L. George and Robert O. Keohane, "The Concept of National Interests: Uses and Limitations," in *Presidential Decisionmaking in Foreign Policy: The Effective Use of Information and Advice*, ed. Alexander L. George (Boulder, Colo.: Westview, 1980), 224.

39. Waltz, *Theory*, 167.

40. Robert Jervis, "Cooperation under the Security Dilemma," *World Politics* 30, no. 2 (1978): 168. On the role of uncertainty in international politics, see Dale C. Copeland, "The Constructivist Challenge to Structural Realism: A Review Essay," *International Security* 25, no. 2 (2000): 199–206.

Whether this struggle for control ends in unification or integration largely depends on how power is distributed within the coalition.[41] If it is distributed asymmetrically, with one of the members considerably more powerful than its partners, the leading state can seize control, thereby bringing about unification. If power is distributed symmetrically, however, no one can take charge, and the coalition members agree to share control— they opt for integration and form a community. Mancur Olson captured the logic well in a different context: "Autocracy is prevented and democracy permitted by the accidents of history that leave a balance of power or stalemate—a dispersion of force and resources that makes it impossible for any one leader or group to overpower all of the others."[42]

Integration is attractive, above all, because it promises to maintain the existing, relatively even distribution of power within the coalition.[43] In the military realm, member states raise forces in proportion to their overall weight in the coalition, and because they have roughly the same amount of power, they field comparably sized militaries. This numerical equality is reinforced by their adoption of similar policies in matters of conscription and training, officer recruitment and instruction, territorial and reserve organization, and general staff organization, among others. Finally, integration means the creation of a single command structure and joint decisions on operational and strategic matters, thereby ensuring that no member state can gain a meaningful advantage over its partners.[44]

Economic integration, meanwhile, promises to perpetuate the existing distribution of economic power. It is generally agreed that economic growth is a function of resources, specifically capital and labor, and technological innovation, which includes the introduction of new products, new production processes, and new organizational forms.[45] Thus, because it

41. For a theory of institutional origins that privileges the distribution of power, see Jack Knight, *Institutions and Social Conflict* (Cambridge: Cambridge University Press, 1992). See also Kenneth N. Waltz, "Structural Realism after the Cold War," *International Security* 25, no. 1 (2000): 18–27.

42. Mancur Olson, "Dictatorship, Democracy, and Development," *American Political Science Review* 87, no. 3 (1993): 573.

43. Scholars have identified the so-called relative gains problem as one of the principal impediments to interstate cooperation. A state will be reluctant to cooperate because it fears that its partner may gain more from their cooperative efforts and use its enhanced power to hurt the first state down the road. Because integration allows for a distribution of gains that roughly maintains the pre-cooperation distribution of power, it provides a partial solution to the problem. See James D. Fearon, "Bargaining, Enforcement, and International Cooperation," *International Organization* 52, no. 2 (1998): 296–97.

44. For a similar argument, albeit with reference to stabilizing the peace after civil wars, see Caroline Hartzell and Matthew Hoddie, "Institutionalizing Peace: Power Sharing and Post-Civil War Conflict Management," *American Journal of Political Science* 47, no. 2 (2003): 318–32.

45. On the determinants of economic growth, see Robert Solow, "A Contribution to the Theory of Economic Growth," *Quarterly Journal of Economics* 70, no. 1 (1956): 65–94.

gives states equal access to resources and technologies and subjects them to the same policies, integration ensures that they grow at similar rates. Of course, even within states, which are highly integrated entities, some regions grow faster than others. But the origins of this differential growth lie in historical accident.[46] There is nothing about integration itself that triggers divergent growth rates. Therefore states have good reasons to assume that economic integration can maintain the current balance of power among them.

International Institutions

Once they decide to integrate, states establish institutions—rules that prescribe and proscribe acceptable and unacceptable forms of behavior—to make their agreement run as smoothly as possible.[47] In order to cooperate effectively, states need to know what issues are covered, what is expected of them, what they can expect from their partners, how policy decisions are going to be made, and so on.

In the case of integration, the key issues are centralization and joint control. Aspiring integrators must therefore develop two sets of rules: one assigning authority over policymaking to a central actor, and another dictating that none of them can control that actor. Both requirements are met when member states agree to abide by decisions reached through a majority voting procedure. An arrangement of this kind ensures that no state can control the policymaking process by forcing its preferences on others or by unilaterally blocking the implementation of policies agreed to by a majority of its partners. The twin requirements of centralization and joint control are also met when coalition members agree to delegate decision-making authority to a supranational actor.[48] Simply put, integrating states "delegate or pool decision-making power in authoritative international institutions."[49]

It should be apparent that I view most institutions as largely reflecting the balance of power. States decide to integrate because of their extreme weakness compared to a nearby great power and the relatively even distribution of power within their coalition. This decision then leads them to

46. On this point, see Paul Krugman, *Geography and Trade* (Cambridge: MIT Press, 1991), 8–10, 25, 66–67, 99–100.

47. This definition is based on Robert O. Keohane, *After Hegemony: Cooperation and Discord in the World Political Economy* (Princeton: Princeton University Press, 1984), 57–61; and John J. Mearsheimer, "The False Promise of International Institutions," *International Security* 19, no. 3 (1994): 8–9.

48. Strictly speaking, delegation to a supranational actor means universal noncontrol—none of the members can control policymaking—rather than joint control. However, because both are designed to prevent any single state from controlling the policymaking process, I treat them as equivalent measures.

49. Andrew Moravcsik, *The Choice for Europe: Social Purpose and State Power from Messina to Maastricht* (Ithaca: Cornell University Press, 1998), 67.

develop a set of rules mandating that decisions must be taken by a central actor beyond the control of any one of them.

It follows that different distributions of power are associated with different kinds of institutions. If one of the coalition members is much stronger than its partners, for example, then the rules are likely to look quite different from those governing a coalition of equally matched states. Specifically, they are likely to be crafted so as to give the most powerful state decisive control over the policymaking process. In short, as Stephen Krasner argues, the best explanation for the "nature of institutional arrangements" is the "distribution of national power capabilities."[50]

Nonintegration

Minor powers confronting an overwhelming adversary usually have no alternative to integration. But because it involves surrendering sovereignty, they never undertake it with enthusiasm. This reluctance is particularly pronounced in two situations. First, they are especially opposed to integrating their militaries. Second, they try to avoid integrating and let their partners do it instead when only a subset of their group needs to join forces to establish a viable counterweight to a nearby great power.

States are more reluctant to integrate their militaries than their economies. The main reason is that they place a greater premium on autonomy in areas that clearly impinge on their security than in those with less immediate security relevance. "In areas of key importance to the national interest," argued Stanley Hoffmann in an early analysis of integration, "nations prefer the certainty, or the self-controlled uncertainty, of national self-reliance, to the uncontrolled uncertainty of the untested blender."[51]

This reluctance to surrender military sovereignty is exacerbated by the knowledge that integration does not bring a sure improvement in security. States cooperating with one another—and integration is simply a particular form of cooperation—must worry that their partners may cheat on their agreement to gain an advantage over them. This fear is especially acute in military affairs because defection can happen quickly and the costs of being cheated on are potentially much graver in the military sphere than the economic one. As Charles Lipson points out, there is a "special peril of defection" in military affairs.[52] Of course, states can cheat on economic agreements as well, but the consequences of being betrayed are less likely to be immediately devastating. As a result, states are especially reluctant to engage in military integration.

50. Stephen D. Krasner, "Global Communications and National Power: Life on the Pareto Frontier," *World Politics* 43, no. 3 (1991): 337. See also Mearsheimer, "False," 13–14; and Waltz, "Structural," 18–27.

51. Stanley Hoffmann, "Obstinate or Obsolete? The Fate of the Nation-State and the Case of Western Europe," *Daedalus* 85, no. 3 (1966): 882.

52. Charles Lipson, "International Cooperation in Economic and Security Affairs," *World Politics* 37, no. 1 (1984): 14.

Competitor

Within-coalition balance of power		Superior	Overwhelming (Coalition viable)	Overwhelming (Not viable)
	Symmetric	Balancing/ buck-passing	Integration (Balancing)	Bandwagoning/ hiding
	Asymmetric	Balancing/ buck-passing	Unification (Balancing)	Bandwagoning/ hiding

Figure 1. Predicted responses to powerful competitors

Some states are less likely to integrate than others. The key to understanding why this is the case and who these states are lies in the distribution of power and geography. If the only way to avoid a gross mismatch is for every single minor power in the region to join forces, then each understands that none of them can avoid joining a coalition and establishing a central governing authority. But if it only takes some of them to establish a viable counterweight, then each state has an incentive to convince the others to integrate and deal with the great power while it remains outside the coalition and retains its sovereignty. In short, the balance of power determines whether all the minor powers work together or try to pass the buck to each other.

If the distribution of power explains whether or not the minor powers try to buck-pass, then geography accounts for the identity of the buck-passers. Weak states in close proximity to the great power realize they have little choice but to form a coalition. On the other hand, states that are further away from their adversary, or separated from it by other states, mountain ranges, or large bodies of water, are not as fearful of being conquered and are therefore more likely to pass the buck to their more vulnerable peers.[53] We should, of course, expect them to support the others' integrative efforts, since this promises to contain the great power. But they are unlikely to surrender sovereignty and integrate themselves.

To conclude, the balance of power explains why states cooperate and accounts for the form their cooperation takes (see figure 1). If they face a superior competitor, they cooperate in a decentralized fashion or eschew cooperation entirely and seek to buck-pass to one another. If they face an overwhelming opponent, on the other hand, and power realities on the ground afford them both the means and the opportunity to balance against it, they usually establish a centralized coalition. The precise arrangements

53. Jervis, "Cooperation," 194–95; Mearsheimer, *Tragedy*, 114–28; and Walt, *Origins*, 23–24.

that follow from the decision to install a central governing authority are likewise determined by the balance of power, this time within the coalition. An asymmetric distribution of capabilities leads to unification, whereas a relatively even balance of power prompts the member states to integrate.

Alternative Explanations

My argument contrasts sharply with the two explanations of integration that currently dominate the debate. Andrew Moravcsik's *The Choice for Europe* attributes the construction of the European Community to the influence of domestic interest groups. These groups responded to high levels of economic or geopolitical interdependence by calling for integration, and because they were politically powerful, their governments faithfully carried out their demands. Craig Parsons focuses on ideational entrepreneurship in *A Certain Idea of Europe*. Integration came about, he argues, because key policymakers believed that the best way to ensure peace and prosperity was to transcend the nation-state system and install a supranational community instead.

Interest Groups and Interdependence

The interest group argument holds that economic cooperation is best understood as a response to the demands of powerful domestic producer groups.[54] A simple insight lies at the core of the argument. Internationally competitive producers stand to benefit from commercial liberalization and they therefore put pressure on their governments to cooperate with others in the removal of tariffs, quotas, and regulatory barriers to trade. Moravcsik makes the point clearly: "To a first approximation, the greater the exports and export opportunities and the more competitive are domestic export producers, the more intense the pressure for trade liberalization."[55]

These demands prompt governments to pursue economic cooperation. Decisions to cooperate are "preceded by pressure from domestic producers." This is not to say that policy coordination happens all the time, but producer groups are especially powerful political actors and often get their way. The reason is that they have "intense, certain, and institutionally represented and organized interests," which gives them a marked advantage over other societal groups, including consumers and taxpayers. It is also not the case that governments promote producer interests at all costs. They

---

54. My description of the argument relies on Moravcsik, *Choice*, 3–10, 24–27, 35–41, 49–50, 67–68, 73–77. Note that I do not lay out his argument about monetary integration because the cases in this book deal with industrial, commercial, and military integration only.

55. Ibid., 38.

must be attentive to fiscal and regulatory constraints. But these are relatively loose in the areas of agricultural and industrial trade liberalization. Thus, "international policy coordination" can be viewed essentially as "a means to secure commercial advantages for producer groups, subject to regulatory and budget constraints."[56]

Internationally competitive producer groups call for liberalization and governments answer those calls when interdependence is high. "Trade liberalization," writes Moravcsik, "is driven primarily by opportunities for profitable international trade and investment." Intra-European cooperation reflected "the imperatives induced by interdependence and, in particular, the large exogenous increase in opportunities for profitable cross-border trade and capital movements in the postwar period." These opportunities are, in turn, the product of high levels of trade or "interdependence." Rising "interdependence and new opportunities for profitable cross-border transactions" give states powerful "incentives to deepen trade liberalization." In fact, in the postwar European case, trade volumes rose "very early in the postwar period, before significant trade liberalization had occurred."[57]

In sum, governments cooperate to advance the interests of producer groups whose preferences are driven by international interdependence. As Moravcsik puts it, "European integration resulted from a series of rational choices made by national leaders who consistently pursued economic interests—primarily the commercial interests of powerful economic producers . . . that evolved slowly in response to structural incentives in the global economy."[58]

States integrate and pool authoritative decision making in international institutions or delegate decision making to them rather than engage in more traditional forms of cooperation when the expected benefits from cooperation are especially high. Governments create institutions, Moravcsik argues, to prevent the familiar cheating problem: they ensure that cheaters are caught and raise the costs of defection. But they pool and delegate their sovereignty in these institutions only when they want to "assure a particular level of agreement." When would they want to ensure a "higher level of compromise"? When "joint gains are high and distributional conflicts are moderate." On the other hand, if mutual gains are limited or conflicts are severe, then states eschew integration and "reserve unanimity rights." Thus, integration is the preferred option when the expected gains from cooperation are large, something that is more likely when interdependence is high.[59]

56. Ibid., 36, 37, 38.
57. Ibid., 38, 26, 50, 40.
58. Ibid., 3.
59. Ibid., 74, 75.

The domestic interest group argument can, in principle, also be applied to military integration. Although he does not deal with military integration in his book, Moravcsik argues elsewhere that his framework "applies equally to . . . economic and national security affairs."[60] Presumably, this means that states cooperate in military matters when powerful domestic interest groups—in this case, the chief executive, the ministry of defense, and top military officials—demand intergovernmental coordination.[61] These actors call for cooperation when the states they represent are militarily interdependent and, specifically, when they confront a common adversary.[62] To take the argument a step further, the closer and more powerful the mutual opponent, the greater their interdependence and potential gains from cooperation, and therefore the more likely they are to engage in integration. In short, Moravcsik argues that we can view the European Community "as a series of pragmatic responses to economic and geopolitical interdependence."[63]

Ideational Entrepreneurship

In contrast to the balance of power and interest group arguments, the ideational entrepreneurship approach holds that integration cannot be understood as a response to objective geopolitical or economic imperatives.[64] The cold war and rising interdependence surely gave the Europeans good reasons to cooperate, but neither drove them to integrate. "Confronted by the two great wars and a fundamentally reconfigured environment," writes Parsons, "many Europeans began to reconsider long-held assumptions about the costs, benefits, and appropriate form of international cooperation. The new environment did *not* dictate their response, however." In fact, the "ideational" approach holds that "structural circumstances rarely dictate a specific course of action."[65]

60. Andrew Moravcsik, "Taking Preferences Seriously: A Liberal Theory of International Politics," *International Organization* 51, no. 4 (1997): 515.

61. My list of key interest groups is based on Helen V. Milner, *Interests, Institutions, and Information: Domestic Politics and International Relations* (Princeton: Princeton University Press, 1997): 191–96; and Andrew Moravcsik, "Armaments among Allies: European Weapons Collaboration, 1975–1985," in *Double-Edged Diplomacy: International Bargaining and Domestic Politics*, ed. Peter B. Evans, Harold K. Jacobson, and Robert D. Putnam (Berkeley: University of California Press, 1993), 130–32.

62. See Celeste Wallander, *Mortal Friends, Best Enemies: German-Russian Cooperation after the Cold War* (Ithaca: Cornell University Press, 1999), 28–29.

63. Andrew Moravcsik, "Despotism in Brussels? Misreading the European Union," *Foreign Affairs* 80, no. 3 (2001): 117.

64. My description of the argument relies on Craig Parsons, *A Certain Idea of Europe* (Ithaca: Cornell University Press, 2003), 1–28, 232–35. Note that I do not lay out his argument about how community institutions themselves furthered the integration process because he argues that this process began after the establishment of the EEC and therefore after the events discussed in this book.

65. Parsons, *Certain*, 1, 5. Emphasis added.

Instead, European integration came about because leaders with "pro-community" ideas periodically came to power in France and the Federal Republic.[66] Although he takes no position on why individual leaders came to power, Parsons is clear that they did not do so based on their views about the proper way to organize western Europe. In France, for example, they "achieved power on other issues." Their ideas about Europe simply had no bearing on whether or not they became major political players. When they did ascend to power, however, their views mattered a great deal. Leadership gave them an opportunity to step "beyond the demands of their allies and supporters" and work to "assemble support behind their personal ideas on Europe." If that idea involved integration, they pursued community projects, and if they could gain enough support for them, integration advanced. In this way, the ideational argument holds that "ideas are autonomous factors in politics, and certain institutions arise because of the ideas actors hold."[67]

Pro-community leaders advocated integration because they saw it as a means to transcend the nation-state system. The early postwar period was an epochal moment that triggered a battle of ideas about how to organize Europe. Most thinkers "defended solutions within the existing nation-state system, or in less radical departures from it." Proponents of the "traditional model located the enduring structures of power and legitimacy solely in the nation-state" and focused on intergovernmental arrangements. Supporters of a "confederal" model "also saw nation-states as lasting realities." Community model advocates, on the other hand, drew a more radical conclusion from their situation: "Legitimacy followed welfare functions; to maximize Europeans' long-term security and prosperity, their fractious nation-states had to be modified." What mattered most was the welfare of individuals and social groups. Historically, nation-states had provided it. But two wars and an economic depression had cast doubt on their ability to deliver. Simply put, "independent nations tended inevitably toward conflict; they also divided Europe's economic markets into small, inefficient pieces." This being the case, community thinkers came to believe that some core functions could be better "organized above the national level."[68]

66. In his book, Parsons focuses on French decision making only. However, his argument is, in principle, a general one and he finds evidence for it in the German case as well. I thank him for discussing this point with me.

67. Parsons, *Certain*, 2, 5, 25.

68. Ibid., 1, 23–24, 44. For a similar argument, see Ernst B. Haas, *The Uniting of Europe: Political, Social, and Economic Forces, 1950–1957* (Notre Dame: University of Notre Dame Press, 2004), xvi; Wilfried Loth, "Sources of European Integration: The Meaning of Failed Interwar Politics and the Role of World War II," in *Crises in European Integration: Challenge and Response, 1945–2005*, ed. Ludger Kühnhardt (New York: Berghahn, 2009), 19–23; and Ole Waever, "Insecurity, Security, and Asecurity in the West European Non-War Community," in *Security Communities*, ed. Emanuel Adler and Michael Barnett (Cambridge: Cambridge University Press, 1998), 82–83.

In sum, ideational entrepreneurship determines the form of international cooperation. Given the opportunity, leaders devise arrangements that reflect their ideas about how best to organize interstate relations. In the case at hand, community-minded thinkers came to power in the 1950s and brought about European integration.

The three arguments laid out in this chapter offer divergent explanations for the construction of the European Community. Broadly speaking: I attribute integration to a specific distribution of power; Moravcsik argues that it follows from the demands of interest groups that are themselves responding to interdependence; and Parsons claims that it is a product of certain leaders' desires to transcend the nation-state. Underlying each of these arguments are different causal logics and predictions about what we should find in the documentary record. It is to an evaluation of these competing logics and predictions that I now turn.

3. Origins

Heavy-Industry Integration, 1945–1950

On May 9, 1950, Foreign Minister Robert Schuman of France announced that his government intended to place "French-German production of coal and steel . . . under a joint high authority, within an organization open to the participation of other European nations." He hoped that an arrangement of this sort would represent the first step toward a "European federation."[1] Later that day, Konrad Adenauer, chancellor of the Federal Republic of Germany, called a press conference and endorsed the proposal unreservedly. The following year, on April 18, 1951, France and Germany, together with Italy and the Benelux states, signed the Treaty of Paris inaugurating the European Coal and Steel Community and in so doing embarked on the process of integration.[2] The British never even entered into negotiations with the Six. In fact, only three weeks after Schuman's announcement, they declared that although they were prepared to "make a helpful, constructive and practical contribution," they could not join because they did not accept "the principles underlying the French proposal."[3] The continental states would take the first step on the road to integration without them.

This chapter is organized around three questions: Why did the French call for the creation of the ECSC only five years after the bloodiest war in

1. Bonbright to Webb, May 9, 1950, *Foreign Relations of the United States* (hereafter *FRUS*), 1950, vol. 3 (Washington, D.C.: GPO, 1977), 693.
2. I use the terms Germany and West Germany interchangeably to refer to the British, French, and American occupation zones of Germany prior to September 21, 1949, and to the Federal Republic of Germany (FRG) after that.
3. Younger to Harvey, June 2, 1950, *Documents on British Policy Overseas* (hereafter *DBPO*), ser. 2, vol. 1 (London: HMSO, 1986), 146.

history? Why did the Germans embrace the French proposal? And why did the British refuse to go along?

My central claim is that these events are best understood as the product of balance of power politics. Specifically, the prevailing distribution of power made west European cooperation possible, and the major players embraced or refused integration based on balance of power calculations.[4] The distribution of capabilities made cooperation possible. The Soviet Union was an overwhelmingly powerful competitor and the European states therefore feared for their survival. Moreover, although not one of them could stand up to Moscow on its own, they calculated that they had the capability to do so collectively. Their efforts would have come to nothing, however, without the U.S. commitment to defend them from the Soviets while they put their coalition into place. They did not believe they could count on U.S. protection forever—hence the imperative of joining forces and establishing an independent power complex—but in the short term the American presence gave them an opportunity to establish a viable coalition.

Within this structural context, France and Germany opted for integration in order to balance against the Soviet Union and one another. Decision makers in Paris and Bonn understood that they could only hope to contain the Soviets if they constructed a centralized unit of power in the western half of the continent. At the same time, however, neither wanted the other to control the coalition, and because they were evenly matched, the outcome of their ensuing struggle for leadership was an agreement to share control of the group. The British saw things differently. Believing that they were in less immediate danger of being conquered and that a purely continental grouping could provide a viable counterweight to the Soviet Union, they buck-passed to their allies. European integration was good for British security and therefore deserving of their support, but there was no reason for them to surrender sovereignty and actually join the emerging community.

Motive, Means, and Opportunity, 1945–1950

In order to establish the initial plausibility of my argument, I must demonstrate that the prevailing distribution of power gave the Europeans the motive, means, and opportunity to establish a balancing coalition. Specifically, I need to show that (1) the Soviet Union was the only great power in Europe, and was thus an overwhelming competitor; (2) although none of them could balance against the Soviets alone, a combination of European states would have the capability to do so; and (3) they had an opportunity to build a coalition without being destroyed by their eastern neighbor.

4. I use the terms European and west European interchangeably to refer to the states of western Europe.

Motive

The Soviet Union held an overwhelming material advantage over the states of western Europe between 1945 and 1950. The belief that the USSR had the capability to dominate the entire continent was widespread even before the defeat of Nazi Germany. "Russia will emerge from the present conflict as by far the strongest nation in Europe and Asia," noted the Office of Strategic Services (OSS) in 1945, "strong enough . . . to dominate Europe and at the same time to establish her hegemony over Asia."[5] The termination of hostilities only increased fears of Soviet hegemony. The Joint Intelligence Committee summed up the predominant view in a memorandum for Major General Alfred Gruenther in January 1946: "The USSR [is] the leading military power on the Eurasian landmass. . . . None of these countries is capable singly of waging a successful defensive war against the USSR."[6] The Soviet Union, argued the Joint Chiefs of Staff (JCS), had been left as "the sole great power on the Continent—a position unique in modern history."[7] Nor were such judgments restricted to military circles. Well before he laid out his strategy of containment, George Kennan warned that the Soviet Union would "constitute a single force far greater than any other that will be left on the European continent."[8] President Harry Truman's speechwriter, Joseph Jones, concurred: "There existed not even a semblance of a balance of power in Europe."[9]

The Soviet Union's potential for domination derived from its staggering military and economic superiority over the other European states. Because of their rapid postwar demobilization, the Soviets held only a 2:1 military advantage over the British in 1947, but by 1950 the Soviet Union was six times more powerful than Britain (see table 1).[10] Worse still, the British faced formidable power projection problems because they were separated from the continent by the English Channel.[11] The other major European states were even weaker by comparison: the Soviet Union's advantage over France grew from 6:1 in 1947 to 9:1 in 1950, and Germany had no military forces at all. Coupled with the fact that the Red Army was a highly effective fighting

5. Quoted in Dale C. Copeland, *The Origins of Major War* (Ithaca: Cornell University Press, 2000), 151.

6. JIC, Estimate of Soviet Intentions and Capabilities, 1948–1955, January 2, 1946, *Records of the Joint Chiefs of Staff* (hereafter *RJCS*), pt. 2, 1946–1953, The Soviet Union (Lanham, Md.: University Publications of America, 1979), reel 2.

7. Quoted in Melvyn P. Leffler, *A Preponderance of Power: National Security, the Truman Administration, and the Cold War* (Stanford: Stanford University Press, 1992), 67.

8. Quoted in Copeland, *Origins*, 151.

9. Joseph M. Jones, *The Fifteen Weeks* (New York: Viking, 1955), 41.

10. On Soviet demobilization, see Matthew A. Evangelista, "Stalin's Postwar Army Reappraised," *International Security* 7, no. 3 (1982): 112–15.

11. On the problems associated with projecting power across water, see John J. Mearsheimer, *The Tragedy of Great Power Politics* (New York: W. W. Norton, 2001), 114–28.

TABLE 1
The European Balance of Power, 1947–1960

	1947	1948	1949	1950	1951	1952	1953	1954	1955	1956	1957	1958	1959	1960
Ratio Soviet military power to														
Britain	1.9	3.6	4.6	6.4	6.2	5.8	6.1	6.6	7.0	6.3	6.4	6.6	7.1	7.5
France	5.5	9.7	8.7	8.8	8.6	8.1	7.8	8.0	8.6	6.6	6.2	6.2	6.5	6.5
Germany	—	—	—	—	—	—	—	—	22.5	24.4	38.6	28.8	12.7	12.2
Ratio Soviet economic power to														
Britain	1.1	1.2	1.4	1.5	1.7	1.9	2.0	2.0	2.0	2.2	2.3	2.6	2.8	2.7
France	2.4	2.4	2.6	3.0	3.0	3.1	3.5	3.6	3.9	3.9	4.2	4.4	4.7	4.6
Germany	3.4	2.6	2.2	2.1	2.1	2.1	2.3	2.3	2.2	2.2	2.4	2.7	2.6	2.5
Ratio Soviet overall power to														
Britain	1.5	2.4	3.0	4.0	3.9	3.9	4.0	4.3	4.5	4.2	4.3	4.6	4.9	5.1
France	3.9	6.1	5.6	5.9	5.8	5.6	5.7	5.8	6.3	5.3	5.2	5.3	5.6	5.6
Germany	—	—	—	—	—	—	—	—	12.4	13.3	20.5	15.7	7.7	7.3
Ratio Soviet military power to														
Big three coalition	1.1	1.9	2.1	2.5	2.4	2.3	2.3	2.4	2.5	2.3	2.2	2.3	2.3	2.3
Continental coalition	1.9	2.9	2.8	3.0	2.9	2.8	2.7	2.8	3.0	2.4	2.2	2.3	2.4	2.4
Ratio Soviet economic power to														
Big three coalition	0.6	0.6	0.6	0.7	0.7	0.7	0.8	0.8	0.8	0.9	0.9	1.0	1.0	1.0
Continental coalition	0.8	0.8	0.8	0.8	0.8	0.8	0.9	0.9	1.0	1.0	1.1	1.2	1.2	1.1
Ratio Soviet overall power to														
Big three coalition	0.8	1.3	1.4	1.6	1.6	1.5	1.5	1.6	1.7	1.6	1.5	1.6	1.6	1.6
Continental coalition	1.3	1.8	1.8	1.9	1.9	1.8	1.8	1.9	2.0	1.7	1.6	1.7	1.8	1.7

Sources: Correlates of War, National Material Capabilities, 1816–2001, http://www.correlatesofwar.org; and Brian R. Mitchell, *International Historical Statistics: Europe, 1750–1993*, 4th ed. (London: Macmillan, 1998).

Note: To generate the military ratios, I calculated the ratio of Soviet military personnel and expenditure to that of the relevant state or coalition and averaged the personnel and expenditure ratios. I generated the economic ratios in the same way using data for steel production and energy consumption (electric energy output, 1947–1954). Finally, I calculated overall ratios by averaging the military and economic figures. Germany did not have a military force before 1955. Big three coalition refers to Britain, France, and Germany. Continental coalition refers to the Six. The coalition calculations assume that West Germany would be able to make the same military effort as France (adjusted for population). Figures report the ratio of Soviet power to the relevant state or coalition.

force—as it had demonstrated during the course of the war—these mismatches meant that no west European state could hope to put up any meaningful resistance to the Soviet Union on its own.[12]

The Soviet Union also had the most powerful economy in Europe after 1945. Although it had only a small lead over Britain in terms of industrial might in 1947, it had a 1.5:1 advantage by 1950. Its advantage over France was even greater, growing from just over 2:1 in 1947 to 3:1 in 1950. Germany, meanwhile, recovered rapidly from the war, but was still at a more than 2:1 disadvantage as the 1940s came to a close.[13]

Most analysts believed this capability advantage would only increase over time given the Soviet Union's vast natural resource base and huge population. In a letter to President Franklin Roosevelt in May 1944, Admiral William Leahy referenced "the recent phenomenal development of heretofore latent Russian military and economic strength—a development which ... has yet to reach the full scope attainable with Russian resources."[14] Similarly, the OSS remarked that "the major *long-term* factors are all more favorable to Russia than to Britain or even to America."[15] The basic view was spelled out at length in a Joint Intelligence Staff report, which concluded with a warning that "the large human and natural wealth of the Soviet Union offers possibilities of practically unlimited economic expansion."[16] Another report, written in November 1946, provided compelling evidence to back up these claims: the Soviet Union's "war industries" were projected to dwarf those of the European states by 1956.[17]

In sum, there is good evidence that western Europe's former great powers confronted an overwhelming opponent in the Soviet Union—given its massive military and economic advantages, none of them could hope to deter or defeat it alone. Worse still, the power gap between them and the

---

12. On the effectiveness of the Red Army and its victory over Nazi Germany, see David M. Glantz and Jonathan M. House, *When Titans Clashed: How the Red Army Stopped Hitler* (Lawrence: University Press of Kansas, 1995); and Richard J. Overy, *Russia's War* (New York: Penguin, 1998).

13. For accounts of the Soviet Union's emergence as an industrial powerhouse in the course of World War II, see Paul M. Kennedy, *The Rise and Fall of the Great Powers: Economic Change and Military Conflict from 1500 to 2000* (New York: Random House, 1987), 352–57; and Richard J. Overy, *Why the Allies Won* (New York: W. W. Norton, 1996), chap. 6.

14. Excerpt from Letter of Admiral Leahy, May 16, 1944, *FRUS*, 1945, Malta and Yalta, 107.

15. OSS, Russian Aims in Germany and the Problem of Three-Power Cooperation, May 11, 1944, *O.S.S. / State Department Intelligence and Research Reports* (hereafter *OSS*), pt. 6, The Soviet Union (Washington, D.C.: University Publications of America, 1977), reel 2. Emphasis in original.

16. JIS 85/26, Capabilities and Intentions of the USSR in the Postwar Period, July 9, 1946, *RJCS*, pt. 2, 1946–1953, The Soviet Union, reel 1.

17. JIC 374/1, Intelligence Estimate Assuming that War Between Soviet and Non-Soviet Powers Breaks out in 1956, November 6, 1946, ibid., reel 1.

Soviets showed no sign of shrinking. Consequently, the Europeans had a strong incentive to join forces to ensure their security.

Means

Although Britain, France, and West Germany could not deter or defeat the USSR alone, a European coalition would be powerful enough to balance effectively against the Soviet Union. Assuming that Germany could devote the same fraction of its population as France to building military forces, a putative coalition comprising Britain, France, and West Germany would be at only a 2.5:1 military disadvantage to the Soviet Union. At the same time, it would be economically stronger than the USSR. In terms of overall (military plus economic) power, the coalition would be at significantly less than a 2:1 disadvantage to the Russians (see table 1).

A hypothetical continental combination including France, West Germany, and the smaller west European states (Italy, Belgium, the Netherlands, and Luxembourg), but excluding Britain, also would have the wherewithal to stand up to Moscow. Such a group would be slightly weaker than one comprised of the three major west European players. But in terms of overall power, it would not be significantly weaker than the Soviet Union and would certainly not be on the wrong end of a gross power mismatch. Moreover, neither grouping would have much to fear in the future. A "big three" combination would be at a 1.3:1 population disadvantage, and a "continental" group would be at a mere 1.2:1 disadvantage, thereby ensuring that they would be able to keep pace with the Soviets militarily and economically over the longer term.[18]

The conviction that a united Europe would be able to balance effectively against the Soviet Union comes through clearly in the statements of American policymakers early in the postwar period, even as the Europeans struggled to recover from the ravages of war. The general line of reasoning was captured in a JCS memorandum of April 1947. If unity were achieved, it argued, then the new combination would have huge potential: "The potential military strength of the Old World in terms of manpower and in terms of war-making capacity is enormously greater than that of our area of defense commitments."[19] Similarly, John Foster Dulles, the Republican Party's foreign policy spokesman, argued that a west European combination would have "immense" potential. After all, the Europeans had "a population of over 250 million" as well as "large resources of such basic things as coal and iron." If they could combine those resources, they would create "one of the great units of power in the world" along with the United States

---

18. The population ratio is for 1955. For the data, see Correlates of War, National Material Capabilities, 1816–2001, http://www.correlatesofwar.org.

19. JCS 1769/1, United States Assistance to Other Countries from the Standpoint of National Security, April 29, 1947, *FRUS*, 1947, vol. 1, 739.

and the Soviet Union. Indeed, "it could be so strong that no other nation or likely group of nations would feel that it could be aggressive toward them with impunity."[20]

State Department officials shared these views, believing that Europe had the aggregate resources to become a "third force" in the world fully capable of balancing against the Soviet Union without American assistance. In January 1948, John Hickerson, the director of the Office of European Affairs, told a British delegation that the United States "envisaged the creation of a third force . . . strong enough to say 'no' both to the Soviet Union and the United States, if our actions should seem so to require."[21] Six months later, Kennan told European officials that U.S. policymakers anticipated "an economically self-supporting Europe . . . militarily capable of taking care of itself" when Marshall Aid ended.[22] This sort of claim was commonplace and reflected the Policy Planning Staff (PPS) view that if the "free nations of Europe" could establish "some form of political, military and economic union," then they would be able "to hold their own against the people of the east united under Moscow rule."[23]

In short, the Europeans had the means as well as the motive to balance against the USSR. A hypothetical coalition—be it of the big three or continental variety—would have more than enough resources to avoid a gross power mismatch vis-à-vis the Soviet Union.

Opportunity

Of course, the Soviet Union was likely to oppose the formation of a powerful coalition in the western half of the continent. The USSR pursued a straightforward strategy in the early cold war years: security through the domination of its neighbors. By 1946 it controlled virtually all of eastern Europe including Poland, Bulgaria, Romania, and the eastern part of Germany. As Winston Churchill put it in a much-publicized speech at Fulton, Missouri, in March 1946, "an iron curtain" had "descended across the Continent," to the east of which Moscow's rule was absolute.[24] A policy of permanent weakening went hand in hand with the establishment of this

20. John Foster Dulles, The Unification of Western Europe, April 7, 1948, *Correspondence Series and the Speeches Series of the Personal Papers of John Foster Dulles (1888–1959)* (Wilmington, Del.: Scholarly Resources, 1993) (hereafter *JFD*), reel 10.

21. Memorandum of Conversation by Hickerson, January 21, 1948, *FRUS*, 1948, vol. 3, 11. For evidence that Hickerson was accurately reflecting the State Department view, see the 1948 unpublished history of the Marshall Plan quoted in Max Beloff, *The United States and the Unity of Europe* (Washington, D.C.: Brookings Institution, 1963), 28.

22. Minutes of the Fifth Meeting of the Washington Exploratory Talks on Security, July 9, 1948, *FRUS*, 1948, vol. 3, 177.

23. PPS/23, Review of Current Trends: U.S. Foreign Policy, February 24, 1948, *FRUS*, 1948, vol. 1, 510.

24. Winston Churchill, *Never Give In! The Best of Winston Churchill's Speeches*, ed. Winston S. Churchill (New York: Hyperion, 2003), 420.

sphere of influence. Nowhere was this more apparent than in the Soviet occupation zone of Germany, where the Russians carried out an aggressive reparations policy designed to eliminate Germany's war potential for good.[25]

There was, then, ample reason to believe that the Soviet Union would resist west European unity. Indeed, having analyzed the Soviet documentary record, Vladislav Zubok concludes that "the consensus [in Moscow] was that the USSR should remain an unchallenged land power in Europe, without even a shadow of countervailing power represented by another state or a group of smaller states."[26] Contemporary observers saw the situation much the same way. "The Soviet Government," observed U.S. diplomat Charles Bohlen even before the war ended, "is violently opposed to the creation of any federations in eastern, southeastern and central Europe."[27] The Soviets dispelled any remaining doubts on this score soon after the war ended. In response to various calls for European unity, the government-controlled media quickly condemned the "threat of a reactionary and aggressive Western bloc." Meanwhile, supporters of such schemes were accused of having "sinister ideas" and trying to build a "union directed against the USSR."[28]

Given this state of affairs, it was the U.S. commitment to balancing against the Soviet Union that gave the Europeans the opportunity to construct a viable coalition. Although the American security guarantee did not ensure that they would put a balancing coalition in place, it gave them that option. Had there been no guarantee, it is reasonable to assume that the major west European states would have quickly bandwagoned to Moscow, or that they would have tried to form a coalition only to be subjugated or destroyed.

The United States was clearly committed to defending Europe in the short term. This was evident immediately after the defeat of Nazi Germany. Indeed, as Melvyn Leffler has noted, "containment was the policy of the United States before George Kennan's famous long telegram arrived from Moscow in February 1946."[29] Initially, however, the strategy was not

25. See Carolyn Woods Eisenberg, *Drawing the Line: The American Decision to Divide Germany, 1944–1949* (Cambridge: Cambridge University Press, 1996).

26. Vladislav Zubok, "The Soviet Union and European Integration from Stalin to Gorbachev," *Journal of European Integration History* 2, no. 1 (1996): 85. See also Andrei Grachev, "The Soviet Leadership's View of Western European Integration in the 1950s and 1960s," in *Widening, Deepening and Acceleration: The European Economic Community, 1957–1963*, ed. Anne Deighton and Alan S. Milward (Baden-Baden: Nomos, 1999), 33–36.

27. Memorandum by Bohlen, December 15, 1943, *FRUS*, 1943, Cairo and Tehran, 847.

28. Quoted in Walter Lipgens, *A History of European Integration* (Oxford: Oxford University Press, 1982), 102.

29. Leffler, *Preponderance*, 61. On this point, see also Copeland, *Origins*, 149–65; and Marc Trachtenberg, *A Constructed Peace: The Making of the European Settlement* (Princeton: Princeton University Press, 1999), 41.

practiced aggressively. The major fear was not that the USSR would use military force to take over the continent, but that the Europeans would simply capitulate to the Soviets through sheer misery and exhaustion. So the Americans devoted most of their efforts to rebuilding the west Europeans' war-torn economies, culminating in the offer of aid through the Marshall Plan in June 1947.[30] Following the failure of the London Conference of Foreign Ministers (CFM) in December 1947, the Prague coup of February 1948, and the Soviet initiation of the Berlin blockade in June 1948, however, the United States moved to solidify and formalize its military commitment, culminating in the creation of NATO in April 1949.[31]

Despite stepping in to balance against the Soviet Union, however, the United States was determined to remain in Europe no longer than was required to preserve the peace. The Central Secretariat stated the administration's view in a July 1945 memorandum that was widely circulated in the State Department: "Permanent occupation of Germany . . . by the United States is inconceivable."[32] A month earlier, Joseph Davies had relayed a similar message to the British on Truman's behalf: "So far as holding large armed forces indefinitely in Europe in the present state of our public opinion, no President would be sustained by the country in such a decision, now or for some time to come."[33]

This view was widely shared. Kennan, for example, argued that one of the primary objectives of American foreign policy must be to "get us as soon as possible out of the position of abnormal political-military responsibility in Western Europe which the war had forced upon us."[34] At the same time, Walter Lippmann, whose opinions rarely coincided with Kennan's, declared that the "grand objective must be a settlement which does not call for a permanent American military intervention in Europe to maintain it."[35] The same view informed another of Kennan's major antagonists, Dean Acheson. When asked whether the North Atlantic Treaty meant that the

---

30. On the origins of the Marshall Plan, see Michael J. Hogan, *The Marshall Plan: America, Britain, and the Reconstruction of Western Europe, 1947–1952* (Cambridge: Cambridge University Press, 1987), 26–53; and Melvyn P. Leffler, "The United States and the Strategic Dimensions of the Marshall Plan," *Diplomatic History* 12, no. 3 (1998): 277–306.

31. On the origins of NATO, see Timothy P. Ireland, *Creating the Entangling Alliance: The Origins of the North Atlantic Treaty Organization* (Westport, Conn.: Greenwood, 1981); and Lawrence S. Kaplan, *NATO 1948: The Birth of the Transatlantic Alliance* (Lanham, Md.: Rowman and Littlefield, 2007).

32. Memorandum by the Central Secretariat, July 12, 1945, *FRUS*, 1945, Potsdam, vol. 1, 501.

33. Davies to Truman, June 12, 1945, ibid., 73.

34. Quoted in James McAllister, *No Exit: America and the German Problem, 1943–1954* (Ithaca: Cornell University Press, 2002), 17.

35. Quoted in John Lamberton Harper, *American Visions of Europe: Franklin D. Roosevelt, George F. Kennan, and Dean G. Acheson* (Cambridge: Cambridge University Press, 1994), 77.

United States would have to send a permanent force to Europe, Acheson, who had replaced George Marshall as secretary of state in January 1949, declared: "The answer to that question, Senator . . . is a clear and absolute no."[36] This commitment transcended party lines. As Dulles put it, the Europeans should be disabused of the "illusion that we can be relied upon indefinitely to rescue them from their own errors." This did not mean that the United States should abdicate its responsibility for rebuilding Europe, but the Americans should avoid "tying" themselves "permanently into the European picture."[37]

Taken together, Washington's clear commitment in the short term and desire to withdraw from the continent in the future provided ideal conditions for the formation of a west European combination. The short-term security guarantee provided the Europeans with the opportunity to build a coalition—without it any experiment in unity was unthinkable. Meanwhile, uncertainty about U.S. protection over the longer term gave them an incentive to begin providing for their own security, something they could only achieve by combining their efforts and resources.

In sum, the Europeans had the motive, means, and opportunity to build a balancing coalition against the Soviet Union between 1945 and 1950. The evidence presented to this point only shows that the conditions required for west European cooperation were present during this period, however. It does not prove that the European governments chose to cooperate because they wanted to balance against the Soviet Union and recognized that they had the means and temporary opportunity to do so. Nor have I demonstrated that balance of power calculations prompted them to adopt a particular form of cooperation, namely integration, and, more specifically, that these calculations resulted in the formation of the ECSC. It is to these tasks that I now turn.

France: Opting for Integration, 1945–1950

French policy between the defeat of Nazi Germany and the Schuman announcement can be briefly summarized. First, they were deeply concerned about the Soviet Union's hegemonic potential, and because they did not believe they could count on the U.S. security guarantee indefinitely, they resolved to establish a balancing coalition in the western part of the continent. Second, they came to the conclusion that despite the anxieties that went along with reviving the Reich, the coalition had to include a rebuilt

36. Quoted in Phil Williams, *U.S. Troops in Europe* (London: Royal Institute of International Affairs, 1984), 10. For further evidence on this point, see Michael Creswell, "With a Little Help from Our Friends: How France Secured an Anglo-American Continental Commitment, 1945–1954," *Cold War History* 3, no. 1 (2002): 2, 6–7.

37. John Foster Dulles, Long-Term Aims, undated, *JFD*, reel 8.

west German state. Third, they understood that any putative coalition must be centrally organized if it was to have a realistic chance of standing up to the Soviet Union on its own. Finally, of the centralized arrangements they could have chosen, they opted for integration because it promised to maintain the roughly even within-coalition distribution of power that had emerged between themselves and the Germans thanks to the postwar settlement.

The Balancing Imperative

The French were acutely aware of the Soviet Union's potential for domination.[38] As early as 1943, key officials were convinced that the USSR would be "the only continental state in Europe capable of maintaining the 'engines of modern war'."[39] Then, as Germany stood on the brink of defeat, French president Charles de Gaulle warned that it was "very possible that Russia will take over the entire continent of Europe in due course and in due time." At the same time, Foreign Minister Georges Bidault was asking Jefferson Caffery, the American ambassador to France, "Who is going to stop Attila: he is covering more territory every day." Similarly, the head of French intelligence, Colonel André Dewarin, noted that the president's great fear was "that the Soviet Union with its gigantic population and tremendous power could be a very dangerous instrument under the leadership of a 'mad-man'."[40]

This basic concern continued to inform French thinking for the rest of the decade. In an address delivered at Lille in June 1947, de Gaulle, now the leader of the opposition Rally of the French People (RPF), detected "in Europe the latent elements of a hegemony which, if it were to take definite shape, would be as dangerous a threat to the independence of nations as

---

38. For the basic point and further evidence, see Michael Creswell and Marc Trachtenberg, "France and the German Question, 1945–1955," *Journal of Cold War Studies* 5, no. 3 (2003): 7–13.

39. Quoted in John W. Young, *France, the Cold War, and the Western Alliance, 1944–49: French Foreign Policy and Post-War Europe* (New York: St. Martin's, 1990), 12.

40. Caffery to Acting Secretary of State, April 20, 1945, to Stettinius, May 5, 1945, and to Byrnes, November 20, 1945, *Confidential U.S. State Department Central Files: France, 1945–1950* (hereafter *CUSSDCFF*) (Frederick, Md.: University Publications of America, 1986), reel 3. On de Gaulle's fear of the Soviet Union, see Georges-Henri Soutou, "Le Général de Gaulle et l'URSS, 1943–1945: Idéologie ou équilibre européen?" *Revue d'histoire diplomatique* 108, no. 4 (1994): 347–53. Regarding Bidault's fear of Russia in 1945 and 1946, see Soutou, "Georges Bidault et la construction européenne 1944–1954," *Revue d'histoire diplomatique* 105, no. 3 (1991): 268–69; and Soutou, "La politique française à l'égard de la Rhénanie, 1944–1947," in *Franzosen und Deutsche am Rhein, 1789, 1918, 1945,* ed. Peter Hüttenberger and Hansgeorg Molitor (Essen: Klartext, 1989), esp. 52–61.

any there has been since the dawn of history."[41] Similarly, in March 1948, Bidault told Caffery that he believed Russian thinking "is about like this: 'If we do not take over western Europe in the relatively near future, the Americans may wake up and then we shall be up against it'." This being the case, the Soviets might bid for hegemony sooner rather than later. Bidault conceded that his opinion might seem "extravagant," but then "we are sitting here under the guns."[42] So worried was he, in fact, that he wrote Marshall twice in a matter of months to "point out to him that the Soviet menace now threatened the whole of Western Europe" and that the "Russian armies were only 200 kilometres from the Rhine."[43]

These fears were heightened by the belief that France could not count on American protection indefinitely. As de Gaulle told Caffery in November 1945, "You are far away and your soldiers will not stay long in Europe. It is hard for you to understand the difference: it is a matter of life and death for us; for you, one interesting question among many others."[44] Bidault's fear, meanwhile, was that "we [the United States] might withdraw our occupation forces from Germany at an early date."[45] Such concerns were commonplace in France. For example, Georges Duhamel, the French author and president of the Alliance Française, worried publicly about abandonment: "If you abandon us, all European civilization is lost forever." Similarly, Eve Curie, the foreign editor of *Paris-Presse*, worried about the day that "the Americans pack up and go home."[46] Robert Murphy, the political adviser for Germany, summed up the situation well: "French policy is based . . . on fear that the United States will lose interest, eventually withdraw from Germany, and that some fine morning they will wake up and find themselves face to face with the Russians on the Rhine."[47]

Nor did the French take much comfort on this score from their conversations with American officials. The Ruhr problem, Marshall told Bidault in December 1947, had a short and long term dimension to it. "During the short range period, the occupying powers would be in control of Europe" and thus "no question of security arose." When the "occupational period was over," on the other hand, the Ruhr "might present a problem of security."[48] That the United States envisaged a postoccupation phase can hardly have

41. Charles de Gaulle, Speech Delivered at Lille, June 29, 1947, *Documents on the History of European Integration* (hereafter *DHEI*), vol. 3 (New York: W. de Gruyter, 1988), 50.

42. Caffery to Marshall, March 4, 1948, *FRUS*, 1948, vol. 3, 629.

43. Georges Bidault, *Resistance: The Political Autobiography of Georges Bidault*, trans. Marianne Sinclair (New York: F. A. Praeger, 1967), 155. See also Cyril Buffet, *Mourir pour Berlin: La France et l'Allemagne, 1945–1949* (Paris: A. Colin, 1991), 94, 118.

44. Caffery to Byrnes, November 3, 1945, *FRUS*, 1945, vol. 3, 890.

45. Caffery to State Department, March 23, 1946, *CUSSDCFF*, reel 1.

46. Embassy in Paris to State Department, Current Opinions of Individuals in Journalistic and Other Circles in Paris, March 21, 1945, ibid., reel 3.

47. Murphy to Byrnes, February 24, 1946, *FRUS*, 1946, vol. 5, 506.

48. Memorandum of Conversation by Douglas, December 17, 1947, *FRUS*, 1947, vol. 2, 814.

reassured the French; the Americans might be committed to the continent in the short term, but they clearly hoped to withdraw in the future. Likewise, Truman's March 1948 statement to the effect that he would keep forces in the region "until the peace is secure in Europe" implied an end date to America's commitment—an end date that would be based on American judgment at that.[49] Even the formation of NATO the following year provided scant comfort: although the Americans agreed to treat an "attack against one" as "an attack against them all," they also reserved the right to respond to a Soviet attack in whatever way they deemed "necessary" including the use of nonmilitary means.[50]

Together, the Soviet threat and uncertainty about the U.S. security guarantee contributed to a growing sentiment in Paris that France must take the lead in constructing a European balancing coalition that included Germany.[51] According to Caffery, French thinking was dominated by "a fear of possible European domination by Soviet Russia . . . and a fear that the United States will once again withdraw into its shell of isolation."[52] Because of this, French policymakers concluded that the Europeans had to provide for their own security by joining forces, and that this coalition must include the western half of Germany if it was to have enough power to contain the Soviet Union. The other west European states simply could not deal with the Soviets on their own.

Given Germany's history of aggression, the French had serious reservations about reviving and entering into some kind of compact with it. De Gaulle put the point well: "Consider this: that we are neighbors of Germany, that we have been invaded three times by Germany in a single lifetime, and you will conclude that we want no more of the Reich."[53] Official French policy in the immediate postwar period therefore aimed at Germany's demilitarization and decentralization and the detachment of the industrial Rhineland, Ruhr, and Saar. French negotiators, meanwhile, opposed the installation of central agencies in Germany—a move they thought might quickly lead to the creation of a central government—and increases in the level of industry in the western zones.[54]

49. Address by the President to the Congress, Toward Securing the Peace and Preventing War, March 17, 1948, *Department of State Bulletin* (hereafter *DOSB*), vol. 18, no. 456 (Washington, D.C.: GPO, 1948), 420.

50. For the text of the North Atlantic Treaty, see Kaplan, *NATO*, 251–54.

51. For a similar argument, see Trachtenberg, *Constructed*, 70–78.

52. Caffery to Stettinius, Observations Relating to Certain Aspects of French Foreign Policy, February 3, 1945, *CUSSDCFF*, reel 1. This continued to be the case throughout the 1940s. See, for example, Memorandum of Conversation by MacArthur, January 29, 1948, *FRUS*, 1948, vol. 3, 620.

53. Quoted in Young, *France*, 84.

54. On French policy during this period, see Marie-Thérèse Bitsch, "Un rêve français: Le désarmement économique de l'Allemagne (1944–1947)," *Relations internationales* 51 (1987): 313–29; Buffet, *Mourir*, 19–53; Pierre Gerbet, *Le relèvement: 1944–1949* (Paris: Imprimerie Nationale, 1991), 85–105; and William I. Hitchcock, *France Restored:*

Nevertheless, the French understood that the magnitude of the Soviet threat ultimately left them no option but to rebuild Germany and incorporate it into a west European coalition. Top decision makers concluded quite early on that they had to rehabilitate Germany. Thus in June 1946, Jean Chauvel, the secretary general of the French Foreign Ministry, told Caffery that his government actually supported Anglo-American plans to "organize" the western zones but could not say so publicly "for internal political reasons." To do so would invite the French Communist Party (PCF), which was especially powerful in France, to create "confusion and chaos." Over time, however, a "real agreement" would be possible.[55] Deputy Premier Pierre-Henri Teitgen made the same point in March 1947, informing Caffery that "in principle" the French were "not opposed" to fusing their occupation zone with those of Britain and the United States—a move that represented the first step toward the creation of a west German state—but would prefer to do so informally to "avoid . . . complications with the Communists." A month later, at the Moscow CFM, Bidault told Marshall that "to the American question 'Can we rely on France?'" the French "answer was 'Yes'," thereby indicating that the French, like the Americans, were committed to rebuilding Germany. However, he added, "France needed time and must avoid a civil war."[56]

In 1948, the French openly committed to rebuilding Germany. Schuman set the ball rolling in February, informing the Americans that he had instructed his delegates at the tripartite London conference on Germany to "modify" the French position, reach a "cordial *modus vivendi*" with the other western Allies, and deal with the "unsatisfactory" German situation.[57] Of course, the French had reservations about organizing the western zones. Bidault was concerned that the public "was still extremely sensitive," and worried that the Soviet Union might use force to derail western plans, a concern that grew in the wake of the Prague coup.[58] Nevertheless, on June

---

Cold War Diplomacy and the Quest for Leadership in Europe, 1944–1954 (Chapel Hill: University of North Carolina Press, 1998), 41–71.

55. Caffery to Byrnes, June 11, 1946, *FRUS*, 1946, vol. 5, 566–67. Bidault reiterated the point during his conversations with the Americans in August. See Caffery to Byrnes, August 30, 1946, ibid., 596. For the argument that the French were committed to rebuilding the western half of Germany, but adopted a different public position for domestic political reasons, see Creswell and Trachtenberg, "France," 9–13.

56. Caffery to Marshall, March 25, 1947, and Memorandum of Conversation by Marshall, April 20, 1947, *FRUS*, 1947, vol. 2, 401, 369. See also Caffery to Marshall, November 6, 1947, ibid., 702.

57. Marshall to the Embassy in France, February 19, 1948, *FRUS*, 1948, vol. 2, 70.

58. Bidault, *Resistance*, 156. For examples of these fears, see Caffery to Marshall, January 10 and May 25, 1948, *FRUS*, 1948, vol. 2, 20–21, 281. See also René Girault, "The French Decision-Makers and their Perception of French Power in 1948," in *Power in Europe? Great Britain, France, Italy, and Germany in a Postwar World, 1945–1950*, ed. Josef Becker and Franz Knipping (New York: W. de Gruyter, 1986), 59; Serge Berstein, "French Power as Seen by the Political Parties after World War II," in *Power in Europe?*

1, 1948, after several months of negotiations, the French reached agreement with their allies on the London Recommendations.[59] A constituent assembly would meet no later than September 1 and draft a constitution for the new state. To be sure, this would not be a fully sovereign state—the newly created International Authority for the Ruhr (IAR) would control and monitor the distribution of coke, coal, and steel, and a Military Security Board (MSB) was established to monitor any military activity—but this was an event of fundamental importance. Britain, France, and the United States were going to establish a new state in their part of Germany.

Leading decision makers took it as axiomatic that France and the new Germany would form the nucleus of an anti-Soviet balancing coalition. Thus in January 1947, during Léon Blum's brief tenure as prime minister, officials at the Quai d'Orsay concluded, "in the economic area, but also in the political area, the integration of Germany into Europe has to be taken as the goal for both the allies and the Germans themselves."[60] A few months later, Bidault assured Marshall that "there is no question that Germany is a part of Europe."[61] In July, he went public with his views in the National Assembly. France was committed to balancing against the USSR; "its adherence to the Brussels pact and . . . participation in the programme of European reconstruction" was proof of that. But more important, he expected Germany to join France in its balancing endeavor: "We are living in difficult times, so that we can only speak in terms of Western Europe and West Germany for the moment. Nevertheless, we must build up Europe, and we must find some place in it for Germany. We will do all we can to create a united Europe."[62] At the same time, de Gaulle told the Anglo-American press that he believed the French should take the lead and "re-create the old Europe . . . on a basis of solidarity." Significantly, this Europe would include Germany. Although he wanted "measures to be taken to prevent their committing aggression ever again," he also declared that he was "not one who would exclude them for ever from that Europe of which they are the children."[63]

Great Britain, France, Italy, and Germany in a Postwar World, 1945–1950, ed. Josef Becker and Franz Knipping (New York: W. de Gruyter, 1986), 463–64; and Buffet, *Mourir*, 128.

59. For the key documents, see *FRUS*, 1948, vol. 2, 309–12, 240–41, 260–62, 290–94, 305–7, and for a historical account, see Peter H. Merkl, *The Origin of the West German Republic* (Oxford: Oxford University Press, 1963).

60. Quoted in Trachtenberg, *Constructed*, 75, n. 37.

61. Memorandum of Conversation by Marshall, April 20, 1947, *FRUS*, 1947, vol. 2, 370.

62. Bidault, *Resistance*, 161.

63. Charles de Gaulle, Address to Members of the Anglo-American Press Association, July 9, 1947, *DHEI*, vol. 3, 50–51. See also Charles de Gaulle, *The Complete War Memoirs of Charles de Gaulle*, trans. Jonathan Griffin and Richard Howard (New York: Simon and Schuster, 1972), 872–73, and de Gaulle's comments quoted in Edmond Jouve, *Le Général de Gaulle et la construction de l'Europe (1940–1966)* (Paris: R. Pichon et R. Durand-Auzias, 1967), 147–48.

This basic strategy continued to inform French policy in the following year. In January, Bidault told France's representative on the Allied Control Council (ACC), General Pierre Koenig, "German recovery in the cadre of Europe should take place as rapidly as possible," and he instructed Secretary of State Pierre Schneiter to inform the Germans that France was determined to "play an honorable role in a united and cooperative Europe."[64] Little changed once the negotiations that would lead to the London Recommendations got under way. France's German policy, Bidault explained in February 1948, must now evolve in the context of the cold war. The natural arena of French action, moreover, was "Europe," and it was "within the context of Europe that we must study the German problem." In effect, "the solution—and there are no others" was the inclusion of "a peaceful Germany into a united Europe."[65] President Vincent Auriol backed up his minister: "It is necessary to organize Western Europe, since the rest of it has already been organized."[66] Indeed, in April, the French government informed the Americans by way of a top-secret note that they wanted "to pursue the construction of western Europe in the political, economic and military realms."[67]

The Office of European Affairs echoed these views in an internal memorandum prepared for Schuman in July 1948. Given the international situation, it argued, the "French-German 'duel' can be regarded as having come to an end." Any future war would find France and Germany on the same side. Therefore one could now speak of "a community of fate binding together the French and the Germans," insofar as it was becoming "ever clearer that what is suffered in future by the Germans will also be suffered to an equal degree by the French."[68] The prevailing balance of power, in other words, made France and West Germany natural allies. As Raymond Aron put it in a classic statement of balance of power thinking at the time, the ongoing "organization" of western Europe was hardly surprising; after all, it was not the "first time that unity was emerging from the recognition of a common peril."[69]

64. Quoted in John Gillingham, "Solving the Ruhr Problem: German Heavy Industry and the Schuman Plan," in *Die Anfänge des Schuman-Plans 1950–51*, ed. Klaus Schwabe (Baden-Baden: Nomos, 1988), 408–9; and John Gillingham, *Coal, Steel, and the Rebirth of Europe, 1945–1955: The Germans and the French from Ruhr Conflict to Economic Community* (Cambridge: Cambridge University Press, 1991), 159.

65. Quoted in Buffet, *Mourir*, 78. All translations from the French are my own.

66. Quoted in Berstein, "French," 467.

67. Quoted in Buffet, *Mourir*, 119.

68. Quoted in Franz Knipping, "Que faire de l'Allemagne? French Foreign Policy toward Germany, 1945–1950," in *France and Germany in an Age of Crisis, 1900–1960: Studies in Memory of Charles Bloch*, ed. Haim Shamir (New York: E. J. Brill, 1990), 81; Buffet, *Mourir*, 182; and Mark S. Sheetz, "Continental Drift: Franco-German Relations and the Shifting Premises of European Security," (PhD diss., Columbia University, 2002), 75.

69. Raymond Aron, *Le grand schisme* (Paris: Gallimard, 1948), 68.

In the late 1940s, then, the French came to the conclusion that they must establish a European coalition, including West Germany, to contain the Soviet Union. The reasoning behind their decision was straightforward and based on balance of power considerations: the Soviet Union possessed overwhelming strength, the Americans could not be relied upon indefinitely to deter the Russians, and therefore the Europeans had to come together and balance for themselves. Moreover, a restored Germany must be part of the European effort; without it, no coalition could survive. This decision was not taken lightly given Germany's history of aggression, but the French understood that the geopolitical situation left them no choice. As Marc Trachtenberg has argued, concerns about overwhelming Soviet power ultimately pushed "France to accept the distasteful and dangerous policy of building up Germany" and "building Europe."[70]

Centralization

Although the terminology varied—government officials and political figures tended to refer to federation, confederation, union, and supranationalism without distinction—the French concluded that they must build a centralized political-economic coalition in western Europe because only an entity of this kind would have the wherewithal to stand up to the Soviet Union. In the remainder of this section, I expand on this claim, first by showing that support for centralization was fairly widespread in France and then by demonstrating that this support was based on balance of power reasoning.

Supporting Centralization
Centralization was quite popular among the French political elite in the late 1940s. This is not to say that the French abandoned traditional balancing altogether. The two major west European security agreements concluded during this period—the Dunkirk Treaty (1947) and the Brussels Treaty (1948)—were conventional military alliances.[71] But these treaties were essentially stopgap measures designed to persuade the United States that the Europeans were determined to contribute to their own defense and, in fact, even as they were being negotiated, the French were advocating a more centralized unit of power.

---

70. Trachtenberg, *Constructed*, 74–75.

71. For the argument that despite formally identifying Germany as the principal threat to European security, the treaties were actually directed against the Soviet Union, see Michael Creswell, *A Question of Balance: How France and the United States Created Cold War Europe* (Cambridge: Harvard University Press, 2006), 11. On the Dunkirk Treaty more generally, see Sean Greenwood, "Return to Dunkirk: The Origins of the Anglo-French Treaty of March 1947," *Journal of Strategic Studies* 6, no. 4 (1983): 49–65, and on the Brussels Treaty, see John Baylis, "Britain, the Brussels Pact and the Continental Commitment," *International Affairs* 60, no. 4 (1984): 615–29.

This was clearly the position taken by the Popular Republican Movement (MRP), whose foreign policy committee declared that the "security and prosperity" of western Europe depended on "the establishment of a federation of states" in the region. At its fourth national congress in May 1948, the party noted the threat posed by the Soviet Union and expressed the hope that existing cooperative efforts constituted the beginnings of a European "union" or "federation."[72] Not long after, Bidault, himself a party member, argued that national officials had a "fundamental responsibility" to support the "creation of European institutions."[73] Similarly, Teitgen, who was considered an MRP foreign affairs specialist, suggested "setting up a federal Europe," by which he meant "an organized Europe with a structure similar to that of a state."[74]

The other major party in the *troisième force* governing coalition, the French Socialist Party (SFIO), shared this view. In July 1947, its National Council openly supported the Marshall Plan because it represented the "first step towards a Europe that would henceforth be more than a purely geographical notion." Then, in the fall, Prime Minister Paul Ramadier acknowledged that it was "not easy to establish such a new and unique constitution as that of a united Europe," but argued that it was nonetheless "what we must do" if Europe was to "continue to exist as an independent political and economic force." The party took a virtually identical line at its fortieth congress, committing to "bring about the United States of free Europe."[75]

Remarkably, there was also support for centralization within the RPF, the party most closely associated with the view that France should preserve its independence. According to de Gaulle, speaking at Marseille in April 1948, "almost everyone admits that we must organize the free peoples of Europe in an economic and strategic whole." That he thought this unit ought to be centralized comes through clearly in his response to Adenauer's March 1950 proposal for a Franco-German union. De Gaulle saw no reason, he announced, why France and Germany could not resume "Charlemagne's enterprise"—Charlemagne had established a west European empire and defended it against its eastern competitors—on an "economic, social, strategic, and cultural" basis. Similarly, he rejected more traditional cooperative agreements such as the Organization for European Economic

72. Quoted in Lipgens, *History*, 499; and MRP, Foreign Policy Motion, May 10, 1948, *DHEI*, vol. 3, 68. For further evidence on this general point, see Berstein, "French," 180–82.

73. Quoted in Alain Greilsammer, *Les mouvements fédéralistes en France de 1945 à 1974* (Paris: Presses d'Europe, 1975), 55.

74. Pierre-Henri Teitgen, Between Britain and Germany, July 9, 1949, *DHEI*, vol. 3, 103.

75. Quoted in Lipgens, *History*, 499–500; and SFIO, Resolution on International Action, July 4, 1948, *DHEI*, vol. 3, 80.

Cooperation (OEEC) on the basis that they had no real "powers."[76] De Gaulle's confidants went even further in their support for a single European entity. Gaston Palewski called for a European federation that would "limit the sovereign rights" of member states in matters of defense and economic cooperation and warned that there were two options: "one is European federation, the other is catastrophe." Meanwhile, General Pierre de Bénouville declared, "it is no longer a question of pursuing a policy based on alliances, but of bringing about the federation of Europe."[77] In short, the RPF view was that a "federal organization of Europe" aligned with the United States was "an imperative necessity for the maintenance of peace and the safeguarding of the essential values of civilization."[78]

Support for centralization was so widespread by 1948 that 169 parliamentary deputies signed a motion calling on the government to convene a European constituent assembly that would "establish the permanent institutions of a democratic European federation." The motion failed to gain a majority in the foreign affairs committee, where doubts were expressed about the feasibility of achieving union via a constituent assembly, but in July the committee invited the government to convene an assembly of national representatives tasked with drawing up plans that would "make it possible to draw up a federal constitution for the democratic nations of Europe."[79]

This kind of thinking was especially strong in the Quai, where the Fourth Republic's foreign policy was made.[80] By early 1948, it was taken for granted that Europe was "on the road to federalism."[81] Foreign Ministry officials responded by arguing that France should take the lead in this process. Thus Jacques Tarbé de Saint-Hardouin, the French political adviser in Germany, told Bidault that he thought Paris should work toward building a "European federation."[82] A few months later, policymakers envisaged "federating" Europe and creating a "European union."[83] Moreover, they

76. Jouve, *De Gaulle*, 148; Charles de Gaulle, *Discours et messages: Dans l'attente, février 1946–avril 1958* (Paris: Plon, 1970), 350; and Pierre Gerbet, "Les origines du Plan Schuman: Le choix de la méthode communautaire par le gouvernement français," in *Histoire des débuts de la construction européenne (mars 1948–mai 1950)*, ed. Raymond Poidevin (Brussels: Bruylant, 1986), 203.

77. For the quotations and further evidence, see Gerbet, "Origines," 202.

78. RPF, Between Federation and Confederation, February 9, 1949, *DHEI*, vol. 3, 87.

79. National Assembly, Motion for the Convening of a European Constituent Assembly, March 19, 1948, and Report of the Foreign Affairs Committee, July 28, 1948, ibid., 65, 67.

80. For the claim that the Foreign Ministry dominated the foreign policy process, see Girault, "French," 51–55; and Gerbet, *Relèvement*, 233–35.

81. Quoted in Hitchcock, *France*, 91.

82. Ibid., 92.

83. Quoted in Raymond Poidevin, "La France devant le danger allemand (1944–1952)," in *Deutsche Frage und europäisches Gleichgewicht*, ed. Klaus Hildebrand and Reiner Pommerin (Cologne: Böhlau, 1985), 261.

concluded that intergovernmental arrangements such as the Brussels Treaty could not meet Europe's needs. What was required instead was a "set of procedures such that the progress made toward federation will be irreversible."[84]

Schuman shared the pro-centralization view in his ministry. Soon after the creation of the Council of Europe—a traditional intergovernmental body—he informed Teitgen, "it had to be done, but we should not expect great things from it." What was required instead was the construction of "something around the Franco-German union" and a "system in which we would not only commit our words, but also our interests."[85] Jean Monnet, who would become a prime mover in the integration process, agreed, arguing that "the idea that sixteen sovereign nations will co-operate effectively is an illusion," and that the Europeans could prosper strategically and economically only through a genuinely joint effort, something that required "a *federation* of the West." Indeed, this kind of thinking made its way into the first draft of what was to become the Schuman declaration: "Europe must be organized on a federal basis. A Franco-German union is an essential element in it."[86]

Balance of Power Reasoning

French support for centralization derived from straightforward balance of power calculations. Only a coalition with a central authority, they reasoned, would be powerful enough to stand up to the Soviet Union. To be sure, advocates of centralization did not always couch their support for it in precisely these terms. Often their ostensible reason for supporting a centrally organized coalition was that such an entity would be "independent" of *both* superpowers. But the kind of independence they aspired to was different depending on the superpower in question. In the case of the United States, it meant not having to rely on the unpredictable Americans for their defense, whereas in the Soviet case it meant deterring the Red Army. In other words, independence from both great powers boiled down to being able to balance against the USSR without American help. The same was true of claims that a centralized grouping would contribute to world "peace." The peace they envisaged was a cold one born of Europe's ability to deter a Soviet attack.

This view was quite widespread among the French political elite. André Philip, a leading member of the SFIO, laid out the general argument in March 1949. Western Europe faced two problems in his opinion: creating

84. Quoted in Marie-Thérèse Bitsch, "Le rôle de la France dans la naissance du Conseil de l'Europe," in *Histoire des débuts de la construction européenne (mars 1948—mai 1950)*, ed. Raymond Poidevin (Brussels: Bruylant, 1986), 171.

85. Quoted in Gerbet, "Origines," 214.

86. Jean Monnet, *Memoirs* (Garden City, N.Y.: Doubleday, 1978), 272–73, 295. Emphasis in original.

economic recovery and ensuring world "peace." The solution to the latter problem was building a "third force equally independent of both" the United States and the Soviet Union. This being the case, he advocated the creation of an "authority" that would look "beyond particular interests to those of our continent as a whole." If Europe was to be a significant player on the global stage alongside the superpowers, not reliant on the United States and capable of containing the Soviet Union, then the Europeans would have to establish "an authority, composed of men who can rise above national interests, [and] 'think European'."[87]

The Radical Party, also a part of the governing coalition, took a similar line. As early as September 1947, its foreign affairs spokesman, Auguste Pinton, asserted that if the Europeans wanted to "be an element of equilibrium and peace," each state had "to make the necessary sacrifice of sovereignty and to take the first steps towards a European federation." In a "world that is more and more merciless to the small and weak," only centralization would enable them to create "a great political reality, equal to the others . . . and capable of providing the element of stability that is so essential to the maintenance of peace."[88]

De Gaulle and his followers operated under similar assumptions. Pointing to the "growing rivalry between the two great masses," the general predicted a "colossal conflict from which . . . no nation and no human being would be safe." In order to avert such a conflict, Europe must come together "organized as a single system" capable of withstanding "any possible claim to hegemony" and providing "an element of a balance" in the cold war.[89] Gaullist deputy René Capitant was more specific in a rapturously received speech to the National Assembly in July 1949. Noting that Europe faced a powerful threat from the Soviet Union, he declared that the solution lay in centralizing authority: "There is no salvation . . . except by restricting national sovereignty . . . and by establishing European political organs." This was not to say that a "United States of Europe" would "arise all of a sudden like the USA"—there would have to be a "confederal phase" first—but France must aim for a "true European federation" including a "single army" and a "political union."[90] In short, in a world dominated by the superpowers, only a centralized coalition could be secure.

This kind of reasoning was quite popular on the eve of the Schuman declaration, and in April 1949 a representative cross-section of the French political elite made the case forcefully in a leaflet titled "Appeal for the Creation of a European Political Authority." The signatories—including seventeen

---

87. André Philip, The Economic Unification of Europe, March 1949, *DHEI*, vol. 3, 93–94.

88. Auguste Pinton, In Favor of a "Marshall Plan" Europe, September 18, 1947, ibid., 55.

89. Charles de Gaulle, Address to Members of the Anglo-American Press Association, July 9, 1947, ibid., 50.

90. René Capitant, For a Federal Europe, July 9, 1949, ibid., 104.

National Assembly deputies, former prime ministers Blum, Ramadier, Paul Reynaud, and Joseph Paul-Boncour, current and former government ministers including Philip, Teitgen, René Mayer, and Guy Mollet (the leading socialist in the country), and several ambassadors, senators, and delegates to European institutions—viewed a centralized unit of power as the only option if Europe was to survive as an independent force. Pointing to "Russian expansionism and totalitarianism, [and] the development of the cold war," they argued that France must "give a firm direction to the common destiny of Europe." To do that, moreover, Paris was going to have to establish a centralized political-economic coalition. "Only the creation of a common authority," they asserted, "will make it possible to adopt the cultural, social, economic and military measures that will turn our small countries into a prosperous union—powerful, respected, peace-loving and brotherly—which will . . . ward off the dangers that now threaten our basic freedoms and the fruits of our labor."[91] As Aron, one of the signatories, had noted soon after the end of the war in Europe, the world was now populated with "multinational, continental states" and the west Europeans would have to establish a similar entity if they wished to survive.[92]

Observations like these reinforced the assumptions of an administration primed to recognize the geopolitical logic of centralization. Monnet made the case in a letter to Schuman. "Europe," he asserted, "cannot long afford to remain almost exclusively dependent on . . . American strength." Therefore the Europeans had to come together, and—if they were to contain the Soviet Union—this cooperation had to be closer than it had been in the past. It was therefore his "profound conviction" that "to face the dangers that threaten us . . . the countries of Western Europe must turn their national efforts into a truly European effort. This will be possible only through a *federation*."[93] Schuman understood perfectly. Looking back on events leading up to his famous announcement, he noted that Europe faced a "political crisis" in its relations with the Soviet Union. Worse still, it was poorly equipped to deal with the Russian threat due to its fragmentation into "twenty or so states . . . at precisely the time that the rest of the world was organizing itself into enormous economic blocs."[94]

Thus, by 1950 many French policymakers had concluded that only a centralized west European coalition could provide a viable counterweight to Soviet power. Some reached this conclusion based on simple calculation: all else being equal, a centralized coalition would be more powerful than a decentralized one. Most, however, employed an imitation logic. If Europe was to survive, it had to look more like the great powers.

91. French Council of the European Movement, Appeal for the Creation of a European Political Authority, April 22, 1950, ibid., 114–15.
92. Raymond Aron, The Age of Empires, July 1945, ibid., 31.
93. Monnet, *Memoirs*, 272–73. Emphasis in original.
94. Robert Schuman, *Pour l'Europe* (Paris: Editions Nagel, 1963), 153, 156–57.

Integration

French decision makers ultimately settled on integration as the best arrangement for establishing and maintaining a roughly even balance of industrial power within western Europe. Indeed, the Schuman Plan is best understood as the direct product of this kind of thinking.

Supporting Integration

Although Schuman did not announce his plan until May 1950, the idea "was in the air" two years earlier.[95] When Lewis Douglas, the American ambassador to London, suggested in February 1948 that international control of the Ruhr give way to a "regime" that controlled "not only [the] Ruhr but also similar industrial regions of Western Europe," the French replied that the "suggestion merited serious consideration." In doing so, they indicated that they were not opposed in principle to the construction of a regional heavy-industrial community.[96]

Monnet and his closest associates began to discuss the details of a "western economic union" with officials at the Quai soon after the meeting with the Americans.[97] Integration seems to have been the principal topic of debate during these discussions. At a private dinner in July 1948, for example, MRP deputy Pierre Pflimlin suggested the formation of "an 'energy complex,' which would include France and the Benelux nations as well as Germany and be run by a European authority." Monnet agreed and, to the approval of others present including the economist Henry Laufenberger, suggested that the issue be discussed with Dulles.[98] The choice of Dulles was significant: even though the future secretary of state did not have a role in the U.S. government at this point, he was one of the most important, visible, and influential proponents of an integrated west European coalition.[99]

To be sure, the French did not have a fully developed vision of integration at this point, but the outline was there. So in August 1948, several prominent personalities were dispatched to the western zones of Germany to float the idea of an organization "charged with controlling all of Europe's primary resources, coal, steel, as well as all forms of energy."[100] Meanwhile, the French daily *Le Monde* declared that "Europe" would only become a reality if the "coal of Rhine-Westphalia" became a "common good" and if

95. Pierre Gerbet, "La genèse du Plan Schuman: Des origines à la déclaration du 9 Mai 1950," *Revue française de science politique* 6 (1956): 526; and Raymond Poidevin, "La France et le charbon allemand au lendemain de la deuxième guerre mondiale," *Relations internationales* 44 (1985): 377.

96. Douglas to Marshall, February 28, 1948, *FRUS*, 1948, vol. 2, 99–100.

97. Poidevin, "Danger," 262.

98. Gillingham, *Coal*, 160.

99. McAllister, *Exit*, 137–40.

100. Quoted in Poidevin, "Danger," 262.

"all the states of western Europe, including Germany" had "free and equal access to it."[101]

By the end of the year, there was growing support for integration both within the Quai and among important public figures. In November, for example, the head of the Office of European Affairs, Jacques-Camille Paris, and his collaborator Romain Gary, called for the "integration of Franco-German coal and steel resources, in joint companies under the control of a public authority." A month later, the office suggested that France take the lead in establishing a "European steel pool in which France and Germany would sit as equals and exercise common control over the steel production of Europe."[102] While these debates were going on behind the scenes, prominent Frenchmen were making the same case publicly. At the foreign affairs committee of the National Assembly, Teitgen suggested that the internationalization of the Ruhr—code for control by the western Allies—give way to its "Europeanization." Philip followed up with a proposal for an international commission tasked with overseeing coal and steel exports not only from Germany, but from the other west European states as well. Schuman himself indicated his approval for these and similar arrangements in December, though he cautioned that more work remained to be done on the details.[103] Then in January, with the backing of the Quai, Philip and André François-Poncet—soon to be named French high commissioner for Germany—were dispatched to discuss the issue with German officials and reporters.[104]

The steady pro-integration drumbeat continued into 1949. Philip led the charge, first appealing for a "European public institution" that would govern the coal, steel, electricity, and transportation industries and then supporting a similar proposal by the chairman of the foreign affairs committee, Edouard Bonnefous, that the Europeans "place their natural resources in common" and establish a "common international administrative body" to manage them.[105] The Quai also made its support for integration public, albeit through a series of intermediaries. In September, Jacques Gascuel, a close confidant of Monnet, published an article calling for a "great industrial combination comprising the metallurgical centers of eastern France,

101. Quoted in Raymond Poidevin, *Robert Schuman: Homme d'Etat, 1886–1963* (Paris: Imprimerie Nationale, 1986), 251.

102. Quoted in Sheetz, "Continental," 81–82; and Raymond Poidevin, "Le facteur Europe dans la politique allemande de Robert Schuman (été 1948–printemps 1949)," in *Histoire des débuts de la construction européenne (mars 1948–mai 1950)*, ed. Raymond Poidevin (Brussels: Bruylant, 1986), 320.

103. Gerbet, *Relèvement*, 298. Schuman made the same point to Adenauer in the fall of 1949. See Minutes of Cabinet Meeting, November 3, 1949, *Die Kabinettsprotokolle der Bundesregierung* (hereafter *KB*), vol. 1, 1949 (Boppard am Rhein: Harald Boldt, 1982), 170.

104. Poidevin, *Schuman*, 211; and Poidevin, "Facteur," 325–26.

105. Quoted in Gerbet, "Genèse," 527–28.

the Ruhr, Luxembourg, eastern Belgium, and south-eastern Holland."[106] Three months later, based on a suggestion by J-C Paris, the National Assembly's economic committee adopted a motion demanding the creation of "European Companies" that would operate free of restrictions across state lines.[107] Perhaps most important, Schuman weighed in on the matter, telling the foreign affairs committee that he believed France should propose "a set of rules to which all European states would submit themselves." These would not be unilaterally imposed, but rather "structured in the interest of the European economy" as a whole.[108]

Balance of Power Reasoning

This support for integration was based on balance of power thinking. Key decision makers in Paris understood that the cold war settlement, by dividing Germany, had brought about rough material parity between France and Germany, and they were determined to maintain it. They also recognized that Germany's ability to upset the balance of power depended on whether or not it could recover exclusive control over its industrial resources. Given these facts, integration was an appealing arrangement: rather than putting Germany's industrial potential back in German hands, it would require all the west European states, including Germany, to share their resources and control them jointly, thereby formalizing and perpetuating the rough power equality wrought by the postwar settlement.

World War II had done more than remove the west European states from the ranks of the great powers; it had also established a roughly even balance of power between France and Germany, a situation virtually without precedent since the unification of Germany. In the three decades prior to the German invasion of France in the summer of 1940, the Reich had between a 1.5:1 and 2:1 population advantage over France. Following the war, however, Germany was cut in half and its population advantage over France was reduced to less than 1.2 to 1.[109] In terms of basic potential, there was little difference between the two states in the late 1940s. J-C Paris summed up the prevailing view, claiming that "Germany's division into two parts" presented France with "some major advantages."[110] Nor could West Germany count on its traditional superiority in industry. Its industrial heartland had come under allied control in the spring of 1945 and was still under tripartite western control on the eve of Schuman's declaration. Even the establishment of the Federal Republic did not alter this state of affairs. In November 1949, two months after its formal creation, Adenauer signed the

---

106. Quoted in Poidevin, *Schuman*, 252.
107. Quoted in Gerbet, "Génèse," 528.
108. Quoted in Poidevin, *Schuman*, 254.
109. For the data, see Correlates of War, National.
110. Quoted in Buffet, *Mourir*, 189. See also Sheetz, "Continental," 77–78; and Thomas A. Schwartz, *America's Germany: John J. McCloy and the Federal Republic of Germany* (Cambridge: Harvard University Press, 1991), 39.

Petersberg Protocol and agreed that the IAR would continue to monitor the production, distribution, and management of its coal and steel industries.[111] As Aron observed in January 1949, West Germany would "never be more powerless."[112]

The French fear, however, was that even a truncated Germany could quickly become the mightiest state in western Europe if given exclusive control of its industrial regions. Although they recognized the need to rebuild Germany and join forces with it, the decision was not taken lightly. After all, if rebuilding meant removing restrictions including the IAR, then the Germans would regain the industrial and thus military potential to dominate a European coalition. As the Central European desk at the Quai noted in October 1948, it was "difficult for us to compete at equal strength with Germany on the economic plane. She already produces nearly as much steel as we do, and soon she will produce more."[113] The following month, Schuman declared his desire to prevent "a reconstitution of this economic and industrial concentration" under the exclusive control of a German government.[114] Indeed, more than a decade after he had come to be regarded as "an apostle of a federal Europe," and therefore having no incentive to reveal his past realpolitik calculations, he recalled that, "while recognizing the necessity of restoring the German economy and progressively returning Germany's independence, we were at the same time preoccupied with imposing durable restrictions."[115] Without such limits, the French feared that the within-coalition distribution of power would move against them: "Yesterday's enemy, who now poses as our ally, could soon become our rival, and even perhaps our master."[116]

Faced with the twin imperatives of building a centralized balancing coalition and freezing the unexpected parity brought on by the war, key French policymakers opted for integration. By creating a Franco-German resource pool and assigning the two states joint control over it, integration would establish and perpetuate a roughly even balance of power between them. Restoring exclusive German control of the Ruhr and Rhineland would be tantamount to inviting domination. What was required instead was a system in which German and French assets were combined and managed jointly. In this way, neither state would have an intrinsic advantage or develop one over time.

111. McCloy to Acheson, November 22, 1949, *FRUS*, 1949, vol. 3, 343–46. For an account of the discussions, see Terence Prittie, *Konrad Adenauer, 1876–1967* (Chicago: Cowles, 1971), 154–55; and Schwartz, *America's*, 80–83.

112. Raymond Aron, A Realistic View of Britain, January 26, 1949, *DHEI*, vol. 3, 86.

113. Quoted in Hitchcock, *France*, 104.

114. Quoted in Poidevin, "Facteur," 313.

115. Schuman, *Pour*, 155. For the popular depiction of Schuman as an apostle of integration, see Alan S. Milward, *The European Rescue of the Nation-State* (London: Routledge, 1992), 325.

116. Quoted in Buffet, *Mourir*, 230.

This perspective began to take hold in the fall of 1948. In November, Gary and J-C Paris argued that preventing the revival of Germany because of the attendant security fears was out of the question. Rather, the French must place themselves "into an economic and political association with Germany." Specifically, they recommended the integration of French and German coal and steel resources in joint companies under public authority. Such an agreement would, they argued, allow France to "control . . . this [German] reconstruction."[117] In arguing that they wanted to "control" German industry, Gary and J-C Paris were not calling for "limits" on production. A powerful Germany was, after all, essential to the defense of western Europe, and they had taken the option of preventing the revival of Germany off the table earlier in the memorandum. Instead, they thought of integration as a means of maintaining an even balance of power between France and Germany by giving them equal access to, and assigning them joint control over, the region's industrial resources.

The chief of the German-Austrian section at the Foreign Ministry, Pierre de Leusse, endorsed this logic in a lengthy memorandum the following month. His point of departure was the same: limiting German industrial production in order to preserve French security was not an option. At the same time, however, giving the Germans unfettered access to the industrial resources of the Ruhr and Rhineland would allow them to dominate the coalition. In order to square the circle, he recommended "a European steel pool, in which French and Germans would operate equally and exercise a common control over the production of European steel." This task would require France to surrender sovereignty, but it would "associate ourselves with our former enemy through contractual links which would bind them as well as us." He concluded with a plea that his colleagues act quickly since "in waiting, we run the risk of seeing the balance of forces shift against us." For de Leusse, in other words, integration was to be the tool that established and maintained material equality within western Europe.[118]

The Office of European Affairs reached the same conclusion in a memorandum prepared in January 1949. Quickly dismissing the utility of the IAR for French security, officials asserted that France must associate "Germany in a larger context, that of Europe." That they meant integration when they referred to "Europe" is clear: "Ruhr steel would not be German steel, but a part of European steel. France would be associated, on an equal footing with Germany . . . in the direction of this steel cartel." The attraction of this solution lay in its implications for the distribution of power. France would "have her say, a better say than she would have under an international control system, in German steel questions." West Germany would not be allowed the exclusive control of the Ruhr and Rhineland that

---

117. Quoted in Sheetz, "Continental," 81–82.
118. Quoted in Hitchcock, *France*, 109–10.

the Reich had enjoyed in the past. An arrangement of this kind would require France to "abdicate a part of her sovereignty," but if the Germans did the same, they would be "bound" just as much as the French were. France could therefore "assure herself the security guarantee that she seeks." In fact, integration would turn "Germany's economic power" into a "support rather than a threat."[119]

The head of the office, François Seydoux, reiterated the argument in April 1950. West Germany could not be left "indefinitely in a position of inferiority," he declared. At the same time, it would be foolish from a power perspective to "return to her the privileges of sovereignty." As a result, he was driven inexorably to the same conclusion as his colleagues: a "supranational authority" would have to be created, able "to impose its decisions upon Western Europe." The downside was a loss of autonomy, but the benefit was that the Germans would not recover their "complete independence," and consequently their traditional power advantage. "From her present régime of trusteeship," he continued, "would follow without transition another régime under which other limitations would restrain her liberty." Again, the intention was not to limit German industrial production, but to ensure that the Germans did not gain exclusive control over western Europe's industrial assets. By placing the Federal Republic and France under the same authority, they could ensure that Germany would not be "master of her destiny."[120] The Ruhr would not "once again fall under the domination of its masters of yesteryear," and the Germans would not be able to dominate the western half of the continent.[121]

The French were quite open about the power calculations underpinning their support for integration. In July 1949, Teitgen told the National Assembly that France must "see to it that if Germany enters a European union, that union is so constituted that she cannot acquire within it the authority and independence that would enable her to evade her obligations." Like the Quai, Teitgen believed the greatest danger lay in an independent West Germany in control of its own resources. This meant that the French would have to form a "federation" and give up their own autonomy, but at least there would be no "recrudescence of the German peril."[122] Capitant articulated it even more plainly. If France were to create a federal Europe, he asserted, then "it becomes a possible solution for the future of Germany and for French and European security, because the controls to which, for the time being, she is rightly subjected . . . can in this way be absorbed into the normal authority of the federal power over all European states, so that Ger-

119. Quoted in Gerbet, "Origines," 209.

120. Quoted in Hitchcock, *France*, 123.

121. François de Clausonne Seydoux, *Mémoires d'outre-Rhin* (Paris: B. Grasset, 1975), 144.

122. Pierre-Henri Teitgen, Between Britain and Germany, July 9, 1949, *DHEI*, vol. 3, 103–4.

many too is solidly attached and integrated into Europe."[123] Neither of them referred specifically to industrial integration, but the claim that integration could maintain material parity within the coalition was there for all to see.

Perhaps the clearest statement of this view came from Monnet in a memorandum for Bidault and Schuman on May 3, 1950, in which he advocated the creation of what was to become the ECSC. Because the cold war was the dominant fact of international life, he argued, the restoration of Germany was inevitable. But an unrestrained Federal Republic would grow rapidly, France would fall "into the rut of limited production," and the Germans would once again be the masters of Europe. This being the case, Monnet had come up with an alternative plan—France must offer to "put all Franco-German coal and steel production under a common High Authority in an organization open to all the other countries of Europe." Such an agreement would create "the conditions for the common expansion of German, French, and European industry with competition," but, crucially, "without domination." In this way, integration promised to put French "industry on the same starting basis as German industry," and maintain that equality over time. It would establish a roughly even balance of power within western Europe and "eliminate the problem of German industrial domination." Failure to integrate, on the other hand, would have terrible consequences: "Germany will develop rapidly . . . France will be seized by her former Malthusianism [restricted production] and this will inevitably lead to her eclipse."[124]

Similar thinking appears in Monnet's account of the decision-making process leading up to the memorandum. The essence of the security problem in Europe, he declared, was that French and German coal and steel lay in a "triangular area artificially divided by historical frontiers." Given this state of affairs, neither France nor Germany could feel secure "unless it commanded all the resources—i.e., all the area," because only control of the area would give it a preponderance of power. But Monnet believed there was an alternative to unilateral control: "joint sovereignty over . . . their joint resources" or, simply, integration. An arrangement of this sort would eliminate security fears on both sides by establishing a durable and even balance of industrial power. Because "coal and steel were at once the key to economic power and the raw materials for forging weapons of war," he observed, "to pool them across frontiers would reduce their malign prestige and turn them instead into a guarantee of peace."[125]

123. René Capitant, For a Federal Europe, July 9, 1949, ibid., 107.

124. Monnet Memorandum, May 3, 1950, reproduced in *Le Monde*, May 9, 1970. See also Monnet Memorandum, May 1, 1950, reproduced in Henry Beyer, *Robert Schuman: l'Europe par la réconciliation franco-allemande* (Lausanne: Fondation Jean Monnet pour l'Europe, Centre de recherches européennes, 1986), 153–60.

125. Monnet, *Memoirs*, 293. For the claim that both Monnet and Schuman saw the coal and steel pool as a means to establish an "industrial balance of power" between France and Germany, see Schwartz, *America's*, 104.

In his announcement, Schuman called explicitly for the establishment of an even balance of power within western Europe. Accordingly, his declaration was faithful both to the Monnet memorandum and to the prevailing view in the Quai d'Orsay. In justifying his call for a coal and steel pool, the foreign minister argued that its chief purpose would be to set up "common bases for economic development" in western Europe. It would establish a "powerful production unit" that would furnish "on equal terms to all countries thus united the fundamental elements of industrial production." In turn, war between France and Germany would become "not only unthinkable, but in actual fact impossible." What did Schuman mean by "unthinkable" and "impossible"? In the speech he appears to claim that war would become unthinkable because integration would establish a "deeper community of interest."[126] This statement is not an expression of balance of power logic. But as he noted looking back on his announcement, the integration of the region's coal and steel industries made war between the integrating parties impossible "because one does not make war when one no longer has free disposal of energy and steel, which underpin the entire war making enterprise."[127] Like his colleagues at the Foreign Ministry, he viewed integration as a balance of power tool and, specifically, as a means to prevent West Germany from regaining a material advantage over France.

Schuman justified the community to his colleagues in these terms. "The aim of the system," he told an MRP leadership meeting, "is to make Germany work with us, and thus to control her much more directly, and to incorporate her progressively into Europe." He rejected the suggestion that he was embarking on a major reorientation of French foreign policy and ignoring the balance of power: "The methods are perhaps new, but the direction is unchanged." He intended to "solve the political problem through economic means. Without this settlement, Germany will grow more unsettling every day."[128] These balance of power calculations did not go unnoticed among astute observers. As Lord Brand told the House of Lords, the question of control of the Ruhr was the vital issue for France and it "must be settled as between France and Germany on as firm, unbreakable, and concrete a foundation as possible; and this, it seems to me, was the reason for the 'high authority' and all the paraphernalia of control."[129]

This view is shared by several historians. Writing less than a decade after the Schuman announcement, William Diebold had no doubt that the French decision was based on power considerations: "Schuman was saying,

126. For a translation of the Schuman declaration, see Bonbright to Webb, May 9, 1950, *FRUS*, 1950, vol. 3, 692–94.
127. Schuman, *Pour*, 164.
128. Quoted in Hitchcock, *France*, 132.
129. Quoted in William Diebold, *The Schuman Plan: A Study in Economic Cooperation, 1950–1959* (New York: Praeger, 1959), 53.

in effect, 'We shall deal directly with the Germans and offer them equal status in return for mutual safeguards, not on paper but in the mines and factories of the Ruhr and Lorraine'."[130] William Hitchcock reaches a similar conclusion. The key issue for Schuman was "to find a way to consolidate a Franco-German balance of power while an agreement to that effect still appealed to the Germans." The coal and steel pool "provided such a mechanism."[131]

Hans-Peter Schwarz argues that Monnet shared Schuman's basic view. He saw the plan as an instrument "to counter a threatening German preponderance. His formula was for joint expansion in mutual competition, but without either side predominating. French industry should thus be brought to the same level as German." The High Authority "would work for a balanced relationship, and would be based on a treaty which could be negotiated with Germany while the country was still weak."[132] In sum, the French viewed heavy-industry integration as the central plank of a balance of power strategy.

West Germany: Embracing Integration, 1945–1950

West Germany's enthusiastic reaction to Schuman's proposal was also based on balance of power calculations. German policymakers viewed the Soviet Union as an overwhelming competitor and believed their security depended on membership in a European balancing coalition, a belief strengthened by the suspicion that the U.S. security guarantee was only temporary. Moreover, the Bonn government was convinced that any west European grouping must be centrally organized if it was to stand any chance of deterring or defeating the USSR. Regarding control of that coalition, German goals were relatively modest. West Germany was a defeated and occupied state, and the French were determined not to allow the Germans exclusive control over their industrial resources. The best that Germany could hope for, then, was joint control of the emerging combination. When that opportunity presented itself in the form of the ECSC, the Germans seized it.

The Balancing Imperative

Fear of Soviet power was the most important determinant of German foreign policy in the late 1940s. Indeed, Adenauer, who dominated policymaking

130. Ibid., 11.
131. Hitchcock, *France*, 127.
132. Hans-Peter Schwarz, *Konrad Adenauer: A German Politician and Statesman in a Period of War, Revolution, and Reconstruction*, vol. 1 (Providence, R.I.: Berghahn, 1995), 510.

at the time, gives pride of place to the Russian threat in the relevant section of his memoirs.[133] Soviet Russia, he observed, "stood in the middle of Germany, on the Elbe. The European balance of power was destroyed; therefore Western Europe, including the part of Germany not handed over to the Soviets, was in constant serious peril."[134] Although made several years after the fact, this statement likely reflects Adenauer's actual thinking in the immediate postwar period. In March 1946, in a personal letter to Wilhelm Sollmann, he warned, "the danger is great. Asia stands at the Elbe."[135] Then, in a December speech, he openly referenced his fear of a "vast power governed by a genius and a way of thinking totally different from our West European traditions."[136]

This basic concern remained central to Adenauer's thinking for the next five years. In a meeting with Schuman in January 1950, he expressed deep concern that the "Russians might one day propose that all four occupying powers should leave Germany." This was a terrifying prospect: if the western Allies were to agree, then "the Russians would be very close." Schuman, who shared Adenauer's outlook, agreed that "he would see this as a great danger." Two months later, Adenauer warned that the "incentive to make war is greater for Soviet Russia than is generally assumed." Conquest of the continent was "worthwhile" from the Soviet point of view—it would bring all of western Europe "under her power" and hand the USSR the "mind and working potential" of the region. Worse still, it could "happen in many ways."[137] In other words, he believed that the Soviet Union had the capability and the desire to control the continent. This calculation clearly informed Adenauer's subsequent acceptance of the Schuman Plan. Germany was committed to making the proposal "a reality," he told Monnet, because "Germany is now under direct pressure from the East and it knows that its fate is tied to the fate of Western Europe."[138] Of course, he may simply have been telling the French what they wanted to hear, but he had made the same case privately to his cabinet on the day of the Schuman

133. On Adenauer's domination of foreign policy, see Michael Balfour, *Germany: The Tides of Power* (New York: Routledge, 1992), 133–35; Wolfram F. Hanrieder, *West German Foreign Policy, 1949–1963: International Pressure and Domestic Response* (Stanford: Stanford University Press, 1967), 95; and Sabine Lee, "German Decision-Making Elites and European Integration: German 'Europolitik' during the Years of the EEC and Free Trade Area Negotiations," in *Building Postwar Europe: National Decision-Makers and European Institutions, 1948–63*, ed. Anne Deighton (New York: St. Martin's, 1995), 40–43.

134. Konrad Adenauer, *Memoirs* (Chicago: Henry Regnery, 1966), 192.

135. Quoted in Schwarz, *Adenauer*, 319.

136. Quoted in Manfred Overesch, "Senior West German Politicians and Their Perception of the German Situation in Europe 1945–1949," in *Power in Europe? Great Britain, France, Italy, and Germany in a Postwar World, 1945–1950*, ed. Josef Becker and Franz Knipping (New York: W. de Gruyter, 1986), 125.

137. Adenauer, *Memoirs*, 237, 246.

138. Quoted in Sheetz, "Continental," 115.

announcement, arguing that the Soviet threat was the overriding concern of the day.[139]

Adenauer's views were shared by top-ranking military officials. Adolf Heusinger and Hans Speidel, two former Wehrmacht generals whom Adenauer relied on for advice in matters of security, believed that Moscow was determined to dominate the continent and worried that the Red Army could quickly overrun western Europe.[140] Even Social Democratic Party (SPD) leader Kurt Schumacher, Adenauer's bitter political rival, told the Americans "it was silly to talk about German neutrality in the East-West struggle . . . Germany was in the fight with the West against the totalitarianism of the Soviets." This did not mean that Schumacher agreed with the details of American policy toward Russia—quite the contrary—but he "was opposed to German industrialists and politicians . . . who took the line that Germany could be neutral."[141]

Fears about the Soviet Union's potential for domination were accentuated by the belief that the United States would not protect Europe indefinitely. In his letter to Sollmann, Adenauer complained that the Americans were "not inclined to interest themselves in European affairs," and implored him to convince the Americans that the "salvation of Europe is equally vital for the United States."[142] Three years later, he informed fellow members of the Christian Democratic Union (CDU) that Germany "might be sold out by the Americans at any minute."[143] And in conversations with the French, he noted that security against the Soviets would come not from a questionable American commitment, but from European unity.[144]

These concerns took on even greater urgency after the Soviets detonated their first atomic weapon in the fall of 1949. At one of his first cabinet meetings, Adenauer worried that the Americans would now be less likely to defend Europe: "This fact will perhaps make the United States disposed

139. Minutes of Cabinet Meeting, May 9, 1950, *KB*, vol. 2, 1950, 370, and vol. 3, 1950, 67–69; and Schwarz, *Adenauer*, 505–6.

140. Manfred Messerschmidt, Christian Greiner, and Norbert Wiggershaus, "West Germany's Strategic Position and Her Role in Defence Policy as Seen by the German Military, 1945–1949," in *Power in Europe? Great Britain, France, Italy, and Germany in a Postwar World, 1945–1950*, ed. Josef Becker and Franz Knipping (New York: W. de Gruyter, 1986), 355–67.

141. Hays to Acheson, May 8, 1950, *Confidential U.S. State Department Central Files: Germany, 1950–1954* (hereafter *CUSSDCFG*) (Frederick, Md.: University Publications of America, 1986), reel 1. See also Schwartz, *America's*, 80.

142. Quoted in Overesch, "Senior," 126; and Hans-Peter Schwarz, *Erbfreundschaft: Adenauer und Frankreich* (Bonn: Bouvier, 1992), 99.

143. Quoted in Sheetz, "Continental," 86. On this point, see also Wilfried Loth, "German Conceptions of Europe during the Escalation of the East-West Conflict, 1945–1949," in *Power in Europe? Great Britain, France, Italy, and Germany in a Postwar World, 1945–1950*, ed. Josef Becker and Franz Knipping (New York: W. de Gruyter, 1986), 524.

144. Sheetz, "Continental," 86.

to comply more with Russian claims."[145] As his principal biographer has written, "Adenauer was . . . convinced, from the end of the Second World War onwards, that the presence of American forces on the continent did not at all represent the natural order of things, but was rather a longer or shorter intermediate phase that would one day belong to the past."[146] Although the chancellor was somewhat ahead of general opinion, he was not alone. In a diary entry on January 1, 1950, Herbert Blankenhorn, the cabinet's private secretary, wrote that one of his two overriding foreign policy concerns as the decade began was the danger of "a new appeasement policy on the part of the Americans . . . at the expense of central Europe, i.e., Germany."[147]

Soviet power and the unreliability of the American security guarantee led to a desire to create a west European balancing coalition. As early as October 1945, Adenauer pointed out that because Europe was now divided, it was "in the best interests not only of the part of Germany which is not occupied by Russia, but also of Britain and France, to unite Western Europe under their leadership."[148] Later, he reiterated his claim: "Only an economically and spiritually regenerated Western Europe . . . can check the further advance of the Asian spirit and power, a Western Europe to which belongs, as an integral element, the part of Germany that is not occupied by Russia."[149] To be sure, there is some evidence that he had not yet given up on the possibility of a united Germany, but he made it clear that, failing progress toward unification, he supported the amalgamation of the western zones and their incorporation into a west European coalition.[150]

Other German decision makers shared Adenauer's views. In April 1948, Minister-President Hans Ehard of Bavaria argued that Europe must "defend itself on the Elbe and Danube." Since Russia was "detached from Europe," and "none of the Western countries" had the power to defend the western half of the continent on its own, he called for "the union of all free European countries in a defensive community."[151] Ehard's endorsement of Adenauer's plans is not surprising since he too was a Christian Democrat. However, even SPD member Carlo Schmid, who vigorously opposed the division of the continent in the immediate aftermath of the war, abandoned "his basic resistance against German participation in designing Europe starting from the West" in the late 1940s. Indeed, as one historian has noted, most politically influential Germans favored the creation of a western

145. Minutes of Cabinet Meeting, September 24, 1949, *KB*, vol. 1, 1949, 315. All translations from the German are my own.

146. Schwarz, *Erbfreundschaft*, 101.

147. Quoted in Schwarz, *Adenauer*, 488.

148. Quoted in Lipgens, *History*, 245.

149. Quoted in Loth, "German," 523.

150. Schwarz, *Adenauer*, 381–82.

151. Hans Ehard, The European Situation and German Federalism, April 3, 1950, *DHEI*, vol. 3, 508–9.

balancing coalition including Germany once it became clear there was going to be a west German state in the summer of 1948. In their eyes, building Europe was now vital because the "victors and the vanquished" of the war were "in the same boat."[152]

German enthusiasm for Schuman's proposal derived at least in part from the conviction that it would bring France and the Federal Republic a step closer to the creation of a viable balancing coalition. As Adenauer told American journalist Benedict Kingsbury-Smith in a highly publicized interview only two months before the French announcement, the survival of western Europe rested on convincing the Russians that "there was still strength left in Europe." The Soviets had to be convinced of Europe's "firm determination" to resist, which in turn depended on building a "union between Germany and France."[153] Given these premises, the Germans were bound to greet the heavy-industry proposal with enthusiasm. To Adenauer's mind, it laid the foundation for a European coalition that could one day become a "third force" in international politics.[154] As he told his colleagues, lasting security against the Soviet Union depended on the construction of a strong European combination, and Schuman's plan was a step in that direction.[155] The cabinet saw the logic of his argument; in the context of the cold war, they agreed, "it must be our aim to create a third force in a united Europe." This force might not "measure up to these two great powers," but it would "have enough political and economic strength to put its weight into the scales for the preservation of peace."[156]

Centralization

Most Germans agreed that the third force must be centralized to be an effective counterweight to Soviet power. They were not always explicit about this, and sometimes claimed to support centralization because it would make Europe independent of both superpowers or ensure world peace. But like their counterparts in Paris, their primary reason for supporting centralization was that it would enable the Europeans to establish a unit of power capable of containing the Soviet Union without American support. Also like the French, they reached this conclusion through a mix of innovation and imitation. Many calculated that something more than a traditional coalition would be needed to balance Russian power. Others concluded

---

152. Loth, "German," 531 (for the quotation), 533. See also Hanns Jürgen Küsters, "West Germany's Foreign Policy in Western Europe, 1949–58: The Art of the Possible," in *Western Europe and Germany: The Beginnings of European Integration, 1945–1960*, ed. Clemens A. Wurm (Oxford: Berg, 1995), 56.

153. Adenauer, *Memoirs*, 246.

154. Prittie, *Adenauer*, 180; and Sheetz, "Continental," 113–14.

155. Minutes of Cabinet Meeting, May 9, 1950, *KB*, vol. 2, 1950, 370, and vol. 3, 1950, 67–69.

156. Adenauer, *Memoirs*, 258–59.

that western Europe must organize itself as a statelike entity to generate enough power to hold its own in the cold war.

The earliest calls for centralization came soon after Germany's defeat. Writing in the *Frankfurter Hefte* in 1946, Walter Dirks declared that "Europe, the poor continent, can only count and subsist, if it pulls itself together: if it collects its mineral resources, its means of production and its working power in a planned organization." What was required was a "confederation of the European nations." Because he wanted to avoid antagonizing the Soviets, Dirks argued that the confederation was not intended to be "against other non-European powers." His underlying message was clear, however: only a centralized coalition would have the power to "achieve a new balance" and guarantee "European freedom."[157] Liberal politician Henry Bernhard was equally careful in his word choice, arguing that he wanted a "united Europe" to maintain "world peace." But he too noted that only a centralized unit of power would be able to act effectively on the international political scene. "Just as the Western hemisphere consists of a union of American states, and . . . just as Eastern Europe and large parts of Asia form a union of Soviet republics," he declared, "so the future of Europe can and must consist of an organic and for ever indissoluble union of European democracies." This union must provide for common foreign and economic policies and "other joint institutions."[158]

The idea that only a centralized coalition could balance against the Soviet Union became quite popular in Germany. Late in 1947, Schmid argued that the west Europeans could "cooperate with the two great political continents on a basis of equal rights and equal influence" only if they abandoned the "principle of sovereignty" and established a "supranational community." The community must, in turn, control foreign policy, defense, economic planning, and the management of major industries.[159] In other words, the existence of vast political units such as the United States and the Soviet Union gave the Germans a strong incentive to establish a similar entity in western Europe. Indeed, the logic of size and centralization was so powerful that they called for a European federation even before it was clear there was going to be a west German state.

As the cold war intensified and the western Allies moved to create the Federal Republic, the Germans ramped up their calls for centralization. Ehard worried that Europe had become a "multiplicity of incomplete formations, none of which can any longer throw its weight fully into the scale of world politics." Worse still, the "disunited, incoherent world of the former European great powers and medium-sized states" was now confronted by the "imperialistic ambitions of a huge empire." Given this situation, he

157. Quoted in Loth, "German," 517.
158. Henry Bernhard, For European Unity, May 1, 1946, *DHEI*, vol. 3, 467.
159. Carlo Schmid, German-French Relations and the Third Partner, November–December 1947, ibid., 504.

advocated a "genuine European association which will transcend national divisions and transfer a due measure of national sovereignty to a supranational power." Only by creating a "confederation" of this kind could the "balance of world affairs be restored."[160]

Such thinking transcended party lines. Thus, while he viewed the Brussels Treaty as a positive step toward preserving the region's independence, Schmid argued that the Europeans could only play a significant "role in international affairs" if they established a "federation" with "sole competence in foreign affairs and for the defense of federal territory." In addition, the entire region must "form a single economic and customs area." Similarly, members of the Free Democratic Party (FDP), the second largest party in West Germany's governing coalition, believed that the "fragmentation of Europe into national states must be overcome by means of a federal union." Establishing an entity of this kind would strengthen the "productive forces and welfare of the Western world," and persuade the Soviet Union to "adopt a policy of peace and restraint."[161] In short, there was an emerging consensus that any balancing coalition must be centrally organized if it was to stand up to the Russians.

Crucially, Adenauer himself was a strong believer in the need for centralization. This conviction was clear as early as 1946: "The aim of all work in Europe must be: to establish the United States of Europe or a similar structure." Although he did not have a specific plan for bringing such a union into being, he had no doubt as to its importance and purpose. The significance of a "European federation . . . cannot be underestimated," he declared in May 1948, adding that it would constitute a "third power" able "to resolve tensions and to mediate between these very great powers."[162]

This reasoning continued to inform his decisions once he became chancellor. He was proposing a Franco-German union, he told Kingsbury-Smith in March 1950, because it was the only way Europe would be able to deter the Soviet Union. Just as the small German states had united to form the most formidable great power on the continent in the late nineteenth century, a Franco-German union would provide the core of a west European great power in the middle of the twentieth. A few days later, he told his colleagues that West Germany had to decide whether it wanted to "see Europe split up between the great power blocs . . . and divided up into nation states warring with each other" or whether it wanted to achieve "political and economic unification which will endow it with a weight of its own."[163] He had little trouble persuading his ministers. At a cabinet meeting on the day

160. Hans Ehard, The European Situation and German Federalism, April 3, 1948, ibid., 511–12.

161. Carlo Schmid, Europe: Only Possible as a Federation, May 1948, and Parliamentary Group of the FDP: Guidelines on Foreign Policy, March 26, 1950, ibid., 514, 536.

162. Quoted in Schwarz, *Adenauer*, 387, 390.

163. Adenauer, *Memoirs*, 246–47, 256.

of the Schuman announcement, no one disagreed with Minister of the Interior Gustav Heinemann's declaration that Germany "must not say no" to a European "federation."[164]

Integration

There was little debate within German political circles that France and Germany would integrate and share control of a centralized European coalition. The reasoning behind this consensus rested on balance of power calculations: a system of joint control would maintain the prevailing roughly even distribution of power within western Europe.

Supporting Integration

German support for integration was so strong that they were calling for it publicly even before the French and well before the founding of the Federal Republic. One of the key figures was Karl Arnold, the minister-president of North Rhine-Westphalia, whose state produced most of Germany's coal and steel. As early as October 1947, he suggested making "the Ruhr, with its basic and key industries, the core of European reconstruction, by closely integrating the interrelated industries of the neighboring countries, particularly of France, Belgium and Luxembourg."[165] His interior minister, Walter Menzel, made essentially the same point the following year, telling the French that the German public would have been far more favorable to the controls placed on the Ruhr had they been "presented as a first step toward the inter-Europeanization of primary resources." Arnold followed up in person during his own conversation with the French in August 1948, expressing his support for a "common European organization . . . tasked with controlling all the essential primary resources of Europe" before going public with his views in a radio broadcast in January 1949.[166] Reflecting on the "new order in foreign relations," he suggested the creation of an "international body . . . on a cooperative basis" rather than "unilateral control of the Ruhr." All the west European states would contribute their heavy industry to this "association." Ownership rights would be assigned based on the size of each state's contribution, and these rights would be "supplemented by an appropriate legal construction, a kind of modern version of 'eminent domain'."[167] Here, then, were the basic features of the coal and steel pool more than a year before Schuman proposed it.

164. Minutes of Cabinet Meeting, May 9, 1950, *KB*, vol. 3, 1950, 68.

165. Quoted in Dietmar Petzina, "The Origin of the European Coal and Steel Community: Economic Forces and Political Interests," *Journal of Institutional and Theoretical Economics* 137, no. 3 (1981): 463.

166. Quoted in Poidevin, "Facteur," 319.

167. Karl Arnold: Radio Broadcast, January 1, 1949, *DHEI*, vol. 3, 520.

The pro-integration view was by no means restricted to officials in Germany's industrial heartland. In late 1947, in the same speech in which he called for the centralization of western Europe, Schmid suggested that France and Germany would be taking a significant step if they were to "place their heavy industrial complexes under mutual international control."[168] A year later, the minister-presidents of Germany indicated that they would be prepared to accept the "internationalization" of the Ruhr as long as the other west European mineral basins were placed under the same authority.[169]

German support for heavy-industry integration was so widespread, in fact, that it was commonly reported in the press. On January 15, 1949, the *Economist* reported that the "Germans have fastened" on the "pious affirmations" of the other west European states that they intended to "adopt similar measures" to the IAR "for themselves." Indeed, the consensus German view "from right to left" was that "international control of heavy industry is acceptable, and even progressive, provided it is not imposed on Germany alone."[170] The editors of *Le Monde* concurred: the Germans were enthusiastic about internationalizing the Ruhr, by which they "really mean the pooling of the heavy industry of the Ruhr, Lorraine, Luxembourg, and Belgium."[171]

Perhaps no one endorsed industrial integration more than Adenauer, who went to great lengths to persuade the French to take the initiative. In calling for the union of western Europe during a speech in Bern in March 1949, he suggested that the IAR and its fifteen-man regulatory board form the basis for an all-European authority. It could, he argued, "represent the beginning of a European federation."[172] Upon becoming chancellor, he expanded on the theme, claiming he would "agree to an authority that supervised the mining and industrial areas of Germany, France, Belgium, and Luxembourg."[173] Similarly, in an interview with *Die Zeit* in November 1949, he noted that the Ruhr authority was "either an extremely deep degradation, or . . . the first step toward the control of the whole of West European heavy industry," and clearly indicated that he preferred the latter.[174] So strong was his support for integration, in fact, that in March 1950 he suggested that France and Germany go beyond industrial integration and move immediately to full economic integration. The proposal did not elicit

168. Carlo Schmid, German-French Relations and the Third Partner, November–December 1947, ibid., 505.

169. Poidevin, "Facteur," 319–20.

170. "Britain, France and Germany," *Economist*, January 15, 1949.

171. "Tension franco-allemande," *Le Monde*, January 24, 1950.

172. Adenauer, *Memoirs*, 196.

173. Monnet, *Memoirs*, 283.

174. Adenauer Interview with *Die Zeit*, November 3, 1949, *Die Bundesrepublik Deutschland und Frankreich: Dokumente, 1949–1963* (hereafter *BDF*), vol. 1 (Munich: K. G. Saur, 1997), 61.

much of a reaction, but it is indicative of his commitment to integration prior to the Schuman announcement.[175] These views were popular within the governing coalition, and especially with Heinrich von Brentano, who would become foreign minister in 1955. "We see in the Ruhr statute," he explained, "the beginnings, albeit incomplete, of coal internationalization in the European economy." What West Germany must do was "take the first step" and accept the statute in the expectation that the other European states would "have to follow."[176]

Balance of Power Reasoning

Germany's support for integration was based on balance of power considerations. The Germans understood that the French would not allow them to regain exclusive control of the industrial resources physically within their territory. To do so would be to reestablish German superiority within western Europe. At the same time, policymakers in Bonn did not want the French to assume control of the coalition and perhaps shift the balance of power in their favor. These twin calculations led to the conclusion that Germany must demand joint control of the coalition, but no more. Fortunately for the Germans, they were in a good position to hold out for such an arrangement: the French understood that no European combination would be able to contain the Soviet Union without Germany and that the Germans would have little incentive to contribute their share unless they were granted decision-making control commensurate with their contribution.

The Germans were aware that the most they could ask for was joint control of a European federation. Max Brauer, the mayor of Hamburg, was convinced that German leadership was impossible because the western Allies would not allow it: "Certainly no leading role will devolve on the Germans in this movement." Given their contribution to the coalition, however, they had a strong claim to equality. West Germany could and should "be a member on equal terms" in a united Europe, "serving and helping" but, crucially, "also sharing the benefits." Arnold agreed, noting that the Germans could not aspire to complete independence—they would have to "be the first to surrender certain sovereign rights to a European authority"— while arguing at the same time that this surrender must be a prelude to their partners doing the same. He could envisage a renunciation of autonomy "provided it led to a general agreement on a footing of equality."[177]

Brentano appears to have shared this understanding. According to Seydoux, he believed the future of Europe lay in Franco-German reconciliation,

175. Adenauer, *Memoirs*, 244–48; and Schwarz, *Adenauer*, 496.

176. Minutes of CDU-CSU Meeting, November 15, 1949, *BDF*, vol. 3, 75. See also Paul Legoll, *Konrad Adenauer et l'idée d'unification européenne janvier 1948–mai 1950: Un homme politique "européen" et son environnement dans le contexte international* (Bern: P. Lang, 1989), 222.

177. Max Brauer, The Results of the European Congress in Brussels, March 6, 1949, and Karl Arnold: Radio Broadcast, January 1, 1949, *DHEI*, vol. 3, 524, 521.

which in turn depended on Germany being granted "equality of rights."[178] The German press quickly latched on to this line of argument. As *Die Zeit* put it, although France needed West Germany for European defense and so could not contemplate disarmament, there was equally "no way back to the old form of German national sovereignty." Consequently, there was "only one way forward: Europe."[179] In short, West Germany was an important component—probably the most important component—of any west European coalition, but it was also a defeated state without sovereignty. The most it could ask for, then, was equality within that coalition.

Adenauer's own pursuit of equality within the emerging west European group was unrelenting. In a letter to a friend just before becoming chancellor, he indicated his commitment to "ensuring that Germany is accepted as quickly as possible as a member of the European federation with equal rights and equal obligations."[180] This was also his public position. As he told the United Press in April 1950, equality of rights was Germany's condition for entering a European federation.[181] But it is his correspondence with Schuman in May 1950 that is most revealing. Responding to the French foreign minister's letter detailing the contents of his forthcoming declaration, Adenauer emphasized something Schuman had not: the notion of equality. The plan, he wrote, would be popular in Germany because "for the first time since the catastrophe of 1945, Germany and France are to work with equal rights on a common task."[182] This emphasis was not lost on observers at the time. The British immediately noted that the plan would be "acceptable to Germany . . . since it places Germany on the same footing as France."[183]

The logic underpinning the chancellor's proposals mirrored that of other German spokesmen: Germany was an important part of the coalition and could not be kept in permanent submission, but the French would not allow them exclusive control over the foundations of their former power. Accordingly, the Federal Republic must be content with joint control.

Adenauer understood that West Germany was an essential element of any coalition and therefore demanded some measure of decision-making authority within it. Less than a year after the war, he made it clear that he did not believe France could be considered the "guiding power" in western Europe.[184] The western zones of Germany were "indispensable" to the "creation of a strong Western Europe." Germany was so important, in fact, that

178. Seydoux, *Mémoires*, 122.
179. Friedländer Article in *Die Zeit*, December 8, 1949, *BDF*, vol. 3, 84.
180. Quoted in Schwarz, *Adenauer*, 475.
181. Gerbet, "Genèse," 536.
182. Quoted in Schwarz, *Adenauer*, 505. See also Adenauer, *Memoirs*, 259–60.
183. Memorandum by Kirkpatrick, May 11, 1950, *DBPO*, ser. 2, vol. 1, 32. See also Seydoux, *Mémoires*, 126, 136.
184. Quoted in Schwarz, *Erbfreundschaft*, 95.

he was convinced the "fetters" imposed by the western Allies "would gradually fall away."[185]

At the same time, there was no prospect of the Germans being allowed to control the coalition. As Adenauer noted in his memoirs, Franco-German relations would forever be colored by the fact "that between Bonn and Paris lie the gigantic graveyards of Verdun." Therefore Germany could "neither demand nor expect full confidence" and had to "avoid everything that might reawaken mistrust."[186] Indeed, he was acutely "aware of the anxieties of Germany's Western neighbors." The French dreaded the prospect of a German state in control of its former industrial heartland and it was impossible to "reassure them by pointing to the present balance of political power in Europe." Coupled with Germany's indispensability, knowledge of this fear led to the conclusion that the "aim should be to participate on an equal footing in the peaceful cooperation of peoples in a union of nations."[187]

Adenauer was explicit about the link between Germany's contribution, French concerns about the balance of power within western Europe, and joint control of the coalition. As he noted in his memoirs, his goal was equality because "it would have been undignified and wrong to follow a policy of slavish submissiveness," but equally "stupid, unwise, and futile to harp on our indispensability."[188] He said much the same thing at the time, noting that France and Germany had to come to a mutually acceptable compromise: the former could not ask for too much in the way of security and the latter could not offer too little.[189] The Schuman Plan struck that balance by pooling Franco-German resources and assigning the parties joint control over them.

This interpretation of German calculations is consistent with that of most historians of the period. In his analysis of West German foreign policy in the early cold war, Wolfram Hanrieder argues that Adenauer's overriding goal was the restoration of German sovereignty. But this did not mean sovereignty in the sense of complete autonomy or independence: "The sovereignty that Adenauer sought to have restored to the West German state was thus of a rather special kind: he was willing to subsume some of its elements, once they were gained, to contractual agreements that would bind Germany to the West in integrative international structures." What he wanted, in fact, was not sovereignty in the traditional meaning of the term, but "equal legal status in an integrative international structure." He was enthusiastic about Schuman's plan because it replaced the control regime

185. Adenauer, *Memoirs*, 194.

186. Ibid., 194, 363.

187. Konrad Adenauer: Speech at Cologne University, March 24, 1946, *DHEI*, vol. 3, 460–61.

188. Adenauer, *Memoirs*, 194.

189. Adenauer Interview with *Die Zeit*, November 3, 1949, *BDF*, vol. 1, 60.

with "an international organization in which the Federal Republic would participate as an equal member."[190]

Britain: Refusing Integration, 1945–1950

The British decided to buck-pass the integration burden to their allies and therefore declined to enter the negotiations that led to the creation of the ECSC. Like their French and German counterparts, officials in London identified the Soviet Union as a potential regional hegemon and understood that the west Europeans had to establish a balancing coalition to deal with it. However, they believed that a purely continental combination that included France and Germany would eventually have the wherewithal to deter and, if deterrence failed, slow a Soviet attack in central Europe. They also understood that they were more secure than their continental allies because they were protected by the English Channel. So they passed the buck to their more vulnerable partners. Britain would cooperate with the continental states for their common defense, but France and Germany would have to pay the sovereignty costs of forming an effective centralized balancing coalition that could contain the Russians.

The Security Calculus

The British were acutely conscious of the Soviet Union's potential for domination. In fact, this concern predated the defeat of Nazi Germany. "Russia after the war," averred the Joint Intelligence Sub-Committee in late 1944, "will contain within her own frontiers such military and economic resources as would enable her to face without serious defeat even a combination of the major European powers."[191] It was not that the Soviets were viewed with hostility—though some officials, including the British ambassador to France, Duff Cooper, were calling for a western coalition designed to stand up to the Russians as early as mid-1944—but policymakers were concerned that immense resources were now concentrated in the hands of a single European state as never before.[192] By the fall of 1945, these concerns

---

190. Hanrieder, *West*, 50, 60–61. See also Küsters, "West," 55–56.

191. Quoted in Donald C. Watt, "British Military Perceptions of the Soviet Union as a Strategic Threat, 1945–1950," in *Power in Europe? Great Britain, France, Italy, and Germany in a Postwar World, 1945–1950*, ed. Josef Becker and Franz Knipping (New York: W. de Gruyter, 1986), 330. On British fears of Soviet domination in this period, see Anne Deighton, *The Impossible Peace: Britain, the Division of Germany and the Origins of the Cold War* (Oxford: Clarendon, 1990), esp. 5–8, 223–35; and Ritchie Ovendale, "Britain, the U.S.A. and the European Cold War, 1945–48," *History* 67, no. 220 (1982): 217–36.

192. John W. Young, "Duff Cooper and the Paris Embassy, 1945–47," in *British Officials and British Foreign Policy, 1945–50*, ed. John Zametica (Leicester: Leicester University Press, 1990), 99.

were widespread, and most Foreign Office officials were calling for a west European coalition to contain the emerging Soviet bloc.[193]

Concerns about Soviet hegemony only increased over the next few years. The Soviet Union's long-term aim, according to Frank Roberts, the chargé d'affaires in Moscow, was to continue building its strength and expanding its empire until it had "enough strength to embark on aggressive action."[194] Two months later, in May 1946, Foreign Secretary Ernest Bevin, who had previously shown a more relaxed attitude than his Foreign Office subordinates, argued that although Germany remained a danger to peace, "the danger of Russia has become certainly as great as and possibly even greater than that of a revived Germany."[195] By early 1947, this had become the official Foreign Office view. According to an updated version of a 1945 report, "the balance of military strength, particularly in Europe, has altered to the advantage of the Soviet Union."[196] A year later, Bevin endorsed the claim in apocalyptic terms. "Physical control of the Eurasian land mass . . . is what the Politburo is aiming at—no less than that," he declared to the Cabinet in March 1948. So powerful was the Soviet Union that "the immensity of the aim should not betray us into believing in its impracticability."[197]

Although they believed the Soviet Union had hegemonic potential, the British knew the luck of geography had placed them last on the Russian target list and made them the toughest west European state to conquer. In the event of war, officials in London believed that the Russians would overrun the continent and that Britain might even be "immobilised by air and projectile attack," but they did not expect to be conquered quickly because the English Channel provided a significant obstacle to invasion.[198] The experience of World War II had confirmed this view—the Third Reich had

193. Klaus Larres, "A Search for Order: Britain and the Origins of a Western European Union, 1944–55," in *From Reconstruction to Integration: Britain and Europe since 1945*, ed. Brian Brivati and Harriet Jones (Leicester: Leicester University Press, 1993), 78. See also Paul Cornish, "The British Military View of European Security, 1945–50," in *Building Postwar Europe: National Decision-Makers and European Institutions, 1948–63*, ed. Anne Deighton (New York: St. Martin's, 1995), 73; and Anne Deighton, "Britain and the Cold War 1945–55: An Overview," in *From Reconstruction to Integration: Britain and Europe since 1945*, ed. Brian Brivati and Harriet Jones (Leicester: Leicester University Press, 1993), 8.

194. Quoted in Deighton, "Britain," 9.

195. Quoted in Greenwood, "Return," 51.

196. Quoted in Victor Rothwell, *Britain and the Cold War, 1941–1947* (London: Jonathan Cape, 1982), 268.

197. Quoted in David Dilks, "The British View of Security: Europe and a Wider World, 1945–1948," in *Western Security: The Formative Years. Europe and Atlantic Defense 1947–1953*, ed. Olav Riste (New York: Columbia University Press, 1985), 52.

198. Quoted in Geoffrey Warner, "Britain and Europe in 1948: The View from the Cabinet," in *Power in Europe? Great Britain, France, Italy and Germany in a Postwar World, 1945–1950*, ed. Josef Becker and Franz Knipping (New York: W. de Gruyter, 1986), 32.

not come close to mounting an assault on the British Isles.[199] Indeed, in February 1946 the Cabinet Defence Committee issued a report claiming that, for at least the next few years, no European state would be able to build a fleet capable of menacing British security.[200] As late as December 1949, London had "no intention . . . of preparing an estimate of the scale and nature of an invasion . . . because it does not believe that the threat of a full-scale seaborne or airborne invasion is sufficiently serious to justify the work."[201]

Even American strategists working on worst-case scenarios did not expect the United Kingdom to be conquered in short order. In fact, American planning for a future war envisaged the use of Britain as a secure base for counterattacking against Soviet forces that had advanced into western Europe. If the Soviets were to conquer western Europe, argued the JCS in April 1946, "our course of action would reasonably include initiation at the earliest practicable date of strategic air operations against vital areas in the USSR." Britain, they added, "is a firm base for this purpose."[202] Little had changed two years later when the JCS assumed that "British forces will have the capability of defending the United Kingdom to the extent that it could be used initially as an operating base."[203]

In addition to believing they were less vulnerable to conquest, the British also had less reason to fear an American withdrawal from the European theater.

Like their counterparts in Paris and Bonn, policymakers in London worried that the U.S. security guarantee was only temporary. It was this fear, in fact, that prompted Bevin to ask for contingency plans in case the Americans chose to abandon the continent.[204] He was frankly "disturbed by signs of America trying to make a safety zone around herself while leaving us and Europe in No Man's land."[205] The Foreign Office confirmed his worries, warning that the Americans might withdraw from the world

199. For this view, see F. S. Northedge, *Descent from Power: British Foreign Policy, 1945–1973* (London: George Allen and Unwin, 1974), 144–45.

200. Dilks, "British," 37; and George C. Peden, "Economic Aspects of British Perceptions of Power on the Eve of the Cold War," in *Power in Europe? Great Britain, France, Italy, and Germany in a Postwar World, 1945–1950*, ed. Josef Becker and Franz Knipping (New York: W. de Gruyter, 1986), 249.

201. JIC 435/12, Soviet Intentions and Capabilities, 1949, 1956/57, November 30, 1948, *RJCS*, pt. 2, 1946–1953, The Soviet Union, reel 3.

202. JCS 1641/5, Estimate Based on Assumption of Occurrence of Major Hostilities, April 11, 1946, ibid., reel 1.

203. JCS 1844/1, Short Range Emergency Plan, March 17, 1948, ibid., reel 4.

204. Larres, "Search," 77–78. For evidence that the fear of American abandonment predated the end of the war, see Sean Greenwood, "Ernest Bevin, France and 'Western Union': August 1945–February 1946," *European History Quarterly* 14, no. 3 (1984): 320.

205. Quoted in Alan Bullock, *Ernest Bevin: Foreign Secretary, 1945–1951* (New York: W. W. Norton, 1983), 340.

"at any moment."[206] Indeed, their fear of American isolationism was so strong that the British were reluctant to form a west European pact against the Soviet Union in 1948 in case it gave Washington the impression that the Europeans could contain the Soviets without American assistance.[207] In short, British decision makers were as concerned as the French and Germans that the United States might exit the European scene.

On the other hand, and unlike the continental powers, they could take comfort from the knowledge that the United States was bound to return in force if the Soviets attacked western Europe. It was generally accepted that American security depended on denying any single state control of the Eurasian landmass and that the Americans would therefore seek to turn back any Russian bid for regional hegemony. This was of little consolation to the continental powers: the war that followed would be fought on their territory and leave them devastated. In the event of a Soviet attack, the Americans planned "to withdraw to the Channel ports . . . to withdraw to Denmark . . . [and] to withdraw to southern France" before forcing their way back onto the continent.[208] As one British observer put it, the Americans were "content to liberate Europe" rather than defend it.[209] The ensuing counterattack would involve a massive ground assault and bombing campaign that would cause widespread destruction. As Truman told the NATO foreign ministers in April 1949, he was confident the United States would ultimately prevail, but this would "involve an operation of incalculable magnitude in which . . . the consequences to . . . Western Europe . . . might well be disastrous."[210] The United Kingdom, meanwhile, would serve as a base for American bombing operations and escape the devastation of a Soviet-American ground war. All the British had to do, therefore, was take advantage of their geographic position and hold out long enough for the Americans to arrive, as they were bound to do.[211]

In sum, the British had a different view of the security situation in Europe. Officials in London feared conquest less than their counterparts in Paris and Bonn. Moreover, while they shared their partners' concern that the United States would retreat into isolationism, they knew—unlike France and Germany—that in the event of a European war the Americans

206. Quoted in Anthony Adamthwaite, "Britain and the World, 1945–9: The View from the Foreign Office," *International Affairs* 61, no. 2 (1985): 227.

207. Baylis, "Britain," 624.

208. JCS 1641/5, Estimate Based on Assumption of Occurrence of Major Hostilities, April 11, 1946, *RJCS*, pt. 2, 1946–1953, The Soviet Union, reel 1.

209. Memorandum by Air Marshal Eliot, October 19, 1950, *DBPO*, ser. 2, vol. 3, 175.

210. Quoted in Trachtenberg, *Constructed*, 90.

211. Given this kind of thinking, the British were concerned not so much with persuading the Americans to rescue Europe but with getting them to enter an eventual war as quickly as possible. See, for example, Baylis, "Britain," 627; and Warner, "Britain," 32.

would come to their aid before it was too late and rescue them at acceptable cost.

Supporting a European Coalition

Despite their relatively advantageous position, British decision makers understood that their security, as had always been the case, depended on preventing any single state from dominating the continent, which in this case meant balancing Soviet power in Europe.[212] Initially, they were reluctant to balance openly for fear of antagonizing the Soviet Union and precipitating a crisis for which the western powers were unprepared. As Bevin informed his colleagues in the fall of 1945, he "did not wish to talk in terms of a Western Bloc, which would upset the Russians," and he was opposed to a formal Franco-British alliance until he "had more time to consider possible Russian reactions." This reasoning led him to condemn Churchill's "United States of Europe" movement: it was overtly anti-Russian. It was not that he was reluctant to balance against the Soviet Union, but he preferred a loose western grouping until the collapse of the Moscow CFM in 1947.[213] Thereafter, Britain openly committed to containment.

There is some debate among historians about how Europe factored into British balance of power planning.[214] Some focus on Bevin's claim that the Brussels Treaty was "a sprat to catch a mackerel," that is to say it was nothing more than bait to secure an American commitment to defend Europe. In this view, the United States was the key to Bevin's balancing strategy and Europe was of secondary importance.[215] Others point to his statement to the Cabinet in March 1948—and others like it—that he planned to use American aid to create a European combination independent of the United States. Bevin wanted to organize the "middle of the planet" into a power complex co-equal with the United States and Soviet Union.[216] In defending these positions, scholars have tended to obscure the fact that "these

212. For this argument, see Michael E. Howard, *The Continental Commitment: The Dilemma of British Defence Policy in the Era of Two World Wars* (London: Maurice Temple Smith, 1972).

213. Quoted in Sean Greenwood, "The Third Force in the Late 1940s," in *From Reconstruction to Integration: Britain and Europe since 1945*, ed. Brian Brivati and Harriet Jones (Leicester: Leicester University Press, 1993), 61, 63, 68.

214. For a summary of the debate, see Jan Melissen and Bert Zeeman, "Britain and Western Europe, 1945–51: Opportunities Lost?" *International Affairs* 63, no. 1 (1986–87): 81–95.

215. Quoted in Avi Shlaim, Peter Jones, and Keith Sainsbury, *British Foreign Secretaries since 1945* (Newton Abbot: David and Charles, 1977), 48.

216. Quoted in Greenwood, "Third," 64. See also John Kent, "Bevin's Imperialism and the Idea of Euro-Africa, 1945–49," in *British Foreign Policy, 1945–56*, ed. Michael Dockrill and John W. Young (London: Macmillan, 1989), 47–76.

explanations are not mutually exclusive."[217] Faced with an overwhelming opponent, Britain responded by simultaneously working to secure an American commitment and encouraging a more united Europe.

A west European coalition, including Germany, figured prominently in British plans for opposing the Soviet Union throughout the late 1940s. Specifically, policymakers in London embraced the wartime belief that a European combination would provide for "the enhancement of British security through 'defence in depth'."[218] Britain could "not afford to have as a buffer between us and a potential enemy a ring of weak neutral states liable quickly to be overrun."[219] Therefore, British officials were determined to build up the continental states and ally with them. In August 1945, soon after becoming foreign secretary, Bevin unveiled his "Grand Design," informing officials that he hoped to forge a west European coalition based on an Anglo-French understanding. He wanted to "establish close relations between this country and the countries on the Mediterranean and Atlantic fringes of Europe," an endeavor that must "start with France."[220] A few months later, he went as far as to tell Secretary of State James Byrnes that he envisaged the creation of "three Monroes," or spheres of influence, the third of which would include a west European group backed by Britain and the Commonwealth.[221] Churchill, then leader of the opposition, vigorously endorsed the government view: "The safety of the world requires a new unity in Europe." Significantly, he believed that Germany ought to be an integral part of the west European system. He conceived of the new entity as one "from which no nation should be permanently outcast."[222] Six months later, in a speech at the University of Zurich, he reiterated the point, calling for a "United States of Europe" that would rest on a "partnership between France and Germany."[223]

This basic aspiration remained central to British policy until the eve of the Schuman declaration. In June 1947, the military Chiefs of Staff still thought that a west European coalition offered defense in depth: "We should wish to see a closely knit Western European Association in alliance with ourselves, capable of preventing an enemy reaching the west coast of Europe."[224] This was Bevin's view as well. In a memorandum to the Americans in January 1948, he called for a "Western democratic system

217. David A. Gowland and Arthur Turner, *Reluctant Europeans: Britain and European Integration, 1945–1998* (New York: Longman, 2000), 28.

218. Baylis, "Britain," 616.

219. Quoted in Dilks, "British," 28–29.

220. Quoted in Greenwood, "Third," 61.

221. Greenwood, "Bevin," 329; Greenwood, "Third," 64; and Larres, "Search," 78.

222. Churchill, *Never*, 421.

223. Ibid., 429.

224. Quoted in Geoffrey Warner, "The Labour Governments and the Unity of Western Europe, 1945–51," in *The Foreign Policy of the British Labour Governments, 1945–1951*, ed. Ritchie Ovendale (Leicester: Leicester University Press, 1984), 63.

comprising, Scandinavia, the Low Countries, France, Italy, Greece and possibly Portugal." The western half of Germany "without whom no Western system can be complete" should be added, "as soon as circumstances permit."[225] Then, in his "Western Union" speech a few weeks later, he called for the "consolidation" of western Europe, something that he argued could be done, at least initially, by extending the Anglo-French treaty to the Benelux states.[226]

The British continued to support the creation of a west European balancing coalition that included Germany in 1949. In July, the Conservative Party echoed Churchill's earlier statements and called for the "establishment of a United Europe" in which Germany must "play her proper part." Britain, they added, "must make the conception of European unity a reality."[227] Similarly, Bevin informed the Cabinet that the Federal Republic must be brought into a west European organization immediately and that it was Britain's duty to sponsor "the process of reconciliation of France and Germany."[228] Then, a little more than a month before Schuman's announcement, Churchill revisited his Zurich speech in the House of Commons: "We should do all in our power to encourage and promote Franco-German reconciliation as an approach to unity, or even perhaps some form, in some aspects, of union."[229]

Key figures took it as axiomatic that the emerging European coalition would be allied with the United States. Bevin made it clear that his plans to establish a European coalition went hand in hand with maintaining the Anglo-American "special relationship."[230] Similarly, Churchill was at pains to point out that only a combination of a "new unity in Europe" and the "special relationship" would deter Soviet expansion.[231] This was still the

225. Inverchapel to Marshall, January 13, 1948, *FRUS*, 1948, vol. 3, 5. Bevin made the same points in a series of memoranda to the Cabinet in the first half of January. See Geoffrey Warner, "Ernest Bevin and British Foreign Policy, 1945–1951," in *The Diplomats, 1939–1979*, ed. Gordon A. Craig and Francis L. Lowenheim (Princeton: Princeton University Press, 1994), 113; and David Dilks, "Britain and Europe, 1948–1950: The Prime Minister, the Foreign Secretary and the Cabinet," in *Histoire des débuts de la construction européenne (mars 1948–mai 1950)*, ed. Raymond Poidevin (Brussels: Bruylant, 1986), 396–97.

226. Stuart Croft, "British Policy towards Western Europe, 1945–51" in *Shaping Postwar Europe: European Unity and Disunity, 1945–1957*, ed. Peter M. R. Stirk and David Willis (New York: St. Martin's, 1991), 85; and Greenwood, "Third," 67–68.

227. The Conservative and Unionist Party, Foreign Policy: Europe, July 1949, *DHEI*, vol. 3, 725. For an analysis of Conservative views on Europe between 1948 and 1950, see Sue Onslow, *Backbench Debate within the Conservative Party and Its Influence on British Foreign Policy, 1948–1957* (London: Macmillan, 1997), 12–77.

228. Quoted in John W. Young, *Britain, France and the Unity of Europe, 1945–1951* (Leicester: Leicester University Press, 1984), 138.

229. Winston Churchill, Franco-German Reconciliation as a Step towards European Unity, March 28, 1950, *DHEI*, vol. 3, 740.

230. Baylis, "Britain," 617; Greenwood, "Third," 61; and Larres, "Search," 77.

231. Churchill, *Never*, 418, 421.

British view early in 1948 when Bevin told the Cabinet that any emerging west European entity must have the backing of the United States and the Commonwealth.[232]

By the fall of 1948, the British were beginning to think of a united Europe as part of a three-pronged balancing effort. In October, the Foreign Office, the Treasury, and the Commonwealth Relations Office defined "Western Union" as a system that would interlock Europe, the United States, and the Commonwealth.[233] Churchill concurred, telling the Conservative Party conference that British security rested on "the existence of three great circles," namely the Empire, the United States, and Europe.[234] Meanwhile, Anthony Eden, the party spokesman for foreign affairs, declared that Britain should promote "the Three Unities: the Unity of Empire, the Unity of Europe and the Unity across the Atlantic."[235]

Cooperation With, Not Integration In

Although committed to cooperation, the British were not prepared to integrate with their continental allies. Their thinking developed along the following lines. Because France and Germany were individually weak and could not count on the United States to defend them over the long haul, they had no choice but to build a centralized unit of power to deter the Soviet Union. If they were successful, British security would be enhanced. Of course, decision makers in London did not believe that Britain could get a completely free ride, and they were determined to coordinate their efforts with the emerging entity. But there was no reason to sacrifice their sovereignty and actually join it. Given that the continental states were in a more precarious security position, they—and not the British—should incur the autonomy costs of providing an adequate defense. In other words, Britain took advantage of its geographic location to buck-pass the balancing burden—a burden that involved centralized cooperation and therefore a surrender of sovereignty—to the French and the Germans.

It is virtually impossible to find anyone in British policymaking circles who was prepared to consider surrendering British autonomy to a European combination in the 1940s. Churchill was explicit about this in his Zurich speech, which, ironically, gained him a reputation as an advocate of Britain's integration into Europe. When it came to an eventual "United States of Europe," he believed "France and Germany must take the lead together."

---

232. R. A. C. Parker, "British Perceptions of Power: Europe between the Superpowers," in *Power in Europe? Great Britain, France, Italy, and Germany in a Postwar World, 1945–1950*, ed. Josef Becker and Franz Knipping (New York: W. de Gruyter, 1986), 447.

233. Young, *Britain*, 121.

234. Winston Churchill, Europe's Place in the System of British World Policy, October 9, 1948, *DHEI*, vol. 3, 718.

235. Conservative and Unionist Party, Debate on European Unity, October 13, 1949, ibid., 733.

The British, meanwhile, "must be the friends and sponsors of the new Europe."[236] The United Kingdom's position was clear: collaboration with, but not membership in, a united Europe.

Even the British European Movement stopped short of endorsing integration for Britain. In a letter to Richard Coudenhove-Kalergi, a key figure in the European federal movement, Leopold Amery, cofounder of the United Europe Movement and a founder member of the United Kingdom Council of the European Movement, observed that "if a definite federal system should emerge" on the continent, the British would "co-operate intimately with it," but "could not be actually inside the structure." The British therefore "reserved" their position, while not wishing "in any sense to stand in the way of the closest possible union of the Continental nations."[237] In other words, decision makers in London had no objection to some kind of centralized coalition, but they did not want to be part of it. Surrendering sovereignty was out of the question.

There was support for this approach from both major political parties. Harold Macmillan, the member of parliament for Bromley, summed up the position of the Conservative Party hierarchy during a debate in October 1949. There was "no question . . . of constitution-making, still less of Federation." What the British meant by "unity" was "the decision to act together by agreement on a number of questions where action taken together can be more effective than taken separately."[238] Thus, leading Conservatives were not prepared to go beyond traditional cooperation. Meanwhile, the ruling Labour Party was prepared to further the cause of unity "based on cooperation by consent between national governments," but refused to "support proposals for European federation." It could not "agree to hand over to a supra-national authority for Western Europe the power to decide, by a majority vote, against our will, questions which we regard as vital to our economic and financial interests."[239] As Bevin remarked, "Western *Union*" was an unfortunate "misnomer." What he was really thinking of was "an *association* of nations on the lines of the Commonwealth." Britain must remain "different in character from other European nations and fundamentally incapable of whole-hearted integration with them."[240]

236. Churchill, *Never*, 430. See also Klaus Larres, "Integrating Europe or Ending the Cold War? Churchill's Post-War Foreign Policy," *Journal of European Integration History* 2, no. 1 (1996): 29.

237. Leopold Amery, The European Movement in Britain, February 2, 1949, *DHEI*, vol. 3, 720.

238. Conservative and Unionist Party, Debate on European Unity, October 13, 1949, ibid., 735.

239. British Labour Members of the Consultative Assembly, The Functional Instead of the Federal Road towards European Unity, November 28, 1949, ibid., 738–39.

240. Quoted in Gowland and Turner, *Reluctant*, 38, n. 26; and Dilks, "Britain," 412–13. Emphasis added.

This kind of thinking had a profound effect on British policy in the late 1940s. The desire to cooperate with the continent was clearly in evidence—the fact that the British signed the North Atlantic Treaty and the Brussels Treaty underlines London's willingness to collaborate with the other west European states. But such cooperation was to be on a strictly intergovernmental basis: Article 5 of the North Atlantic Treaty simply committed Britain to take "such action as it deems necessary," and although the Brussels Treaty went further by requiring signatories to provide "military and other aid" in the event of an attack, Bevin explicitly denied that it entailed "some pooling of sovereignty."[241]

Meanwhile, London rejected at least two initiatives that would have required member states to surrender a degree of sovereignty.[242] The first was the French proposal of July 1948 to set up a European Assembly, essentially a European parliament. Bevin's reaction was to propose that common policies be made by a council of ministers that would operate on the basis of intergovernmental agreement. Ultimately, the Europeans decided to establish both bodies, but—as the British had hoped—the Assembly was subordinated to the council, thereby ensuring that Europe continued to operate on a purely intergovernmental basis.[243] The second initiative came from the Americans, who tried repeatedly to recast the intergovernmental OEEC as a supranational body. The British, however, explained that they could not accept such a solution because it would involve an "impairment of sovereignty."[244] Despite Washington's best efforts, London stood firm and ensured that the OEEC continued to operate as an intergovernmental organization.[245]

The British view on the eve of the Schuman announcement can thus be summarized as a desire to cooperate with the continental powers but a refusal to join any arrangement that required Britain to abandon its sovereignty. As one British official explained to the Americans less than two weeks before the declaration, Britain "distinguished between 'unity' and 'union' of Europe." The first term meant cooperation among "equal partners" and the British were wholeheartedly in favor of it. But "union" involved a "surrender of sovereignty," something they were "not prepared to

---

241. For the text of the North Atlantic and Brussels treaties, see Kaplan, *NATO*, 245–48, 251–54, and for Bevin's comment, see John T. Grantham, "British Labour and The Hague 'Congress of Europe': National Sovereignty Defended," *Historical Journal* 24, no. 2 (1981): 452.

242. For the general argument, see Klaus Schwabe, "Efforts towards Cooperation and Integration in Europe, 1948–1950," in *The Western Security Community, 1948–1950*, ed. Norbert Wiggershaus and Roland G. Foerster (Oxford: Berg, 1993), 29–42.

243. Hogan, *Marshall*, 180–83; Warner, "Britain," 37–39; and Young, *Britain*, 108–17.

244. Douglas to Marshall, September 17, 1947, *FRUS*, 1947, vol. 3, 435.

245. For a summary of the relevant episodes, see Hogan, *Marshall*, 123–26, 156–61, 217–19, 283–86, 289–91.

do."[246] "Britain had defined her main aims" by early 1950, notes John Young, the chief one being "to co-operate with Europe, but preserve British independence."[247]

Declining Schuman's Invitation

Given this attitude, Britain's refusal to enter into the Schuman Plan negotiations was to be expected. This is not to say that the British opposed the proposal. Rather, they viewed it as a useful step toward establishing a viable counterweight to Soviet power on the continent and resolved to associate closely with the new Franco-German combination. At the same time, however, they were not prepared to join as this would mean giving up sovereign prerogatives.

Although caught unawares by Schuman's announcement, many British policymakers reacted favorably to it, believing that the French plan laid the foundation for a Franco-German unit of power that could oppose the Soviet Union. As the Chiefs of Staff noted only two days after the announcement, the Schuman Plan went "a long way towards solving both . . . [of the] problems" that stood in the way of harnessing "the potential of Western Germany for [the] purposes of Western European Defence," namely France's fear of "a resurgence of German armed power," and the "question of what safeguards would be required to prevent the re-emergence of a Sovereign independent Germany." Moreover, although the plan was not without risks, these were not thought to be serious and its implementation would "increase the armament potential of the West." Simply put, "the strategical implications of the French proposal appear to be strongly in favour of Western European defence."[248]

The British high commissioner in Germany, Sir Ivone Kirkpatrick, agreed, arguing that the plan promised to "incorporate Germany into the Western comity of nations." His only concern was that the resulting "third Power" might want to remain neutral in the cold war rather than being allied with the United Kingdom and the United States.[249] Sir Oliver Harvey, the British ambassador to France, was even more enthusiastic, claiming that if the French proposal was adopted, "Franco-German relations and in consequence Western European co-operation, the policy of Western Union and the Atlantic Pact should be set on a steady and hopeful course."[250] In his estimation, the Schuman Plan had the potential to transform the European balance of power. Even Bevin, who feared the plan might shift the leadership of

246. United States Delegation at the Tripartite Preparatory Meetings to Acheson, April 26, 1950, *FRUS*, 1950, vol. 3, 881.

247. Young, *Britain*, 144.

248. Note by the Chiefs of Staff, May 11, 1950, *DBPO*, ser. 2, vol. 1, 29–30.

249. Memorandum by Kirkpatrick, May 11, 1950, ibid., 32–34.

250. Harvey to Bevin, May 19, 1950, ibid., 75.

Europe from Britain to France, expressed his desire "to give the French proposal not only a welcome but a helping hand."[251]

This remained the British view even after they decided not to join in the coal and steel negotiations. In response to American high commissioner John McCloy's accusation that the British were determined to sabotage the Schuman Plan, Kirkpatrick explained that London did not want to do anything to "prejudice" the ongoing negotiations. Quite the contrary: "I repudiated the suggestion that we were afraid of a Franco/German bloc by explaining that the policy of the balance of power was only reasonable in an age when Europe was the umbilical center of the world and European hegemony meant world predominance."[252] Similarly, while he believed that "the success of this process might hold certain dangers and risks for us," Deputy Under-Secretary of State Sir Roger Makins noted that it "would also have advantages since it would tend to strengthen Western Europe and raise its morale and will to resist."[253]

British policymakers were determined to forge a durable link between themselves and the emerging heavy-industry community. Makins, for example, concluded that the British should "take the risk of letting European federal tendencies develop and seek, if anything, to encourage them while looking for ways of associating ourselves as closely as possible with any federal organisations which might develop."[254] Based on this reasoning, the British went to great lengths to work out some form of cooperative arrangement, and they ultimately signed a treaty of "association" with the ECSC in December 1954.[255]

This was, however, as far as the United Kingdom was prepared to go, because the French plan required members of the putative community to surrender their sovereignty. If Schuman's announcement had left any doubt, then Monnet set the record straight when he traveled to London and made it "abundantly clear" that Schuman's proposal envisaged "the surrender of national sovereignty over a wide strategic and economic field."[256] Participants would have to "accept the supranational principle as a *nonnegotiable* basis for talks on the plan." This did not mean they had to accept a supranational solution in advance, but they did have to commit not to

251. Quoted in Bullock, *Bevin*, 774.

252. Kirkpatrick to Gainer, July 11, 1950, *DBPO*, ser. 2, vol. 1, 255.

253. Makins to Strang, July 12, 1950, ibid., 258.

254. Ibid. See also Note by Plowden, June 30, 1950, and Makins to Franks, July 17, 1950, ibid., 231, 263.

255. For accounts of the association process, see Christopher Lord, " 'With but Not Of': Britain and the Schuman Plan, a Reinterpretation," *Journal of European Integration History* 4, no. 2 (1998): 23–46; and John W. Young, "The Schuman Plan and British Association," in *The Foreign Policy of Churchill's Peacetime Administration 1951–1955*, ed. John W. Young (Leicester: Leicester University Press, 1988), 109–34.

256. Note of a Meeting with Monnet, May 16, 1950, *DBPO*, ser. 2, vol. 1, 60.

discuss any other institutional arrangement.[257] Moreover, they believed that in entering discussions they would be committing to not reject an eventual draft treaty solely on the grounds that it infringed state sovereignty.[258] Given these strictures, the British announced they could not be a party to the negotiations.

The sovereignty issue proved to be determinative. A little more than a week after the Schuman announcement, the economic adviser to the British high commissioner in Germany concluded it would be difficult to engage in discussions on a supranational basis because the project was "so nebulous and the one thing that is clear about it is that some abatement of sovereignty is involved."[259] Bevin concurred with the basic sentiment, stating that the British government would "adopt a positive attitude towards the French proposals," but adding that if the French insisted "on a commitment to pool resources and set up an authority with certain sovereign powers . . . His Majesty's government would reluctantly be unable to accept such a condition."[260] A month later, when the British had already rejected the French invitation to enter into talks on the coal and steel pool, the Cabinet met and reiterated the point. Britain was "prepared in principle to support all reasonable plans for promoting closer economic co-ordination in Europe." But it was also determined to "reject any proposal for placing these industries under the control of a supra-national authority whose decisions would be binding on Governments."[261]

There was more to the British decision than a deep attachment to sovereignty. Key policymakers also believed there were important security implications to surrendering autonomy. The basic fear was that by integrating their economy with those of the continental states they might become dependent on them for vital war-making materials and products. If this happened, Britain would be unable to survive the fall of the continent—by quickly overrunning continental Europe, the Soviets would be able to deny the United Kingdom the resources it would need to hold out until the Americans arrived in force. This concern predated the Schuman announcement. During a meeting of high-level officials in January 1949, the participants agreed that Britain's policy ought to be one of "limited liability." The British could not "assist the Europeans beyond the point at which our own viability was impaired." Nor could they "embark upon measures of cooperation which surrender our sovereignty and which lead us down paths along which there is no return."[262]

257. Young, *Britain*, 152. Emphasis in original.
258. Strang to Younger, June 2, 1950, *DBPO*, ser. 2, vol. 1, 133.
259. Stevens to Macready, May 20, 1950, ibid., 77.
260. Bevin to Harvey, May 26, 1950, ibid., 99.
261. Extract from Conclusions of a Meeting of the Cabinet, June 22, 1950, ibid., 211.
262. Quoted in Gowland and Turner, *Reluctant*, 39. See also Young, *Britain*, 153.

This kind of thinking became especially acute after Schuman's announcement. The Ministry of Defence worried that if "it were decided by some supra-national authority that we should abandon certain of our manufactures which were admittedly uneconomical, we might find that our war potential was crippled because we were dependent on supplies from abroad, and these supplies were not forthcoming." The real risk, they pointed out, was that "Europe would be speedily over-run in another war."[263]

The Labour government's decision not to enter the coal and steel negotiations under the conditions laid out by the French was relatively uncontroversial. On the face of it, some Conservatives were more willing to consider heavy-industry integration for Britain. In June 1950, for example, Churchill argued that the United Kingdom ought to have joined the talks, declaring that "those who are absent are always in the wrong."[264] But as Bevin noted, it was clear that the French conditions, that is to say, "supranational authority and federalism," were "unacceptable to all parties."[265] Meanwhile, Labour politician R. W. G. Mackay regretfully informed the European Consultative Assembly that "whether it is the Labour party or the Tory party which is in power in Britain . . . neither party will accept any supra-national authority in this matter."[266] Striking proof of this came in August, when Macmillan brought a proposal to the Council of Europe that, rather than breaking with Labour policy, simply reiterated British desires to turn the Schuman Plan into an intergovernmental project with national vetoes.[267] As Monnet put it, Macmillan's proposal did not envisage true integration, but sought to establish "a coordinating mechanism between national governments with a voting system that would make Britain preponderant."[268] Two days later, Schuman dismissed the Macmillan Plan as insufficiently supranational.[269]

263. Note by the Ministry of Defence, May 11, 1950, *DBPO*, ser. 2, vol. 1, 31.

264. Quoted in Sean Greenwood, *Britain and European Cooperation since 1945* (Oxford: Blackwell, 1992), 39.

265. Note by Hall-Patch, June 30, 1950, *DBPO*, ser. 2, vol. 1, 229.

266. Quoted in Martin Ceadel, "British Political Parties and the European Crisis of the Late 1940s," in *Power in Europe? Great Britain, France, Italy, and Germany in a Postwar World, 1945–1950*, ed. Josef Becker and Franz Knipping (New York: W. de Gruyter, 1986), 157.

267. Greenwood, *Britain*, 39.

268. Quoted in Raymond Poidevin, "Le rôle personnel de Robert Schuman dans les négociations CECA," in *Die Anfänge des Schuman-Plans 1950–51*, ed. Klaus Schwabe (Baden-Baden: Nomos, 1988), 106.

269. Northedge, *Descent*, 159. See also Harold Macmillan, *Tides of Fortune: 1945–1955* (London: Macmillan, 1969), 201–19; and Monnet, *Memoirs*, 325–26, 334–35.

Alternative Explanations

Having established the plausibility of my theory, I now turn to an evaluation of its competitors. In order to make the analysis more tractable, I focus on French and German decision making regarding the ECSC.

Interest Groups

Although Moravcsik does not test his theory on the ECSC case, he classifies it as an example of integration. In describing the failure of the EDC in 1954, he notes that it crushed any hope that the ECSC "would lead automatically to deeper integration." The implication is that the heavy-industry community involved shallow integration at the very least. Elsewhere he makes a stronger case, noting that the common market, which he treats as the first major integration bargain, involved less pooling and delegation of sovereignty than the ECSC. Given that he takes these features to be the hallmarks of integration, this suggests that he views the coal and steel pool as an example of integration. Indeed, at one point he makes precisely this case, describing the ECSC as a "supranational" institution.[270]

If the interest group argument is correct, there should be good evidence that French and West German coal and steel producers called for a heavy-industry pool and that their governments then pursued the ECSC on their behalf.

The French case offers no support for these claims. To begin with, it is clear that French business did not lobby the government for a coal and steel pool. All the evidence suggests that the Foreign Ministry, and especially Monnet and his confidants, worked alone on the ECSC initiative, with no input from industry. Monnet's memoirs paint a picture of a small group of officials working secretly on what was to be presented to the world as the Schuman Plan. Indeed, he states that his group "could go no further in our technical proposals, because no experts were to be let into the secret."[271] Acheson had no doubt that this was the case. The "merger proposal," he observed, had been drafted following discussions with a "limited number of French Ministers." The steel industry had simply "not [been] consulted."[272]

French industry was uniformly opposed to the ECSC proposal when it was made public. As Henry Ehrmann noted in his detailed analysis of the

270. Andrew Moravcsik, *The Choice for Europe: Social Purpose and State Power from Messina to Maastricht* (Ithaca: Cornell University Press, 1998), 86, 112.

271. Monnet, *Memoirs*, 293–98. The quotation is from ibid., 298.

272. Acheson to Webb, May 12, 1950, *FRUS*, 1950, vol. 3, 697, 699. For further evidence on this point, see Henri Brugmans, *L'idée européenne, 1920–1970*, 3rd ed. (Bruges: De Tempel, 1970), 164–65.

Schuman Plan negotiations, "most of the French trade associations directly or indirectly affected by the Coal and Steel Treaty bitterly resented its provisions."[273] Virtually every consequential producer group quickly lined up against the Plan. Foremost among them were the National Association of Steel Industries, the National Associations of Iron Ore Mines, the National Association of Non-ferrous Metals, the Association of Engineering and Metal-processing Industries which alone represented over ten thousand firms, and the National Council of French Employers (CNPF), an organization Moravcsik refers to as the "leading French business association."[274] Even the usually antagonistic wings of the employers' movement put aside their differences and "united in their opposition to the treaty."[275]

Business opposition intensified during the negotiation and ratification phases. The industry delegate to the Schuman negotiations quickly withdrew from the process, denouncing the coal and steel pool as "socialistic, inconsistent, antipatriotic, and unnecessary."[276] Similarly, in a series of meetings in January 1951 with one of Monnet's most important collaborators, Etienne Hirsch, the directors of France's major steel companies made no effort to disguise their opposition to the Schuman Plan. The minutes of these meetings provide "indisputable evidence that the frequent and heated protests made by official leaders . . . were representative of steel producer sentiment as a whole."[277] Then in March 1951, A. Aron, the "leader of the French Steel Industry," Pierre Ricard, the vice president of the CNPF, and Robert Lacoste, the former industry and commerce minister, met with the Americans and reiterated their intense opposition to the Plan.[278] John Gillingham summarizes the business attitude to the negotiations in his magisterial study of the ECSC: "Monnet negotiated on behalf of France without the active support of any organized interests in the private sector and in the face of bitter opposition from virtually all of it."[279] Then, when the time came for ratification, members of the French National Assembly described being inundated with a "flood" of anti–Schuman Plan propaganda from the major trade associations.[280]

French producer opposition to the ECSC was rooted in two factors. First, they did not believe they were competitive with their German counterparts, and assumed that the creation of a common market for coal and steel would "result in the closing-down of French steel mills and coal pits, with ensuing unemployment and other dislocations of the economy." Sec-

273. Henry W. Ehrmann, "The French Trade Associations and the Ratification of the Schuman Plan," *World Politics* 6, no. 4 (1954): 453.

274. Ibid., 453–58; and Gillingham, *Coal*, 237. Moravcsik's claim is from *Choice*, 108.

275. Ehrmann, "French," 458.

276. Quoted in Gillingham, *Coal*, 237.

277. Ibid., 289.

278. Goldenberg to State Department, March 14, 1951, *FRUS*, 1951, vol. 4, 98–101.

279. Gillingham, *Coal*, 236.

280. Ehrmann, "French," 469.

ond, they were opposed to the supranational setup of the community, maintaining that it should be "controlled by decentralized and hence 'democratic' contractual agreements among the producers rather than by an authoritarian bureaucracy." The "threat of a sinister 'technocracy' . . . was constantly evoked."[281] In other words, producers were opposed to cooperation in coal and steel in general and to supranational integration specifically.

In sum, and contrary to the interest group explanation, the French government appears to have pursued integration in the face of producer opposition, not as a response to producer pressure. Even Moravcsik is forced to this conclusion. The position of "French industry," he admits, was one of "opposition to the ECSC."[282]

The German decision to enter into the coal and steel negotiations also cannot have been driven by business interests—Adenauer approved Schuman's proposal immediately without consulting anyone. "I informed Robert Schuman at once," he notes in his memoirs, "that I accepted his proposal wholeheartedly."[283] Indeed, Acheson described the response as coming "an embarrassingly short time after Schuman's announcement."[284] This does not entirely invalidate the interest group argument, however. Moravcsik argues that business can exert what he terms "structural" rather than direct pressure on policymakers. It is possible, in other words, that Adenauer endorsed the coal and steel pool knowing that the German coal and steel industries would support it.[285]

The problem with this argument is that German industry was opposed to the coal and steel pool. Although big business was enthusiastic about liberalization, it was adamantly opposed to integration and any kind of supranational arrangement. In his overview of German industry's attitude toward integration, Werner Bührer notes that the Iron and Steel Association was highly critical of the "dirigistic" implications of the Schuman Plan. Similarly, the Federation of German Industries (BDI) "took a rather critical view of the negotiations."[286] This finding is significant given that Moravcsik describes the BDI as being the "most influential economic interest group in postwar Germany," and therefore, presumably, the group most likely to have dictated government policy.[287] " 'Pro-European' sentiment," noted Ernst Haas, "was widely mingled with anti-supranational demands,

281. Ibid., 459–63. See also Acheson to Webb, May 12, 1950, *FRUS*, 1950, vol. 3, 697–99.

282. Moravcsik, *Choice*, 108.

283. Adenauer, *Memoirs*, 257.

284. Acheson to Webb, May 12, 1950, *FRUS*, 1950, vol. 3, 698.

285. Moravcsik, *Choice*, 36.

286. Werner Bührer, "German Industry and European Integration in the 1950s," in *Western Europe and Germany: The Beginnings of European Integration, 1945–1960*, ed. Clemens A. Wurm (Oxford: Berg, 1995), 102.

287. Moravcsik, *Choice*, 96.

indicating that for many businessmen integration meant little more than the removal of Allied controls."[288] The last word on the issue goes to Gillingham: "German manufacturers were no more willing to sacrifice their basic industries or entrust their fortunes to a supranational authority than were the French."[289]

Given this evidence, it is hard to make the case that West Germany embraced the Schuman Plan because important economic producers were in favor of integration. Thus, there are good reasons to doubt the explanatory power of the interest group argument. Even Moravcsik appears to recognize this, noting that Fritz Berg, the head of the BDI, later commented that the ECSC was a "typical example of how *not* to do European integration."[290]

Ideational Entrepreneurs

There are several points of agreement between my account and the ideational entrepreneurship argument. For example, I agree with Parsons' claim that following World War II, "many Europeans began to reconsider long-held assumptions about the costs, benefits, and appropriate form of international cooperation." Moreover, I do not dispute his intuition that the story of European integration is "about the assertion of certain [pro-integration] ideas by an elite minority." Finally, we agree that European decision makers pursued integration because they thought it would ensure "peace."[291]

But we differ in our claims about the reasoning behind various actors' support for integration. My argument is that Schuman, Monnet, Adenauer, and others promoted integration for balance of power reasons. They wanted to establish a counterweight to Soviet power while maintaining an even balance of power between France and Germany. It was by balancing power, they believed, that they could avert a future war. Parsons, on the other hand, argues that these same decision makers supported integration because they viewed it as a means to transcend the nation-state. Without nation-states there would be no war. In other words, we differ not on whether there were pro-integration elites in Europe, and not on what they wanted to achieve by integrating, but on the reasoning underlying their pro-community stance.

Several Europeans endorsed integration as a means to transcend the nation-state.[292] This view was most closely associated with the "federalist" movement and the associations it spawned, notably the Union of European Federalists (UEF), the United Europe Committee, the European

288. Ernst B. Haas, *The Uniting of Europe: Political, Social, and Economic Forces 1950–1957* (Notre Dame: University of Notre Dame Press, 2004), 165.

289. Gillingham, *Coal*, 285.

290. Moravcsik, *Choice*, 97. Emphasis in original.

291. Craig Parsons, *A Certain Idea of Europe* (Ithaca: Cornell University Press, 2003), 1, 44.

292. This paragraph is based on Brugmans, *L'idée*, 81–172; and Lipgens, *History*.

Parliamentary Union, and the International Committee of the Movements for European Unity.[293] Certainly, there were important differences among self-proclaimed federalists. Some saw supranational institutions as a means to improve aggregate welfare, others thought they would safeguard distinctively European values, and still others wanted the region to have a voice in international politics.[294] But as Walter Lipgens points out in his study of the federalist movement, many of them supported integration because they believed it would eliminate the nation-state. For them, federation was a "reaction to the catastrophe into which the Continent was plunged by the system of nation states." The two world wars had shown that "consultative machinery was not enough and that Europe must be united in a true federation if it was to avoid internecine wars."[295] Henri Brugmans, meanwhile, traces the postwar federalist impulse to the resistance view that past wars were attributable to "the existence . . . of thirty sovereign states," and that the Europeans had to "remedy this anarchy by creating a federal union."[296]

There is scant evidence, however, that prominent political figures and important decision makers subscribed to this kind of thinking. Brugmans and Lipgens provide no clear-cut evidence that the most powerful French supporters of centralization—Auriol, Bidault, Capitant, de Gaulle, Mayer, Mollet, Palewski, Pflimlin, Philip, Pinton, Ramadier, Reynaud, Schuman, and Teitgen—advocated it as a means to transcend the nation-state. The same applies to West Germany. Although Adenauer, Arnold, Brentano, Ehard, Heinemann, and Schmid all advocated centralization, they do not appear to have done so because they wanted to eliminate nation-states from western Europe. Indeed, historians of the federalist movement have identified only two examples of prominent actors engaging in this kind of reasoning. Wilfried Loth notes Blum's conviction that World War II would "not be the last war" unless the Europeans "set up . . . a super-state on a level above national sovereignties."[297] And Brugmans points to a note from Monnet to the French Committee of National Liberation in August 1943 to the effect that there would "be no peace in Europe if the states reestablish themselves on the basis of national sovereignty, with all that this implies by way of prestige policies and economic protectionism."[298] He does not

293. Brugmans, *L'idée*, 122–28.

294. For a sense of federalists' various motivations, see Alain Greilsammer, *Les mouvements fédéralistes en France de 1945 à 1974* (Paris: Presses d'Europe, 1975); and Lipgens, *History*, 1–58.

295. Lipgens, *History*, 685.

296. Brugmans, *L'idée*, 98.

297. Quoted in Wilfried Loth, "Sources of European Integration: The Meaning of Failed Interwar Politics and the Role of World War II," in *Crises in European Integration: Challenge and Response, 1945-2005*, ed. Ludger Kühnhardt (New York: Berghahn, 2009), 20–21.

298. Quoted in Brugmans, *L'idée*, 157.

argue, however, that Monnet continued to harbor such views in the lead up to the Schuman proposal.

Alan Milward has, in fact, convincingly refuted the ideational argument. Milward acknowledges that "the founding fathers of the European Community appear in most histories as the harbingers of a new order in which the nation no longer had a place." His review of the evidence, however, suggests that these histories provide a flawed account of the views of the key players in the integration process. For example, he rejects the view that Schuman and Adenauer were "less committed to the nation-state" than their contemporaries as a "persistent cliché." Even after Schuman became a public "apostle of supranationality the nation remained the basis of his political thought." Indeed, he believed "the new edifice was to be built" in order to ensure the "security of the nation-states." Adenauer shared this basic conviction. "Within this context of western European unity," argues Milward, "a German state still had to exist as the prime protector of its people." Monnet, finally, "was a most effective begetter of the French nation-state's post-war resurgence," even as he posed as the "father of European integration."[299]

The evidence in this chapter buttresses Milward's claim that the major protagonists had no desire to transcend the nation-state. Their thinking remained traditional, stressing balance of power calculations. Monnet's memorandum of May 3, 1950, and his own description of the thinking that led him to write it clearly reflected balance of power thinking. Schuman's acceptance of the memorandum as the basis for his announcement a few days later was driven by the same kind of considerations. Similar calculations come through clearly in Adenauer's memoirs, despite strong incentives for him not to tarnish his legacy as a founding father by admitting to them.

Parsons' own review of the historical record also offers little support for the claim that European leaders were determined to go beyond the nation-state. His account describes Schuman as being motivated by a desire to find "a basis for Franco-German reconciliation," and Monnet as having "long entertained the belief that Europe's future lay in unification." Neither description suggests a powerful desire to integrate so as to do away with the nation-state. But even if they did, the evidence Parsons cites does not support such a claim. His discussion of Schuman rests on French historian Pierre Gerbet's claim that the foreign minister pursued integration as a means to "guarantee the security of our country." And his description of Monnet's motives relies on the latter's memoirs, which lay out a fairly straightforward balance of power argument.[300]

---

299. Milward, *European*, 318, 327, 329, 330, 334.

300. On Schuman and Monnet's motives, see Parsons, *Certain*, 51, 55, and for the sources Parsons uses to come to these conclusions, see ibid., 51, n. 41 (Monnet's memoirs), and 55, n. 58 (Gerbet). The Gerbet quotation is from "Origines," 222.

Nor is there much support for Parsons' argument in the primary source he puts front and center as an exemplar of community thinking in the late 1940s: "It is by a voluntary abdication of one part of the sovereignty of states, by an association of interests of these states that France believes it possible, in thus tying down Germany, to be assured of the security guarantee she seeks. . . . German economic power will become a support rather than a menace."[301] Even if this is not a balance of power argument—and a strong case can be made that it is—it surely does not suggest a desire to transcend the nation-state.

Conclusion

The evidence presented in this chapter lends powerful support to my argument. The French understood that, in view of the Soviet threat, their security depended on reviving Germany and incorporating it into a centralized balancing coalition. At the same time, they remained mindful of Germany's industrial potential and settled on integration as the best way to maintain a roughly even balance of power within the emerging community. West Germany's enthusiastic reaction to the coal and steel pool can also be explained by balance of power reasoning. Believing that integration promised to build a centralized unit of power capable of balancing against the Soviet Union and realizing that the most that the Germans could hope for was joint control of that coalition, Adenauer immediately accepted Schuman's proposal for a heavy-industry community. The British, conversely, benefited from the luck of geography and buck-passed the integration burden to their allies. My argument is also more persuasive than its competitors. Major producer groups opposed integration, and the evidence suggests that their governments did not consult them prior to making their decisions. Meanwhile, the key decision makers were not motivated by a desire to transcend the nation-state.

Thus, the evidence suggests that the origins of integration lie in the realm of power politics. Even as they put their industrial community in place, however, the Europeans faced the possibility of extending integration to the military realm. It is to those negotiations that I now turn.

301. Parsons, *Certain*, 51.

4. Setback

Military Integration, 1950–1954

On June 25, 1950, less than a week after delegates of the Six met in Paris to begin the negotiations that would lead to the creation of the ECSC, North Korea attacked South Korea. Because it was assumed that the Soviets had approved the invasion in advance, western planners feared that events on the peninsula foreshadowed Russian aggression in Europe. The American response was swift, and at the tripartite conference of foreign ministers in New York in September, Secretary of State Dean Acheson informed the British and the French that the United States intended to send a Supreme Allied Commander (SACEUR) and four to six additional divisions to Europe. The only condition was that the Europeans must agree to create German military units and incorporate them into a European defense force.[1]

The French responded to Acheson's announcement with a plan of their own. On October 24, Prime Minister René Pleven called for the creation of a "European army" made up of nonnational contingents of European soldiers under a European defense minister, who would himself be responsible to a European assembly.[2] Despite the apparent similarities between the two plans, weeks of debate ensued before the western Allies agreed to the Spofford compromise, an agreement that provided for two sets of parallel

1. For details of the debates in New York, see *Foreign Relations of the United States* (hereafter *FRUS*), 1950, vol. 3 (Washington, D.C.: GPO, 1977), 1188–1247, and for the final resolution, see Acheson to Webb, September 26, 1950, ibid., 350–52. For an account of American thinking at the time, see Christopher Gehrz, "Dean Acheson, the JCS and the 'Single Package': American Policy on German Rearmament, 1950," *Diplomacy & Statecraft* 12, no. 1 (2001): 135–60.

2. For the text of the speech, see Pleven Declaration, October 24, 1950, *Die Bundesrepublik Deutschland und Frankreich: Dokumente, 1949–1963* (hereafter *BDF*), vol. 1 (Munich: K. G. Saur, 1997), 379–82.

negotiations.[3] The first set of negotiations, designed to examine how West Germany would contribute to NATO, opened at the Petersberg Hotel near Bonn on January 9, 1951. The second set of talks, intended to lay the groundwork for a European army, opened in Paris on February 15. Although progress at the Paris meeting was initially quite slow, the conferees eventually produced an interim report in July 1951, recommending "that the countries participating pool their military forces and resources under a European defense commissioner responsible to a supranational cabinet and parliament." Then, on May 27, 1952, the foreign ministers of the Six signed the Paris Treaty establishing the European Defense Community.[4] Again, the British refused to enter into negotiations with their allies.

Before the community could come into existence, however, all the signatories had to ratify the treaty. This never happened. Despite intense pressure from the Americans and ratification by four of their five partners, the French National Assembly rejected the EDC treaty on a technical, procedural motion on August 30, 1954, by a vote of 319 to 264. Thereafter events moved quickly, and by the terms of the Paris Agreements of October 1954, West Germany became a member of NATO and the WEU, a purely European, intergovernmental coalition that included the Six plus Britain and was charged with controlling the German military establishment.[5]

In this chapter, I seek to answer four questions: Why did the French agree to create a military community in 1952? Having signed the EDC treaty, why did they subsequently refuse to ratify it and instead seek German membership in the WEU and NATO in 1954? Why did West Germany welcome the French proposal for a European army and sign and ratify the EDC treaty? And why did Britain refuse to become involved in the EDC negotiations?

My central claim is that these events are best understood as the consequence of balance of power politics: the power configuration that made European cooperation in heavy industry possible remained in force, and each state chose to engage in or forego integration based on balance of power calculations. The global distribution of power made cooperation possible. Most important, the west European states continued to confront an overwhelming competitor and therefore had good reason to fear for their survival. Moreover, although they did not have the power to stand up to the USSR singly, they did have the capability to do so together. In other words, power realities gave them the motive and the means to establish a balancing coalition. This would not have been enough, however, had the

3. For details of the Spofford compromise, see *FRUS*, 1950, vol. 3, 457–64.

4. Quoted in Robert McGeehan, *The German Rearmament Question: American Diplomacy and European Defense after World War II* (Urbana: University of Illinois Press, 1971), 137–38. For an analysis of the contents of the treaty, see Edward Fursdon, *The European Defence Community: A History* (London: Macmillan, 1980), 150–88.

5. For the key documents, see *FRUS*, 1952–1954, vol. 5, 1345–66, 1435–57.

United States not continued to defend western Europe, thereby giving them an opportunity to establish a third force.

In this environment, the Germans pursued integration because they believed that only a centralized military force could balance effectively against the Soviet Union, and that the best they could hope for was joint control of it.

The French reaction was to pursue a different kind of coalition. If they were going to be left to deal with the Soviets and the Germans alone, they reasoned that an integrated military was the best solution. There was a better option from a balance of power perspective, however: a continued U.S. commitment to the continent. If the Americans remained in Europe in great numbers, the Soviets would be deterred and the Germans contained. Moreover, the NATO alternative had the singular virtue of not requiring them to surrender their military sovereignty. Of course, even if the Americans agreed to the French proposal, they might withdraw in the future, so France planned to supplement NATO with the WEU, a purely European alliance that included the Six plus Britain. The WEU was designed to serve a twofold purpose. First, it provided the framework for a west European military organization that could be converted into a centralized coalition capable of defending itself against the Soviet Union if the United States pulled out of the region. By coordinating their efforts through the WEU in the short term, France, Germany, and the others would be well prepared to form an integrated military should the need arise. Second, the WEU would keep the Germans from becoming too powerful because it had the authority to control their rearmament. As it happened, the Americans gave the French what they wanted, and Europe's experiment in military integration came to an end.

British policy also rested on balance of power thinking. Like their continental allies, decision makers in London viewed the Soviet Union as a potential regional hegemon in the early 1950s and favored the creation of a coalition to contain it. Thus, they supported the French and the Germans when it appeared they were going to establish an integrated European force. However, although they were keen to cooperate, they had no intention of surrendering their sovereignty and actually joining a European army. A centralized military-industrial combination comprising the six ECSC states would have a good chance of standing up to the Soviet Union. This being the case, the British opted to buck-pass the containment burden to the Six, while promising to cooperate with them if need be.

Motive, Means, and Opportunity, 1950–1954

The European power situation remained essentially unchanged in the early 1950s. The Soviet Union continued to be an overwhelming competitor, the Europeans continued to have the collective resources to establish a viable balancing coalition, and the United States continued to deter the Soviets from taking over the western half of the continent. In other words, the west Europeans still had the motive, means, and opportunity to establish some kind of collective counterweight to Soviet power.

Motive

The Soviet threat was as great as ever in the early 1950s. Between 1950 and 1954, it consistently had a 6:1 military advantage over Britain, its nearest competitor, and an 8:1 advantage over France. Truly staggering, however, was the growth of the Russian economy. Despite the French and West German economic booms of the early 1950s, the Soviet Union's advantage in industrial power increased steadily throughout the period. By 1954, its industrial economy was twice as powerful as those of Britain and West Germany, and its advantage over France had grown to more than 3:1. In terms of overall power, the former great powers were hopelessly overmatched. Britain, which continued to be the most powerful state in the region, was at a 4:1 disadvantage throughout the period, and France's inferiority was on the order of 6:1 (see table 1).

This increase in relative power did not go unnoticed. In August 1952, for example, the U.S. National Security Council (NSC) produced a comprehensive study of Soviet policy and capabilities. According to the document's authors, the Soviet Union now possessed "formidable military capabilities," including an "army of about 2½ million men organized into about 175 divisions." Moreover, the Soviets now had atomic weapons. It was estimated that they already had a stockpile of thirty such weapons in 1951, and this number could rise to as many as three hundred by mid-1955. Worse still, the Soviet Union was quickly expanding its economy. "Particular attention," warned the NSC staff, "is apparently being given to capital construction, chiefly in the heavy industries and in the electrical, transportation, and communications fields." The Soviet Union was increasing "not only its actual production but—more important—its basic industrial potential."

Given this state of affairs, the Americans were convinced that none of the west European states were in a position to put up any meaningful resistance to the Soviet Union. The "free world" was unlikely to "have the capability by mid-1953 of holding more than lodgement areas in Europe against a determined Soviet assault." So great was the Russian power advantage that the United States "would be the primary arsenal of the entire free world to an even greater degree than was the case in World War II."[6]

Thus, the Europeans continued to have ample reason to join forces to balance against the Soviet Union in the early 1950s. The evidence clearly

6. Annex to a Report to the National Security Council by Lay, August 22, 1952, *FRUS*, 1952–1954, vol. 2, 98–99, 101, 103–5, 107.

suggests that the USSR was an overwhelming opponent—given the trends in military and economic might, the chance that any of them could deter or defeat the Soviet Union alone was lower now than at any time since the end of the war. The pressure to engage in some form of joint action was as strong as ever.

Means

Although Britain, France, and West Germany could not deter or defeat the USSR alone, a putative European coalition would have the wherewithal to balance against the Russians. West Germany was still disarmed, but assuming that it would be permitted to devote the same fraction of its population as France to raising military forces, a big three coalition would provide stiff resistance to the Soviet Union. Even though it would be at a more than 2:1 military disadvantage, it would have slightly more economic might than the USSR and would only be at a 1.5:1 disadvantage in terms of overall (military plus economic) power. A hypothetical continental combination that included the six ECSC signatories, but excluded Britain, would also have the capability to stand up to the Soviets. A group of this kind would be slightly weaker than one comprised of Britain, France, and West Germany, but it would still be at a less than 2:1 disadvantage overall and would certainly not be on the wrong end of a gross mismatch (see table 1).

It is worth noting that the data likely understate west European power. By 1954, the United States had approximately 350,000 troops on the ground in Europe. Presumably, if these were to be withdrawn, the Europeans would make up the shortfall from their own resources—they certainly had the population to do so. Were they to raise these additional troops and increase their military spending accordingly, then a big three combination would be at a 1.4:1 disadvantage and a continental combination would be at a 1.7:1 disadvantage overall.[7]

Given these figures, top American officials remained convinced that a European coalition had the capability to stand up to Moscow. At a White House meeting in January 1951, General Dwight Eisenhower, who was serving as SACEUR, reminded his colleagues that western Europe had "about 350 million people, tremendous industrial capacity, and a highly skilled and educated population." The only thing the Europeans lacked was "unity." If they were to achieve this, "most of the danger" from the Soviet Union "would end." The general feeling was that the Europeans "could tell Russia to go to hell if they only would get together, raise enough men, and produce enough equipment."[8] He made the same point as president two

7. For the data used to calculate these figures, see Correlates of War, National Material Capabilities, 1816–2001, http://www.correlatesofwar.org.
8. Notes on a Meeting at the White House, January 31, 1951, *FRUS*, 1951, vol. 3, 450–51.

years later, arguing that if the United States "could get Europe to go in for political and economic union" then "conceivably it could by itself defeat Russia."[9] This view was widely shared. Like Eisenhower, policy planners in the State Department were convinced that Europe had the wherewithal to be a "separate entity of great potential power."[10]

It was commonly agreed, then, that the Europeans had the means to balance against the Soviet Union provided they joined forces. A hypothetical coalition, be it of the big three or continental variety, would be weaker than the USSR, but not at such a disadvantage as to be unable to defend itself. As far as the Americans were concerned, a west European regional grouping continued to have the potential to be a "third force" in the international system.

Opportunity

As had been the case in the late 1940s, the anticipated Soviet response was an important impediment to the development of a west European combination. Balance of power logic meant that the Russians were unlikely to tolerate the consolidation of a powerful coalition in the western half of the continent. Any doubts in this regard were decisively disconfirmed by the Soviet reaction to the Schuman announcement. "The Schuman Plan is not a plan for peace," asserted the west European Communist parties, no doubt under Moscow's direction, "it is a plan for war." Its core purpose, they argued, was to "make western Germany, which has been placed under American control, a political, economic and military base in Europe which is essential for the third world war."[11] The western powers were under no illusion as to Soviet thinking. The Soviet Union's "first preoccupation," noted the deputies to the North Atlantic Council (NAC), was "to prevent the establishment in Europe or Asia of forces capable of threatening the USSR." Consequently, Moscow was determined to "prevent Western Germany from being effectively integrated into Western Europe."[12]

The Soviet Union opposed military integration as soon as it was proposed. Joseph Stalin's reaction to the news emanating from the New York conference was to assert that he simply "would not accept the renaissance in western Germany of a regular German army." The Kremlin followed up, announcing that it "would not tolerate" German rearmament.[13] These were

9. Memorandum of the 157th Meeting of the National Security Council, July 30, 1953, *FRUS, 1952–1954*, vol. 2, 437.

10. Draft Paper Prepared by Davies and Tufts, June 26, 1951, *FRUS, 1951*, vol. 1, 99.

11. French Note, Analysis of the Arguments against the Schuman Plan put forward by Communist Propaganda, undated, http://www.ena.lu/mce.swf?doc=6597&lang=2.

12. Report by the Council Deputies to the North Atlantic Council, February 6, 1952, *FRUS, 1952–1954*, vol. 5, 281–82.

13. Quoted in Michael Creswell, *A Question of Balance: How France and the United States Created Cold War Europe* (Cambridge: Harvard University Press, 2006), 31.

not viewed as idle threats. Even before Stalin's statement, France's foreign minister, Robert Schuman, cautioned that the Soviets would vigorously oppose German rearmament, and he suggested that a German contribution should come only "when our strength was sufficient to prevent action by the USSR." Similarly, British foreign secretary Ernest Bevin wanted to delay German rearmament until the western powers were "sure of our own strength."[14] Although they had brought up the whole issue of German rearmament and were determined to carry through on it, the Americans shared these fears. As early as June 1950, the American high commissioner for Germany, John McCloy, warned that the Soviets would regard West German rearmament "as sufficiently provocative to warrant extreme countermeasures."[15]

The Soviets followed up with a diplomatic offensive. In two notes, on November 3 and December 30, 1950, Moscow accused the western Allies of establishing a "regular German army" composed of "whole divisions." Moreover, they appeared to be in negotiations with the Federal Republic "concerning the inclusion of these divisions in the so-called 'united armed forces'." The formation of a unified military force of this kind was unacceptable, and the Russians demanded that the four occupying powers meet and discuss the "fulfillment of the Potsdam Agreement regarding the demilitarization of Germany."[16] In other words, the USSR left little doubt that it rejected the creation of a west European military force.

Perhaps the best evidence that the Soviet Union opposed the formation of a balancing coalition in the western half of the continent came in March 1952.[17] By late 1951, it was clear that France and West Germany were close to agreement on the contours of the EDC. Stalin's response was to issue a Soviet note on March 10, 1952, calling for a united, neutral Germany. The proposal was designed explicitly to appeal to the Germans. The country would be reunified, occupation forces would be withdrawn, the Germans would be allowed to raise their own forces, and the new state would not be part of either bloc. Why would Stalin make such an offer? The evidence

14. Minutes of a Private Conference of the French, British, and United State Foreign Ministers and Their High Commissioners for Germany, September 14, 1950, *FRUS, 1950*, vol. 3, 297, 300.

15. Quoted in Marc Trachtenberg and Christopher Gehrz, "America, Europe, and German Rearmament, August–September 1950: A Critique of a Myth," in *Between Empire and Alliance: America and Europe During the Cold War*, ed. Marc Trachtenberg (Lanham, Md.: Rowman and Littlefield, 2003), 3.

16. Soviet Note of November 3, 1950, *Department of State Bulletin* (hereafter *DOSB*), vol. 24, no. 600 (Washington, D.C.: GPO, 1950), 12; and Soviet Note of December 30, 1950, ibid., no. 602, 91–92.

17. On this episode, see Vojtech Mastny, *The Cold War and Soviet Insecurity: The Stalin Years* (Oxford: Oxford University Press, 1996), 134–40; James McAllister, *No Exit: America and the German Problem, 1943–1954* (Ithaca: Cornell University Press, 2002), 219–22; and Gerhard Wettig, "Stalin and German Reunification: Archival Evidence on Soviet Foreign Policy in Spring 1952," *Historical Journal* 37, no. 2 (1994): 411–19.

suggests the note was a last ditch attempt to sabotage European military integration. Because they believed the German "masses" longed for reunification and neutrality, the Russians calculated that western rejection of their proposal would bring down the Adenauer government, thereby wrecking the EDC. "In confidentially explaining the purpose of the Soviet note to party activists," notes Vojtech Mastny, "the East Berlin politburo made no qualms about its being intended to derail the obnoxious agreements," namely the treaties ending the allied occupation regime and establishing the EDC.[18]

Given the Soviet Union's hostility, it was the American security guarantee that gave the Europeans the opportunity to build a counterweight to Soviet power without fear of retaliation. Before 1950, that guarantee was almost entirely atomic—the Americans had less than eighty thousand troops on the ground in Europe and relied on their atomic monopoly to deter the Red Army. As late as September 1950, Acheson reassured Schuman and Bevin that the Soviets would not launch a "preventive war" to thwart the formation of a European balancing coalition because they were "deterred . . . by the fear of atomic bombing."[19] The Soviet detonation of an atomic device in August 1949 and the North Korean attack in June 1950 led to a major reassessment of this position. American planners quickly concluded that Europe "had to be defended on the ground, and as far to the east as possible."[20] The western powers would have to cut into the Soviet Union's massive lead at the conventional level. The problem was that raising German troops would be a long and complex process, and the French had a paltry five combat-ready divisions on the continent. In the short term, the Europeans simply could not provide for their own security.[21] Therefore the Americans concluded that they would have to send forces to Europe in great numbers and do so quickly. The number of American troops assigned to European Command increased from approximately 80,000 in 1950, to 260,000 in 1952, to 350,000 in 1954.[22]

Despite the troop buildup, deemed unavoidable given the condition of indigenous European forces, the United States did not want to maintain a

18. Mastny, *Cold*, 137. For evidence that the French understood the logic behind the Soviet offer, see French Foreign Ministry Note, March 12, 1952, *BDF*, vol. 1, 128–30.

19. Minutes of a Private Conference of the French, British, and United State Foreign Ministers and Their High Commissioners for Germany, September 14, 1950, *FRUS*, 1950, vol. 3, 298. For this argument, see Michael Creswell, "Between the Bear and the Phoenix: The United States and the European Defense Community, 1950–54," *Security Studies* 11, no. 4 (2002): 95.

20. See Marc Trachtenberg, *A Constructed Peace: The Making of the European Settlement* (Princeton: Princeton University Press, 1999), 96–103. The quotation is from ibid., 100.

21. The French division figure is from William I. Hitchcock, *France Restored: Cold War Diplomacy and the Quest for Leadership in Europe, 1944–1954* (Chapel Hill: University of North Carolina Press, 1998), 149.

22. For the American force figures, see Daniel J. Nelson, *A History of U.S. Military Forces in Germany* (Boulder, Colo.: Westview, 1987), 45.

permanent presence in the region. "From such [a] long term view point," argued Acheson in June 1951, "it is probably neither practical nor in the best interests [of] Eur[ope] or [the] US that there sh[ou]ld be a US Commander in Eur[ope] or substantial numbers of US forces on [the] Continent."[23] A month later, he noted that although a European military force would have to be "strengthened and stiffened by British and American contingents" for some time, "it would be a force which . . . would not have to be changed in any fundamental way whenever the time came that the overseas contingents might be withdrawn."[24] The U.S. ambassador to France, David Bruce, agreed, telling Acheson that a solid European political structure was essential for the day that "US commander and US troops are withdrawn" from the continent.[25] The Americans were, in fact, quite open about their preferences. President Harry Truman used his 1952 State of the Union address to assert that the United States wanted a "Europe freed from any dependence on our aid," and the State Department followed up, declaring that Washington looked forward to "the day when Europe will be able to maintain her forces without further assistance from us."[26] In the summer of 1952, Acheson hailed the EDC treaty as presaging "the unification of Western Europe into a federal organization which will be large enough to be strong, vigorous and, we hope in time, to take over its own defense on the basis of a strong economic foundation."[27]

The change of administration in 1953 did nothing to alter the basic thrust of U.S. policy toward Europe. This was due, at least in part, to Eisenhower's selection of John Foster Dulles as secretary of state. Perhaps more important, however, was the president's own desire to exit the European scene in the not too distant future. As he told Edward Bermingham in February 1951, the key question was "how to inspire Europe *to produce for itself those armed forces that, in the long run, must provide the only means by which Europe can be defended.*" The defense of western Europe, he added, could not rest "exclusively or even materially upon the existence, in Europe, of strong American units." Therefore, "if in ten years, all American troops stationed in Europe for national defense purposes have not been returned to the United States, then this whole project will have failed."[28] He made broadly the same point when asked about future force levels in Europe by the Senate Committee on Foreign Relations: "I do not know if you could get to

23. Acheson to the Embassy in France, June 28, 1951, *FRUS*, 1951, vol. 3, 802.

24. Memorandum by Acheson, July 6, 1951, ibid., 816.

25. Bruce to Acheson, July 3, 1951, ibid., 806.

26. Quoted in McGeehan, *German*, 171.

27. Quoted in McAllister, *Exit*, 222.

28. Eisenhower to Bermingham, February 28, 1951, *The Presidential Papers of Dwight David Eisenhower* (hereafter *PPDDE*), vol. 12 (Baltimore: Johns Hopkins University Press, 1970), 76–77. Emphasis in original. See also Eisenhower to Hazlett Jr., June 21, 1951, ibid., 369.

zero, but that would be the objective in any planning in which I took part."[29]

Eisenhower continued to nurture similar hopes throughout his presidency. "From the beginning," he asserted in the fall of 1953, "the stationing of American troops abroad was a temporary expedient. It was a stop-gap operation to bring confidence and security to our friends overseas."[30] It was, "properly speaking . . . an emergency measure not intended to last indefinitely."[31] This was also the view of the JCS: "The United States had always considered that it would withdraw its own contribution to the NATO forces at such time as the European states had achieved the capacity to defend themselves."[32] Robert Cutler, special assistant to the president for national security affairs, summed up the administration view in his list of cardinal "points for consideration" when making foreign policy. The United States must "concentrate on creating . . . strong, independent, and self-sufficient groupings of nations, friendly to the United States, centered on Western Europe," and confine its assistance "to progressively lessened support of the regional grouping . . . as it becomes self-sufficient."[33]

The powerful but avowedly temporary nature of the American security guarantee provided the Europeans with an ideal opportunity to continue building their nascent power complex. In the short term, they could count on the Americans to deter Soviet attempts to frustrate any coalition-building efforts. Uncertainty over America's long-term staying power, however, meant they had a powerful incentive to try to provide for their own security, something that would require combined action.

In sum, the European states continued to have the motive, means, and opportunity to put a balancing coalition in place in the early 1950s. The only remaining question was what kind of combination they would build. It is to this issue that I now turn.

West Germany: Embracing Integration, 1950–1954

German policy between 1950 and 1954 can be briefly summarized. First, top German officials were deeply concerned about Soviet capabilities and were determined to build a west European coalition in order to balance against it. Second, they concluded that any combination must be centrally organized to stand a chance against the USSR. Third, they judged that the

29. Quoted in McAllister, *Exit*, 212.
30. Memorandum by Cutler to Dulles, September 3, 1953, *FRUS*, 1952–1954, vol. 2, 456.
31. Memorandum of Discussion at the 165th Meeting of the National Security Council, October 7, 1953, ibid., 527.
32. Memorandum of Discussion at the 160th Meeting of the National Security Council, August 27, 1953, ibid., 454.
33. Memorandum by Cutler, July 31, 1953, ibid., 440.

best they could hope for given their current status was joint control of the emerging coalition. Indeed, an arrangement of this kind was quite attractive—Germany might not become fully sovereign by integrating, but it would become France's equal and regain considerable control over its military affairs. In short, the Germans were driven to embrace military integration for balance of power reasons.

The Balancing Imperative

Chancellor Konrad Adenauer, who at the time had almost complete control over German defense policy, understood that no west European power had the wherewithal to deter or defeat the Soviet Union alone, and that the Europeans therefore had to join forces to survive. "The time was gone," he noted in his memoirs, "when one of the relatively small nations of Western Europe could believe that it could manage by itself."[34] This was also his view in the early 1950s. "The Soviet danger stands right at the heart of Europe, equipped with all the military and administrative weapons of which the Soviet Union possesses an abundance," he warned an American audience in April 1953. "The countries of Western Europe are helpless in the face of the huge power of the Soviets. None of them can resist it standing alone." Consequently, the Europeans had to "unite in an economic, political and defense community."[35] Similarly, in a speech to the European Council in Strasbourg in May 1954, he declared that Europe's "tragic historical heritage" had taught him that none of the west European states was in a position "to protect its own existence on its own." This being the case, they could "only stand together."[36] He adopted a more apocalyptic tone in a review of the cold war situation: "When we consider what an imbalance of power now prevails, we see what a disastrous situation we are faced with and how catastrophic the consequences will be if we do not take prompt and appropriate countermeasures."[37] Those measures included the European army. States that, "taken singly," would offer little resistance to Moscow "were now to be combined for the preservation of peace."[38]

The belief that the Americans could not be counted on to protect Europe indefinitely added urgency to the balancing imperative. As early as August 1949, Adenauer was calling for German rearmament within the context of a European army because "the American taxpayer will not agree to have part of the United States Army, or at least a unit strong enough to defend . . .

---

34. Konrad Adenauer, *Memoirs* (Chicago: Henry Regnery, 1966), 279.

35. Konrad Adenauer, *Journey to America: Collected Speeches, Statements, Press, Radio and TV Interviews* (Washington D.C.: German Diplomatic Mission, 1953), 111.

36. Quoted in Anneliese Poppinga, *Konrad Adenauer: Geschichtsverständnis, Weltanschauung und Politische Praxis* (Stuttgart: Deutsche Verlags-Anstalt, 1975), 76.

37. Konrad Adenauer, *World Indivisible, with Liberty and Justice for All* (New York: Harper and Brothers, 1955), 16.

38. Adenauer, *Memoirs*, 427. See also ibid., 416.

Western Europe, permanently stationed in Germany." He went public with his concerns two years later, telling other west European leaders that he feared "the United States would not for ever keep troops in Europe and Europe itself must therefore take lasting and effective measures against Soviet expansionism." Because NATO was designed to deal with the "present threat" and would not be able to "meet the long-term need," the west Europeans could only hope to survive over the long haul if they were "genuinely united."[39] He made virtually the same point in his memoirs, arguing that "the time would certainly come when America would withdraw from Europe," at which point "European formations would . . . be needed." After all, NATO "had been a response to present tensions" while the "European army was intended for a longer period."[40] Contemporary observers believed these statements were genuine. In March 1954, French high commissioner André François-Poncet noted that an American troop reduction announcement had caused consternation in Bonn, where decision makers interpreted it as the prelude to an American withdrawal from Europe.[41]

Given this perspective, Adenauer was committed to German rearmament and the formation of a European balancing coalition.[42] He was so committed, in fact, that he first suggested rearmament before the creation of the Federal Republic, at a time when the Germans were forbidden from discussing military matters. Thus, in a July 1949 meeting with the Allied High Commission (AHC), he argued that the Germans must be given the opportunity to "defend their country in the event of an emergency." He followed up a week later, informing a group of officials from the Office of Military Government for Germany (OMGUS) that he was in favor of German membership in NATO and rearmament in the context of a European army. This basic approach was to continue in the early months of his chancellorship. In late 1949, he gave two interviews—to *L'Est Républicain* and to the *Cleveland Plain Dealer*—affirming West Germany's desire to provide contingents for a future European military force. In a meeting with the AHC in June 1950, armed with a memorandum from General Gerhard Graf von Schwerin, he asserted that Germany must be allowed to rearm if Europe was to stand any chance of defending itself against a Soviet attack.[43]

39. Quoted in McAllister, *Exit*, 175, 215.

40. Adenauer, *Memoirs*, 356.

41. Creswell, *Question*, 143.

42. For the claim that he was the first important German politician to hold this view, see David Clay Large, *Germans to the Front: West German Rearmament in the Adenauer Era* (Chapel Hill: University of North Carolina Press, 1996), 49.

43. See McAllister, *Exit*, 175; Thomas Alan Schwartz, *America's Germany: John J. McCloy and the Federal Republic of Germany* (Cambridge: Harvard University Press, 1991), 118, 127 (for the quotation); and Hans-Peter Schwarz, *Konrad Adenauer: A German Politician and Statesman in a Period of War, Revolution, and Reconstruction*, vol. 1 (Providence, R.I.: Berghahn, 1995), 522, 527.

The Korean War strengthened Adenauer's commitment to placing a re-armed West Germany within a European coalition. Following Winston Churchill's call for the creation of a European army in August 1950, Mc-Cloy asked Adenauer whether the Federal Republic would contribute a contingent to such a force, and predictably, the chancellor replied in the affirmative. West Germany was prepared to "place its human reserves and its material reserves for the protection of Western freedom at the disposal of an international army, which under some circumstances will have the task of repelling a Soviet Russian attack."[44] He reiterated the point for domestic consumption in a speech to the Bundestag a couple of months later. The Germans could not "expect the United States . . . and the countries of western Europe to assume the sacrifices that arise from the creation of a defense front" alone—every German had a duty to "defend his country and his liberty" and to contribute to the common effort.[45]

The chancellor's view of the EDC was clearly informed by similar considerations. As he argued during the ratification debate in December 1952, the treaty's primary virtue was that it promised to establish a viable balancing coalition and thereby enhance German security. The Federal Republic was in a precarious position, "disarmed and defenseless, bordered by a colossus who is trying to enslave and swallow her." The Germans therefore faced a choice between "slavery and freedom." If they wanted freedom they had to ratify the treaty. Otherwise, the "Soviet Union would be done the greatest imaginable service."[46] It was "only by such associations" that the Europeans could hope to "defend peace, to rebuild Europe, [and] to save European culture," in the face of a state "far larger, far more powerful and far more totalitarian" than Nazi Germany.[47] Adenauer continued to hold this view even after the French rejected the EDC. "I am still of the opinion," he asserted just days after the no vote in the French National Assembly, "that the fate of France and the fate of Germany are indivisible. Either both of us will fall into the hands of Russia, or we shall both remain free."[48] In his opinion, the very survival of Europe depended on a functioning Franco-German coalition.

There was considerable support in Germany for Adenauer's views. His military advisers had been advocating rearmament and the incorporation of German units into a western coalition since the beginning of 1950. In October, they produced the Himmerod Memorandum recommending a German defense contribution of twelve heavy armored divisions.[49] Indeed, building an effective coalition was deemed so important that one former

44. Quoted in Schwarz, *Adenauer*, 550–51.
45. Quoted in F. Roy Willis, *France, Germany, and the New Europe, 1945–1967* (Stanford: Stanford University Press, 1968), 154.
46. Quoted in ibid., 174–75.
47. Adenauer, *World*, 2–3.
48. Quoted in Fursdon, *European*, 309–10.
49. Schwartz, *America's*, 212; and Schwarz, *Adenauer*, 527.

general was prepared to agree to a French commander for the EDC "because building up defensive strength for Western Europe as a whole was more important than matters of national prestige."[50] Despite surface appearances, this was also Kurt Schumacher's view. Although the SPD leader wanted the western Allies to build up their own forces first to deter a Russian attack before the Federal Republic rearmed, he nevertheless agreed that the Soviet Union represented an overwhelming threat and that the Germans must rearm and join some kind of coalition.[51] As his successor, Erich Ollenhauer, stated in response to the possibility of German neutrality in February 1951, West Germany had "made its decision for the West and . . . no one should doubt the commitment of the SPD on this point."[52]

The balancing imperative was so strong that it dictated German attitudes toward reunification. Adenauer was horrified by the Soviet suggestion in November 1950 that they might consider German reunification. Acceptance of the Soviet proposal that Germany be reunified, neutralized, and demilitarized, he argued, would pose the "greatest danger" to Germany and to Europe as a whole. Germany would be defenseless, there would be no west European coalition, and the Soviet Union would dominate the continent. The Soviet plan would result in Europe's "abandonment to the Soviet sphere of power." The same logic applied almost eighteen months later. Tasked with responding to the latest Soviet note, Felix von Eckhardt and Theodor Blank declared that the Soviet aim was to prevent the formation of an effective west European coalition so that they could "exert the decisive influence" on the continent.[53] In a similar vein, Adenauer told the CDU Evangelical Working Group that the prospect of reunification must not interfere with the formation of a defensive coalition: "We must make the most of every opportunity to create a reorganization of Western Europe."[54] Nothing, not even the prospect of reunification, was to interfere with the overriding goal of creating a European coalition designed to safeguard Germany's security.

In sum, facing an overwhelming opponent in the form of the Soviet Union, the Germans sought to rearm and join forces with their western neighbors. As Adenauer put it looking back on events in the early 1950s, the "persistent Russian danger" meant that Germany had "to make common cause with the West and to take her place in a free Europe." It was, he observed in a textbook statement of balance of power reasoning, "a policy of pure self-preservation."[55]

50. Hans Speier, *German Rearmament and Atomic War: The Views of German Military and Political Leaders* (Evanston, Ill.: Row, Peterson, 1957), 55.

51. Schwarz, *Adenauer*, 590.

52. Quoted in Ronald J. Granieri, *The Ambivalent Alliance: Konrad Adenauer, the CDU/CSU, and the West, 1949–1966* (New York: Berghahn, 2003), 54.

53. Quoted in Schwarz, *Adenauer*, 602, 652.

54. Quoted in Granieri, *Ambivalent*, 54.

55. Adenauer, *Memoirs*, 431.

Centralization

As he had done throughout the late 1940s, Adenauer continued to assert that any future coalition must be centralized to be effective in containing the Soviets. The Federal Republic, he told the *Cleveland Plain Dealer* in December 1949, was prepared to contribute to the defense of western Europe only "in the context of a European army or, to put it differently, to the army of a European federation." Using slightly different language, the chancellor later asserted that the "unification" of Europe "had become a political necessity of the first order" in light of the tremendous power of the Soviet Union.[56] This would be true, he noted in April 1953, even if "current tensions disappeared or were greatly diminished." The Soviet Union was simply "too strong" and the Europeans "by themselves too weak," thereby making the "unification of Western Europe along military, political and economic lines . . . a necessity."[57]

Adenauer's support for the EDC was clearly rooted in his conviction that it would lead to the creation of a "confederation" whose members would renounce their "most important sovereign right" and transfer it "to a supranational authority." In his mind, the community was the "foundation . . . for the political and economic unification of Europe." Indeed, without an arrangement of this kind, western Europe would be subject to "decay and perdition."[58] Of course, he did not believe that a union could be "created in one day." After all, the United States of America "needed . . . decades before they were consolidated into one country." But a "United States of Europe" ought to be the goal, and its "crowning achievement . . . must be the establishment of a European army and of a European Political Community."[59] Adenauer was so convinced of this that he informed the U.S. National Press Club in April 1953 that "every single rational argument" pointed to the construction of a "United States of Europe."[60]

Although he used the terms federation, confederation, unification, and union indiscriminately, the logic behind Adenauer's support for a centralized arrangement was eminently consistent: only a military coalition of this kind could compete in a world of centrally governed superstates. This rationale comes through clearly in his memoirs. "The preservation of peace . . . and defence were tasks of such magnitude, due to the world situation," he wrote, "that their solution could be found only in the framework of comprehensive communities."[61] As he told the Senate Foreign Relations Committee during his trip to the United States, "the impressions I have re-

56. Ibid., 270, 416.
57. Adenauer, *Journey*, 78.
58. Adenauer, *Memoirs*, 424, 436.
59. Adenauer, *Journey*, 122–23.
60. Adenauer, *Memoirs*, 453.
61. Ibid., 393.

ceived here ... strengthen my conviction that if Europe does not unite, it will fall to pieces, because in view of the magnitude of your country, and the enormousness of its means, and resources ... [the] European national states, the European structure as it is now, appears rather obsolete." Similarly, he informed the American Committee on United Europe that "measured by modern power standards, the present political structure of Europe appears to be made up of *small states*." If Europe continued to be "divided into a great number of states and exposed to the suction of the power system of Soviet Russia," it was "doomed."[62]

Adenauer made the same competitive effectiveness claim in advocating the defense community specifically. "The last war, [and] the development of weapons technology ... had created new conditions in the world," he noted. "There were now two world powers: the United States and Soviet Russia. . . . The countries of Western Europe ... were no longer in a position to save European culture if each country acted by itself." Therefore, and this was the purpose of the defense community, "the peoples of Western Europe had to unite politically, economically and culturally. It was the only policy that could enable them to protect the peace." Failure to centralize, on the other hand, would have disastrous consequences. In the context of the cold war, "to insist upon holding high the traditional concepts of nationalism," by which Adenauer meant states trying to procure their "own military protection," was "to surrender Europe."[63] Given that the "danger ... from the East is so great," the Europeans had to form a union even if this meant "relinquish[ing] some of their past and their cherished traditions."[64] He was convinced that unless the Europeans abandoned traditional forms of cooperation and established a centralized unit of power, they were unlikely to survive.

Integration

Top German officials agreed that the Franco-German military force, like the industrial community before it, must be an integrated one—that is to say, one in which the Federal Republic and France would be equally represented and share decision-making control. Adenauer was clear about this from the moment a German defense contribution was broached. In November 1949, he asserted that the Federal Republic wanted to join a European defense system with a joint high command. A month later, he told the press that Germany would contribute to the defense of western Europe as a member of a European army "under European command." Although he

---

62. Adenauer, *Journey,* 52, 143. Emphasis in original.
63. Adenauer, *Memoirs,* 437, 453.
64. Adenauer, *Journey,* 34.

did not say so explicitly, a "European" command clearly implied one in which all member states had some say in decision making.[65]

The chancellor's support for an integrative solution gathered momentum following Pleven's announcement. Germany, he repeated over and over again, ought to "have the same duties but also the same rights as all other participating countries." It was for this reason that the French assurance of November 1950 that "Germany was to be completely equal with the other partners" in a putative defense community gave Adenauer "great satisfaction."[66] And it was for the same reason that he soured on the EDC concept a month later. West Germany's minimum requirement of "full equality of rights with the others as regards armaments and the structure of command" was not being met, and he feared he would soon "be in the unhappy position of having to reject it." Indeed, had the French carried through on their promise of integration and "equality of rights," the west Europeans would have already been well on the way to establishing a European army.[67] The press shared the chancellor's reservations, asserting that the Germans refused to become "foreign legionnaires under a high command where everyone commands but us."[68] To be sure, these statements focused heavily on German demands, but they logically implied a jointly controlled defense effort. After all, if all member states, including the Federal Republic, were to have equal rights, the defense community would be jointly controlled.

Adenauer continued to support military integration throughout the early 1950s, culminating in his address to the French diplomatic and foreign press in Paris on December 11, 1953. Making his now familiar claim that no single European state was "in a position to resist on its own the conquest of Europe planned by Soviet Russia," he declared that they had no option but to engage in "integration" through the EDC. That the chancellor took integration to mean joint control of a centralized coalition comes through clearly in the remainder of his speech. "Any integration of Europe," he asserted, "demands of its participants the surrender of rights; this is of the essence of integration." All member states would be expected to give up those rights to an entity he called "integrated Europe." Put somewhat differently, they would "surrender part of their rights," in this case their military decision making, "to the community to which they belong." Adenauer understood that this was not a particularly welcome prospect because "each state . . . wants to surrender as few of its rights as possible; this is in the nature of things." But the alternative was to "remain in isola-

65. Adenauer, *Memoirs*, 268.

66. Ibid., 297, 299.

67. Kirkpatrick to Bevin, December 12, 1950, *Documents on British Policy Overseas* (hereafter *DBPO*), ser. 2, vol. 3 (London: HMSO, 1989), 354–55.

68. Quoted in Mark S. Sheetz, "Continental Drift: Franco-German Relations and the Shifting Premises of European Security" (PhD diss., Columbia University, 2002), 155.

tion," fail to centralize, refuse to integrate, and "become—one to-day, another to-morrow—Russian satellite states."[69]

The Germans strongly endorsed military integration because they understood that joint control of the emerging European army was the best outcome they could hope for.

German control was simply out of the question; the French would not allow it, and they had the backing of Britain and the United States. Knowing this, Adenauer went out of his way to reject arrangements that might conceivably lead to German domination of western Europe, lest he raise suspicion that this was his intention. Thus, although he was quite open about his desire for German rearmament, he consistently argued that it should take place within the context of an "integrated . . . European army," and he categorically rejected "a national German army."[70] As he put it in December 1950, if the "Allies demanded that we should take part in the defence of Western Europe, I should be in favour, not of an independent Wehrmacht but of a German contingent in a European force."[71] Little had changed when he addressed the American Council on Foreign Relations in April 1953. "The German people," he announced, "welcome the fact that we are aiming not at a national army but at an integrated European army." Germany was committed to "merging into a larger community."[72]

At the same time, however, the West Germans argued that their contribution to the common effort entitled them to equal standing with the French. After all, they could not be expected to bear an equivalent burden and yet have no say in the running of the coalition. Thus, they had no qualms about asking that their military contribution be reflected in equality of status within any west European coalition. Adenauer was explicit about trading a German military contribution for equality. Speaking at the CDU conference in December 1949, he made it clear that the Germans were prepared to contribute to European defense, but not as "mercenaries." They would have to "take part in the same way as Englishmen, Frenchmen, and other nationalities." His "precondition" for German participation in the common defense was "complete equality," because "equal duties presupposed equal rights." He made the same point in his interview with the *Cleveland Plain Dealer:* West Germany was prepared to contribute to a European army, but only as an "equal member." In other words, he viewed rearmament as "the way to gaining full sovereignty for the Federal Republic."[73]

The chancellor, his generals, and the press continued to make the case for equality of status in the summer of 1950. In the Spiedel-Heusinger

---

69. Konrad Adenauer, *For Europe—Peace and Freedom* (Cologne: Press and Information Office of the Federal Government, 1954), 6.

70. Adenauer, *Memoirs*, 394.

71. Quoted in Fursdon, *European*, 64.

72. Adenauer, *Journey*, 126.

73. Adenauer, *Memoirs*, 270.

memorandum, prepared for Adenauer in August, top military officials observed that Germany's commitment to the defense of the West was "not matched by a readiness on the part of the Western world to incorporate West Germany on equal terms."[74] The implication was clear: if Germany was to rearm in earnest, it must be granted equal status. Adenauer made precisely this point to the AHC later in the month. "It would be extremely difficult to impose additional burdens on [the] German people such as would be required for defense," he declared, "if they had no assurance that Germany was being received as [an] equal partner by the western nations."[75] Meanwhile, the German press welcomed the idea of a European military force, but made it clear that the Federal Republic would only participate if it was accorded "equal rights and equal obligations with other nations."[76]

The Federal Republic toughened its stance in the fall, using the threat of domestic unrest to extract concessions. In a November meeting with the AHC, Adenauer declared that the German people would contribute to western defense only if there were "at least the prospect of obtaining complete freedom." The Germans had to believe that their "sacrifices are . . . worthwhile." In practice, this meant that relations between the western Allies and West Germany had to be "progressively regulated by a system of contractual agreements." Although Adenauer denied it, McCloy was left with the impression that "his paper was a condition put forward as a sort of trade for [a] German contribution."[77] As François-Poncet observed in a communication to Paris, the Germans were now insisting that "the recognition of the principle of absolute equality of rights . . . precede German rearmament."[78] Sir Ivone Kirkpatrick, the British high commissioner, also reported a "hardening of [the] German line." Adenauer was now bidding for a "contractual agreement and [the] promise of ultimate equality as [the] price of [a] German contribution to defence."[79]

As if to confirm these suspicions, Adenauer took advantage of an interview with Benedict Kingsbury-Smith in December to assert that although he was not particularly concerned about equality of numbers, he was committed to equality of rights. German troops could not be treated as "cannon-fodder" or "second-class soldiers."[80] Herbert Blankenhorn, who acted as the chancellor's foreign policy spokesman, soon tightened the screw, insisting that "what was now needed was . . . a statement of principle that Germany would be given its sovereignty," lest the German people "drift to-

74. Quoted in Schwarz, *Adenauer*, 540.

75. Hays to Acheson, September 1, 1950, *FRUS*, 1950, vol. 4, 715–16.

76. Quoted in Fursdon, *European*, 86.

77. McCloy to Acheson, November 17, 1950, *FRUS*, 1950, vol. 4, 780–81, 784.

78. Quoted in Hitchcock, *France*, 245, n. 47.

79. German Attitude on Controls and Defence, December 1–4, 1950, *DBPO*, ser. 2, vol. 3, 309.

80. Quoted in Fursdon, *European*, 96.

ward neutralism."[81] Simply put, equality was the price of rearmament and adherence to a western coalition. As Wolfram Hanrieder notes, "Adenauer never allowed the connection between rearmament and sovereignty to go unnoticed."[82]

Given this emphasis on equality, the Germans were initially unhappy with the European army conference in Paris, which they did not see as leading to the creation of a truly integrated military force. Adenauer told McCloy that the French plan seemed "so deficient that he had taken steps to avoid any leaks about it for fear of adverse German public reaction." As it stood, the plan was unacceptably discriminatory. McCloy had to reassure him that the French intended to create an army "on the basis of real equality."[83] His assurances did little to calm German fears, however. In June 1951, Walter Hallstein, a top-ranking civil servant in the Federal Chancellery, worried that the European army was "just a dodge to make sure that any German troops which may be raised are placed under French command" rather than a sincere attempt to establish an integrated military.[84] This was also the view of the SPD. In July, Carlo Schmid asserted that he did "not accept the Pleven plan, since it is based on the principle of German inequality." Any "German contingent would be only a Foreign Legion."[85]

German attitudes changed when it began to look as if the European army was going to be an integrated force in which the Federal Republic would be the equal of France. The West Germans had come to embrace the defense community idea, argued McCloy in February 1952, because it appeared to respond to their "almost hysterical attitude . . . on the discrimination issue."[86] French deputy high commissioner Armand Bérard observed that the Germans were jubilant; they believed that, thanks to the EDC, they now stood "alongside the victors" for the first time in decades.[87] The evidence from the German side certainly appears to support these views. Adenauer rejoiced because the signing of the treaty meant "the turning of a new leaf." West Germany was on the verge of creating a "community in which we shared all rights but also all duties with our partners."[88] Franz-Josef Strauss, soon to be minister for special affairs, saw the treaty as the culmination of a new policy recognizing the Federal Republic as a "partner of the West."[89] Even at this juncture, however, the Germans continued to

81. McCloy to Acheson, January 16, 1951, *FRUS*, 1951, vol. 3, 1452.

82. Wolfram F. Hanrieder, *West German Foreign Policy, 1949–1963: International Pressure and Domestic Response* (Stanford: Stanford University Press, 1967), 96.

83. McCloy Telegram, March 3, 1951, *FRUS*, 1951, vol. 3, 771, n. 5.

84. Quoted in McAllister, *Exit*, 205–6.

85. Quoted in McGeehan, *German*, 74.

86. McCloy to State Department, February 1, 1952, *FRUS*, 1952–1954, vol. 5, 15.

87. Quoted in Hitchcock, *France*, 168.

88. Adenauer, *Memoirs*, 417.

89. Quoted in Speier, *German*, 158–59.

insist on the principle of equality. Although the Bundestag approved of Adenauer's intention to sign the EDC treaty on February 8, 1952, it demanded that the government ask for equal rights within the community, the end of the occupation, and the restoration of sovereignty.[90]

Because the EDC treaty satisfied West German demands for equality and therefore involved the restoration of a measure of decision-making authority, ratification proved to be fairly uncontroversial.[91] To be sure, some SPD party members opposed it on the grounds that membership in the EDC would "widen [the] gulf between [the] Federal Republic and East Germany," effectively reducing the chances of reunification. Moreover, they argued that the treaty "did not give Germany equality."[92] But they were in the minority. Most decision makers supported Adenauer's contention that by joining the EDC the Federal Republic would be establishing a powerful balancing coalition within which it would be France's equal. The Bundestag duly ratified the treaty on March 19, 1953, and the Bundesrat did the same on May 15.

France: Flirting with Integration, Choosing Alliance, 1950–1954

French policy between 1950 and 1954 was driven by straightforward power and sovereignty calculations. The key goal was to establish a favorable balance of power vis-à-vis Germany and the Soviet Union, and to do so without giving up sovereignty if possible. By 1950, this had largely been achieved— the United States had agreed to keep forces in Europe until the peace was secure and signed the North Atlantic Treaty, thereby committing to defend western Europe. For the time being, the French could rely on American power to deter the Soviets and control the Germans. But the Soviet threat continued to loom large, and when the Americans called for the rearmament of Germany in 1950, France did not oppose the plan in principle. If the Europeans were to balance effectively against the Soviet Union, it stood to reason that Germany had to be rearmed. French officials were, however, uncomfortable with the American demand that they agree to rearm the Federal Republic openly and immediately. So in October 1950, they proposed the Pleven Plan—an unworkable initiative that discriminated against Germany—in an attempt to delay German rearmament.

France's shift from the Pleven Plan to an agreement to establish an integrated military force—the EDC—in May 1952 rested on balance of power thinking. The principal consequence of Pleven's announcement was that the French found themselves negotiating the terms of a European army. This was not, as we shall see, necessarily an outcome they wanted. But they

90. Willis, *France*, 155–56.
91. For an account of the process, see ibid., 172–78.
92. Dulles to State Department, February 6, 1953, *FRUS*, 1952–1954, vol. 5, 1568.

reasoned that if there was going to be a European military force, then it must be centralized, and France and Germany must share control of it. Only by integrating in this way could they establish an effective bulwark against the Soviet Union and ensure a roughly even balance of power within western Europe.

But balance of power calculations also meant that the EDC was never especially popular in France. Even as they negotiated the defense community, the French were having second thoughts. Although the EDC would establish a fairly *favorable* balance of power, it would not establish a *sure* balance of power, because the Germans could secede from the community at any time. Worse still, this precarious situation would come at considerable cost—joining a European army meant surrendering military sovereignty, something that France vehemently opposed. Accordingly, the French were never really sold on the EDC.

Similar considerations ultimately led Paris to call for Germany's rearmament and membership in NATO and the WEU. In balance of power terms, an American military commitment to the continent was more attractive than the EDC: the Soviets would be deterred and the rearmed Germans would be contained, all while the French retained their cherished sovereignty. Of course, even if the Americans committed now, the French feared they might leave in the future. Therefore, France hoped to supplement an American presence with a purely European arrangement that included Britain and had the authority to control German rearmament. A coalition of this kind would ensure that the Germans did not become too powerful, thereby maintaining an even balance of power within western Europe. It would also lay the foundation for a centralized combination capable of defending itself against the Soviets in the event of an American withdrawal. So the French rejected the EDC in August 1954, informing their allies that they would support German rearmament provided it was accompanied by a strengthened American commitment and the creation of a European alliance including Germany and Britain—the WEU—which would be subordinate to NATO.

The Americans and British gave the French what they wanted, and continental Europe's experiment in military integration came to an end. Had Washington and London not agreed to France's terms, we can reasonably assume that the French would have been forced back to the military integration option or something like it. But they did and the point was moot. In October 1954, the Americans reiterated their pledge to keep forces in Europe, and Germany was admitted to NATO and the newly established WEU. There was no need for the French to revisit the integration option.

The American Commitment

In the late 1940s, the French government worked hard to secure an American commitment to the region, culminating in the establishment of the

NATO system for the defense of western Europe.[93] With American power deployed on the continent, the Soviets would be deterred and the Germans controlled. This is not to say that NATO was viewed as a perfect solution in Paris. French decision makers continued to worry that the Americans might withdraw from Europe down the line or fail to follow through on their commitments in the event of a Soviet attack. But as long as NATO functioned as advertised, Europe and France would be more secure.

The French desire for an Atlantic alliance that included the United States was in evidence soon after the war ended. In November 1945, President Charles de Gaulle expressed an interest in cooperating with the Americans and acknowledged that France had to secure such an alliance if it "wished to survive."[94] In fact, top decision makers were interested in negotiating a "secret military agreement" with the British and Americans against the Soviet Union.[95] The French view did not change with de Gaulle's departure from office. In March 1947, Foreign Minister Georges Bidault made it clear to Secretary of State George Marshall that France was opposed to plans to demilitarize Germany because these might be regarded as a "substitute" for what they really wanted: an American presence in Europe.[96] Later in the year, the French sent General Pierre Billotte to the United States to negotiate a "Franco-American military agreement."[97] Marc Trachtenberg puts the point well: "From the start the French were strong supporters of a western defense system under American command. They wanted the American commitment to Europe to be as strong and as 'organic' as possible."[98]

French officials ramped up their efforts to secure an American defense commitment in 1948. Their decision to conclude the Brussels Treaty in March was driven at least in part by the belief that overcoming American skepticism about Europe's ability to contribute to its own security was vital to persuading the United States to commit to the continent. Meanwhile, the Prague coup in February and the Berlin Blockade, which began in June, led to explicit calls for the Americans to step up their involvement. Between March and April, Bidault repeatedly asked Washington for an American-

---

93. The argument in this section is based on Michael Creswell, " 'With a Little Help from Our Friends': How France Secured an Anglo-American Continental Commitment, 1945–54," *Cold War History* 3, no. 1 (2002): 1–7; Georges-Henri Soutou, "La sécurité de la France dans l'après guerre," in *La France et l'OTAN*, ed. Maurice Vaïsse, Pierre Mélandri, and Frédéric Bozo (Paris: Editions Complexe, 1996), 21–52; and Trachtenberg, *Constructed*, 66–86.

94. Quoted in Irwin M. Wall, *The United States and the Making of Postwar France, 1945–1954* (Cambridge: Cambridge University Press, 1991), 42.

95. Georges-Henri Soutou, "Le Général de Gaulle et l'URSS, 1943–1945: Idéologie ou équilibre européen?" *Revue d'histoire diplomatique* 108, no. 4 (1994): 353.

96. Bidault-Marshall Meeting, March 13, 1947, *FRUS*, 1947, vol. 2, 247.

97. Quoted in Trachtenberg, *Constructed*, 83.

98. Ibid., 84.

British-French alliance.[99] Then, in June, he informed the American ambassador, Jefferson Caffery, that the "present danger is the weakness of the Western European powers," a situation that could be remedied only if the United States were to cooperate with Europe. What was needed was "not a spectacular system of guarantees, but an effective and concrete system of assistance."[100]

The United States soon complied with French wishes. In March 1948, President Truman declared that U.S. troops would remain in Europe until the peace was secure, a commitment later codified in the London three-power agreement on Germany.[101] At the same time, Marshall informed Bidault that the United States was ready to discuss the establishment of an Atlantic security system, a point he reiterated three months later, telling his French counterpart that the Americans wanted to go ahead with negotiations on the "nature of [the] US association . . . with European security arrangements."[102] Exploratory talks convened in Washington in July, and the North Atlantic Treaty was signed in April 1949.

Although decision makers in Paris continued to worry about the permanence of the American commitment, they welcomed the NATO system because it enhanced French security. As Trachtenberg notes, they believed that the American troop presence served two goals simultaneously: it "would not just protect western Europe from Soviet aggression, it would also automatically set limits on how far the Germans could go."[103] This was obvious to observers at the time. Bevin told Marshall that the French would be more likely to stand up to the Soviets and revive Germany if they were offered a "really workable Security System," by which he meant an "Atlantic System."[104] The Americans understood this clearly. Charles Bohlen noted that the "one faint element of confidence which [the French] cling to is the fact that American troops . . . stand between them and the Red Army," and that a weakening of America's commitment to the continent would "have a most unfavorable reaction in France," where there was acute concern about "returning power to [the] Germans at the present juncture."[105]

99. Creswell, *Question*, 11.

100. Caffery to Marshall, June 29, 1948, *FRUS*, 1948, vol. 3, 142.

101. Address by the President to the Congress, Toward Securing the Peace and Preventing War, March 17, 1948, *DOSB*, vol. 18, no. 456, 420; Paper Agreed Upon by the London Conference on Germany, Report of the London Conference on Germany, and Communiqué of the London Conference on Germany, June 7, 1948, *FRUS*, 1948, vol. 2, 291, 312, 316.

102. Marshall to Bidault, March 12, 1948, and Marshall to the Embassy in France, June 23, 1948, *FRUS*, 1948, vol. 3, 50, 139. See also Marshall to Inverchapel, March 12, 1948, ibid., 48.

103. Trachtenberg, *Constructed*, 77.

104. Memorandum of Conversation by Marshall, June 14, 1948, *FRUS*, 1948, vol. 3, 138.

105. Quoted in John Lewis Gaddis, *The Long Peace: Inquiries into the History of the Cold War* (Oxford: Oxford University Press, 1987), 65.

Meanwhile, Acheson informed Senators Tom Connally and Arthur Vandenberg that the alliance "would give France a greater sense of security against Germany as well as the Soviet Union."[106]

The Balancing Imperative and German Rearmament

Events on the Korean Peninsula accentuated French fears of the Soviet Union and led to the view that rebuilding the German economy was insufficient— the Federal Republic had to be rearmed and incorporated into the western defense system. The military leadership had been pleading for some form of cooperation with Germany for some time, arguing that it was "inconceivable that the Germans would not also pay the blood price for their safety." It would be impossible to defend Europe effectively if the West Germans were reduced to the role of "spectators."[107] Following the outbreak of war in Asia, civilian officials endorsed this view as well, arguing that "it would be ridiculous" for France to "make substantial, additional military efforts" in the defense of Europe without the Federal Republic playing its part. What was needed was a "truly common effort." One way to accomplish this would be to make the Germans "soldiers in an Atlantic community army or even a European army."[108]

The view that Europe must defend itself by coming together remained central to French decision making throughout the early 1950s. As Bérard put it in October 1950, there was a "certain parallelism between the position of France and that of West Germany with regard to the defense of the West" in that both were "concerned above all with making sure that they are not invaded and that their territory does not serve as a battleground."[109] In a diary entry three months later, Ambassador Hervé Alphand asserted that the core precept of French strategic planning was that "we are trying to build, as far east as possible, with the help of the Germans, a barrier against eventual aggression."[110] Schuman made broadly the same point when he opened the European army conference in Paris: "In their concern for their common future, nations once deeply divided are meeting round

---

106. Memorandum of Conversation by Acheson, February 14, 1949, *FRUS*, 1949, vol. 4, 109.

107. Quoted in Pierre Guillen, "Les chefs militaires français, le réarmement de l'Allemagne et la CED (1950–1954)," *Revue d'histoire de la deuxième guerre mondiale* no. 129 (1983): 4. See also Georges-Henri Soutou, "France and the German Rearmament Problem, 1945–1955," in *The Quest for Stability: Problems of West European Security, 1918–1957*, ed. R. Ahmann, Adolf M. Birke, and Michael E. Howard (Oxford: Oxford University Press, 1993), 497.

108. Bruce to Acheson, July 28, 1950, *FRUS*, 1950, vol. 3, 157.

109. Quoted in Trachtenberg and Gehrz, "America," 4.

110. Hervé Alphand, *L'étonnement d'être* (Paris: Fayard, 1977), 224.

the same table [to establish] . . . a common army that will be able to act only in defense of their common civilization."[111]

This was a decision imposed on the French by the European power architecture. Although not a single French policymaker wanted to rearm Germany for its own sake, almost all of them understood that rearmament was essential if they were to balance against the Soviet Union. As the Radical politician Yvon Delbos pointed out, it was "hard, after the Hitlerian horrors, to accept the rearmament of Germany," but it was an absolute necessity if they were to confront the "Soviet peril."[112] Similarly, Pierre Mendès France, in one of his first speeches after becoming prime minister, noted that although German rearmament and "participation in a common defense organization" was a "sore trial for the French people," it was nonetheless "required by the international situation."[113] Looking back on events, François Seydoux said much the same thing. The French understood in the fall of 1950 that "nothing was going to stand in the way" of German rearmament. The "cold war" had pushed the Federal Republic into the western camp, and the West "needed Germany's military collaboration." French negotiators might debate the details with their allies, but they had "already conceded the principle." The issue now was not whether Germany would participate in the common defense, "but how it would participate in it."[114]

Given this mindset, there was no fundamental opposition to Acheson's call for West German rearmament in September 1950.[115] "Regarding the participation of Germany in the defense effort," argued Schuman in a statement that echoed those of top military officials, "it would seem illogical for us to defend Western Europe, including Germany, without contributions from Germany."[116] Bérard concurred, arguing that it was "both normal and necessary that Germany contribute to her own defense."[117] As Michael Creswell observes, the French "did not reject the German rearmament proposal in principle" at the tripartite foreign ministers conference.[118]

Key decision makers continued to hold this view after the New York meeting. As a Quai memorandum put it in November, France and the United States agreed that Germany should provide "her own contribution" to the defense of western Europe. There was *"agreement on the principle of*

111. Quoted in Willis, *France*, 134.

112. Quoted in ibid., 165.

113. Quoted in Jacques Fauvet, "Birth and Death of a Treaty," in *France Defeats EDC*, ed. Daniel Lerner and Raymond Aron (New York: Frederick A. Praeger, 1957), 157.

114. François de Clausonne Seydoux, *Mémoires d'outre-Rhin* (Paris: B. Grasset, 1975), 157.

115. For the basic argument, see Creswell, *Question*, 26–35.

116. United States Minutes, Private Meeting of the Foreign Ministers, New York, September 12, 1950, *FRUS*, 1950, vol. 3, 1200.

117. Quoted in Sheetz, "Continental," 141.

118. Creswell, *Question*, 29.

'German rearmament'."[119] Bevin interpreted matters the same way: "The French have agreed to the principle of a German contribution . . . and that this being so, it is unnecessary to press them . . . to commit themselves to it more openly."[120] Confirmation came in December, when Schuman informed him that France "did not object to the principle of German participation." Indeed, France "could not conceive of defending Germany on the Elbe without sacrifice and effort from the Germans." There was no question that the western powers "must advance quickly" on the rearmament issue; the only matter for discussion was how they could "do so most surely."[121]

What the French did object to was Acheson's demand that they commit to West German rearmament immediately and publicly. For both domestic and international reasons, top decision makers wanted to delay rearmament and keep their assent to it secret. Schuman was deeply concerned that precipitate rearmament would give the "Russians a chance to interpret such a move as aggravating an international situation," and might even provide a "reason for starting a war." Thus, he wanted to delay discussion of a German contribution until western "strength was such that we could stop any moves which the Russians might take."[122] A public declaration would also have domestic repercussions: "No French Government could face the French Assembly or French public opinion with the proposition of reestablishing at this time German units." Simply put, a rearmament announcement would pose a "serious psychological problem in France." Therefore, the French wanted to keep the decision to rearm the Federal Republic confidential, and in order to calm public opinion, they thought it best to build up the other members of the western alliance system before rearming Germany.[123]

This desire to delay German rearmament led directly to the Pleven announcement. The prime minister's eponymous plan was not intended to lay the foundation for an integrated European military force, although it was presented as such. During his speech, Pleven said he wanted a "united European army, made up of forces from the various European nations" that would "pool all of its human and material components under a single

119. Quoted in Michael Creswell and Marc Trachtenberg, "France and the German Question, 1945–1955," *Journal of Cold War Studies* 5, no. 3 (2003): 17. Emphasis in original.

120. Bevin to Franks, October 28, 1950, *DBPO*, ser. 2, vol. 3, 232.

121. Attlee-Bevin-Pleven-Schuman Meeting, December 2, 1950, ibid., 312–13.

122. Minutes of a Private Conference of the French, British, and United States Foreign Ministers and Their High Commissioners for Germany, September 14, 1950, *FRUS*, 1950, vol. 3, 296–97.

123. Acheson to Truman, September 14, 1950, and United States Minutes, Private Meeting of the Foreign Ministers, New York, September 12, 1950, ibid., 301, 1200. See also Jebb to Younger, September 13, 1950, *DBPO*, ser. 2, vol. 3, 36.

political and military European authority."[124] But a close reading of the proposal revealed that the plan was militarily inefficient. Eisenhower dismissed it as being as "cockeyed an idea as a dope fiend would have figured out." It seemed to him "almost inherently, to include every kind of obstacle, difficulty, and fantastic notion that misguided humans could put together in one package."[125] Moreover, rather than being based on the principle of equality, it clearly discriminated against Germany.[126] This was certainly Adenauer's view, as we have seen, and others saw things the same way. Acheson was convinced that the plan was designed to give Germany "permanently second class status." The Germans were being "openly, in fact blatantly, labeled as inferiors."[127]

The plan was unacceptable by design: the French hoped it would lead to long negotiations and delay German rearmament even though they did not want to prevent it. This is, in fact, how French officials described the plan to their counterparts in London. One French diplomat described it as "a '*canard*' to deflect [the] Americans from [the] immediate rearmament of Germany." He hoped that the British would not "insist too much on the obvious inherent difficulties" in it, but rather "regard it as [a] long term plan which might ultimately have useful features." The French ambassador to London, René Massigli, also implied that the plan was "devised as [a] delaying tactic."[128] The British understood what they were being told. Bevin, for example, concluded that the plan had probably "been devised largely for electoral and tactical reasons."[129] Similarly, Minister of Defence Emanuel Shinwell observed that the French accepted "the principle of German rearmament," and had come up with the Pleven proposal as " 'a way out' of their difficulties."[130] This was the American view as well: Ambassador Bruce believed the plan was "mainly the concoction of politicians designed to meet political difficulties."[131] Acheson, meanwhile, was convinced that the proposal was intended to postpone the German "participation problem for many months."[132]

124. Pleven Declaration, October 24, 1950, *BDF*, vol. 1, 381. For a summary of the plan, see Acheson to Bruce, October 27, 1950, *FRUS*, 1950, vol. 3, 410–12.

125. Quoted in Thomas A. Schwartz, "The 'Skeleton Key'—American Foreign Policy, European Unity, and German Rearmament, 1949–1954," *Central European History* 19, no. 4 (1986): 380; and Pascaline Winand, *Eisenhower, Kennedy, and the United States of Europe* (New York: St. Martin's, 1993), 27.

126. See Creswell, "Bear," 102; and McAllister, *Exit*, 195.

127. Acheson to the Embassy in France, October 27, 1950, *FRUS*, 1950, vol. 3, 412.

128. Interpretation of Pleven Plan by French Embassy, October 25–31, 1950, *DBPO*, ser. 2, vol. 3, 220.

129. Bevin to Franks, October 28, 1950, ibid., 231.

130. British Joint Services Mission in Washington to Ministry of Defence, October 28, 1950, ibid., 227.

131. Harvey to Dixon, October 31, 1950, ibid., 240.

132. Acheson to the Embassy in France, October 17, 1950, *FRUS*, 1950, vol. 3, 385.

In short, France remained committed to rebuilding Germany and incorporating it into a European coalition directed against the Soviet Union. French decision makers differed from their allies on matters of timing and preferred to keep their plans secret but agreed on the essentials. German rearmament, however distasteful, was crucial if western Europe was to hold its own against Moscow.

Centralization, Integration, and the EDC Treaty

The French negotiated and signed the EDC treaty, which envisaged the creation of an integrated European military force, based on balance of power thinking. Among other things, the Spofford compromise provided for negotiations aimed at the creation of a European army.[133] As we shall see, this was not France's optimal outcome. Nevertheless, during the Paris negotiations, which ran from February 1951 to May 1952, the French reasoned that if such a force were to come into being, it must be centralized and subject to joint Franco-German control. Only a centralized unit of power would be able to hold its own against the Soviet Union. Moreover, to maintain a roughly even distribution of military power within western Europe, they would have to share control of the European army with the Germans. On the basis of these calculations, French negotiators opted for an integrated European military.

French policymakers believed that if it came down to it only a centralized European coalition could compete effectively with the Soviet Union. Even before the Pleven announcement, Socialist deputy André Philip, who had been an ardent proponent of heavy-industry integration, argued that the west European powers could not deal with the "danger of totalitarianism" by simply "juxtaposing small national armies which, as at present constituted, are no more than children's toys." A traditional alliance system would not suffice. What was required instead was "a European army financed by a European fund fed by European taxes." This army "would be an army responsible for defending the whole territory of Europe, with all the citizens of Europe." Failing the construction of such a force, he warned, a "divided Europe, a barren Europe, will inevitably attract the conqueror."[134] Pierre-Henri Teitgen, who would soon become president of the MRP, agreed, calling for the construction of a "European Army of United Europe."[135]

Jean Monnet expressed similar reasoning as he considered a European army in the fall. History, he observed, was full of examples of the dangers

133. For the claim that the French were forced into the negotiations by the United States, see Large, *Germans*, 97.

134. André Philip, For a Political Authority, August 8, 1950, *Documents on the History of European Integration* (hereafter *DHEI*), vol. 3 (New York: W. de Gruyter, 1988), 120–21, 123.

135. Quoted in Willis, *France*, 132.

inherent in alliances, of "juxtaposed national armies." The problem was that "at critical moments national concerns sweep them up and the solidarity that one had hoped for falls apart." The British had rushed to defend the Channel ports in World War I, thereby allowing Germany to pierce the Allied front in 1918. The lesson was clear: the Europeans must guard against these problems by abandoning national armies and establishing a centralized military force.[136]

France's top military officers shared this understanding of centralization. Just before the Paris conference opened, the Chiefs of the General Staff Committee asserted that any future European military force must be an "instrument" of a "unified" Europe. "Placed at the disposition of a European federal government," they continued, "this army would find its moral force and its cohesion in an enlarged patriotism and in the conviction that the interests of each state are better guaranteed by a complete association."[137] In other words, they believed that military effectiveness required a centralized political structure.

French officials also stressed the importance of centralization in conversations with their partners. In the Pleven Plan speech, which was directed as much to France's allies as to his domestic audience, the prime minister argued that a European military force could not be "created simply by placing national military units side by side, since, in practice, this would merely mask a coalition of the old sort." After all, "tasks that can be tackled only in common must be matched by common institutions." Therefore France proposed a "united European army, made up of forces from the various European nations," that would "pool all of its human and material components under a single political and military European authority."[138] Schuman took essentially the same line in opening the Paris negotiations. The French, he declared, wanted to "construct a military tool of sure efficiency." What was required was a centralized military force, an army "with cohesion and vigor at least as great as in [the] case of national armies."[139]

French decision makers quickly decided that integration was the best form of centralized cooperation. Monnet took the lead, telling Pleven that France must apply the principles of the Schuman Plan to the military realm. What the government must strive for, he wrote in October 1950, was a "Western Europe, federated around an enlarged Schuman Plan." Less than two weeks later, he clarified his views and suggested that the French government propose a military arrangement in the "same spirit" as the coal and steel pool, by which he meant "the establishment of a European Army

---

136. Quoted in Philippe Vial, "Jean Monnet, un père pour la CED?" in *Europe brisée, Europe retrouvée: Nouvelles réflexions sur l'unité européenne au XXe siècle,* ed. René Girault and Gérard Bossuat (Paris: Publications de la Sorbonne, 1994), 213.

137. Quoted in Guillen, "Chefs," 10.

138. Pleven Declaration, October 24, 1950, *BDF,* vol. 1, 381.

139. Bruce to Acheson, February 15, 1951, *FRUS,* 1951, vol. 3, 768.

with a single High Command, a single organization, unified equipment and financing, and under the control of a single supranational authority."[140] He made essentially the same argument in a series of letters to Schuman at around the same time. German rearmament must be achieved, he wrote in September, "within the general European context of the Schuman Plan."[141] As he noted in his memoirs, he had hoped to delay the process of military integration, but "now, the federation of Europe would have to become an immediate objective." Western Europe's military assets would "have to be placed simultaneously under joint sovereignty."[142]

There was considerable support among top policymakers for Monnet's conclusion that France and Germany must integrate and share control of an eventual European army. Claiming to speak for Pleven, Schuman, and Minister of Justice René Mayer, Quai officials Bernard Clappier, Roland de Margerie, and Jacques Bourbon-Busset informed the Americans that France was considering a military "initiative comparable in every respect to the Schuman plan." Crucially, it would embody the principle of joint control: "Germany would enjoy a status of equality."[143] The integration option had found its way into the military realm.

The French endorsed integration because it would enable them to establish and maintain an even balance of military power within the west European coalition. The reasoning behind this belief was straightforward: because each state would contribute to a European force in proportion to its share of total group resources, German forces would not outnumber those of France at the outset, and because all relevant decisions would be taken jointly, the Federal Republic would not be able to adopt policies that enabled it to dominate the coalition over the long haul. In short, integration offered to maintain a fairly even within-coalition distribution of power.

One of the chief attractions of an integrated military force was that the West Germans would be a minority within it and would therefore be less likely to overturn the balance of power in western Europe. The fear that Germany would become the dominant power in the region if it was fully autonomous was common in French decision-making circles. An unfettered Germany would inevitably be more militarily powerful than France owing to its "demographic superiority . . . the rapid recovery of the Ruhr industries and of the . . . economy as a whole," factors that Schuman described as "elements of unbalance."[144] As Acheson reminded Truman just before the signature of the EDC treaty, the French had a basic "fear of being quickly outdistanced by their German neighbors" and had "an inferiority

140. Jean Monnet, *Memoirs* (Garden City, N.Y.: Doubleday, 1978), 346.

141. Monnet to Schuman, September 14, 1950, *Jean Monnet–Robert Schuman correspondance, 1947–1953* (hereafter *Monnet-Schuman*) (Lausanne: Fondation Jean Monnet pour l'Europe, 1986), 56.

142. Monnet, *Memoirs*, 343.

143. Bohlen to Acheson, October 15, 1950, *FRUS*, 1950, vol. 3, 378–79.

144. Schuman to Acheson, January 29, 1952, *FRUS*, 1952–1954, vol. 5, 9.

complex relative to the German birth rate and industriousness."[145] If a European military force was established, on the other hand, then the coalition members, including Germany, would contribute to it according to some equitable formula, and regardless of the formula employed, West Germany would raise only a fraction of the total force because it constituted only a fraction of western Europe as a whole.

This logic clearly appealed to the French ambassador to the United States, Henri Bonnet, who noted that the attraction of an integrated military was that it would contain "substantial numbers of Belgian, French and Dutch divisions," in addition to West German units. Similarly, officials at the Quai were reassured that "the members of the Brussels Treaty have a population of more than 100 million people and there is thus no fear that German troops will outnumber the troops of these countries."[146] As it happened, the Europeans settled on national income as an appropriate metric. According to the July 1951 interim report on the European army, each participant's troop contribution would be related to its "expenditures on the European Army," which would in turn be "shared according to . . . the economic capabilities of each state."[147] At the time, the Federal Republic accounted for 30 percent of the gross national product of the Six, a figure reflected in the EDC negotiations: West Germany would contribute twelve out of forty-three land divisions in the proposed European army.[148] Thus, the French used the principle of equality as a means to limit German rearmament at the outset and prevent the Germans from overturning the balance of power within western Europe.

In addition to establishing an equal balance of power within the coalition, integration would perpetuate that balance by denying the Germans decision-making autonomy in military matters. France's fear was not of a rearmed Germany per se, but of an autonomous Federal Republic. The reason autonomy was so frightening was that West Germany would be free to make its own military decisions and perhaps overturn the balance of power in western Europe. Pleven was clear about this: "The formation of . . . a German Ministry of Defense, would sooner or later be bound to lead to the rebuilding of a national army and, by that token, to the revival of German

---

145. Acheson to Truman, May 26, 1952, ibid., 682.

146. Quoted in Sheetz, "Continental," 149–50.

147. Quoted in Creswell, *Question*, 66. For the report itself, see Interim Report of the Delegations to the Conference for the Organization of a European Defense Community to the Participating Governments, July 24, 1951, *FRUS*, 1951, vol. 3, 843–46.

148. The gross national product calculation is based on Susan B. Carter et al., *Historical Statistics of the United States: Earliest Times to the Present*, vol. 5, *Governance and International Relations* (Cambridge: Cambridge University Press, 2006), 567–72; and Brian R. Mitchell, *International Historical Statistics: Europe, 1750–1993*, 4th ed. (London: Macmillan, 1998), 905–28. For the division figures, which were agreed at the Paris conference in November 1951, see Report by Schuman to the North Atlantic Council, November 27, 1951, *FRUS*, 1951, vol. 3, 938.

militarism."[149] This fear remained four years later, when Mendès France worried that were France to approve a sovereign Federal Republic, it would be exposing itself to "unlimited, unilateral, and uncontrolled" German rearmament.[150]

Military integration would go some way to solving this problem. According to Seydoux, one of the key features of the planned European army was that it would establish "an international régime limiting the sovereignty of all the states of western Europe." As a member of that organization, the Federal Republic would have no purely national military institutions and would therefore be unable to adopt policies that worked to its advantage.[151] The belief that the creation of a European force would allow for greater control over German military policy was widespread. France should not challenge American attempts to rearm Germany, argued the Foreign Ministry in September 1950, but rather prepare "modalities permitting the retention of sufficient control on the part of the French government over German rearmament." The ECSC provided a good model for this.[152] Similarly, Schuman endorsed the Pleven Plan in November 1950 on the grounds that it would prevent the Germans from having "national" armed forces "freely available" to them. At no time would "German units" ever be "at the disposition of a German government."[153] Although he focused on the consequences of not establishing a European army, Edouard Bonnefous made basically the same point in his capacity as chairman of the foreign affairs committee. If Germany were to "return to strength . . . in an unorganised Europe," it might become "the dominant element of the present day mosaic of European powers."[154] Meanwhile, SFIO leader Guy Mollet left no doubt that when it came to the "human participation of Germany . . . in giving Europe a defensive capacity," he preferred the "participation by Germans in a European army" to the "rebirth of a German army."[155]

Monnet laid out the logic most clearly in a memorandum to Schuman in September 1950. German rearmament was "indispensable to the defense of the West" and therefore inevitable. The key issue was whether German forces would have "all the attributes of sovereignty," or be "incorporated into continental Western Europe in the same fashion as the Schuman Plan." The dangers associated with a "national" solution were manifest: a rearmed

149. Pleven Declaration, October 24, 1950, *BDF*, vol. 1, 380.

150. Quoted in Pierre Guillen, "La France et l'integration de la RFA dans l'OTAN," *Guerres mondiales et conflits contemporaines* no. 159 (1990): 83.

151. Quoted in Hitchcock, *France*, 144.

152. Quoted in Wall, *United States*, 199.

153. Quoted in McGeehan, *German*, 65, 85.

154. Quoted in Fursdon, *European*, 71.

155. Quoted in Denis Lefebvre, "The French Socialist Party, 1954–1957," in *Socialist Parties and the Question of Europe in the 1950s*, ed. Richard T. Griffiths (New York: E. J. Brill, 1993), 43, n. 2.

West Germany "fortified by its industrial and demographic potential" would be free to pursue "national goals thanks to its recovered sovereignty." In other words, an autonomous Germany would have both the "freedom of action" and the material assets to build up its military strength at will and upset the balance of power on the continent. But if West Germany's participation was "organized within the framework of a supranational Europe" in a sort of "enlarged Schuman Plan," the French might be able to control its rearmament and secure a roughly even balance of power within western Europe.[156] After all, the virtue of the Schuman proposal was that it "makes possible a positive solution of the German problem which substitutes the integration of West Germany . . . for existing controls and restrictions."[157]

The view that integrating West Germany into a European force was preferable to establishing an autonomous German military continued to resonate even after most French decision makers turned against the EDC. In April 1952, the director for political affairs at the French High Commission, Louis de Guiringaud, argued that military integration was the only way that the French could hope to "control . . . the rebirth of German military power." In the absence of the EDC or something like it, West Germany would be free to "reconstitute the Wehrmacht and set up whatever armament industry it wishes."[158] This was also the view at the Quai d'Orsay, where officials prepared a memorandum arguing that only a supranational defense community could serve as a "control mechanism over Germany."[159] Similarly, Jean Chauvel, the French ambassador to Switzerland, argued that, together with the coal and steel pool, Germany's membership in the emerging defense community was one of France's few "guarantees against the rebirth of the German peril."[160] Parliamentary deputy Alfred Coste-Fleuret made broadly the same point in a last-ditch attempt to save the EDC treaty: "The two sources of power of modern Germany in recent times, are the Ruhr arsenal (to neutralize it we have constructed the C.E.C.A. [ECSC]) and the national German army, which we also want to neutralize by integrating German soldiers into the discipline of a supranational army. German growth is a fact, but the question is to control its direction."[161]

In sum, the French signed the EDC treaty because, from a power perspective, they preferred integrating Germany into a European coalition to establishing an autonomous German military force. Military integration

156. Monnet to Schuman, September 16, 1950, *Monnet-Schuman*, 58–59.
157. Monnet to Schuman, September 9, 1950, ibid., 53.
158. De Guiringaud Note, March 4, 1952, *BDF*, vol. 1, 126.
159. Hitchcock, *France*, 175.
160. Chauvel Memorandum, May 7, 1953, *BDF*, vol. 1, 150.
161. Quoted in Alfred Grosser, "Germany and France: A Confrontation," in *France Defeats EDC*, ed. Daniel Lerner and Raymond Aron (New York: Frederick A. Praeger, 1957), 66.

offered to establish and maintain an equal balance of power within the west European combination, whereas building a sovereign German army did not. The key, as Acheson observed, was that the EDC brought the West Germans "into the common defense under the control of common institutions."[162] Because France and Germany would have equal rights and operate under the same rules, the treaty promised to create and perpetuate a roughly even balance of power between them.

Integration's Discontents

Although integration was more attractive than establishing an independent German military force, the French signed the Paris Treaty with grave reservations. President Vincent Auriol made this abundantly clear at the time, reminding his interlocutors that "signing is not ratifying."[163] France's first concern was that the Germans might break out of the community at a later date. Because the EDC was an institution, there was nothing to stop the Federal Republic seceding from it and asserting national control over its military units and policy at a later date. In other words, the EDC was a fragile instrument for maintaining a favorable balance of power. The second problem was that joining the community would require the French to surrender their military autonomy. France would effectively cease to be a sovereign state. Try as they might, successive administrations were unable to resolve either the secession or the sovereignty issue, and the National Assembly failed to ratify the EDC treaty.

The French were painfully aware that West German membership in the EDC rested on a promise that, like all promises, could be broken. If the Federal Republic reneged on its commitments and broke the EDC rules, France would be confronted quite suddenly with a dangerous scenario: a powerful West German military.

Of course, no institution, not even the recently ratified ECSC, could prevent a state from breaking its promises, but the situation was more dangerous in the military realm. The French would be able to spot German defection from the coal and steel agreement, and it would take time for the Germans to ramp up industrial production and translate it into military might. As Schuman explained to Adenauer in May 1950, if the West Germans broke out of the heavy-industry agreement, the French would quickly become aware of their intentions and would have ample time to respond. "Rearmament," he wrote, "always showed first in an increased production of coal, iron, and steel." The ECSC would allow the French "to detect the first signs of rearmament," and afford them the time to organize their

---

162. Acheson to Truman, May 26, 1952, *FRUS*, 1952–1954, vol. 5, 681.
163. Quoted in Creswell, *Question*, 93.

response. As a result, the coal and steel pool had "an extraordinarily calming effect in France."[164]

The situation was quite different in the military realm: a decision to defect from the EDC would almost immediately establish a German army and might place France in great peril. To be sure, the defense community agreement ensured there was no German general staff, thereby providing some reassurance. But the treaty also envisaged the creation of West German divisions, or "groupements," which could be reorganized to form an independent German army.[165] Moreover, by the terms of the treaty, Germany and France would contribute roughly the same number of troops to the European army. This even balance of power was important to France, as we have seen, but it also meant that the French would not possess the overwhelming military advantage required to control or coerce the Germans if they withdrew from the community. In other words, if the Federal Republic were to defect, France could suddenly be confronted by an autonomous military equal. These fears took on an added urgency in the light of historical experience: although prohibited from doing so and under close scrutiny by the other European powers, the Germans had carried out a substantial rearmament campaign in the interwar period.[166]

French officials tried to overcome the defection problem in two ways. First, they sought to limit the size of German contingents in the EDC. When negotiations began, they wanted to restrict the size of German units to between five thousand and six thousand men.[167] Their logic was simple: if the Germans were organized in small units, then their eventual defection from the EDC would result in a military force comprised of small, inefficient fighting contingents rather than a full-fledged German army. France favored German rearmament, argued Defense Minister Jules Moch, but "under the condition that . . . these units be not large units."[168] If the Germans were allowed to contribute divisions to the EDC, however, their eventual defection could prove devastating. The creation of large West German units, explained Alphand, would be the same as establishing a latent German army which might be used "to unleash war" with little warning.[169]

Second, Paris worked hard to persuade the British to join the EDC, believing that this would provide a counterweight to German power and discourage defection. De Gaulle laid out the basic argument in a speech in November 1953. Were Britain to be part of the equation, he argued, then the

164. Adenauer, *Memoirs*, 257.

165. Report by Schuman to the North Atlantic Council, November 27, 1951, *FRUS*, 1951, vol. 3, 937–38.

166. See Gordon A. Craig, *The Politics of the Prussian Army, 1640–1945* (Oxford: Oxford University Press, 1956), 382–467; and Wilhelm Deist, *The Wehrmacht and German Rearmament* (Toronto: University of Toronto Press, 1981).

167. Creswell, *Question*, 54–55.

168. Quoted in ibid., 31.

169. Quoted in Sheetz, "Continental," 156.

EDC members could "influence, shape, and if necessary resist" West Germany's "impulses."[170] The French government shared this view. President Auriol, for example, told Anthony Eden, the British foreign secretary, that the French would likely support the EDC if the British elected to participate. Without them, however, Europe would be "a sort of Holy Alliance where Germany will dominate."[171] As Bidault told the Americans, the absence of a "British counter-weight" in the EDC was a "real problem psychologically."[172]

Unable to limit the size of West German units or convince the British to join, the French concluded that the defense community offered little more than a paper guarantee against swift and potentially devastating defection. "It would be very difficult," Schuman informed Acheson even before the EDC treaty was signed, "to get the French Parliament to accept a community treaty from the obligations of which Germany could any day withdraw with the help of the supremacy which she would have been permitted to reestablish at our expense."[173] He was quick to confirm Eden's hunch "that one of the fundamental French concerns was over the possibility that Germany might, after beginning re-armament, secede from [the] EDC."[174] Other members of the French elite were even more forceful. The president of the National Assembly, Edouard Herriot, put little stock in the EDC because "obligations agreed on paper are insufficient," while de Gaulle asserted that "limitations written on paper count for nothing."[175] The Americans, for their part, understood the French position. As Ambassador Bruce noted early in 1952, France's great fear was that "German irredentism may, when it suits national designs, cause secession from EDC."[176]

In addition to doing comparatively little for French security, the proposed defense community entailed a surrender of sovereignty in the most sensitive realm of all, defense. There had been opposition to military integration because of the associated autonomy cost from the beginning. In November 1950, Schuman asserted that the Pleven Plan was not a call for a "European 'super-state' vested with the power to make war, but simply for the establishment of European administrations to recruit, train, and arm the European force."[177] A few months later, Gaullist deputy Jacques Soustelle noted regretfully, "Only France among the great powers is expected to sacrifice its national army on the altar of the European army."[178]

170. Charles de Gaulle, *Discours et messages: Dans l'attente, février 1946–avril 1958* (Paris: Plon, 1970), 590.

171. Quoted in Sheetz, "Continental," 180.

172. Dunn to State Department, February 3, 1953, *FRUS*, 1952–1954, vol. 5, 1558.

173. Schuman to Acheson, January 29, 1952, ibid., 8.

174. Memorandum by Acheson, February 15, 1952, ibid., 41.

175. Adenauer, *Memoirs*, 413 (for the Herriot quotation); and de Gaulle, *Discours*, 571.

176. Bruce to State Department, February 1, 1952, *FRUS*, 1952–1954, vol. 5, 12.

177. Trachtenberg, *Constructed*, 120.

178. Quoted in Large, *Germans*, 141.

The view that military integration involved an unacceptable surrender of sovereignty really gathered momentum after the signing of the Paris Treaty. In June 1952, de Gaulle condemned the defense community on the grounds that France was being asked to "give man-power, arms and money to a stateless melting pot." Worse still, France was alone in suffering this indignity: "France is, of all the great nations which have their own army today, the only nation which is to lose hers."[179] Herriot made broadly the same argument in October, condemning the treaty on the grounds that it involved "an abandonment of national sovereignty without reciprocity. Certain advantages accrue to Germany but none to France."[180] It was time, declared French Senate member Michel Debré, "to tell all the theologians of little Europe point-blank: Europe is not a nation; it is an aggregate of nations. Europe is not a state; it is a grouping of states."[181]

Government officials shared this aversion to surrendering French autonomy. In a January 1953 memorandum, Guy le Roy de la Tournelle, the director general of the Quai, asserted that the defense community would eliminate France "as an independent world military power." As if this was not bad enough, he explained that this loss of sovereignty would not be compensated by an increase in security because the EDC would not control Germany. "Is it right," he asked rhetorically, "to practice a policy which will not block the restoration of German military power, but which will at the same time be for us a source of weakness and confusion? Is it wise, in the false hope of binding our neighbor in chains, to chain ourselves up as well?"[182] The memorandum was written for Bidault, who shared de la Tournelle's concerns. In a series of meetings with the Americans and the British in Bermuda in December 1953, he was at pains to point out that although France was keen to "build Europe," it had no intention of being "engulfed by it and thereby lose its individual personality so that . . . France would no longer be considered except through the European Community." It would be a tragedy if joining the community meant that "it would be a European who would sit in the place he had the honor to occupy."[183] As Schuman put it looking back on the failure of the EDC, the one issue that bound almost all its opponents together was the fear that "France would be diminished."[184]

These concerns were so great that successive administrations concluded that they would have to eliminate the supranational features of the treaty if they were going to push it through the French National Assembly. In January 1953, the Mayer government forwarded additional protocols to the

179. Quoted in Fauvet, "Birth," 134, n. 2.
180. Quoted in Fursdon, *European*, 201.
181. Quoted in Willis, *France*, 168–69.
182. Quoted in Hitchcock, *France*, 177–78.
183. United States Delegation Minutes, December 6, 1953, *FRUS*, 1952–1954, vol. 5, 1799.
184. Quoted in McGeehan, *German*, 235.

EDC Interim Committee that would "permit the French army to retain as much autonomy as possible."[185] Although Mayer fell from power in May 1953, French concern about the sovereignty implications of military integration remained high, and at the Brussels conference on August 19, 1954, Mendès France presented the other five signatories with a series of proposed amendments designed to eliminate the defense community's supranational features. Had they been implemented, the provisions would have permitted member states unilaterally to reject any decision taken by the EDC Commissariat for the next eight years; provided for national rules to remain in effect regarding recruitment, promotion, training, and discipline until the member states unanimously agreed otherwise; allowed France, and France alone, to retain national military forces; and prevented the creation of a European Political Community (EPC).[186] As Edward Fursdon explains, "The general message of the Protocol was brutally undisguised. Mendès-France was 'asking for a European Army for the Germans and a French Army for the French.' "[187] The other conferees immediately rejected the French demands, noting that they were "seriously damaging [to the] supranational character of [the] EDC."[188]

Mendès France's failure to eliminate its supranational features and to obtain a British guarantee against West German secession meant there was little appetite for the EDC treaty, and he duly put it to the National Assembly knowing it would fail. That defection and sovereignty concerns were the key impediments to the community's acceptance in France is abundantly clear in Seydoux's account of the entire affair. "I refused to admit the necessity of . . . subtracting from our sovereignty," he asserted, before adding that the defense community project would have succeeded had "Britain been the seventh member."[189] Or as Mendès France himself put it in September 1954, the two most important problems with the EDC were its "overly supranational character and the absence of Britain."[190]

Back to the American Commitment . . . and the WEU

The obvious alternative to the EDC was to secure a strong American presence on the continent and rearm Germany within the Atlantic alliance system. From a balance of power perspective, the NATO option was preferable to the EDC. A large American troop presence would protect western

---

185. Willis, *France*, 164.
186. For an explanation of the provisions, see Foreign Ministry Explanatory Note, August 13, 1954, *Documents diplomatiques français* (hereafter *DDF*), 1954 (Paris: Imprimerie Nationale, 1987), 147–50.
187. Fursdon, *European*, 284–85.
188. Conant to State Department, August 16, 1954, *FRUS*, 1952–1954, vol. 5, 1042, n. 4.
189. Seydoux, *Mémoires*, 162.
190. Mendès France to Diplomatic Representatives, September 18, 1954, *DDF*, 1954, 396.

Europe from the Soviet Union and also contain the Germans, who could therefore be rearmed to the benefit of the West without threatening France. This course of action was also clearly superior to the defense community option in terms of sovereignty since France would not have to surrender military autonomy to a supranational institution.

There was considerable support in France for strengthening NATO throughout the EDC affair. While the treaty was being negotiated, officials at the Quai wondered whether they were unnecessarily "complicating and delaying" matters, when it would be "so simple" to accept Germany into the Atlantic alliance without "displeasing the Allies."[191] This was the military view as well. In the fall of 1951, France's highest-ranking military officer, Marshal Alphonse Juin, openly called for a German contribution to an alliance system that included the United States and Britain.[192] Indeed, Georges-Henri Soutou argues that this view was widespread even as France signed the EDC treaty: "One may even wonder if the EDC was really what they wanted, or whether they might not have preferred a simpler system, closer to the American and German concepts."[193]

Support for the NATO option gathered momentum after the Treaty of Paris. During an important debate in the upper house of the French parliament, the Conseil de la République, in October 1953, the Socialists accepted German rearmament as long as the United States reinforced its security guarantee to Europe. Meanwhile, the Gaullists, led by Debré, called openly for the incorporation of West German forces into the Atlantic pact.[194] As they had done during the EDC negotiations, top military officials endorsed this position. In a series of speeches in the spring of 1954, Juin informed listeners that the military wanted Germany rearmed and controlled within the Atlantic alliance: NATO was to be the "sole master of the use of re-armed German forces."[195]

Crucially, this was also the position of the key decision makers. According to one historian, Bidault believed that Germany's incorporation into NATO "counted far more than the EDC. . . . He felt that a close understanding with the United States was far more important than the building of an integrated Europe."[196] This remained the basic view under Mendès France. Like his predecessors, the prime minister understood the need to rearm West Germany in order to enhance the security of western Europe. As he told Bonnet, "It has always seemed to me that it was indispensable to keep Germany in the bonds of a western alliance."[197] But his administration

191. Guillen, "France," 76. See also Seydoux, *Mémoires,* 163.

192. Guillen, "France," 76.

193. Soutou, "France," 502.

194. René Massigli, *Une comédie des erreurs, 1943–1956: Souvenirs et réflexions sur une étape de la construction européenne* (Paris: Plon, 1978), 396–97.

195. Quoted in Guillen, "Chefs," 32.

196. Soutou, "France," 507–8.

197. Mendès France to Bonnet, August 13, 1954, *DDF,* 1954, 142.

was not wedded to the EDC. Philippe Baudet, Mendès France's principal private secretary, explained that the defense community was an element of the kind of defense system France desired, but it was not an "irreplaceable" element.[198] The other option, with which France was increasingly comfortable, was a rearmed Germany as a member of the Atlantic pact. Indeed, Mendès France told the Americans that he expected the National Assembly to "vote against EDC," at which point the western powers "must move very promptly" to bring about "German entry into NATO."[199]

French support for the NATO alternative was based on straightforward balance of power reasoning. Pleven laid out the argument for Bruce in August 1950. The key to the entire enterprise was an American commitment to the continent: the United States must "exercise [a] preponderant role . . . in the Atlantic defense effort." If it did so, then the western powers would be able to "withstand [Soviet] aggression." Moreover, if the United States committed forces to the continent, this would reduce French fears of being overwhelmed by Germany and persuade them to proceed with German rearmament. An American presence would reduce the inevitable "alarm" associated with the "recreation of the German military establishment," and lead the French "to accept [the] participation of Western Germany in [the] NAT [North Atlantic Treaty] defense effort." And German rearmament would, in turn, make Europe more powerful and more secure.[200] In short, an American military presence would resolve the twin problems of Soviet and German power in Europe.

French opinion continued to run along these lines even after the Paris Treaty. Bidault made the case when the French met with the Americans and British in Bermuda in December 1953. The presence of "unintegrated Atlantic forces"—by which he meant American and British troops—on the continent was essential. For one thing, they would deter the Soviet Union: they would "guarantee the security of the Continent and the security of the world." Moreover, they would serve as a "counterweight" to German forces in the region. This is not to say that the French wanted to prevent Germany from rearming. In fact, they believed German rearmament was "indispensable . . . for the defense of the Continent." But they wanted to ensure that the Germans could not dominate western Europe. Therefore "the strength of U.S. and U.K. forces stationed in Europe should . . . have a definite proportion relationship to the German forces." In this way, the Germans would add "new divisions" to the common defense rather than "replace the troops of old allies." The French, then, saw a strong Anglo-American commitment as a solution to France's twofold balancing problem. As Bidault put it: "There was an overriding problem which contained the key of all solutions

198. Baudet Note, July 21, 1954, ibid., 5.
199. Dillon to Department of State, August 24, 1954, *FRUS*, 1952–1954, vol. 5, 1074.
200. Bruce to Acheson, August 1, 1950, *FRUS*, 1950, vol. 3, 171–72.

and that was the problem of the U.S. and U.K. forces stationed on the European continent."[201]

Mendès France also wanted a strengthened NATO for balance of power reasons. As Churchill noted less than a week before the National Assembly vote, the French prime minister seemed to be "much keener about N.A.T.O." than the defense community. And he suspected that the reasoning behind his support was based on power considerations. There was a "deep feeling in France that in [the] E.D.C. they will be bound up in civil and military affairs with the much more active and powerful Western Germany, whereas in the N.A.T.O. system the United Kingdom and the United States of America counter-balance Germany to her proper proportions."[202] Creswell and Trachtenberg concur in this assessment, arguing that Mendès France believed that if West Germany were to join NATO it "would pose no threat but could still contribute to the defense of the West as a whole."[203]

German rearmament within NATO was also infinitely more attractive than the defense community on sovereignty grounds. The French military supported the NATO approach because, unlike the EDC, it would allow the French army to "remain intact."[204] Bidault made essentially the same point at Bermuda. As a member of NATO's Standing Group, France would be sovereign, but as a member of the EDC she would lose her sovereignty. The great French fear was that the creation of the defense community would "separate France . . . from the association of the Big Three."[205]

Despite these attractions, the French had two concerns about the NATO option. The first was that if the Federal Republic was simply admitted directly to the Atlantic pact, as the British suggested, France would not be able to control German rearmament.[206] NATO, observed Mendès France, was an organization composed of "fully sovereign states" dedicated to maximizing western military might. It would therefore be difficult to "count on NATO effectively to exercise the controls and limitations that we want to impose on Germany." It would not be long before the Germans demanded that all restrictions on them be removed, and their allies would likely acquiesce.[207] Bonnet put the problem well: "In principle NATO members could raise and equip troops without limitations. How could one refuse

201. United States Delegation Minutes, December 6, 1953, *FRUS*, 1952–1954, vol. 5, 1799–1800.

202. Churchill to Dulles, August 24, 1954, ibid., 1077.

203. Creswell and Trachtenberg, "France," 24.

204. Soutou, "France," 503.

205. United States Delegation Minutes, December 6, 1953, *FRUS*, 1952–1954, vol. 5, 1799.

206. For the British view, see De Crouy-Chanel to Margerie, August 24, 1954, and Massigli to Mendès France, August 25, 1954, *DDF*, 1954, 206–7, 209–10.

207. Mendès France to Diplomatic Representatives, September 18, 1954, ibid., 395–98. Bidault had expressed the same fear in December 1953 (Second Plenary Tripartite Meeting of the Heads of Government, December 5, 1953, *FRUS*, 1952–1954, vol. 5, 1785).

this privilege to Germany without imposing a discrimination on her that she would reject?"[208] France would be exposed to "unlimited, unilateral, uncontrolled" German rearmament.[209] Top military officials saw things much the same way. Although they were keen to rearm Germany as part of the Atlantic alliance, they worried that once the Germans had raised the requisite number of forces, they would offer to raise even more, and the Americans might not "resist this offer."[210]

The second fear had plagued the French since 1949—NATO could not prevent an American withdrawal from the continent. To be sure, the United States appeared to be committed to Europe for the time being, but the French did not believe they could depend on this over the long haul. Indeed, the EDC affair had heightened their fears about the durability of the American security guarantee. In December 1953, Dulles told the NAC that if the EDC "should not become effective . . . that would compel an agonising reappraisal of basic United States policy," by which he meant the withdrawal of American forces from West Germany to bases on the periphery of Europe.[211] He repeated the same threat to Mendès France in person the following July. Nonratification of the Paris Treaty, he warned, would prompt the United States to write off Europe as a "noble but unproductive experiment," and "engage in a peripheral form of defense."[212] Even without such statements, American behavior gave the French good reason to worry about the permanence of the commitment. The Americans were going to extraordinary lengths to get the EDC treaty ratified, alternately promising to stay if the Europeans established a defense community and threatening to leave if they did not. Why was this the case? The obvious conclusion was that they hoped a fully functioning defense community would balance the Soviet Union on its own, thereby allowing them to depart the European scene. Withdrawal, the French had to suspect, was the ultimate objective.

To address these concerns, the French advocated the establishment of a purely European organization including the Six plus Britain, subordinate to NATO and endowed with the authority to control West German rearmament. Such an arrangement promised to address all of France's fears simultaneously: the continuation of NATO would ensure a favorable balance of power on the continent; German rearmament would be effectively

208. Bonnet to Mendès France, August 24, 1954, *DDF*, 1954, 198.
209. Quoted in Guillen, "France," 83.
210. Quoted in Guillen, "Chefs," 32.
211. Statement by Dulles to the North Atlantic Council, December 14, 1953, *FRUS*, 1952–1954, vol. 5, 463. On the agonizing reappraisal, see Brian R. Duchin, "The 'Agonizing Reappraisal': Eisenhower, Dulles, and the EDC," *Diplomatic History* 16, no. 2 (1992): 201–21; and Kevin Ruane, "Agonizing Reappraisals: Anthony Eden, John Foster Dulles and the Crisis of European Defence, 1953-54," *Diplomacy & Statecraft* 13, no. 4 (2002): 151–85.
212. Memorandum of Conversation by MacArthur, July 13, 1954, *FRUS*, 1952–1954, vol. 5, 1020.

controlled, thereby maintaining an even Franco-German balance of power; and the European states would establish a powerful seven-state coalition that could be converted into a centralized European defense force capable of defending itself against the Soviet Union in the event of an American withdrawal.

A solution of this kind was in the air even before the National Assembly rejected the EDC. In early August 1954, Alexandre Parodi, secretary general of the French Foreign Ministry, called for the "creation of a European defense organization, a 'grand alliance,' grouping the six members of the community and Britain." This organization was to be "subordinated" to NATO and would "conserve certain essential guarantees" with respect to West Germany. Specifically, the Federal Republic would be denied "operational autonomy, logistical autonomy, [and] autonomy in setting force levels."[213] A week later, top military officials demanded a similar system: Germany must be admitted to NATO, but within a "framework limiting and controlling it." Perhaps, they added, this could take the form of a "European grouping of the Six, with a pact defining terms of association and commitments."[214] The French plan was to "combine the two, the Atlantic solution and the European solution."[215]

Toward the end of the month, just before putting the defense community treaty to the National Assembly, Mendès France floated the idea to France's allies. In a meeting with the British on August 23, he told Churchill and Eden that the EDC would be rejected and that he hoped to establish "a sort of coalition of the six European states that Britain would also join," which would be structured to "contain Germany." It would, he concluded, be a question of "constructing a small box inside the big NATO box."[216] Lest there be any doubt, he conveyed the same message to the Americans.[217]

Two weeks later, the French had developed a concrete plan. Mendès France laid out the essentials for Massigli in an important memorandum written on September 8. France wanted West Germany (and Italy) to join the existing Brussels Treaty Organization (BTO), which would now have the authority to "limit force levels for all participants as well as Germany," and exercise some "form of control over armaments." An arrangement of this kind had two major benefits. First, the Federal Republic could be controlled without discrimination because the rules would apply to all members equally. The result would be a fairly even distribution of power within the coalition. The arrangement, Mendès France noted, would "assure among the different members the equality, which the Germans as well as

213. De Beaumont Note, August 6, 1954, *DDF*, 1954, 96–97.

214. Quoted in Guillen, "Chefs," 32.

215. De Crouy-Chanel to de Margerie, August 24, 1954, *DDF*, 1954, 207.

216. Memorandum of Conversation between Mendès France, Churchill, and Eden, August 23, 1954, *DDF*, 1954, Annexes, 138.

217. Dillon to Department of State, August 24, 1954, *FRUS*, 1952–1954, vol. 5, 1071–77.

the French, for different reasons, had such a strong attachment." Second, the British would not have to surrender their sovereignty because limitations would be determined by "unanimity vote," and would apply to force levels in the European theater only. This would, in turn, clear the way for Britain to join the scheme, thereby establishing a formidable, purely European grouping in the event that the United States decided to withdraw from the continent. This did not mean Mendès France was giving up on the United States. The revamped BTO had to come into being as part of the Atlantic pact: "Appropriate commitments would have to be made between the members of the European Union and the other members of the Atlantic pact, especially the United States." Germany, in other words, was to be re-armed in a system ultimately dominated by U.S. power.[218]

There was a reasonable chance that the United States and Britain would agree to the French plan. To be sure, the Americans did not want to stay in Europe longer than they had to, but between 1950 and 1954 they assured the French that they would remain on the continent for the time being. When the Paris Treaty was signed, the United States government expressed its "resolve to station such forces on the continent of Europe . . . as they deem necessary and appropriate to contribute to the joint defense of the North Atlantic Treaty area, having regard to their obligations under the North Atlantic Treaty, their interest in the integrity of the European Defense Community, and their special responsibilities in Germany."[219] Then, in April 1954, President Eisenhower informed the Europeans that the United States would maintain necessary and appropriate forces in Europe for the joint defense of the NATO area; consult with its allies regarding force levels under the command of SACEUR; closely enmesh its forces with those of the Europeans; regard a threat to the EDC as a threat to the United States; and issue a firmer guarantee of continued American membership in NATO.[220]

Although these assurances could ultimately be dismissed as cheap talk designed to persuade the Six to ratify the EDC, the growing American troop presence in Europe gave the Europeans greater confidence that, at least in the short term, the United States would remain on the continent. This had not been the case in September 1950 when Acheson first broached the European army topic. At the time, the United States had less than one hundred thousand troops in Europe, and the North Atlantic defense system was still in the planning stages. Things had changed by 1954, however.

218. Mendès France to Massigli, September 8, 1954, *DDF*, 1954, 313–15. On the non-discrimination issue, see Mendès France to Diplomatic Representatives, September 18, 1954, ibid., 396–97. The precise commitments expected of the United States appear in Mendès France to Diplomatic Representatives, September 18, 1954, ibid., 400–401.

219. Tripartite Declaration, May 27, 1952, *FRUS*, 1952–1954, vol. 5, 687.

220. U.S. Assurances Concerning EDC, April 15, 1954, *DOSB*, vol. 30, no. 774, 619–20.

Eisenhower had arrived in Europe as the first SACEUR, the number of American troops on the continent had gone over 350,000, and the NATO system had gradually been set up. The United States had made a tangible and not immediately reversible commitment to the region.[221]

The French had reason to believe that the British and Americans would also support the BTO portion of their plan. For one thing, the British were far more likely to agree to extend the Brussels Treaty to West Germany than to join the EDC, since it did not require them to give up their sovereignty. As Mendès France observed, membership in the new organization simply did not "demand any new sacrifices of Britain."[222] Moreover, neither Britain nor the United States disagreed with the basic reasoning behind the BTO solution, namely that German rearmament must be controlled. From the beginning of the German rearmament negotiations, the Americans had made it clear that they wanted "to work out a plan which will give Ger[many] substantial polit[ical] freedom and equality at such time as she w[ou]ld enter [the] defense arrangements." The use of the term "substantial" was intentional—officials in Washington never planned to give the Germans complete autonomy, even if they were admitted directly into NATO. Acheson did not plan to "give up supreme authority" in the Federal Republic.[223] The British concurred. In the event that the French failed to ratify the Paris Treaty, Churchill planned to bring a rearmed Germany into NATO subject to "certain restrictions" on force levels and armament production.[224] Eden was also sympathetic to the view that the Germans could not be left to their own devices. If the Federal Republic was to be disarmed, he asked the House of Commons in February 1954, "who will keep Germany disarmed?" Alternatively, if the Germans were to be kept neutral, "who will keep Germany neutral?"[225]

Given the attraction and plausibility of the French plan, Mendès France's decision to allow the parliament to kill the defense community and propose a NATO-cum-expanded-BTO arrangement can be seen as a calculated maneuver. If Britain and the United States agreed to his suggestion, France would be placed in an ideal situation. If not, then Paris would have to revisit the integration option or something like it.

Fortunately for the French, Mendès France's gambit paid off. By the terms of the Paris Agreements of October 1954, West Germany was admitted to

---

221. For the troop figures, see Nelson, *History*, 45.

222. Mendès France to Massigli, September 8, 1954, *DDF*, 1954, 315.

223. Acheson to Embassy in the United Kingdom, December 14, 1950, and United States Delegation Minutes of the Meeting of the Foreign Ministers of the United States, United Kingdom, and France, December 19, 1950, *FRUS*, 1950, vol. 4, 801, 809.

224. De Crouy-Chanel to Margerie, August 24, 1954, *DDF*, 1954, 207.

225. Quoted in Kevin Ruane, *The Rise and Fall of the European Defence Community: Anglo-American Relations and the Crisis of European Defence, 1950–1954* (London: Macmillan, 2000), 149.

an expanded BTO—now known as the WEU—and NATO.[226] An important American commitment lay at the heart of the agreements: they would "maintain in Europe, including Germany, such units of its armed forces as may be necessary and appropriate to contribute [to] . . . the joint defence of the North Atlantic area while a threat to the area exists."[227] Moreover, they agreed to take an active role in controlling German military power. As the French had hoped, the German army was to be incorporated into NATO and put at the disposal of a strengthened American SACEUR.[228] For the time being, the Americans would do the heavy lifting with regard to balancing German and Soviet power on the continent.

The American commitment was to be supplemented by the WEU, an institution to which the French attached great importance. For one thing, it was given the authority to restrict the size and character of the West German military, thereby allaying French fears about German rearmament. Specifically, it was tasked with establishing an even balance of power between France and the Federal Republic by ensuring that the "German defence contribution will conform to the contribution fixed for E.D.C."[229] Moreover, because it included all of western Europe's major powers, it provided the foundation for a formidable west European coalition that would have a fighting chance of defending itself against the Soviet Union should the need arise.[230] The WEU was not an alternative to the Atlantic pact— NATO had to be the dominant institution for reasons of operational effectiveness—but it provided a solid basis for a purely European solution in the event of an Americans withdrawal. This had been the French intention all along. Mendès France had insisted that the European organization "must not be merely [a] paper control or window dressing but must have real substance."[231] The French plan was for the "association of the seven" to be the "political and military basis of the future Europe."[232] Thus, the Paris Agreements ensured that the Brussels Treaty was "strengthened and ex-

226. For the documents comprising the Paris Agreements, see *FRUS*, 1952–1954, vol. 5, 1345–66, 1435–57. Initially, the French wanted Germany admitted to the BTO only, but they quickly agreed to German membership in NATO. See Dillon to the Office of the United States High Commissioner for Germany, September 16, 1954, ibid., 1198.

227. Final Act of the Nine-Power Conference, October 3, 1954, ibid., 1351.

228. For the French position, see Mendès France to Diplomatic Representatives, September 18, 1954, *DDF*, 1954, 400–401.

229. Final Act of the Nine-Power Conference, October 3, 1954, *FRUS*, 1952–1954, vol. 5, 1346. For evidence of French concerns about the within-coalition balance of power, see Guillen, "France," 83.

230. Protocols to the Brussels Treaty, October 22, 1954, *FRUS*, 1952–1954, vol. 5, 1441–56.

231. Dillon to the Office of the United States High Commissioner for Germany, September 16, 1954, ibid., 1198.

232. Mendès France to Bonnet, September 19, 1954, *DDF*, 1954, 405. See also Dillon to the Office of the United States High Commissioner for Germany, September 16, 1954, *FRUS*, 1952–1954, vol. 5, 1198.

tended to make it a more effective focus of European integration."[233] As a report summarized Eden's remarks during the negotiations, "there will be created [the] nucleus of [an] organization which may eventually develop along [the] lines [of the] EDC."[234]

Had the Americans and British not acquiesced to French demands—and it was not a foregone conclusion that they would—France likely would have had to reconsider the EDC option or something similar. In the event, however, the British and the Americans met virtually every French condition. To be sure, they did not do so with good grace. Dulles, especially, was "sullen and resentful."[235] But the bottom line was that they agreed to the NATO-WEU alternative, and Europe's flirtation with military integration came to an end.

A Contradictory Case?

On the face of it, French decision making between 1950 and 1954 might appear to contradict the claim that, given the opportunity, states facing overwhelming adversaries form centralized balancing coalitions. France was confronted by a surpassingly powerful Soviet Union and was protected by the United States, but it could not count on American support over the long term. Surely if they were attentive to balance of power imperatives, the French should have embraced the EDC solution just as they opted for the ECSC.

Upon closer inspection, however, French behavior in the defense community case does not contradict the logic of my argument. The key point is that states are extremely reluctant to centralize because it involves giving up sovereignty. Nevertheless, weak states confronted by an especially powerful opponent often have no alternative: they can deal with it only by joining forces and centralizing decision making. In cases such as these, centralization may be unattractive but it is the only option available to them. It is not, however, *always* the only possible strategy, and when other possible arrangements exist that offer to establish a favorable balance of power without requiring a surrender of sovereignty, we should expect states to avoid centralization. This is what happened in 1954. A substantial Anglo-American troop presence on the European mainland promised to establish a more favorable balance of power than a putative defense community without requiring the French to give up their sovereignty.

But why did the French opt to rely on an American force commitment when they thought there was a good chance that the United States would withdraw from the region in the future? Germany might secede from the

233. Final Act of the Nine-Power Conference, October 3, 1954, ibid., 1346.

234. Dillon to the Office of the United States High Commissioner for Germany, September 16, 1954, ibid., 1200.

235. Trachtenberg, *Constructed*, 125.

EDC and this made the defense community strategically unattractive, but the American security guarantee was no more certain. The answer is that the French did not entirely put their faith in an American security guarantee. To be sure, they believed that the Americans would defend them from the Soviets and control the West Germans in the short term. After all, the United States now had more than 350,000 troops in Europe and the NATO system was up and running. Over the longer term, however, they feared an American pullout and therefore established the WEU as an insurance option. If the Americans left, the WEU could be converted into a self-sufficient, purely European defense system.

Even if this interpretation is correct, an apparent inconsistency remains: although the security environment remained the same between 1945 and 1955, French decision making did not. Specifically, they *actually constructed* a centralized industrial complex (the ECSC), but *merely planned* for the contingency of a centralized military force (the WEU). What matters here is time. It takes approximately the same amount of time to *establish* centralized economies and militaries—it took a year to negotiate both the ECSC and EDC treaties. But it takes longer for the *power enhancing effects* of centralization to manifest themselves in the economic realm. In military affairs, provided that the relevant forces are already cooperating with one another in some fashion as the west Europeans were in the WEU and NATO, a decision to centralize can quickly increase a group's fighting power by providing improved coordination, especially at the operational and strategic levels. In economic affairs, on the other hand, it takes a considerable amount of time for the competition engendered by a large, single market to generate larger scale production, a greater variety of products, and technological advances.

Because it takes longer for centralization to lead to power enhancements in the economic sphere, groups of weak states that think they may have to balance against an overwhelming adversary in the future have powerful incentives to establish a centralized economy at the earliest possible date. Given that its future fighting power depends on the size and sophistication of its economic base, a coalition that fails to establish a single economy in the short term will be at a severe disadvantage down the line. Its members will not benefit from the economies of scale and innovations accruing to larger economic areas. As separate, small economies they will fall even further behind the great power, which will benefit from its possession of a large, unified economic space in the interim. In short, they must centralize now in order to compete effectively in the future.

This timing issue accounts for the French decision to integrate via the ECSC and merely prepare to integrate via the WEU. In the 1950s, the Europeans were not sure that the Americans would continue to protect them and feared that they might have to balance against the Soviet Union on their own at some point in the future. To prepare for that eventuality, they had to establish a large single economy that could keep pace with the USSR and compete with it effectively if and when they were left to fend for themselves. When it came to military matters, on the other hand, putting an embryonic European military in place was sufficient. In the event of a future American withdrawal, they could quickly centralize that military and benefit from doing so in fairly short order.

Britain: Refusing Integration, 1950–1954

The British declined to enter the European army negotiations and chose to buck-pass the integration burden to the continental powers instead. Like the French and Germans, they viewed the Soviet Union as a hegemonic threat and concluded that the west Europeans had to establish a balancing coalition to protect against it. Thus, when it appeared that France and Germany were going to establish a European army, they supported those efforts and were determined to cooperate with the emerging entity. But they also understood that they were less likely to be conquered than their allies due to their geographic location, and so resolved not to join the EDC, reasoning that their more vulnerable partners should bear the sovereignty costs of establishing a viable counterweight to Soviet power.

An Unchanged Security Situation

In the early 1950s, British decision makers continued to believe that their security depended on balancing Soviet power. Important officials were acutely concerned about the Soviet Union's potential for continental domination. Indeed, they were so worried that earlier fears about a future German threat were pushed aside. The Chiefs of Staff summed up the common view in October 1950: "The threat now confronting the Western world is the real threat from Russia, rather than a hypothetical threat from a rearmed Germany."[236] Consequently, the western powers had to form some sort of coalition. "There must be created," declared Churchill in the summer of 1950, "a real defensive front in Europe. . . . It is by closing the yawning gap in the defences of the Western Powers in Europe that we shall find the surest means, not only of saving our lives and liberties, but of preventing a third world war."[237]

A continental European coalition featured prominently in these balancing calculations. By 1950, it was a core precept of British strategic planning that Europe had to be defended as far to the east as possible. According to top military officials, holding "the enemy east of the Rhine is vital to the defence of the United Kingdom, which is the first 'pillar' of British strategy,

---

236. Extract from a Brief by the Chiefs of Staff, October 20, 1950, *DBPO*, ser. 2, vol. 3, 180.
237. Quoted in Fursdon, *European*, 75.

and that the defence of the United Kingdom and of Western Europe must therefore be considered together."[238] Indeed, by the time Pleven made his announcement, the British had concluded that "our defence lies along a land line in Europe, as far east as we can make it." It was also taken for granted that this line had to be defended primarily by the continental powers, and especially the Germans. Any gap in defenses could "only be filled by a German contribution."[239] Arguing that western Europe was a "vital area—vital to the survival of . . . the United Kingdom" and that it must be "defended—not liberated," the military brass pointed to the "the urgent necessity for German military participation in the defence of Western Europe."[240]

Civilian leaders took essentially the same line. Bevin, for example, "pressed hard and successfully for government acceptance of the need for German rearmament."[241] For his part, Minister of Defence Shinwell informed the House of Commons that he doubted whether the British people would tolerate a situation in which western forces "were engaged in the defense of German territory without some contribution from the German people."[242] In short, a continental coalition that included Germany was essential to deterring the Soviets and, if deterrence failed, providing defense in depth.

Even as they fretted about the security situation, however, the British understood that they were less endangered than their continental allies. As had been the case before 1950, the Red Army was expected to overrun continental Europe, but western planners did not believe the Russians would be able to mount an attack on the British Isles. "At present the Soviet system has the military capability of overrunning large portions of continental Europe," noted the NSC in August 1952. Nevertheless, "The Soviet system does not now have adequate naval forces and sufficient shipping to enable it to make large overseas amphibious type attacks. The USSR does not now appear capable of occupying the U.K."[243]

Another basic continuity from the late 1940s was the conviction that Britain was more likely than France or Germany to be rescued by the Americans at acceptable cost in the event of a European war. This is not to say that British decision makers were less concerned about the temporary nature of the American security guarantee. In January 1951, Bevin informed Prime Minister Clement Attlee that he was worried that the United States

---

238. Memorandum for the Permanent Under-Secretary's Committee, April 27, 1950, *DBPO*, ser. 2, vol. 2, 164.

239. Memorandum by Elliott, October 19, 1950, *DBPO*, ser. 2, vol. 3, 178.

240. Extract from a Brief by the Chiefs of Staff, October 20, 1950, ibid., 180.

241. David Weigall, "British Perceptions of the European Defence Community," in *Shaping Postwar Europe: European Unity and Disunity 1945–1957*, ed. Peter M. R. Stirk and David Willis (New York: St. Martin's, 1991), 93.

242. Quoted in Fursdon, *European*, 94.

243. NSC 135/1 Annex, August 22, 1952, *FRUS*, 1952–1954, vol. 2, 109–10.

might retreat into "a kind of armed isolation," a problem that "must not be underrated."[244] There is also ample evidence that Eden, who became foreign secretary in October 1951, took Dulles's threat to withdraw American troops from Europe quite seriously. As he noted in his memoirs, it would have been "reckless" to treat the security guarantee as a "natural right." The Europeans could not "assume that it could never be withdrawn."[245]

Nevertheless, the British took comfort in the knowledge that in the event of a Soviet attack the United States would return in force and rescue them at acceptable cost. The U.S. battle plan did not reassure Paris and Bonn. As had been the case in the late 1940s, the Americans intended to allow France and Germany to fall to the Soviets before fighting their way back onto the continent. The two states would thus be the battleground in a devastating war. American strategy in 1954, for example, called for destroying targets in France and Germany "so as to deny additional military capabilities to the enemy." This being the case, "the expectations of [the] Europeans of the probable consequences to them of an all-out war are horrendous enough, and with justification."[246] Britain, on the other hand, would serve as the base for these bombing operations and largely escape the destruction of a prolonged ground war. In short, although the United Kingdom was far from invulnerable, the British were more secure than their continental allies.

"With" But Not "of" the European Army

Given this situation, the British supported the creation of a European army and were committed to cooperating closely with it, but they were equally determined not to join it. If the continental powers wanted to establish a centralized military force, this was all to the good: such a force would go a long way to deterring the Soviet Union and providing defense in depth. So when the Six began negotiating the EDC, the British offered their support and promised to cooperate closely with an eventual European defense force. But they were not prepared to incur the sovereignty costs of participation. France and Germany might have no choice but to build a centralized coalition. If they failed to do so, they would not be able to balance effectively against the Soviet Union. But this did not mean that the British had to follow suit. Instead, they could free ride and allow their more endangered allies to incur the sovereignty costs of establishing a centralized military.

244. Quoted in Ruane, "Agonizing," 161.
245. Anthony Eden, *Memoirs: Full Circle* (London: Cassell, 1960), 58. For the claim that his Foreign Office subordinates shared these fears, see Ruane, "Agonizing," 161.
246. Paper Prepared by Fuller, September 10, 1954, *FRUS*, 1952–1954, vol. 5, 1171–72.

This dynamic was already in evidence before the EDC affair. *European Unity*, a pamphlet produced by the Labour Party in the summer between the Schuman and Pleven announcements, summarized the approach. Its authors began with a familiar premise: the Soviet Union was an overwhelming rival and the Europeans therefore had to cooperate in order to ensure their survival. "Since no country in Western Europe feels strong enough to resist Soviet aggression by its own unaided efforts," they asserted, "all recognize the need to combine their resources of manpower, industrial potential and human skill in the service of a single policy. . . . The survival of Western Europe in any form will depend on achieving adequate solidarity in [the] face of Soviet expansionism." The key question was what constituted "adequate solidarity." For the continental powers it meant centralization: "Some people believe that the required unity of action . . . must be imposed by a supra-national body with executive powers." France and Germany wanted to establish a "union" by "surrendering whole fields of government to a supra-national authority." The British view was different. Noting the "unprecedented progress" that had been made through intergovernmental institutions, they preferred "co-operation between governments by mutual consent," and opposed surrendering "to a supranational authority . . . the constitutional powers which they exercise at present."[247] Because it came soon after Schuman's proposal, *European Unity* was a source of considerable embarrassment for British officials. Nevertheless, it accurately represented the government's position—both Attlee and Bevin had approved it ahead of time. It reflected the view of the Foreign Office as well. Although the permanent under-secretary, Lord Strang, lamented that it was "ill-timed and in places ill-expressed," he also admitted it was "in its main thesis along the true line of British policy."[248]

The Conservative Party took essentially the same stance, though this was not altogether clear at the time. Claims that the Conservatives favored British membership in an integrated European force rest on Churchill's assertion at Strasbourg, in August 1950, that the British should declare themselves "in favour of the immediate creation of a European Army under a unified command and in which we should all bear a worthy and honourable part."[249] But although Churchill was sincere in his desire for a European force, he did not envisage Britain actually being part of it. As he explained to Anthony Nutting, "I meant it for them, not for us."[250] Well-informed observers understood this clearly at the time. MRP politician Maurice Schumann, for example, was convinced that Churchill expected

247. Manifesto by the National Executive Committee of the British Labour Party on European Unity (May 1950), http://www.ena.lu/manifesto_national_executive_committee_british_labour_party_european_unity_1950-2-28436.

248. Quoted in David A. Gowland and Arthur Turner, *Reluctant Europeans: Britain and European Integration, 1945–1998* (New York: Longman, 2000), 53, n. 26.

249. Quoted in Fursdon, *European*, 75.

250. Quoted in Weigall, "British," 94.

the continental states to integrate, but "was 'anti' and remained consistently so" when it came to British membership.[251] Thus, as Klaus Larres has observed, "as far as Europe was concerned and despite all party political rhetoric, Churchill's views hardly differed from the perspective of Prime Minister Attlee and Foreign Secretary Ernest Bevin."[252]

This thinking—support for integration and a desire to cooperate with, but not join, whatever entity emerged from discussions on the continent—continued after the Pleven announcement. To be sure, there was some hesitation: Bevin worried that if the European army project concluded successfully, the Americans might feel that they could withdraw from the continent. He viewed the Pleven Plan as "out of harmony with our general policy of building up the Atlantic community as the major grouping for the future." It would be a "cancer in the Atlantic body" and might "discourage instead of encouraging continuing American concern with the security of Europe." As a result, he thought it best to "nip it in the bud." But Attlee quickly affirmed that the United Kingdom would pursue its established policy. If the continental states wanted to create an integrated military force, he asserted in a meeting with the Cabinet Defence Committee in November 1950, it was "not . . . for us to veto their attempt." Moreover, if a European army actually came into being, the British ought to cooperate with it. The defense of western Europe would then rest on "the United States, Great Britain . . . and the Federated European Force." However, he was "totally opposed" to British membership. The Chiefs of Staff recorded their full agreement with his decision.[253]

Herbert Morrison, who replaced Bevin as foreign secretary in March 1951, agreed. In a document circulated to the Cabinet in July, he argued that the Pleven Plan had the virtue of leading to German rearmament, which was essential to the security of the United Kingdom. British officials should therefore "counter the impression . . . that we are hostile to all schemes of integration" and register their strong support for the defense community. Nevertheless, he recognized that British support must not go too far. The United Kingdom would, of course, "remain outside" any integration schemes.[254]

---

251. Quoted in Fursdon, *European*, 77.

252. Klaus Larres, "Integrating Europe or Ending the Cold War? Churchill's Postwar Foreign Policy," *Journal of European Integration History* 2, no. 1 (1996): 30.

253. Memorandum by Bevin, November 24, 1950, and Minutes of a Meeting of the Defence Committee of the Cabinet, November 27, 1950, *DBPO*, ser. 2, vol. 3, 293–94, 302.

254. Quoted in Geoffrey Warner, "The Labour Governments and the Unity of Western Europe, 1945–51," in *The Foreign Policy of the British Labour Governments, 1945–1951*, ed. Ritchie Ovendale (Leicester: Leicester University Press, 1984), 76. For evidence that others supported Morrison's conclusions, see Spencer Mawby, *Containing Germany: Britain and the Arming of the Federal Republic* (New York: Palgrave, 1999), 65.

Perhaps the clearest statement of British policy came in a memorandum Attlee prepared for the Cabinet in August 1951. Like Morrison, the prime minister supported the European army because he believed it allowed for the simultaneous rearmament and control of West Germany and therefore enhanced British security.[255] As long as the plan could be "made militarily effective," he wanted the government to "give every encouragement to it." As for Britain's relationship with the defense community, he again advocated cooperation and support but rejected membership. The United Kingdom was "willing to play an active part in all forms of European cooperation on an inter-governmental basis but cannot surrender our freedom of decision and action to any supranational authority." British officials did not oppose integration for the continental states. They were "quite ready to encourage Continental countries who feel disposed to adopt such plans" and were "also ready to look very sympathetically on the European Army Plan."[256] But because it would impinge on British sovereignty, membership was out of the question.

The British went public with their views in September, when they issued a joint statement on the EDC with the French and the Americans in Washington. Simply put, they favored "the inclusion of a democratic Germany . . . in a Continental European Community," and intended to "establish the closest possible association with the European continental community at all stages of its development."[257] The language was crucial: the "community" was explicitly "continental" and Britain would merely be "associated" with it. Internal British documents support this interpretation. The Washington declaration was judged to have provided "formal recognition . . . of our inability to integrate fully with Europe," and made it clear that "while we cannot join the 'European Community' we nevertheless wish to be closely associated with it."[258] As David Clay Large has observed, "Britain adopted a stance of 'benevolent neutrality' . . . Britain would not oppose the Europeans' efforts to achieve unity in military matters, but would refuse to be part of a European army."[259]

The thinking underlying British policy remained unchanged when the Conservatives came to power in October 1951.[260] Upon his arrival at the Foreign Office, Eden received a brief outlining British policy toward integration and toward the EDC specifically. Although Britain was "ready to

255. Saki Dockrill, *Britain's Policy for West German Rearmament, 1950–1955* (Cambridge: Cambridge University Press, 1991), 76.

256. Quoted in Warner, "Labour," 77.

257. Quoted in John W. Young, *Britain and European Unity, 1945–1992* (Basingstoke: Macmillan, 1993), 37.

258. Quoted in Warner, "Labour," 78.

259. Large, *Germans*, 124.

260. John W. Young, "British Officials and European Integration, 1944–1960," in *Building Postwar Europe: National Decision-Makers and European Institutions, 1948–63*, ed. Anne Deighton (New York: St. Martin's, 1995), 93.

play an active part in all plans for integration on an inter-governmental basis," a variety of considerations prevented it from delegating "control of policy to any European supranational authority." This did not mean that the British opposed integration for the Europeans. They had "encouraged those countries who feel able to go ahead with such plans" and "assured them of our good-will." However, Britain's relationship with any integrated entity was to be purely cooperative since membership would involve a loss of autonomy. Foreign Office officials wanted to be "closely associated . . . short of actual membership."[261]

Eden, who dominated foreign policy after October 1951, quickly adopted the position outlined in the brief.[262] Like Attlee and Morrison, he supported continental military integration, believing that a powerful Franco-German force would enhance British security through defense in depth. In December 1951, for example, he flatly rejected Churchill's proposal for an intergovernmental European force on the grounds that it would destroy the EDC, whose principal virtue was that it made German rearmament more acceptable to the French.[263] The defense community would play a crucial "anchoring" role with respect to the Federal Republic and keep it on the right side in the cold war, a role even "more important than the question of a German military contribution."[264] Thus, he fully supported the European army project. Given that "so much of Europe wants to federate," he wrote Churchill, "it would not be right—or good policy—to try to stop the others." At the same time, he took it to be axiomatic that the United Kingdom could not actually join a European federation. He recommended that Britain "find the most practicable and useful means of establishing close relations" with whatever emerged.[265] His general approach was simple: "We want a united Europe. . . . It is only when plans for uniting Europe take a federal form that we cannot ourselves take part."[266]

The Permanent Under-Secretary's Committee took basically the same line in an important memorandum written in December 1951. European integration, the committee argued, would enhance British security: "The effect of the Schuman Plan should be to strengthen the economy of Western Europe; of the Pleven Plan, to provide for its effective defence." For this

261. Brief for Eden, October 31, 1951, *DBPO*, ser. 2, vol. 1, 743.

262. For the claim that Eden dominated foreign policy making during this period, see John W. Young, "Churchill's 'No' to Europe: The 'Rejection' of European Union by Churchill's Post-War Government, 1951–1952," *Historical Journal* 28, no. 4 (1985): 923–37; and John W. Young, "German Rearmament and the European Defence Community," in *The Foreign Policy of Churchill's Peacetime Administration 1951–1955*, ed. John W. Young (Leicester: Leicester University Press, 1988), 82–83.

263. Young, "Churchill's," 931; and Mawby, *Containing*, 73. For evidence that Eden's views were widely shared in December 1951, see ibid., 76.

264. Quoted in Ruane, "Agonizing," 156.

265. Eden to Churchill, March 18, 1952, *DBPO*, ser. 2, vol. 1, 847.

266. Quoted in Gowland and Turner, *Reluctant*, 56.

reason, there was considerable "advantage in encouraging the movement," though, needless to say, the British "cannot seriously contemplate joining in European integration." The only concern was the familiar one that Europe might become so powerful and "self-contained" that the Americans would have an excuse to withdraw their troops from the continent.[267]

Crucially, Eden managed to secure Churchill's approval. Although the prime minister feared that the defense community project was unworkable—he referred to the European army as a "sludgy amalgam"—he nonetheless endorsed it because it had the potential to enhance British security by establishing a powerful Franco-German force on the continent.[268] As he told Eisenhower after the fact, his support for the EDC project had been based on the belief that "it was the only way in which the French could be persuaded to accept the limited German army which was my desire." Throughout the affair, he had kept "one aim above all others ... namely a German contribution to the defence of an already uniting Europe."[269] He was prepared to be quite favorable to the EDC, arguing in a Cabinet memorandum that he was "not opposed to a European Federation," and that Britain "should not ... obstruct but rather favour the movement to closer European unity." At the same time, he did not plan to join in the European project. "I never thought," he argued in November 1951, "that Britain ... should ... become an integral part of a European Federation, and have never given the slightest support to the idea."[270] His attitude was therefore in line with the conventional view: "We help, we dedicate, we participate, but we do not merge and we do not forfeit our insular or Commonwealth character."[271] The British would "help the European Army all it can, mingle with it, and should it be necessary, fight and die with it," but they would not join.[272]

British policy between 1952 and 1954 mirrored these internal discussions. Officials worked hard to persuade the continental powers to establish a European army. The key impediment was the French fear that the Germans might secede from the EDC. In response, the British promised to keep forces on the continent after the community came into being and to defend any member who came under military attack. On May 27, 1952, they signed a declaration committing them to defend the EDC against any threat to its integrity and to keep forces on the continent as long as they were deemed necessary. Meanwhile, by the terms of the Anglo-EDC treaty, which came into effect on the same day, they promised to come to the

267. Memorandum by the Permanent Under-Secretary's Committee, December 12, 1951, *DBPO*, ser. 2, vol. 1, 786–87.

268. Quoted in Gowland and Turner, *Reluctant*, 59.

269. Quoted in Weigall, "British," 94–95.

270. Quoted in Dockrill, *Britain's*, 81.

271. Quoted in Christopher Lord, "With but not of: Britain and the Schuman Plan, a Reinterpretation," *Journal of European Integration History* 4, no. 2 (1998): 23.

272. Quoted in Ruane, *Rise*, 28.

assistance of any defense community member attacked by another state.[273] Then, in April 1954, in a last-ditch effort to get the French to ratify the EDC, the British government agreed to station "such units of its armed forces as may be necessary and appropriate" to defend the North Atlantic area, and to keep them there as long "as the threat exists to the security of Western Europe and of the European Defence Community."[274]

The British also indicated that they were determined to cooperate with a continental defense community if and when it came into being. In their first major statement of policy in December 1951, Churchill and Eden declared that Britain would "stand together in true comradeship" with an EDC force. United Kingdom forces would be "linked with those of the European Defense Community for training, supply and operation by land, sea and air." The following year, the foreign secretary reiterated the point: "British forces on the Continent will operate as closely as possible with the European defense forces and be linked with them in matters of training, administration and supplies."[275] Then, on April 13, 1954, London signed an Agreement on Association with the EDC, which provided for a wide variety of institutional links between Britain and the defense community, and on the following day Eden announced that the United Kingdom would transfer an armored division to EDC command.[276] The agreements entailed such close cooperation that Housing Minister Harold Macmillan worried France was being offered "almost everything but marriage."[277]

At every turn, however, British decision makers made it clear that although they were committed to cooperation, membership was a bridge too far. Typical of the approach was the 1952 Eden Plan, a proposal that the intergovernmental Council of Europe should become an umbrella organization over the federated Six and Britain.[278] As Eden explained, the plan was ideal because it allowed the "federalists to federate," while keeping Britain "associated" and therefore autonomous.[279] He expressed the same reasoning in a speech to the House of Commons: "We have established a formal and special relationship between the United Kingdom and EDC. This clearly shows that, although we cannot join that community, we are linked with its future and stand at its side."[280] A year later, Churchill confirmed the basic thrust of British foreign policy. "We are not members of the EDC, nor do we

273. Mawby, *Containing*, 79.

274. Quoted in Ruane, *Rise*, 75.

275. Quoted in Fursdon, *European*, 133, 140.

276. For the text of the Association Agreement, see U.K. Association with EDC, April 13, 1954, *DOSB*, vol. 30, no. 774, 620–21, and for the Eden announcement, see Ruane, *Rise*, 75.

277. Quoted in Gowland and Turner, *Reluctant*, 65.

278. For a description of the plan, see ibid., 62.

279. Brief for Eden, March 8, 1952, *DBPO*, ser. 2, vol. 1, 835, n. 7.

280. Quoted in F. S. Northedge, *Descent from Power: British Foreign Policy, 1945–1973* (London: George Allen and Unwin, 1974), 163.

intend to be merged into a Federal European system," he declared. "We are 'with' them but not 'of' them. We will exchange officers for command and training and co-operate in many other ways. . . . We have stationed our largest military force on the Continent. . . . What more is there we could give, apart from completely merging ourselves with the European military organization?"[281] In short, Britain was prepared to guarantee the integrity of the defense community and to be closely associated with it, but it would not be merged into a supranational community.

In view of subsequent claims by some of the major protagonists, it is worth noting that no one in British decision-making circles disputed this basic policy. Looking back on Britain's refusal to join the defense community, "Tory Strasbourgers," including Macmillan, Sir David Maxwell-Fyfe, and Robert Boothby, claimed that they were more favorably disposed to integration than Churchill's administration and castigated Eden for failing to take Britain into Europe. Rhetorically, there does appear to have been a split. In a widely circulated memorandum, Macmillan warned of the dangers that would ensue from the "collapse of the European idea," and exhorted the government to further the cause of European "unity." At no point, however, did he recommend that the United Kingdom surrender its sovereignty and integrate with the Six. By his own admission, Britain could not, "of course, join a Federation." What he was suggesting instead was a "European Union or Confederation" along the lines of the intergovernmental Commonwealth. So there was basic agreement that Britain could not be integrated into Europe. Eden wanted the continental powers to integrate and then associate with them, and Macmillan wanted to come up with a nonfederal arrangement that Britain and the continentals could all join. But neither expected Britain to surrender its sovereignty and join an integrated European entity.[282] As Kevin Ruane notes, "even those who . . . urged a more imaginative pro-European line, never went so far as to propose . . . military federation for Britain."[283]

Sovereignty concerns clearly lay at the heart of this approach. Indeed, the British were quite open about this. Surrendering sovereignty, Eden announced in a speech at Columbia University, was "something which we know in our bones we cannot do."[284] Similarly, Lord Henderson told Adenauer that although Britain would "not withhold her sympathy" if the Europeans "wanted to draw up their own Schuman or Pleven Plans," she was "not prepared to give up her national sovereignty."[285] This fact was not lost on observers at the time. As the American diplomat Leon Fuller put it in 1953: "The British stand aloof for much the same reason—for them, as for

---

281. Quoted in Weigall, "British," 97.
282. Note by Macmillan, January 16, 1952, *DBPO*, ser. 2, vol. 1, 814.
283. Ruane, *Rise*, 21.
284. Quoted in Young, *Britain*, 39.
285. Adenauer, *Memoirs*, 384.

us, merger of national sovereignty respecting defense in a supra-national federation is unthinkable."[286]

Perhaps the best evidence that this was the British position lies in the United Kingdom's quick acceptance of the NATO-WEU alternative. Given the opportunity to join a defense arrangement that resembled the EDC in most respects, except that it was intergovernmental, British decision makers jumped on board. Eden, in fact, was instrumental in selling the French plan to the Americans.[287] From the British perspective, there could be no better system than one in which they were intimately involved in the defense of western Europe without surrendering sovereign prerogatives.

Alternative Explanations

The EDC episode is an anomalous case for both the domestic interest group and ideational entrepreneurship arguments because both predict that the EDC should have been a success rather than a failure. If followed to their logical conclusions, they imply that the French should have supported the European army plan, thereby leading to the creation of an integrated west European military force.

Interest Groups

Although Moravcsik focuses exclusively on economic integration, he claims that his argument is equally applicable to military affairs. It should therefore be able to account for the failure of the EDC, which he describes as potentially involving "deeper integration" than the coal and steel pool.[288] To reiterate, he argues that governments cooperate when powerful domestic interest groups demand it and these groups call for cooperation when interdependence is high. Moreover, when interdependence is especially high, governments go one step further and integrate rather than simply cooperate with one another.

It certainly seems that important domestic interest groups in France—including the chief executive, the ministry of defense, top military officials, and the defense industry—wanted to cooperate with West Germany. Moreover, they demanded cooperation because they believed France and the

286. Quoted in Larres, "Integrating," 39.

287. See Anne Deighton, "The Last Piece of the Jigsaw: Britain and the Creation of the Western European Union," *Contemporary European History* 7, no. 2 (1998): 181–96; Ruane, *Rise*, 111–72; Large, *Germans*, 215–20; and Trachtenberg, *Constructed*, 124.

288. For Moravcsik's claim that his argument applies to military and economic affairs, see Andrew Moravcsik, "Taking Preferences Seriously: A Liberal Theory of International Politics," *International Organization* 51, no. 4 (1997): 515, and for his characterization of the EDC, see *The Choice for Europe: Social Purpose and State Power from Messina to Maastricht* (Ithaca: Cornell University Press, 1998), 86.

Federal Republic were militarily interdependent: only together could they balance against the USSR effectively, and neither could hope to balance against it alone.

Most important government decision makers between 1950 and 1954 understood that West Germany had to be rearmed and incorporated into the western alliance system against the Soviet Union. The prime ministers and foreign ministers of the day—including Pleven, Antoine Pinay, Mayer, Joseph Laniel, Schuman, Bidault, and Mendès France—may have disagreed about the details, but none of them opposed the principle of German rearmament. If the western powers were going to balance effectively against the Soviet Union, then the Germans were going to have to play their part. Top military officials shared this view and were, in fact, more strident in their demands that the Germans be rearmed and attached to the western camp. French producer groups were not focused on the balance of power implications of German rearmament, but they too favored Franco-German cooperation. The CNPF, which Moravcsik identifies as the most important French business association, "discreetly supported proposals to merge European armaments production" on behalf of the leading sectors of French industry.[289]

Their support for integration, however, was lukewarm at best. The EDC was never France's clear number-one option. As we have seen, Pleven and Schuman found themselves negotiating the terms of a European army because of the Spofford compromise rather than a real desire to establish an integrated military force. Similarly, officials at the Quai were advocating German rearmament in a context other than the European army quite early on.[290] After the treaty was signed, Laniel, Bidault, and Mendès France worked hard to secure an American commitment to the continent and turn the defense community into an intergovernmental organization that included Britain. The French military took a more negative stance, beginning with Juin's call for a German contribution to the Atlantic alliance in 1951, and culminating in his campaign to replace the EDC with a nonsupranational NATO alternative in March 1954.[291] Then in the summer, the CNPF, which had consistently supported "industrial ententes" rather than "supranational dirigism," turned against the defense community, arguing that

289. Paul M. Pitman, "Interested Circles: French Industry and the Rise and Fall of the European Defence Community, 1950–1954," in *La communauté européenne de défense, leçons pour demain?* ed. Michel Dumoulin (Brussels: P.I.E.–Peter Lang, 2000), 53.

290. For the claim that they opposed the EDC from 1952 onwards, see Craig Parsons, *A Certain Idea of Europe* (Ithaca: Cornell University Press, 2003), 76.

291. Creswell, *Question*, 138; Guillen, "Chefs," 32; and Guillen, "France," 76. See also Claude d'Abzac-Epezy and Philippe Vial, "French Military Elites and the Idea of Europe, 1947–1954," in *Building Postwar Europe*, ed. Anne Deighton (New York: St. Martin's, 1995), 1–20; and Raymond Poidevin, "La France devant le problème de la CED: Incidences nationales et internationales," *Revue d'histoire de la deuxième guerre mondiale* no. 129 (1983): 35–57.

French industry would not be competitive in this kind of arrangement.[292] Thus, as Helen Milner argues in a defense of the interest group argument, France's rejection of the EDC can be attributed to "lack of endorsement from key domestic actors."[293]

This support for cooperation but opposition to integration is at odds with the basic interest group claim that governments opt for integration when interdependence is especially high. If interdependence "refers to situations characterized by reciprocal effects among countries or among actors in different countries," then states facing a common powerful opponent are militarily interdependent and those facing an overwhelmingly powerful adversary—as France and West Germany were in the early 1950s—are highly interdependent.[294] Thus, if the interest group argument is correct, the French should have pursued integration rather than preferring mere cooperation.

There are four possible responses to this anomaly, but none is convincing. First, Moravcsik could claim that his argument does not apply in the military realm, but as we have seen, he does not do so. Similarly, Milner states that the distinction between the two realms, and between the ECSC and EDC specifically, is untenable: both "had important security implications."[295] Second, Moravcsik could argue that the case actually lends support to his argument—domestic interest groups wanted cooperation rather than integration and got it. But this version of events contradicts his causal logic, which holds that these groups tend to support integration rather than cooperation when interdependence is high. Third, he could argue that important domestic interest groups opted for cooperation rather than integration because of the sovereignty costs attached to the latter course of action. Elsewhere, however, he does not assign a powerful influence to sovereignty concerns: "It is not uncommon for states knowingly to surrender sovereignty."[296] Finally, he could claim that these same interest groups turned against the EDC because they worried that it could not prevent German secession. But this does not square with his core argument that states establish international institutions precisely because they believe that they can prevent others from cheating on their agreements.[297]

292. Pitman, "Interested," 58–61.
293. Helen Milner, *Interests, Institutions, and Information: Domestic Politics and International Relations* (Princeton: Princeton University Press, 1997), 200.
294. Robert O. Keohane and Joseph S. Nye, *Power and Interdependence: World Politics in Transition* (Boston: Little, Brown, 1977), 8.
295. Milner, *Interests*, 181.
296. Moravcsik, "Taking," 520.
297. Moravcsik, *Choice*, 73–75.

Ideational Entrepreneurs

Parsons accounts for the failure of the EDC by pointing out that it was unpopular with French bureaucrats, the military, and a clear majority of French politicians.[298] I agree with this assessment, although I lay more emphasis on the existence of an attractive NATO-based alternative.

The problem is not that Parsons has misread the evidence, but that it flatly contradicts the ideational entrepreneurship argument, which logically predicts enthusiastic and widespread support for the defense community. If the French were truly going to transcend the nation-state, then surrendering sovereignty over military affairs should have been an attractive proposition—more attractive, in fact, than doing so in economic affairs. As Parsons himself notes, the draft EDC treaty went a long way toward replacing individual nation-states with a supranational arrangement: "[It] was filled with references to supranationality . . . and the goal of 'superimposing a broader European patriotism over national patriotisms.' It provided for negotiations of an additional 'European political authority' to guide the army." The community was, then, a "huge step in federal-style unification."[299] It would, in other words, go further than the coal and steel pool toward transcending the nation-state system in Europe.

Given the anticipated effects of establishing a defense community, Parsons cannot explain the depth and extent of opposition to the EDC. He cannot, for example, account for the fact that most of the French political elite—he claims that the pro-integration group amounted to "Schuman, Monnet, Alphand, and their scattered supporters"—objected to an arrangement that was "supranational" and "equality-based." Nor can he explain why "no political majority, bureaucratic elite, or interest group coalition . . . [drove] the transformation of the Pleven Plan into the EDC." Finally, the ideational argument cannot be squared with the fact that most Frenchmen viewed the prospect of a "European State . . . with horror."[300] If the French were intent on transcending the nation-state system, there should have been little opposition to a "supranational" and "equality-based" European army, strong support for the transformation of the Pleven Plan into the EDC, and a powerful desire to build a "European State."

Conclusion

There is good evidence that my theory can account for the EDC case. West German support for the European army project clearly reflected balance of power thinking. Adenauer was acutely aware that the Soviet Union was an

298. Parsons, *Certain*, 75–81.
299. Ibid., 69, 72.
300. Ibid., 75, 82–83.

overwhelming competitor and that France and Germany would have to establish a centralized military force if they were to balance against the Russians effectively. Moreover, he supported integration because an arrangement of this kind promised to establish rough military parity between Germany and France and give the Germans joint control of the coalition, thereby increasing their decision-making power. The British, on the other hand, were less endangered than the continental powers. They therefore supported Franco-German integration because it would provide them with defense in depth on the continent but made it clear they would not join themselves since doing so entailed a surrender of sovereignty.

With the Germans in favor and the British refusing to become involved, it fell to the French to determine the fate of military integration. Had a purely European solution been their only choice, they would likely have opted for an integrated force. It would have been the only arrangement that established a powerful bulwark against the Soviet Union while maintaining a rough balance of power between France and Germany. This kind of thinking, in fact, led the French to sign the EDC treaty. Even while they were negotiating it, however, they concluded that an Atlantic solution would establish a more favorable balance of power by arraying greater resources against Germany and the Soviet Union at little cost to French sovereignty. And if they could supplement this with an embryonic European defense community, they would ensure themselves against a future American withdrawal from the continent. As it happened, the Americans and the British met these desiderata by agreeing to the NATO-WEU alternative, and France's flirtation with a European army came to an end.

In contrast, the domestic interest group and ideational entrepreneurship arguments cannot account for the failure of the EDC. France and Germany were highly militarily interdependent in the early 1950s and the defense community offered the Europeans an opportunity to move toward replacing the nation-state system with a supranational union. Thus, the two arguments logically predict that the European army project should have ended in success rather than failure.

In sum, balance of power politics calculations appear to explain why the Europeans did not complement their industrial pool with an integrated defense community. Within months of the EDC debacle, however, they embarked on negotiations that would ultimately lead to the establishment of the European Economic Community. It is to an analysis of those events that I now turn.

5. Triumph

Economic Integration, 1955–1957

In the early 1950s, the coal and steel pool was the exception: the Europeans preferred to cooperate rather than establish supranational institutions and integrate their economies.[1] Then in May 1955, only months after the French National Assembly had voted down the European army project, the Benelux states called on their neighbors to "make a fresh advance toward European integration" by constructing a common market and establishing common policies for transport, energy, and peaceful uses of atomic energy.[2] France, West Germany, and Italy took up the Benelux offer, and on June 3, 1955, the Six issued the Messina Resolution in which they declared their desire to "work for the establishment of a united Europe by the development of common institutions, the progressive fusion of national economies, [and] the creation of a common market."[3] They convened a committee of experts headed by Belgian foreign minister Paul-Henri Spaak and tasked it with working out the finer points of the common market as well as an

---

1. I use the term "economic integration" to describe the result of the treaty establishing the EEC in March 1957. In doing so, I distinguish what happened in the late 1950s from the narrower "sectoral" or "heavy-industry" integration involved in setting up the ECSC.

2. For an account of developments prior to Messina, see Pierre Gerbet, "La 'relance' européenne jusqu'à la conférence de Messine," in *La relance européenne et les Traités de Rome*, ed. Enrico Serra (Brussels: Bruylant, 1989), 61–91.

3. The Benelux Memorandum and Messina Resolution are reproduced in Howard Bliss, ed., *The Political Development of the European Community: A Documentary Collection* (Waltham, Mass.: Blaisdell, 1970), 34–39.

atomic energy community.[4] Initially, the British participated in the talks, but they pulled out before the end of the year.

The Spaak Committee completed its report in April 1956, and at the end of the following month the foreign ministers of the Six met in Venice and agreed to begin negotiations aimed at the creation of the European Economic Community, at the core of which lay a common market and a European Atomic Energy Community (Euratom). Negotiations, including several crucial high-level meetings between France and the Federal Republic, took place over the course of the next nine months, and on March 25, 1957, the Six signed the Treaties of Rome establishing the EEC and Euratom. As finally crafted, the EEC treaty set a framework for the creation of a common market and the establishment of a common agricultural policy and embedded it "in a set of quasi-constitutional institutions unique among international organizations."[5] Euratom, however, was "gradually eviscerated" in the course of the negotiations and "was diluted to a minor collaboration."[6]

This chapter is structured around four questions: Why did the Europeans not achieve economic integration in the late 1940s and early 1950s? Why did the Federal Republic welcome the Benelux proposal in 1955 and make substantial concessions to France in order to establish the EEC? Why did the French agree to create a supranational common market so soon after rejecting the defense community and then carry through on their commitment? And why did the British initially join the discussions, quickly pull out, and then propose a competing European industrial free trade area (FTA) in October 1956, before finally seeking to associate their own economic grouping with the common market?

These events, I argue, are best understood as the product of balance of power politics. Specifically, the global distribution of power made European cooperation possible, and the major protagonists endorsed or refused integration based on balance of power calculations.

The international distribution of capabilities made European cooperation possible. As minor powers confronted by an overwhelming competitor in the form of the Soviet Union, the Europeans feared for their survival. Moreover, although it was clear that they could not hope to stand up to the USSR on their own, they did have the combined capability to build a viable balancing coalition. It is unlikely that they would have been able to

---

4. For an account of the Spaak Committee's deliberations, see Michel Dumoulin, "Les travaux du comité Spaak (juillet 1955–avril 1956)," in *La relance européenne et les Traités de Rome*, ed. Enrico Serra (Brussels: Bruylant, 1989), 195–210. Because the customs union proposal developed into a common market during the course of the negotiations, I use the two terms interchangeably throughout.

5. Andrew Moravcsik, *The Choice for Europe: Social Purpose and State Power from Messina to Maastricht* (Ithaca: Cornell University Press, 1998), 86.

6. Craig Parsons, *A Certain Idea of Europe* (Ithaca: Cornell University Press, 2003), 109, 114. See also Moravcsik, *Choice*, 120.

establish one, however, without the American commitment to defend them from the Soviet Union while they put it in place. This protection was not guaranteed over the long term. Indeed, much of the impetus to join forces and establish an independent west European combination can be attributed to the fact that the American security guarantee was uncertain. But, at least in the short term, it provided them with an opportunity to establish a credible counterweight to Soviet power.

Within these structural constraints, officials in Paris and Bonn opted for integration to balance against the Soviet Union and one another. The key decision makers understood that the Soviet Union was an overwhelmingly powerful state and that they could hope to compete with it only if they too were to construct their own centrally organized unit of power. Even as they were driven to this conclusion, however, they were determined not to surrender control to one another, believing this might be the prelude to the within-coalition balance of power shifting against them. Therefore, because they were fairly evenly matched, France and Germany both concluded that the most they could demand, and the most they would concede, was joint control of the group. Simply put, they understood that by integrating and forming a community they would be instantiating and perpetuating a roughly even within-coalition distribution of power.

The British, meanwhile, faced a different geopolitical situation. Because they were less vulnerable than their continental allies, they continued to support continental integration efforts as a means to provide them with defense in depth on the continent. But they saw no reason to surrender their autonomy and actually participate in the emerging community. The sovereignty concessions required to establish a viable counterweight to Soviet power would have to be made by the more endangered continental states.

Motive, Means, and Opportunity, 1955–1957

If my balance of power theory is correct, the west Europeans must have confronted essentially the same geopolitical situation after 1955 that they faced between 1945 and 1954. Specifically, there should be good evidence that the Soviet Union continued to be an overwhelmingly powerful adversary, that the states of western Europe had the combined capability to balance against it effectively, and that the Russians could not prevent them from combining their efforts.

Motive

The Soviet Union continued to be an overwhelming competitor between 1955 and 1960. Despite reducing its military forces from approximately six million men in 1955 to less than four million in 1960, the USSR remained vastly superior to its western neighbors. In the second half of the decade, its military advantage over Britain and France was consistently greater than 6:1, and it had an enormous advantage over a slowly rearming Federal Republic (see table 1). Clearly, none of the west European states had the wherewithal to put up a good fight against the Soviets in an all-out conventional war. Secretary of State John Foster Dulles believed that the Soviet Union was so powerful that "not even the United States, could, out of its own resources, adequately match the strength of a powerful totalitarian state." Any attempt to do so would "bust us."[7]

The Soviet Union's economic growth was a matter of even greater concern. Between 1955 and 1960, Russia's industrial advantage over Britain grew from 2:1 to almost 3:1, its advantage over France grew from almost 4:1 to almost 5:1, and its advantage over the Federal Republic of Germany increased to more than 2.5:1. That this happened when France and West Germany were experiencing their own so-called economic miracles was truly remarkable and did not go unnoticed. In December 1955, State Department officials observed that "despite present surface evidences of recovery, boom, prosperity and growth in Western Europe, the USSR will, by 1975, have overtaken Western Europe's aggregate GNP, unless political and economic decisions are made to increase its power and accelerate its growth."[8] Six months later, Dulles informed the Germans that the situation was bleak. The Soviets had "a rate of industrial growth which is more rapid than that of Western Europe." Moreover, the situation was likely to get worse: "The USSR is transforming itself rapidly . . . into a modern and efficient industrial state." Indeed, he "thought that at the present time the economic danger from the Soviet Union was perhaps greater than the military danger."[9]

In short, the USSR posed an overwhelming threat to western Europe. Given its military and economic superiority, none of the region's former great powers could deter or defeat it alone. Moreover, all indications were that nothing would change in the medium term—because the Soviet economy was growing rapidly, it was likely to maintain its advantage for years to come. Consequently, the incentive to form a balancing coalition remained as powerful as ever.

Means

Although none of them could balance against the Soviet Union on their own, a coalition of European states would be powerful enough to form an

7. Quoted in Marc Trachtenberg, *History and Strategy* (Princeton: Princeton University Press, 1991), 139.

8. Memorandum Prepared in the Office of European Regional Affairs, December 6, 1955, *Foreign Relations of the United States* (hereafter *FRUS*), 1955–1957, vol. 4 (Washington, D.C.: GPO, 1986), 355.

9. Memorandum of a Conversation, Department of State, June 12, 1956, *FRUS*, 1955–1957, vol. 26, 116, 119.

effective counterweight to it. West Germany was still in the early stages of rearmament in the late 1950s, but assuming it would be able to devote the same fraction of its population to building military forces as France, a big three coalition would be weaker militarily but roughly equal to the Soviet Union in economic terms (see table 1). In terms of overall (military plus economic) power, the coalition would be at approximately a 1.5:1 disadvantage to the Russians. A putative continental coalition would also match up well against the Soviet Union and even at its weakest—in 1955—would certainly not have been on the wrong end of a gross power mismatch.

American planners remained convinced that a united Europe would be able to balance effectively against the Soviet Union. President Dwight Eisenhower voiced the conventional wisdom at a NSC meeting in November 1955, arguing that western Europe could become a "solid power mass," or "third great power bloc." So great was its potential, in fact, that its creation would allow the United States "to sit back and relax somewhat" in the cold war.[10] Similarly, he told Major General Alfred Gruenther that he "never doubt[ed] for a minute" that a federated western Europe "would be automatically . . . a third great power complex in the world."[11] As his subordinates noted, the president was convinced that a unified Europe "would constitute a focus of power, in addition to the US and USSR, which would greatly advance the material and moral well-being of European peoples and the security interests of the United States." A few months later, Eisenhower made the point personally to French prime minister René Mayer: "A united Europe consisting of 250 million-odd people, of whom at least 23 million were skilled workers, would create an industrial complex comparable to the United States." It would constitute a "third force" in the world. He relayed the same message to Franz Etzel, who was soon to become Germany's minister of finance, noting that he "strongly supported a united Europe as a third great force in the world."[12]

Dulles pressed the same message in his own meetings with the Europeans. In a conversation with the Germans in May 1956, he announced that the United States supported a common market, because "with the common market Europe would be a third world force along with the US and the Soviet Union." In the absence of unity, however, Europe would "remain weak."[13] Meeting with Chancellor Konrad Adenauer soon after the signing

10. Meeting of the National Security Council, November 21, 1955, *FRUS*, 1955–1957, vol. 19, 150–51.

11. Eisenhower to Gruenther, December 2, 1955, *The Presidential Papers of Dwight David Eisenhower* (hereafter *PPDDE*), vol. 16 (Baltimore: Johns Hopkins University Press, 1970), 1919–20.

12. Memorandum Prepared in the Office of European Regional Affairs, December 6, 1955, Memorandum of a Conversation, February 8, 1956, and Memorandum of a Conversation, February 6, 1957, *FRUS*, 1955–1957, vol. 4, 355, 409, 517.

13. Memorandum of a Conversation, May 14, 1956, ibid., 441.

of the Rome Treaties, he reiterated the point, warning that although the American public was not prepared to incur the costs of supporting a weak and divided Europe, the United States would be a firm friend of a united Europe because such a unit "could be as powerful as the United States or the Soviet Union."[14] Privately, he told American officials that if the west Europeans were to integrate, they "could remove the burden of Europe from the back of the United States . . . and constitute a unified pool of power to balance the USSR." After all, they certainly had the "people and resources so that they can be a real force in the world."[15]

Opportunity

As had been the case since the defeat of Nazi Germany, the Soviet Union opposed the construction of a powerful "third force" in the western half of the continent. Early in 1954, when it was already clear that the French were unlikely to ratify the EDC, Soviet foreign minister Vyacheslav Molotov publicly denounced the idea that "any part of Germany could be part of a group like the European Defense Community, which is clearly a military bloc uniting certain European countries against the others." There was a "complete incompatibility" between Germany's membership in the EDC and European security, he argued, before warning that it could lead to a "new war in Europe."[16] The creation of the common market elicited similar hostility. *Pravda* decried it as the economic counterpart of NATO and suggested that it was part and parcel of an "aggressive North Atlantic bloc." Similarly, General Secretary of the Communist Party Nikita Khrushchev denounced European integration as a project that "menaces the vital interests of all peoples and the cause of peace in the world." Meanwhile, Soviet officials went out of their way to wreck the community by playing to French fears and asserting that integration strengthened West Germany at the expense of France. The common market and Euratom, they argued, would "represent a new and dangerous step on the road to reestablishing German domination in Western Europe."[17] In short, as Marie-Pierre Rey notes, the Soviets may have condemned and sought to sabotage the ECSC

---

14. Memorandum of a Conversation, May 4, 1957, *FRUS*, 1955–1957, vol. 26, 240.

15. Memorandum of a Conversation, January 25, 1956, and Verbatim Minutes of the Western European Chiefs of Mission Conference, May 6, 1957, *FRUS*, 1955–1957, vol. 4, 391, 587.

16. Quoted in Marie-Pierre Rey, "L'URSS et la sécurité européenne de 1953 à 1956," *Communisme* nos. 49–50 (1997): 128–29.

17. Quoted in Marie-Pierre Rey, "Le retour à l'Europe? Les décideurs soviétiques face à l'intégration ouest-européenne, 1957–1991," *Journal of European Integration History* 11, no. 1 (2005): 8–9.

and EDC, but it was "the signature of the treaties of 1957 [that] crystallized their opposition to community projects" in western Europe.[18]

Given this opposition, it was the American security guarantee that prevented the Russians from taking concrete measures to derail west European unity. There were two elements to the guarantee. First, the United States kept between three and four hundred thousand ground forces in Europe between 1955 and 1960.[19] When these troops were added to those provided by the west Europeans themselves, they provided an important deterrent to Soviet aggression. Second, and more important, the Russians were deterred by America's atomic superiority. In 1958, the United States had 1,620 bombers capable of delivering 2,610 warheads, while the Soviet Union had just 85 bombers armed with 250 warheads. Moreover, the United States had 4,122 tactical weapons, while the Soviets had only 600. Given this advantage and the United States' commitment—from December 1954 onward—to the rapid and massive use of nuclear weapons in the event of an attack on western Europe, the Soviets could not threaten or use force to prevent the Europeans from building a powerful balancing coalition.[20]

Although they continued to deter the Soviet Union on western Europe's behalf, the Americans did not plan to remain on the continent longer than they had to.[21] Eisenhower, noted his staff secretary Andrew Goodpaster in the fall of 1956, "considers—as he has from the beginning of the NATO build-up—that the U.S. reinforcements sent to Europe were provided to bridge the crisis period during which European forces were building up."[22] Eighteen months later, the president told NSC officials that he was determined to "bring pressure all around the world so that the local forces in all these countries constitute the first line of defense," while the United States acted as a sort of "mobile reserve."[23] The stationing of American forces in Europe had been a "stop-gap, temporary operation" until the Europeans could "carry their full weight."[24] Indeed, Eisenhower became quite disen-

---

18. Ibid., 7. See also Andrei Grachev, "The Soviet Leadership's View of Western European Integration in the 1950s and 1960s," in *Widening, Deepening and Acceleration: The European Economic Community, 1957–1963*, ed. Anne Deighton and Alan S. Milward (Baden-Baden: Nomos, 1999), 36–38.

19. Daniel J. Nelson, *A History of U.S. Military Forces in Germany* (Boulder, Colo.: Westview, 1987), 81.

20. See Keir A. Lieber, *War and the Engineers: The Primacy of Politics over Technology* (Ithaca: Cornell University Press, 2005), 134–40; and Marc Trachtenberg, *A Constructed Peace: The Making of the European Settlement* (Princeton: Princeton University Press, 1999), 156–69. The warhead figures in this paragraph are from the Natural Resources Defense Council, http://www.nrdc.org/nuclear/nudb/datainx.asp.

21. For this argument, see Trachtenberg, *Constructed*, 146–56.

22. Memorandum from Goodpaster to Dulles, October 2, 1956, *FRUS*, 1955–1957, vol. 19, 360.

23. Memorandum of Discussion at the 400th Meeting of the National Security Council, March 26, 1959, *FRUS*, 1958–1960, vol. 7, 445.

24. Memorandum of Conference with Eisenhower, November 16, 1959, ibid., 519.

chanted with the situation during his second term. As he told American officials in December 1958, he had become "discouraged at the continuing pressure for the retention of sizeable U.S. forces" in Europe.[25] The Europeans were close to "making a sucker out of Uncle Sam," and although he had been happy to provide them with "emergency help" in the past, "that time had passed."[26] The United States must find a way to withdraw its forces from Europe.

Dulles continued to hold basically the same view. In a National Security Council meeting in July 1955, "he said that of course our true objective was to get out of Europe."[27] Then, early in 1957, he laid out his perspective in greater detail. American forces had been sent to Europe as an "emergency measure" and that situation had, unfortunately, "become permanent." But he was not prepared to accept the status quo. The west Europeans ought to be responsible for dealing with "local defense on the ground" and the United States should only have to come in "with air and naval forces."[28] In other words, while Dulles understood that there could be a dire situation in which the Americans would have to respond to a Soviet attack with nuclear weapons, he wanted the Europeans to take primary responsibility for their own security.

Coupled with its short-term security guarantee, the American desire to withdraw from the continent gave the Europeans a strong incentive to build a formidable balancing coalition. Without the security guarantee, they could not have considered establishing a coalition at all—the Soviet Union would likely have threatened or used force to prevent them from coming together. At the same time, the uncertainty surrounding the U.S. commitment over the long term meant that the Europeans had good reason to begin providing for their own security, a consideration that led ineluctably to a decision to join forces.

In sum, the west Europeans had the motive, means, and opportunity to build a balancing coalition against the Soviet Union between 1955 and 1957. They continued to confront an overwhelming competitor, had the wherewithal if they combined their resources to establish a formidable coalition, and could count on the United States to hold the Soviet Union at bay in the short term while they put it in place. In the remainder of this chapter, I show that the Europeans chose to cooperate with one another based on their assessment of the balance of power—that is, that they cooperated because they wanted to balance against the Soviet Union and recognized that

25. Quoted in Robert J. Art, "A Defensible Defense: America's Grand Strategy after the Cold War," *International Security* 15, no. 4 (1991): 23, n. 36.

26. Memorandum of Conference with Eisenhower, November 4, 1959, *FRUS*, 1958–1960, vol. 7, 498.

27. Memorandum of Discussion at the 254th Meeting of the National Security Council, July 7, 1955, *FRUS*, 1955–1957, vol. 5, 274.

28. Memorandum of Discussion at the 314th Meeting of the National Security Council, February 28, 1957, *FRUS*, 1955–1957, vol. 19, 429.

they had the means and temporary opportunity to do so. Moreover, I show that balance of power calculations prompted France and Germany to select a particular variant of cooperation, namely integration, and more specifically that these calculations resulted in the formation of the common market.

Economic Integration before 1955

Before turning to the common market negotiations, a few words are in order regarding the European failure to engage in economic integration prior to 1955. Given that the Europeans were operating in broadly the same strategic environment in the late 1940s as they were in the late 1950s, why did they not build a supranational common market or something like it in the years immediately after World War II?

There is compelling evidence that the timing of integration was a function of balance of power politics. As we have seen, the Federal Republic committed to the principle of integration early in the postwar period and staunchly supported economic integration from the late 1940s onward. In contrast, the British refused to become involved in any economic integration initiatives during this period. Given this split, the French determined the fate of economic integration prior to 1955. Like the Germans, they were convinced of the need to establish a centralized unit of power to balance against the Soviet Union, and they were strong supporters of integration as a means of maintaining rough equality with the Federal Republic. This was the logic underlying the Schuman Plan, and it meant that the French were committed to the principle of integration in the decade after the war. In practice, however, French decision makers believed that their economy was so weak that anything more than sectoral integration might cause its collapse rather than establishing and perpetuating the within-coalition equality of power that they hoped for. Therefore, Paris was unwilling to agree to economic integration prior to the publication of the Benelux Memorandum.

British Refusal

Britain's refusal to integrate extended beyond the industrial and military realms. Once again, the British did not oppose cooperation, but any agreement that required a diminution of sovereignty was out of the question. As a result, the United Kingdom consistently refused to be a party to any and all initiatives that had the potential to bring about economic integration in the late 1940s.

The British reaction to France's proposal of August 1947 that the west Europeans establish a customs union provides perhaps the best evidence of their refusal to countenance economic integration for themselves. The

French proposal was, in many ways, quite innocuous. France indicated that it would take years for a customs union to come into being and suggested that members simply look to the harmonization of national tariffs in the short term. Moreover, British officials believed that Paris was more interested in appeasing the Americans, who wanted to see evidence of economic cooperation in Europe, than in moving quickly to the creation of a customs union. Nevertheless, had the French proposal been adopted, it would have taken the Europeans some way down the path to integration and certainly further than they had been to that point. The thinking in London was that "since a customs union would affect the whole economy, it would probably necessitate a *full economic union*, with results that were hard to estimate."[29]

In response, the British worked hard to ensure that the customs union discussions did not move in a supranational direction. Soon after learning of the French proposal, they persuaded the delegates to the Committee on European Economic Cooperation (CEEC) to establish a European Customs Union Study Group (ECUSG) tasked with discussing the possibility of creating a customs union, but without entering into any formal commitments. Then, in November 1947, they began to slow play the issue by persuading the ECUSG to undertake a comprehensive study of all the possible ramifications of a customs union, a project they confidently predicted would take months to complete. Finally, when the ECUSG met for the third time in March 1948, they suggested that any further discussion of commercial matters should proceed through the intergovernmental OEEC. This request was reiterated in November, whereupon the negotiations collapsed.[30]

Britain's position on economic integration was therefore consistent with its attitude toward integration in other issue areas. Decision makers in London were prepared to cooperate with their continental allies but would go no further and ruled out integration in the form of a supranational customs union. To be sure, there were economic arguments against joining a customs union. As Ambassador Duff Cooper noted, "The mere words 'customs union' produce a shudder in the Treasury and nausea in the Board of Trade." But it was the issue of sovereignty that was determinative. In a memorandum for the Cabinet in January 1947, Foreign Secretary Ernest Bevin asserted that a customs union would probably be economically beneficial, but would also mean an unacceptable loss of policymaking independence. Britain ought to seek looser forms of cooperation since "it may be doubted whether democratic governments, in spite of the economic advantages which the Union might bring with it, can give to an international body the

29. John W. Young, *Britain, France and the Unity of Europe, 1945–1951* (Leicester: Leicester University Press, 1984), 69. Emphasis in original.

30. Wendy Asbeek Brusse, *Tariffs, Trade, and European Integration, 1947–1957: From Study Group to Common Market* (New York: St. Martin's, 1997), 57–60; and Young, *Britain*, 118–22.

ultimate power to . . . exercise some of the . . . controls outlined."[31] By 1948, when the customs union issue was squarely on the table, this position was unquestioned in London: Britain could not accept the creation of supranational authorities that might override British interests and insisted that ultimate control must remain in the hands of member states. "Anything in the nature of a formal customs union or federation," declared Bevin, "was out of the question."[32]

German Enthusiasm

Convinced that integration provided the surest means to balancing against the Soviet Union and establishing parity with France, the Germans were ardent advocates of economic integration from the beginning. Less than six months after the creation of the Federal Republic, Adenauer launched arguably the most ambitious plan for economic integration in the postwar period. At first blush, it seems that he was calling for more than mere integration in his interview with Benedict Kingsbury-Smith on March 7, 1950. What he was suggesting was a "complete Union of France and Germany" that would in time become a "foundation stone for the United States of Europe." There are, however, two reasons to doubt the credibility of his call for complete political and economic union. First, he admitted that his plan "would be difficult to put into practice," and that he was more interested in putting forward "bold ideas" and taking a "visible and decisive step" than making any practical recommendations. Second, there is probably some truth to the French suspicion that he was using the interview to ingratiate himself with the United States and pressure France to return the Saar to Germany.[33]

The best evidence that the chancellor was thinking specifically in terms of economic integration rather than a United States of Europe comes from a follow-up interview that he had with Kingsbury-Smith on March 21. When pressed to outline his plans, he recalled the "formation of the German customs union and the establishment of a customs parliament which ensured the free exchange of goods between those many [German] states" after the Napoleonic Wars. What he had in mind was a similar entity comprising France and Germany: "A start could be made with the gradual merger of the two countries with regard to tariffs and the economy. The instrument for such a union might be a common economic parliament to be formed by members of the two countries' legislative bodies. Both governments could decide on a body that would hold joint responsibility with the economic parliament." Here, then, was the blueprint for economic integration, in-

31. Quoted in Sean Greenwood, *Britain and European Cooperation since 1945* (Oxford: Blackwell, 1992), 16.
32. Quoted in Brusse, *Tariffs*, 59.
33. Konrad Adenauer, *Memoirs* (Chicago: Henry Regnery, 1966), 244–45.

cluding the claim that cooperation of this kind could lead to "unification" and the suggestion that France and Germany "work together and . . . carry joint responsibility."[34]

It is clear, then, that the Federal Republic's support for integration extended to the entire economy. Indeed, the depth of Adenauer's commitment was shown by the fact that he was prepared to express these views publicly when the other European states had grave doubts about Germany's reliability and intentions and might therefore view his announcement in a threatening light.

France: Support in Principle, Reservations in Practice

In the late 1940s, the French gradually came to the conclusion that they could only balance effectively against the Soviet Union and West Germany if they built an integrated west European economy. This kind of thinking resulted in five initiatives between 1947 and 1950: the Franco-Italian Customs Union, the European Customs Union, the Fritalux-Finebel proposal, and the Petsche and Buron plans. Each of them gestured toward economic integration. But there was an important practical problem with going down this road: the French economy might collapse if exposed to German competition. Economic integration implied the reduction of barriers to exchange and most officials believed that the French economy would be seriously damaged by such liberalization and the competition that would ensue. Indeed, integration might well lead to German domination rather than to a rough equality at the heart of the European coalition. As a result, the French backed away from economic integration in each case with the intention of revisiting the issue when their economy became more competitive.

Paris considered several integration plans in the early postwar period. The earliest was the Franco-Italian Customs Union, mooted in July 1947 and signed in March 1949. Although this was a simple bilateral treaty and the French Economic Council immediately rejected it in April 1949 on the grounds that it did not make economic sense, it is worth noting that some officials expected the union to lay the foundation for a wider west European entity. Thus in August 1947, Hervé Alphand, the director general of economic and financial affairs at the Foreign Ministry, suggested that Paris and Rome announce their intention to establish a customs union open to the other states of western Europe. The following year the Italians declared that, like the French, they "conceived of the idea of the Union not as an end in itself but rather as a reasonable central nucleus to put us on the road to larger economic constellations."[35]

34. Ibid., 246–47.

35. Quoted in Enrico Serra, "L'unione doganale italo-francese e la conferenza di Santa Margherita (1947–1951)," in *Italia e Francia (1946–1954)*, ed. Jean-Baptiste Duroselle and Enrico Serra (Milan: Franco Angeli, 1988), 81. See also Pierre Guillen, "Le

The next French initiative, announced in August 1947, was more obviously regional in scope. France was prepared to negotiate with any government that wanted to form a European customs union. The French declaration of intent may not have been entirely sincere, but two customs union proposals in two months suggest at least some interest in exploring the possibility of European economic integration. It is also important that despite difficulties on the domestic front and fear of Soviet reprisals, Alphand informed the Benelux delegates that a customs union could eventually include western Germany.[36]

Just as in the case of heavy industry, France began to think seriously about economic integration in 1949. First came the Fritalux-Finebel plan, which aimed at the removal of quantitative restrictions on the movement of capital, labor, and goods in several sectors.[37] Although the plan originally involved France, Italy, Belgium, and Luxembourg, by the end of the year West German participation was explicitly considered. This was not a full-blown plan for economic integration—there was limited provision for supranational control and members were required only to liberalize certain sectors—but no previous initiative had gone so far in an integrative direction. As Secretary of State Dean Acheson remarked in May 1950, the coal and steel community proposal was "consistent with . . . [the] basic features [of the] Finebel approach."[38]

The next proposal, the Petsche Plan of July 1950, called for member states to remove quotas from a selected list of products and for the creation of a European investment bank tasked with allocating capital to modernize the enterprises that emerged from the ensuing competition.[39] Again, this was a recommendation to expose only selected sectors to competition, but the plan covered a wider range of sectors than the coal and steel proposal and the addition of a European bank implied some supranational management of the process. Indeed, the British viewed the proposal as an "eco-

projet d'union économique entre la France, l'Italie et le Benelux," in *Histoire des débuts de la construction européenne (mars 1948–mai 1950)*, ed. Raymond Poidevin (Brussels: Bruylant, 1986), 143–49; Frances M. B. Lynch, *France and the International Economy: From Vichy to the Treaty of Rome* (New York: Routledge, 1997), 104–7; and Alain Quagliarini, "La nouvelle donne allemande dans les relations franco-italiennes 1949–1951," *Revue d'histoire moderne et contemporaine* 42, no. 4 (1995): 622–57.

36. Brusse, *Tariffs*, 58. See also Michael J. Hogan, *The Marshall Plan: America, Britain, and the Reconstruction of Western Europe, 1947–1952* (Cambridge: Cambridge University Press, 1987), 60–69; and Lynch, *France*, 104–7.

37. On Fritalux-Finebel, see Brusse, *Tariffs*, 60–63; Richard T. Griffiths and Frances M. B. Lynch, "L'échec de la 'petite Europe': Les négociations Fritalux/Finebel, 1949–1950," *Revue historique* no. 555 (1985): 159–93; and Lynch, *France*, 119–22.

38. Acheson to Webb, May 12, 1950, *FRUS*, 1950, vol. 3, 697.

39. On the Petsche Plan, see Gérard Bossuat, *La France, l'aide américaine et la construction européenne, 1944–1954*, vol. 1 (Paris: Imprimerie nationale, 1992), 729–31; and Lynch, *France*, 131–32.

nomic manifestation" of the continental drift toward federation and noted its emphasis on supranational regulation.

Finally, the Buron Plan of December 1950 called for liberalization in certain sectors, as well as the creation of a High Political Authority, an investment bank, and an integration fund. In so doing, it explicitly extended the ECSC model beyond coal and steel to other parts of the economy.[40]

Although they gave careful thought to economic integration, the French ultimately shied away from a Schuman Plan kind of initiative because they feared this would lead to German domination rather than a relatively even Franco-German balance of power. This calculation was certainly at play in the European customs union case. The French supported it, observes Michael Hogan, because they "could work to reduce Germany's prewar tariffs and yet retain the quantitative restrictions on competitive German imports. . . . This was one way to contain Germany."[41]

A similar logic applied to the Finebel project: as the negotiations progressed, it became clear that the French would go ahead only if they could secure numerous guarantees designed to prevent German domination of the group. The French were "cautious and protectionist," observed the Americans, and were working hard to install mechanisms that would constitute "a second line of defense" against the Germans once import quotas and exchange controls were lifted. Meanwhile, Paul Hoffman, the head of the Economic Cooperation Administration (ECA), chastised the French for "dividing" rather than "expanding" markets.[42] Pierre Guillen offers a neat summary of the situation: Finebel was designed to "accustom French industry to competition by a progressive and prudent liberalization of exchanges with France's neighbors."[43]

This cautious approach was also evident in the Petsche and Buron proposals. Both insisted on liberalizing a common but limited list of products under certain conditions in the hope that this would protect the French economy from all-out competition. As Gérard Bossuat has explained, the Schuman and Petsche plans aimed for the same result: "liberalization but with guarantees."[44]

French policymakers clearly had these concerns in mind when deciding how to proceed. According to Bernard Clappier, the director of the cabinet at the Foreign Ministry, the Schuman Plan had succeeded and, presumably,

40. On the Buron Plan, see Bossuat, *France,* 731–32; and Lynch, *France,* 132–33.

41. Hogan, *Marshall,* 65.

42. Quoted in ibid., 281.

43. Guillen, "Projet," 156–57.

44. Gérard Bossuat, "La politique française de libération des échanges en Europe et le Plan Schuman (1950–1951)," in *Die Anfänge des Schuman-Plans 1950–51,* ed. Klaus Schwabe (Baden-Baden: Nomos, 1988), 323. For a similar argument to the one in this paragraph, see Frances M. B. Lynch, "Restoring France: The Road to Integration," in *The Frontier of National Sovereignty: History and Theory 1945–1992,* ed. Alan S. Milward et al. (London: Routledge, 1993), 61–64.

other proposals had failed because it applied to a "restricted domain" in which "precautions could be taken."[45] Jean Monnet and Foreign Minister Robert Schuman shared this caution. The former stressed that the French should focus on their "plan of national effort" before thinking about a "plan of cooperation." France must restore its own economic base before integrating with other states and with Germany in particular. "Cooperation is certainly necessary," he told the cabinet in July 1948, "but it will come later and lean on the national efforts that will precede it and prepare the way for it."[46] Similarly, although Schuman ultimately hoped to establish a single European economy, he believed it would be impossible to integrate "all the sectors of the European economy simultaneously." The reason he opted for coal and steel integration only was that "these two key industries included a restricted number of firms" and it was therefore "possible to coordinate them without excessive difficulties."[47]

Events soon appeared to confirm the wisdom of the French decision to avoid precipitate economic integration.[48] Their brief flirtation with liberalization, which began in late 1949, provoked an economic crisis. By early 1952, when Prime Minister Edgar Faure's government reimposed all quantitative restrictions on trade that had been lifted over the previous two-and-a-half years, France's budget deficit had exploded and inflation had risen above 25 percent. Such was the damage wrought by liberalization, in fact, that it was late 1952 before inflation started to fall and France's balance of trade position began to recover. The lesson the French took from these events was clear: their economy was not ready for major liberalization. This protectionist consensus went unchallenged until the publication of the Benelux Memorandum, as Parsons explains: "Support for this stance was consistent through the Mayer, Laniel, Mendès France, and Faure governments and was almost the only consensual view in Faure's Cabinet in 1955."[49]

Given this kind of thinking, the French were bound to reject the Beyen Plan, a Dutch proposal of February 1953 that called for a supranational customs union that would be combined with the ECSC and EDC in a European Political Community.[50] The French reaction was predictable: because

45. Quoted in Pierre Gerbet, "Les origines du Plan Schuman: Le choix de la méthode communautaire par le gouvernement français," in *Histoire des débuts de la construction européenne (mars 1948–mai 1950)*, ed. Raymond Poidevin (Brussels: Bruylant, 1986), 222.

46. Quoted in Bossuat, *France*, 624.

47. Robert Schuman, *Pour l'Europe* (Paris: Editions Nagel, 1963), 158, 163.

48. For background on this period, see Lynch, *France*, 128–45; and Paul M. Pitman, "France's European Choices: The Political Economy of European Integration in the 1950s" (PhD diss., Columbia University, 1997), 34–67.

49. Parsons, *Certain*, 99.

50. On the Beyen Plan, see Richard T. Griffiths, "The Beyen Plan," in *The Netherlands and the Integration of Europe 1945–1957*, ed. Richard T. Griffiths (Amsterdam: Neha, 1990); Brusse, *Tariffs*, 147–57; and Lynch, *France*, 137–45.

they could not compete in an integrated west European economy of this kind, they could not entertain it. Instead, they determined that the best course of action was to continue to build up their industry behind protectionist barriers until it could compete effectively with the other European states. Mayer's government quickly rejected the plan while the Quai allowed discussions to continue in the belief that the negotiations would highlight the myriad problems associated with giving up economic sovereignty. Then, in March 1954, the French imposed the "super tariff" designed to cushion French industry from the effects of liberalization and fund the modernization of marginal firms. As Wendy Asbeek Brusse has noted, "France could hardly have expressed more clearly that it rejected surrendering its tariffs, which was the essence of Beyen's Plan."[51]

In conclusion, although the French understood the need for economic integration based on balance of power reasoning, they worried about its practical effects. Officials in Paris feared that the French economy would not be able to compete with West Germany's, and that this would upset the balance of power in the western half of the continent. This being the case, they rejected economic integration in the late 1940s and early 1950s. And because only the Germans were enthusiastic about it, the French decision effectively killed any movement in that direction before Messina.

France: Opting for Integration, 1955–1957

Both the Faure government, which held power between February 1955 and January 1956, and Guy Mollet's government, which followed it, endorsed the EEC for balance of power reasons. Their thinking can be briefly summarized. First, they continued to be deeply troubled by the Soviet threat and were resolved to establish a European coalition that included West Germany in order to balance against it. Second, they understood that any coalition must be centrally organized if it was to compete with the USSR effectively. Third, of the centralized arrangements that they could have chosen, they opted for integration because it promised to maintain the roughly even balance of economic power that obtained within western Europe at the time.

Balancing and Centralization

France remained committed to establishing a viable west European balancing coalition in the second half of the 1950s. The imperative of associating with West Germany was as strong as ever. "Without German economic and military support," observed the Quai in a memorandum for Foreign Minister Antoine Pinay before one of his meetings with Adenauer, "the Atlantic

51. Brusse, *Tariffs*, 151.

coalition cannot equal the power of the Sino-Soviet bloc of 800 million men that it is faced with. Such balance is both the condition for peace and for the survival of our conception of the world."[52] This was also Mollet's publicly expressed view in September 1955, almost six months before he became prime minister: "If the German Federal Republic ever becomes part of the Soviet world, all of Europe would before long be subjugated."[53] As Pinay himself observed, a "Franco-German understanding remains the essential condition" for progress toward the "organization of Western Europe."[54]

That the European coalition must be centrally organized was equally unquestioned. On April 12, 1955, Monnet informed the Americans "that the governments of the six CSC [coal and steel community] member countries, including the French, appear willing to take further steps towards creating a united Europe." That he meant centralized when he said united was clear from the context; unity would be achieved through the "extension" of the existing centralized "Community."[55] This was also Pinay's view in his conversations with the British a little more than a week later. France was committed to the "relaunch of the European idea," he told British foreign secretary Harold Macmillan. It was time to show the European publics that "the construction of Europe is not a utopia." Although he used different language, Pinay envisaged the same process as Monnet. The construction of western Europe would involve extending the ECSC model to transportation, conventional energy, and atomic energy.[56] A few months later, Mollet told the American Committee on United Europe that France's "guiding principle for the present is clear: to set in motion new plans for supranational or federal communities among 'the Six'."[57]

As had been the case since the end of the war, this commitment to centralization derived from the belief that only a coalition of this kind could match the superpowers. Monnet articulated the logic clearly in late 1954: "Our countries have become too small for today's world, at the level of modern techniques, at the measure of America and Russia. . . . The unity of the peoples of Europe united in the United States of Europe is the way to raise their standard of living and to maintain peace."[58]

Pinay agreed, and early in 1955 he assured Monnet that he would support the extension of the ECSC model to other sectors because there was

52. Political Desk Note, April 15, 1955, *Documents diplomatiques français* (hereafter *DDF*), 1955, vol. 1 (Paris: Imprimerie Nationale, 1987), 457.

53. Guy Mollet, *The New Drive for European Union* (Paris: American Committee on United Europe, 1955), 8.

54. Pinay to French Diplomatic Representatives Abroad, May 4, 1955, *DDF*, 1955, vol. 1, 573.

55. Memorandum from Merchant to Dulles, April 12, 1955, *FRUS*, 1955–1957, vol. 4, 279.

56. Summary of Conversation between Pinay and Macmillan, April 21, 1955, *DDF*, 1955, vol. 1, Annexes, 28.

57. Mollet, *New*, 9.

58. Quoted in Pierre Gerbet, *La construction de l'Europe* (Paris: Imprimerie Nationale, 1983), 192.

"no other way to save Europe's economy and its freedom."[59] Later, looking back at the events that had led to the construction of the common market, he recalled that he had been a "supporter of . . . Europe" because he was "aware that if we are caught between the two giants of the last war, we shall be crushed, while if we are united, we can talk as equals to equals."[60] Although these comments came after the Rome Treaties, they were probably sincere. After all, Pinay had signed the Messina Resolution, which deemed centralization "indispensable" if western Europe was to "maintain . . . the position that it occupies in the world."[61]

Mollet's government shared this basic reasoning. In an article in *Le Monde* not long before his election, Mollet himself noted that only a united Europe could compete in a world inhabited by superstates: "In the presence of the Russian and American colossi . . . a mosaic of European states leaves Europe's place empty."[62] In July 1956, he elaborated, telling the National Assembly that "only a united Europe will have any authority in the face of the two colossi" because "only that structure—a European community—will assure Europe of stability and power and make it no longer a bone of contention between the two blocs, but a factor for peace."[63] Perhaps his clearest statement of the balance of power logic underpinning his support for a centralized European coalition came in another National Assembly debate in January 1957. He supported a common market because it would form the basis for "a united Europe, which could become a third, independent power in the world." Constructing a third force of this kind was essential because the Europeans operated in a world dominated by an "impulsive" America and a "restless and menacing" Soviet Union.[64] Looking back on the establishment of the EEC, he remarked that "none of our European states" could exert a meaningful influence on international politics. In fact, "only a united Europe can fill [that role]."[65]

Foreign Minister Christian Pineau took essentially the same line. Before the Messina conference, and long before he became foreign minister, he

59. Quoted in Hervé Alphand, *L'étonnement d'être* (Paris: Fayard, 1977), 270.

60. Quoted in René Girault, "Decision Makers, Decisions and French Power," in *Power in Europe? II: Great Britain, France, Germany and Italy and the Origins of the EEC, 1952–1957,* ed. Ennio Di Nolfo (New York: W. de Gruyter, 1992), 83.

61. Quoted in Gerbet, *Construction,* 199.

62. Guy Mollet, "Le Front Républicain et l'Europe," *Le Monde,* December 28, 1955.

63. Quoted in Pierre Guillen, "Europe as a Cure for French Impotence? The Guy Mollet Government and the Negotiation of the Treaties of Rome," in *Power in Europe? II: Great Britain, France, Germany and Italy and the Origins of the EEC, 1952–1957,* ed. Ennio Di Nolfo (New York: W. de Gruyter, 1992), 507.

64. Quoted in Mark S. Sheetz, "Continental Drift: Franco-German Relations and the Shifting Premises of European Security" (PhD diss., Columbia University, 2002), 255. Pineau, Maurice Faure, and Defense Minister Maurice Bourgès-Maunoury made essentially the same case in the course of the debate (Guillen, "Europe," 515).

65. Quoted in Gérard Bossuat, "Guy Mollet: La puissance française autrement," *Relations internationales* no. 57 (1989): 29.

called for "the creation of European organizations" so that the west European states would be assured of "their political independence."[66] Similarly, he urged ratification of the Rome Treaties on the basis that a European union would compensate for "the relative weakness of the Western democracies."[67] His basic position, argues Bossuat, was that "France could not be powerful through national independence but through European interdependence, conducted to the benefit of France and of the European populations. Sacrifices of sovereignty would therefore be necessary."[68]

The Suez crisis, which began with the French, British, and Israeli attack on Egypt in October 1956, strengthened the pro-centralization view. There is some debate about the precise effect of the crisis. One view is that the French had been dragging their feet on the integration issue and that the main lesson of defeat in the Middle East was that they had to pursue the common market and build Europe. Others argue that the major stumbling blocks to integration had been cleared up in the fall of 1956 and that Suez therefore had little impact on French support for integration.[69]

The most plausible interpretation is that the climax of the crisis strengthened a preexisting determination to establish a centralized west European entity. On November 24, Mollet argued that American and Soviet reactions following Suez had "highlighted the need for medium-sized nations to group together if they want to have the necessary authority."[70] Similarly, Pineau observed that Suez made the integration case more compelling by showing the Europeans that "they could hardly defend themselves alone; that America was not as reliable as one might think . . . and that consequently, Europe was more necessary than ever."[71] When these events were coupled with the Soviet Union's invasion of Hungary, they strongly sug-

---

66. Quoted in Jeffrey William Vanke, "Europeanism and the European Economic Community, 1954–1966" (PhD diss., Harvard University, 1999), 65.

67. Quoted in Pierre Guillen, "L'Europe remède à l'impuissance française? Le gouvernement Guy Mollet et la négociation des Traités de Rome (1955–1957)," *Revue d'histoire diplomatique* no. 102 (1988): 333.

68. Bossuat, "Mollet," 34.

69. For the view that Suez was transformational, see Guillen, "Europe," 513–14; Hanns Jürgen Küsters, "The Treaties of Rome (1955–57)," in *The Dynamics of European Union*, ed. Roy Pryce (London: Croom Helm, 1987), 96–98; and Küsters, *Fondements de la communauté économique européenne* (Brussels: Editions Labor, 1990), 211–16, 356; and for the argument that it was not, see Lynch, *France*, 183; and Moravcsik, *Choice*, 119–20. My understanding is close to that of Paul Pitman who concludes that Suez highlighted the need for European unity by "dramatizing long-standing concerns." See Paul M. Pitman, " 'A General Named Eisenhower': Atlantic Crisis and the Origins of the European Economic Community," in *Between Empire and Alliance: America and Europe during the Cold War*, ed. Marc Trachtenberg (Lanham, Md.: Rowman and Littlefield, 2003), 49.

70. Quoted in Serge Berstein, "The Perception of French Power by the Political Forces," in *Power in Europe? II: Great Britain, France, Germany and Italy and the Origins of the EEC, 1952–1957*, ed. Ennio Di Nolfo (New York: W. de Gruyter, 1992), 349.

71. Quoted in Guillen, "L'Europe," 333.

gested that the Europeans ought to make sure that there was "something concrete" west of the iron curtain that would "eventually be able to take a position that did not take account of the Americans or the Soviets."[72] Socialist deputy Jean Le Bail neatly summed up the effects of Hungary and Suez: "We are at present drawn towards pursuing a great-power policy, and we can see that our diplomacy has not the resources for it. . . . What we must do is create Europe."[73]

The French were convinced that only a centralized European coalition could survive in a world dominated by the superpowers. Increasingly aware that they could not count on the United States to protect their interests and that the Soviet Union continued to be a dangerous adversary, they resolved to build "Europe," by which they meant a centralized unit of power in the western half of the continent. As Bossuat has pointed out, "The men behind the European relaunch in the *cabinets* of Guy Mollet or Edgar Faure saw the common market as the starting point for a new European adventure, which would form the basis of an international Third Force."[74]

Integration

The French concluded that integration provided the surest means to establish an even balance of power within the centralized west European coalition that they planned to construct. Indeed, it was precisely this kind of thinking that led them to support both the common market and Euratom.

Supporting Integration

Faure and his colleagues clearly supported Euratom from the beginning. Even before the Messina conference, the prime minister held two press conferences in which he broached the possibility of a European atomic energy community.[75] Though not part of the government at the time, Mollet echoed this view in an article in *Le Populaire* on April 2: "Let us attempt integration 'by sector' both by setting up new specialised communities and by drawing support from the supranational authority that has withstood the test, the Coal and Steel Community."[76] Later that month, in a

72. Christian Pineau, "Debate," in *La relance européenne et les Traités de Rome*, ed. Enrico Serra (Brussels: Bruylant, 1989), 284.

73. Quoted in Berstein, "Perception," 349.

74. Gérard Bossuat, "The French Administrative Elite and the Unification of Western Europe, 1947–58," in *Building Postwar Europe: National Decision-Makers and European Institutions, 1948–63*, ed. Anne Deighton (London: St. Martin's, 1995), 31.

75. Pierre Guillen, "La France et la négociation du Traité d'Euratom," *Relations internationales* no. 44 (1985): 397. For Monnet's support of atomic energy integration, see Gerbet, *Construction*, 194.

76. Quoted in Denis Lefebvre, "The French Socialist Party, 1954–1957," in *Socialist Parties and the Question of Europe in the 1950s*, ed. Richard T. Griffiths (New York: E. J. Brill, 1993), 47.

conversation with Adenauer, Pinay inquired whether the Germans would be interested in integrating Europe's aviation and atomic energy industries.[77] In other words, the French were supportive enough of atomic energy integration to take the lead on the issue.[78]

In contrast, the French had two practical reservations that initially made them more cautious about economic integration. First, the Faure government worried that there was little appetite for integration of any kind in the wake of the EDC debacle. Faure himself feared that loose talk of integration might destroy the "fragile domestic equilibrium."[79] Similarly, Pinay told Macmillan that he was reluctant to entertain any major initiative so soon after the EDC failure because the National Assembly would likely "refuse a new treaty of too great import."[80] Adenauer clearly understood the situation, noting that Pinay was a "friend of integration," but one who had to act cautiously because "this was an election year in France and there was no uniform opinion in France with respect to European integration."[81]

Second, as they had done for almost a decade, key French policymakers feared that integration and the liberalization that it would entail might damage their economy. Pinay considered the German desire for economic integration overly ambitious and dangerous to the French economy, and even Monnet thought that fashioning a common market would prove too difficult.[82] Although the opponents of the common market were more strident in their criticism, they based their opposition on the same basic belief: namely, that France's economy would not be able to compete in a common market.[83] Given these concerns, the French were cautious about embarking on economic integration. It is in this context that Faure's recommendation to Pinay not to go "along the road to an Economic Community, which is quite impossible at the present time" ought to be understood.[84] As Pinay

77. Pierre Guillen, "La France et la négociation des Traités de Rome: L'Euratom," in *La relance européenne et les Traités de Rome*, ed. Enrico Serra (Brussels: Bruylant, 1989), 515.

78. For evidence that this was a fairly broadly held view, see Department Note, May 1955, *DDF*, 1955, vol. 1, 704.

79. Edgar Faure, *Mémoires: Si tel doit être mon destin ce soir* (Paris: Plon, 1984), 216.

80. Summary of Conversation between Pinay and Macmillan, April 21, 1955, *DDF*, 1955, vol. 1, Annexes, 29.

81. Memorandum of Conversation by Lyon, June 14, 1955, *FRUS*, 1955–1957, vol. 4, 297.

82. Jeffrey Glen Giauque, *Grand Designs and Visions of Unity: The Atlantic Powers and the Reorganization of Western Europe, 1955–1963* (Chapel Hill: University of North Carolina Press, 2002), 21; Pierre Gerbet, *La naissance du marché commun* (Paris: Editions Complexe, 1987), 79; and Pineau, "Debate," 282.

83. See, for example, Bossuat, "French," 28–30.

84. Christian Tauch, "The Testimony of an Eyewitness: Christian Pineau," in *Socialist Parties and the Question of Europe in the 1950s*, ed. Richard T. Griffiths (New York: E. J. Brill, 1993), 60.

informed Spaak, France wanted to "make Europe step by step and not at a gallop."[85]

Despite these reservations, the French were conditionally supportive of economic integration in the run up to Messina. When asked by the other five heads of state what the French attitude would be at the upcoming conference, Faure answered that they "could go ahead with the Common Market. France would not give them an unpleasant surprise."[86] Likewise, although he worried about the practicalities of establishing a common market, Mollet believed that the "most logical approach would be to pursue general economic unification, including the harmonisation of economic, social and financial policies and the free movement of goods, capital and people."[87]

Indeed, a consensus gradually began to emerge that France would support a common market if it could be crafted in such a way as to protect the French economy. According to a Quai memorandum in early April, the customs union plans deserved close examination "despite the objections that have been raised against them." Economic integration might even redound to France's advantage if it came with "escape clauses, an appeals tribunal, and perhaps some readaptation and reconversion mechanisms, and an effort . . . to harmonize social costs." Toward the end of the month, another note recommended a reserved attitude until the French could negotiate better terms, since integration might allow France to "control Germany without discriminating against it; obtain a better result in a larger context by combining workers, techniques, financing, production and markets; and make a political move to bring about the unification of Europe." Then, in May, officials did not reject the common market out of hand, but instead suggested that negotiators at Messina demand an in-depth study of the relevant obstacles to agreement.[88]

Perhaps the most striking sign that French officials were prepared seriously to entertain the possibility of economic integration lies not in their statements, but in their behavior during the spring. Because the other five held them responsible for the demise of the EDC, the French believed they could not afford to be seen wrecking another major integrative initiative. Just by going to Messina, then, they were indicating their willingness to consider pursuing economic integration. Nor did they reverse themselves once they got there. Instead, they signed the Messina Resolution advocating the creation of a "common market," and proposed that Spaak—a devotee of economic integration—take charge of the study group.[89]

85. Quoted in Gerbet, *Naissance*, 83.
86. Faure, *Mémoires*, 211.
87. Quoted in Lefebvre, "French," 47.
88. Department Notes, April 7, end of April–beginning of May, and May 1955, *DDF*, 1955, vol. 1, 420–21, 549, 704–5.
89. Gerbet, *Construction*, 199; and Parsons, *Certain*, 104.

Following Messina, the Faure government became a stronger supporter of economic integration while continuing to express concern about its practical effects. In a circular telegram to all diplomatic offices upon his return from Sicily, Pinay announced that integration had to be achieved "progressively and realistically," and that although "difficulties and divergences remain[ed]," he was pleased with what had been achieved. The meeting marked "the first step toward a new development in European integration since August 30, 1954."[90] Although conscious of the thorny economic issues still to be worked out, he was committed to integration in principle.

Other officials appear to have shared this basic outlook. In an important memorandum presented to the Spaak Committee in October, the French raised a series of practical concerns but accepted integration as an organizing concept. Specifically, they endorsed the "supranational notion" and planned to limit future discussions to the Six—that is, the only European states "disposed to subscribe to an organization that grants extended powers to personalities independent of their government[s]."[91] As the Belgians told the Americans, the proposal might not be "audacious," but it was "the first constructive integration proposal emanating from [the] French Government in 3 years."[92]

Although there is some debate about the Faure government's attitude, it is generally agreed that the Mollet administration that followed it supported integration in the form of both a common market and an atomic energy community. In the fall of 1955, Mollet himself linked the two enterprises, announcing that "the creation of a European Authority for Atomic Energy must . . . be the test of the 'new drive' for unity," before adding that the Spaak Committee's "other major concern . . . is to establish a general common market in Europe."[93] He followed up in an article that appeared in *Le Monde* during his election campaign, affirming his support for an atomic energy community in the short term and a "European common market" over the longer term.[94] Then, during his inaugural address to the National Assembly, he announced his intention to "secure the conclusion of a treaty setting up Euratom" and his determination to "get the general common market going" before calling on his colleagues "to make the European idea no longer a subject of misunderstanding, but instead a great unifying factor."[95]

90. Pinay to French Diplomatic Representatives Abroad, June 10, 1955, *DDF*, 1955, vol. 1, 757.

91. Economic and Financial Affairs Desk Note, October 13, 1955, *DDF*, 1955, vol. 2, 658–59.

92. Alger to State Department, October 21, 1955, *FRUS*, 1955–1957, vol. 4, 334.

93. Mollet, *New*, 9–10.

94. Mollet, "Front."

95. Quoted in Lefebvre, "French," 53.

Pineau and France's chief negotiator, Maurice Faure, shared the prime minister's views.[96] Long after the fact, Pineau claimed that he and Mollet were committed to the common market all along but had been forced to move slowly and "throw a discreet veil" over it for fear of arousing too much opposition from those who believed France would be unable to compete in a liberalized economic system.[97] This being the case, Pineau took a cautious line in public. In a speech in February 1956, he was at pains to point out that, although he strongly supported both Euratom and the economic community, he believed "that achieving the Common Market will take much longer . . . [because] it raises financial and other questions, the solutions to which are far from having been developed."[98] As he told the Americans, "he personally was strongly in favor of European integration and of [a] common market," but this would not be possible "without [a] great deal of prior negotiations, and also [a] great deal of education in France."[99] As one historian has concluded, the Mollet government was intent on "a relaunch along supranational lines," but had a narrow margin for maneuver.[100] The evidence supports this claim; when presented with the opportunity to push integration forward, Pineau seized it. At the Venice conference in May 1956, he endorsed both integration projects, recommended that the Six begin negotiations for Euratom and the common market immediately, and suggested that the two projects be merged into a single treaty in order to ease ratification.[101] The government subsequently endorsed his position at a crucial interministerial meeting in September.[102]

Balance of Power Reasoning

France's support for economic integration rested on straightforward balance of power reasoning. Having concluded that they had to build a centralized west European economy, the French were keen to establish and perpetuate an even Franco-German balance of power at the heart of the

96. On Maurice Faure's role, see Bruno Riondel, "Maurice Faure et la négociation des Traités de Rome," in *Europe brisée, Europe retrouvée: Nouvelles réflexions sur l'unité européenne au XXe siècle*, ed. René Girault and Gérard Bossuat (Paris: Publications de la Sorbonne, 1994), 347–64.

97. Tauch, "Testimony," 60.

98. Quoted in Lefebvre, "French," 54.

99. Dillon to State Department, February 7, 1956, *FRUS*, 1955–1957, vol. 4, 407–8. For evidence that he made the same point to the Germans, see Memorandum of Meeting between Pineau and von Brentano, February 11, 1956, *DDF*, 1956, vol. 1, 186.

100. Gilles Cophornic, "Les formations politiques françaises et la création de la communauté économique européenne," in *Europe des élites? Europe des peuples? La construction de l'espace européen, 1945–1960*, ed. Elisabeth de Réau (Paris: Presses de la Sorbonne Nouvelle, 1998), 259. See also Guillen, "L'Europe," 321.

101. Vanke, "Europeanism," 69.

102. Laurent Warlouzet, "Quelle Europe économique pour la France? La France et le marché commun industriel, 1956–1969" (PhD diss., Université Paris Sorbonne, 2007), 53–57.

emerging entity. In this respect, integration was an ideal arrangement because it ensured that as members of the same community, France and West Germany would have equal power in making policy and be subject to the same policies once they were made. The French realized, however, that they would enter the community with a less competitive economy than Germany. Consequently, they were prepared to endorse integration only if special arrangements could be made that would allow them to enter the common market on a roughly equal basis with the Federal Republic. To borrow Monnet's language from the coal and steel negotiations, they wanted to integrate from "the same starting basis." It is as a search for and achievement of initial parity, therefore, that the French negotiating position between 1955 and 1957 should be understood.

As had been the case since the late 1940s, officials in Paris supported integration because it would subject France and the Federal Republic to the same policies, rules, and controls. Monnet, for example, viewed Euratom in exactly the same terms as he had viewed the ECSC. Rather than becoming independent, the Germans would participate as equals with France under a common atomic authority.[103] Officials at the Quai d'Orsay shared this understanding of integration. In debating France's position on a possible European atomic authority, they observed that they were "once again confronted by the doctrinal quarrel which grew up around the notion of 'supranationality' and the creation of a continental Europe." At the heart of this debate, they continued, was a concept that "had been there at the outset of our European policy," namely the idea that integration might enable France to "control Germany without discriminating against it."[104]

Mollet clearly believed that if they chose to integrate, the states of western Europe would be agreeing to adhere to a common set of obligations. As he told the American Committee on United Europe, he was convinced that, like individuals in "organized societies," the Europeans must surrender "some of . . . [their] 'sovereignty'." A putative common market must have "its own working rules and a common Authority—federal in character, independent of governments" that could see to it that "rules are fully observed, to prevent possible mishaps, and to take firm action in periods of adjustment or crisis." In other words, he took a common set of rules and a common authority to be the hallmarks of integration. This was important because the rules and obligations would apply to all member states, including West Germany. His goal was a "Germany, integrated economically and politically into a European Community which would have authority over Germany as well as over the other member countries."[105]

Despite their support for the concept of integration, the French were acutely aware that a common set of policies applicable to all member states

103. Gerbet, *Construction*, 166.
104. Department Note, end of April–beginning of May 1955, *DDF*, 1955, vol. 1, 549.
105. Mollet, *New*, 4, 5, 7. See also Guillen, "Europe," 507; and Bossuat, "Mollet," 29.

would not maintain an even balance of power within western Europe unless the French and West German economies were equally matched from the outset. If France's economy was less competitive than Germany's when the agreement went into force and both were subjected to the same set of rules, then France would quickly fall behind and Germany would come to dominate the emerging community.

As a result, the French were determined to make their economy competitive before taking the integration plunge. This concern about competitiveness, which went back to the late 1940s when it had precluded any progress toward general economic integration, was apparent from the moment Paris became aware of the Benelux Memorandum. As Pinay told Macmillan in April 1955, a common market designed along lines that would be acceptable to the Germans would pose a serious threat to the French economy.[106]

Pinay's views reflected those of his advisers at the Quai. According to the Economic Cooperation desk, a customs union would bring about West German political and economic hegemony in western Europe.[107] In a note written at the end of May, officials argued that the formation of a customs union would make the rich states of the region, such as Germany, richer, and relatively poor states, such as France, poorer. Moreover, a common market agreement would likely lead to an unacceptable reduction in French tariffs, destroy the protective mechanisms that sustained French agriculture, and weaken France's ties with its colonies. Officials reiterated the point in another note a few days later: France was unlikely to cope with the increase in competition that integration would bring.[108]

Given these fears, the French quickly concluded that general economic integration would be acceptable only if it could be managed in such a way as to preserve France's power position in Europe. France's partners would have to agree to a series of measures designed to make the French economy competitive from the outset. Thus, an early memorandum suggested that the French might rally to a customs union if it came with measures that would cushion the French economy from the effects of wholesale competition. Another group of officials made the same point a week before Messina. Although they wanted the government to reject the common market on the grounds of France's lack of competitiveness, they conceded that if this was impossible, then they would like to see the Six study "policies designed to avoid the accentuation of economic inequalities" and to agree to "the coordination of investments to prevent the creation of uncompetitive industries." A third group reiterated the argument: "The best solution would be to demand that our partners define the conditions for establishing an economic community that would not enrich the rich regions and

---

106. Giauque, *Grand*, 21.
107. Lynch, *France*, 170.
108. Department Notes, May 26 and May 1955, *DDF*, 1955, vol. 1, 692, 704–5.

impoverish the poor ones."[109] In short, the French went to Messina intent on negotiating a deal that would put them in a position to compete with the Federal Republic in an economically integrated Europe.

Pinay made it abundantly clear that enhanced French competitiveness must precede integration. At Messina, he insisted that the creation of a common market be subordinated to the study of a number of key "problems." Specifically, any agreement would have to take account of two matters that affected the competitiveness of the French economy. First, because social costs in France were higher than elsewhere in Europe, thereby putting the French economy at a competitive disadvantage, Pinay wanted social policies harmonized among the Six. Second, the French wanted the others to consider creating a European investment fund.[110] Clappier drew up a similar set of conditions in late June. Although positively disposed toward a common market, he wanted to mitigate the effects of opening up the French market by harmonizing social policies and establishing an investment fund. In addition, he emphasized the need for a series of safeguard clauses and insisted that agriculture would need to be organized under separate agreements.[111] A month later, the Economic Council approved a report that called for the harmonization of economic and social policies and stressed the need for France to maintain its imperial ties.[112] By the fall of 1955, then, a set of demands had begun to emerge. Briefly stated, France would agree to create a common market if its partners would agree to harmonize social policies, establish a common agricultural policy, create a European investment fund, and extend special treatment to France's colonies. In other words, the French were looking for an agreement that would eliminate the sources of their economic inferiority before they took the integration plunge.

The French outlined three of their core demands in a document that they presented to the Spaak Committee in October. Although the memorandum introduced several new elements into the equation—French negotiators wanted to include a number of safeguard clauses that member states could invoke unilaterally and insisted that the creation of the common market had to be a two-stage process—the harmonization of social poli-

109. Department Notes, April 7, May 26, and May 1955, ibid., 418–21, 692–93, 705.

110. Pinay to French Diplomatic Representatives Abroad, June 10, 1955, ibid., 756–57.

111. Lynch, *France*, 172; and Pitman, "France's," 285.

112. Pitman, "France's," 288–89. For French demands concerning the harmonization of social costs, see Lise Rye Svartvatn, "In Quest of Time, Protection and Approval: France and the Claims for Social Harmonization in the European Economic Community, 1955–56," *Journal of European Integration History* 8, no. 1 (2002): 85–102, and for their demands regarding their colonial possessions, see René Girault, "La France entre l'Europe et l'Afrique," in *La relance européenne et les Traités de Rome*, ed. Enrico Serra (Brussels: Bruylant, 1989), 351–78; and Pierre Guillen, "L'avenir de l'union française dans la négociation des Traités de Rome," *Relations internationales* no. 57 (1989): 103–12.

cies, the creation of an investment fund, and a common agricultural policy took pride of place.[113] The rough outline of a deal was now on the table; if the others would agree to address the key causes of France's relative weakness, then integration could proceed.

Mollet's accession to power left the general thrust of French policy intact. In his *Le Monde* article, he was at pains to point out that the French had to prepare their economy to "withstand external competition." His government, he added, would require the now familiar concessions from the other members of the Six: social policy harmonization, arrangements for agriculture, and a readaptation fund.[114] These views mirrored those of his subordinates. Indeed, the economic dangers posed by integration and the need for concessions in order to avert them were constant themes in internal discussions in the first half of 1956. A note from the Quai in February 1956, for example, confirmed that the Spaak Committee was planning to advocate for a readaptation fund and a common agricultural policy, but warned that the French would not get full satisfaction on the issue of social harmonization.[115] The following month, the Directorate for Economic and Financial Affairs warned that if the French were to be subjected to free trade, then "entire regions" of the country might become the scene of "economic and social turmoil."[116] At the same time, other officials highlighted the economic problems France would face if it joined a common market without safeguards, while noting that Germany would face no such difficulties. An April memorandum, meanwhile, reminded decision makers that social harmonization, the overseas territories, and a European investment fund were "essential" issues that must be dealt with in any negotiation.[117]

Pineau made these demands explicit when the foreign ministers of the Six met to discuss the Spaak Report in Venice in May. The French position had been worked out at an interministerial working group earlier in the month. The participants came to conclusions similar to those reached by the Faure government in October 1955.[118] First, the Europeans would have to harmonize their social policies if the French were to compete effectively in a common market. The Spaak Report was deemed disappointing in this respect. Second, any agreement must include special provisions for

113. Memorandum of the French Delegation to the Intergovernmental Committee Created by the Messina Conference, October 14, 1955, *DDF*, 1955, vol. 2, 660–63. See also the accompanying note by the Economic Cooperation Desk, October 13, 1955, ibid., 658–60.

114. Guy Mollet, "Front."

115. Economic and Financial Affairs Desk Note, February 2, 1956, *DDF*, 1956, vol. 1, 135–40.

116. Quoted in Edelgard E. Mahant, *Birthmarks of Europe: The Origins of the European Community Reconsidered* (Aldershot: Ashgate, 2004), 77.

117. Economic and Financial Affairs Desk Notes, April 17 and 21, 1956, *DDF*, 1956, vol. 1, 610–13, 636–40.

118. Others have noted the striking similarity between the October 1955 and May 1956 positions. See Mahant, *Birthmarks*, 79; and Pitman, "France's," 337.

agriculture. Third, the other states would have to share the expenses associated with France's overseas territories. Pineau took these demands to Venice, endorsing the Spaak Report as a basis for negotiation but insisting that the negotiators bear in mind the importance of social policy harmonization, overseas territories, agriculture, and a European investment fund.[119] If these issues could be resolved, then France would move forward with the establishment of a common market. As the foreign minister told Dulles, if France's partners would agree to "harmonization of social legislation" and the "inclusion of overseas territories within the Common Market area," then success in the negotiations would be "assured."[120] This position was confirmed at an important internal meeting in September.[121]

Although they were intent on extracting concessions that would level the playing field for France, many key decision makers believed that integration might actually benefit the French economy by exposing it to competition and forcing it to modernize. As the diplomatic editor of *Le Monde*, Jean Schwoebel, put it, French foot-dragging stemmed from a desire to postpone "the disagreeable moment for throwing itself into the cold water it knew to be good for its health."[122] Mollet made the same point in December 1955, arguing that a common market agreement "would be an incomparable stimulant to the rationalization and modernization of our economy."[123] Four months later, a group of officials at the Quai suggested that there was no "formula" other than a common market that could provide "conditions conducive to the modernization and expansion of the French economy."[124]

Upon becoming prime minister, Mollet made the point repeatedly: "Protectionism and closing in on themselves lead a people to decadence." Or as he told the SFIO Congress in June 1957, "Our industrialists must make the necessary effort at investments in order to put themselves in a position to be competitive. That is an effort worthy of a nation that wishes

119. Economic and Financial Affairs Desk Notes, May 3 and May 7, 1956, and Memorandum of Conversation of the Conference of the ECSC Foreign Ministers, June 8, 1956, *DDF*, 1956, vol. 1, 703–5, 725–31, 917–30; and Bousquet to Pineau, September 28, 1957, *DDF*, 1957, vol. 2, 472–77.

120. Memoranda of Conversations, State Department, June 18 and 19, 1956, *FRUS*, 1955–1957, vol. 27, 73–74.

121. Lynch, "Restoring," 84. Some key players concluded that not even these concessions would be enough to level the playing field. Although the final agreement contained all of the concessions that the government demanded, the Mendèsists opposed ratification of the EEC treaty, arguing that it would destroy France's economy. See Moravcsik, *Choice*, 117.

122. Quoted in F. Roy Willis, *France, Germany, and the New Europe, 1945–1967* (Stanford: Stanford University Press, 1968), 246–47.

123. Mollet, "Front."

124. Economic and Financial Affairs General Directorate Note, April 21, 1956, *DDF*, 1956, vol. 1, 637. For a similar argument, see Brusse, *Tariffs*, 173.

to keep its place."[125] In other words, a carefully arranged common market would allow France to match Germany and might even prove to be more beneficial to French than to German industry.[126] The French, declared Maurice Faure, had a choice to make: they could change nothing and accept that they would "always be the feeblest" or they could strive for "economic rehabilitation by Community procedures."[127] Socialist deputy Alain Savary was more explicit in his claim that integration would work to France's advantage: "Protectionism . . . has gone against the country's long-term interests. It would seem that a thorough change in the structures and habits of the French economy ought to be made."[128] This view was quite widespread. As Moravcsik notes, "nearly all French leaders . . . during this period . . . advocated trade liberalization" on the grounds that it "might increase pressure for industrial modernization."[129]

Although the claim that integration would actually benefit France was contentious, the French position was clear by the fall of 1956: they would accept integration if the French and West German economies were placed on a similar starting basis through the elimination of the sources of French economic weakness. The question now was whether Germany would meet France's demands.

West Germany: Embracing Integration, 1955–1957

The Federal Republic acceded to French demands and therefore ensured the success of the Messina initiative. The German decision appears to have been driven by balance of power calculations. Above all, Adenauer was deeply troubled by Soviet power and believed that the west Europeans could only counter the USSR if they formed a centralized balancing coalition. As for the question of running the coalition, the Germans understood that the best they could hope for was joint control. Moreover, because they viewed joint control of an economic community as the prelude to joint control of a political-military community, they were prepared to make significant economic concessions to France in order to bring it about.

The Balancing Imperative

The Soviet danger remained front and center in German decision making in the mid-1950s. During a major address to the Grandes Conférences Catholiques in September 1956, Adenauer warned that "Soviet Russia was

125. Quoted in Guillen, "Europe," 514.
126. Ibid., 510.
127. Quoted in Moravcsik, *Choice*, 117.
128. Quoted in Berstein, "Perception," 349.
129. Moravcsik, *Choice*, 114.

consolidating itself more and more" and might even be more "expansive" than Tsarist Russia had been before it.[130] This was his private position as well. In January 1956, in an important policy-setting memorandum that Economics Minister Ludwig Erhard would later refer to as the "Integration Command" (*Integrationbefehl*), Adenauer demanded a "positive attitude" to European integration in view of the "extraordinary dangers" posed by the Soviet Union.[131] As Winfried Becker has pointed out, the "dominant factor" in his worldview was "the military and ideological threat from the Soviet Union."[132] His great fear was that the Soviets might come to believe that "the free world was not united or was not strong."[133]

This threat loomed even larger due to the growing belief that the United States could not or would not defend the Europeans indefinitely. This grave concern took on epic proportions in July 1956 when the *New York Times* reported that the chairman of the Joint Chiefs of Staff, Admiral Arthur Radford, was reviewing plans to reduce the size of America's conventional forces in Europe and withdraw troops from West Germany. To Adenauer, the implications were clear: the United States and Britain were planning to abandon the region and leave the continental west European powers to fend for themselves.[134] As he told a group of reporters, he was unhappy that America was retreating from the world and becoming "a fortress for itself, because that would mean that we would be outside that fortress."[135] Because of this, the Europeans could no longer count on the United States. As he put it in a letter to Dulles in July 1956, "Europe, including Germany, has lost its confidence in the United States' reliability. These plans are regarded as clear evidence that the United States does not feel itself to be strong enough to keep up the pace with the Soviet Union."[136]

This fear of abandonment was common in West German policymaking circles. In September, one of Adenauer's close party colleagues, Heinrich Krone, wrote him that because "the Americans live far from Germany . . . one should not rest comfortably in the thought that they have to stand with

---

130. Quoted in Hans-Peter Schwarz, *Konrad Adenauer: A German Politician and Statesman in a Period of War, Revolution, and Reconstruction*, vol. 2 (Providence, R.I.: Berghahn, 1995), 237.

131. Adenauer to all Ministers, January 19, 1956, in *Briefe, 1955–1957*, ed. Hans Peter Mensing (Berlin: Siedler, 1998), 139.

132. Winfried Becker, "Views of the Foreign Policy Situation among the CDU Leadership, 1945–1957," in *Power in Europe? II: Great Britain, France, Germany and Italy and the Origins of the EEC, 1952–1957*, ed. Ennio Di Nolfo (New York: W. de Gruyter, 1992), 357.

133. Quoted in Franz Knipping, "'Firm with the West!' Elements of the International Orientation of West Germany in the Mid-1950s," in *Power in Europe? II: Great Britain, France, Germany and Italy and the Origins of the EEC, 1952–1957*, ed. Ennio Di Nolfo (New York: W. de Gruyter, 1992), 520.

134. Pitman, "General," 46.

135. Quoted in Ronald J. Granieri, *The Ambivalent Alliance: Konrad Adenauer, the CDU/CSU, and the West, 1949–1966* (New York: Berghahn, 2003), 88.

136. Quoted in Schwarz, *Adenauer*, 235.

Europe forever." The chancellor agreed, noting that the view that "America will never abandon Europe is false." There was always the chance "that the further development of nuclear weapons will lead to an American withdrawal [and we] must never forget the possibility of 'fortress America'."[137] In a long memorandum written at roughly the same time, government spokesman Felix von Eckhardt put a dismal spin on the situation: "There can hardly be any doubt that in three, at the latest four years, American troops will have left Germany, even the whole of Europe. All good observers of U.S. policies share this opinion." Given this kind of thinking, Adenauer informed Secretary of the Air Force Donald Quarles that he thought it "no exaggeration" to claim that NATO, the key symbol of the U.S. commitment to the continent, was "finished."[138]

The chancellor reserved his most forceful statement about American unreliability for his meeting with Mollet in November 1956. The Americans, he told the French prime minister, had come to believe that they could ensure their security through nuclear deterrence. As Quarles had told him, it was generally agreed that the U.S. "response would be so terrible" that the Russians would never launch a "first strike." Consequently, Adenauer believed that the Americans were no longer particularly interested in defending western Europe, which explained why they had come up with the Radford Plan and were minimizing their role in NATO. His fear was that things would soon get worse—the Americans would lose interest in NATO altogether and pull out of the region. Once that happened, he doubted that they would have the "nerve" to fight a nuclear war to defend Europe. Not everyone at the meeting embraced Adenauer's analysis. Mollet argued that he was being overly "pessimistic," but the chancellor retorted that he was simply being "realistic." In the same vein as Mollet, German foreign minister Heinrich von Brentano argued that the Americans were bound to fight to defend Europe because they knew that after Europe fell the Soviets would turn on them. Again, Adenauer was unmoved. The Americans may have "been of this opinion (in the last war)," but now they felt "certain about their security with their atomic weapons."[139] In short, he had little faith in the American security guarantee.

Given this mindset, the Germans were committed to being part of a west European balancing coalition. Adenauer laid out the logic in his speech to the Conférences Catholiques, explaining that the European states had to reduce their dependence on American "patronage," which could not and should not be permanent. Moreover, differences of opinion were bound to arise between the Europeans and the Americans. Hence the need for a "united Europe." Only a west European coalition could ensure "our spiritual

137. Quoted in Granieri, *Ambivalent*, 89.
138. Quoted in Schwarz, *Adenauer*, 236, 256.
139. Summary of Conversation, Mollet-Adenauer Meeting, November 6, 1956, *DDF*, 1956, vol. 3, 235–36.

and political existence . . . and . . . the maintenance of our voice in the concert of world powers."[140] Europe had "shrunk alarmingly" and "only a dam erected in common by the remaining free nations of Europe . . . can block the further advance of the Communist mass."[141] The Europeans, he argued, ought to construct a "third force" in world politics. They had become too dependent on the United States, and given the brewing Suez crisis, this was "a good time to make a new start for Europe."[142] Later, he was even more forceful, telling a group of journalists that France and Germany were not constituent states of the United States of America and had the right to defend their own interests.[143]

The chancellor made the same argument in private conversations with his own ministers and with the French. In his *Integrationbefehl*, for example, he explained that his support for European integration derived from the fact that it would "cast a single Europe into the balance" against the Russians.[144] In a cabinet meeting in October 1956, he explained his support for a European coalition as follows: "The creation of a third force is necessary if the fate of individual European countries is not going to depend on the power of Russia and the United States alone."[145] He made essentially the same point in another cabinet meeting two months later. "Europe" would have a "longer life than NATO," he told his colleagues, and it was therefore time to "push ahead with the unification of Europe."[146] American unreliability meant that the Europeans had to look to themselves to ensure their security. He delivered the same message to Mollet when they met to discuss Franco-German relations, insisting that the United States had become too inward looking and that the Europeans ought to be "drawing together and tightening the lines which bound them."[147] Then, in their summit meeting the following month, he warned that if the Americans were to leave the continent it would be "necessary for us to unite under some form or other."[148]

Although Adenauer's opinions are of particular interest because he dominated foreign policy making, most German decision makers agreed with his basic position.[149] Walter Hallstein, who was the most important

140. Quoted in Sheetz, "Continental," 239–40.

141. Konrad Adenauer, *World Indivisible, with Liberty and Justice for All* (New York: Harper and Brothers, 1955), 49–50.

142. Quoted in Granieri, *Ambivalent,* 91.

143. Ibid., 92.

144. Adenauer to all Ministers, January 19, 1956, *Briefe,* 139–40.

145. Minutes of Cabinet Meeting, October 3, 1956, *Die Kabinettsprotokolle der Bundesregierung* (hereafter *KB*), vol. 9, 1956 (Munich: R. Oldenbourg, 1998), 609.

146. Quoted in Pitman, "General," 51.

147. Quoted in Mahant, *Birthmarks,* 130.

148. Summary of Conversation, Mollet-Adenauer Meeting, November 6, 1956, *DDF,* 1956, vol. 3, 235–36.

149. For the claim that Adenauer continued to dominate foreign policy making, see Sabine Lee, "German Decision-Making Elites and European Integration: German 'Eu-

figure in the Foreign Ministry, informed the other Messina conferees that integration was essential to create "an equilibrium between East and West."[150] This was a theme that CDU party member Hans Furler would return to repeatedly, arguing that integration would ensure the "protection of Europe's liberty" and calling on Germany's allies to unite economically in order to match the economic power of eastern Europe.[151]

The balancing imperative gained greater urgency as superpower relations seemed to improve. Matters came to a head prior to the Geneva summit of July 1955, when it appeared that the western powers and the Soviet Union might agree to German reunification and neutralization in the interests of relaxing tensions between East and West. The great German fear, as Eckart Conze has explained, was that a neutralized Germany would "without a doubt be sucked into the Russian orbit, and the Soviet Union would have realized its objective: the removal of the U.S. from Europe and the domination of Western Europe's economic and armament potential." Neutralization, argued Adenauer, "poses a very great, indeed deadly danger."[152] There was a real chance that West Germany might cease to exist. Consequently, the Germans were even more determined to establish a balancing coalition and consolidate their position within it. As Adenauer told a group of journalists in December 1958, "This I have always maintained: Firm with the West. I don't think that a country can lie between two blocks without being crushed or torn apart one way or another."[153] This in turn meant that the Germans were prepared to make important sacrifices to move European unity forward, as evidenced by their willingness to make concessions throughout the EEC negotiations.[154] The creation of an anti-Soviet, west European balancing coalition that included the Federal Republic was the cornerstone of German foreign policy in the mid-1950s.

Centralization

As they had done throughout the postwar period, the Germans continued to assert that any European coalition must be centralized. Adenauer himself was convinced that in a world dominated by two great powers, it was

ropolitik' during the Years of the EEC and Free Trade Area Negotiations," in *Building Postwar Europe: National Decision-Makers and European Institutions, 1948–63*, ed. Anne Deighton (New York: St. Martin's, 1995), 40.

150. Quoted in Edelgard E. Mahant, "French and German Attitudes to the Negotiations about the European Economic Community, 1955–1957" (PhD diss., London University, 1969), 53. For the claim about Hallstein's importance, see Lee, "German," 41.

151. Quoted in Mahant, "French," 233.

152. Eckart Conze, "No Way Back to Potsdam: The Adenauer Government and the Geneva Summit," in *Cold War Respite: The Geneva Summit of 1955*, ed. Günter Bischof and Saki Dockrill (Baton Rouge: Louisiana State University Press, 2000), 197. For Adenauer's fears as he himself expressed them, see Adenauer, *World*, 56–60.

153. Quoted in Knipping, "Firm," 520.

154. See Giauque, *Grand*, 20.

"absolutely necessary for a third power to arise." Moreover, this third force must be "constructed on true federative lines."[155]

Most important officials shared Adenauer's views. Thus, when Dulles expressed some concern that West Germany might "weaken its emphasis on the need for the unification of Europe" in June 1955, Erhard, whose vision of what Europe ought to look like was quite different from the chancellor's, nonetheless assured the secretary of state that he was a "believer in a unified Europe." Indeed, "doubts in Germany over unification were not political in nature but rather questioned the method." Others were more enthusiastic. In July, the State Department reported that Carl Friedrich Ophüls, the head of the German delegation to the Spaak Committee, believed that the Europeans ought to "advance beyond cooperation arrangements to Federal institutions, with [the] necessary transfer of sovereign power."[156]

Explicit references to federal institutions were, in fact, quite common among German policymakers. A Foreign Ministry note of October 1956, for example, argued that the Federal Republic ought to move ahead with the other five in the hope that Britain would ultimately agree to join the resulting west European "federation." A month later, Adenauer explained what this would mean in practical terms: greater supranationalism and a strong executive body to represent the entire community and, if necessary, override the resistance of individual member states.[157] Then, in December, he told Senator William Fulbright that all of Europe's institutions would eventually "take on a federal European form."[158]

Their support for a centralized west European coalition derived from the belief that only an entity of this kind could compete with the Soviet Union. Even before the publication of the Benelux Memorandum, Adenauer argued that only a united Europe, by which he meant a centralized Europe, would be able to operate as "an independent, influential factor in world politics again."[159] If the Europeans were to throw their "weight in favor of peace at crucial moments, when the tensions between the two great powers grew too alarming," they would have to establish a federation.[160] He made broadly the same argument in a speech in Mainz shortly after the ratification of the Rome Treaties: "We Europeans should not give in to the illusion that Europe plays a great role in the world today. . . . There are no European great powers anymore, there are only two great powers, the So-

155. Adenauer, *World*, 51–52.
156. Memorandum of a Conversation, June 7, 1955, and Dulles to Embassy in Germany, July 1, 1955, *FRUS*, 1955–1957, vol. 4, 291–92, 308.
157. Giauque, *Grand*, 24.
158. Quoted in Schwarz, *Adenauer*, 239.
159. Quoted in Becker, "Views," 361.
160. Adenauer, *World*, 52.

viet Union and the United States. . . . If Europe wants to exercise cultural and political influence in the future, it must come together."[161]

Although these statements implied a desire to be independent of both superpowers, the main goal was to be powerful enough to deter or defend against the Soviet Union without U.S. help. And, in fact, Adenauer often linked centralization explicitly to physical survival. Europe, he observed in an extended survey of the geopolitical scene, had been "outstripped both economically and militarily by two great powers formed by the amalgamation of great land-masses." This being the case, the Europeans had no option but to follow suit if they wanted to "guarantee . . . [their] citizens' welfare, freedom and territorial integrity." Simply put, "the necessity for union for economic, political and military reasons is incontestable."[162] As he noted in October 1956, "In Europe there were no longer any great powers . . . Europe could only survive economically and politically if she joined together in one form or another."[163]

Most other high-ranking policymakers agreed with the basic sentiment. In July 1956, the cabinet declared that Europe would only "have a chance to become a factor of power between the United States and the Soviet Union" if it was united. Moreover, the expected American withdrawal from the continent meant that "Europe," by which they meant a centralized west European unit of power, had to "become a reality" because it was "only in strength" that the European states could "become a force to be reckoned with."[164]

Integration

There was little debate among German policymakers that the emerging economic entity ought to be an integrated one in which the Federal Republic and France would be equally represented and share control. As early as January 1955, Adenauer was telling the president of the European Parliament, Giuseppe Pella, that the west Europeans must continue the process that had begun with the creation of the ECSC. In April, he made the same point to Pinay, stressing that he was determined to retain the key features of the coal and steel community in any future agreement.[165] Later in the summer, he met with Dulles and confirmed that "such concepts as the Coal and Steel Community were good and should be held on to," before adding that he had instructed Hallstein to push forward on integration at Messina. American observers were clearly convinced, asserting that the "Federal

161. Quoted in Granieri, *Ambivalent*, 96.
162. Adenauer, *World*, 53.
163. Quoted in Knipping, "Firm," 522.
164. Quoted in Sheetz, "Continental," 235–36.
165. Hanns Jürgen Küsters, "The Federal Republic of Germany and the EEC Treaty," in *La relance européenne et les Traités de Rome*, ed. Enrico Serra (Brussels: Bruylant, 1989), 495–97.

Government is firm in its determination to pursue integration as a matter of policy." Meanwhile, the State Department confirmed that Ophüls clearly understood the need for "further pursuing European integration."[166]

This determination to pursue integration persisted into the fall and the following year. In September 1956, Adenauer informed Hugh Gaitskell, the chairman of the British Labour Party, that he was considering the creation of a confederation of west European states. Although he used the term confederation, it was clear that he envisaged an integrative agreement: it would be set up in such a way as to ensure that "no individual member would be conceded a right of veto, in which, however, a minority would have the chance to raise objections."[167] This was confirmed two months later when Adenauer informed Dulles that Germany was "ready to join the common market as well as the atomic energy pool."[168] He quickly followed up with his own subordinates, leaving no doubt that he wanted them to implement the Messina decisions and to establish "joint institutions" in western Europe.[169]

Not everyone supported the chancellor's vision. Erhard, in particular, wanted to pursue "functional" integration, by which he meant increased economic interdependence through the creation of a free trade area with few if any institutions.[170] But there was little support for his views among the important decision makers.[171] Etzel, at the time vice-president of the High Authority of the ECSC, responded to Erhard's plans for "functional integration" by arguing that the Europeans could not rely on a "fully liberalized economy" and an intergovernmental decision-making structure as Erhard advocated because this would amount to recreating the tragic "situation of 1914."[172] Erhard's views were so at odds with those of his colleagues, in fact, that French ambassador Maurice Couve de Murville thought the time had come to tell the economics minister that his position was "compatible with the policies of neither the German nor the French government."[173]

Why did the Germans endorse economic integration? The evidence suggests that their support was based on balance of power considerations. They understood that the French would not allow them to lead the coali-

166. Adenauer-Dulles Conversation, June 14, 1955, and Dulles to Embassy in Germany, July 1, 1955, *FRUS*, 1955–1957, vol. 4, 297, 307–8, 307, n. 3.

167. Quoted in Schwarz, *Adenauer*, 237.

168. Quoted in Hanns Jürgen Küsters, "West Germany's Foreign Policy in Western Europe, 1949–58: The Art of the Possible," in *Western Europe and Germany: The Beginnings of European Integration, 1945–1960*, ed. Clemens A. Wurm (Oxford: Berg, 1995), 68.

169. Quoted in Schwarz, *Adenauer*, 231.

170. Vanke, "Europeanism," 56.

171. Manfred Görtemaker, "The Failure of the EDC and European Integration," in *Crises in European Integration: Challenge and Response, 1945–2005*, ed. Ludger Kühnhardt (New York: Berghahn, 2009), 41.

172. Quoted in Vanke, "Europeanism," 48.

173. Couve de Murville to Pineau, March 16, 1957, *DDF*, 1957, vol. 1, 479–80.

tion or to have unfettered control of their own economic affairs. Given the inherent competitiveness of the Federal Republic's economy, this course of action would reestablish German superiority within western Europe. At the same time, however, policymakers in Bonn were reluctant to allow the French to assume exclusive control of the coalition since this might allow them to shift the balance of power in their favor. These twin calculations led to the conclusion that they could demand joint control of the coalition, but no more.

The Germans understood that the French were not going to allow them to control the emerging coalition. Officials in Bonn were acutely aware of France's enduring fear of the Federal Republic, a fear that would likely increase in the event that the Germans demanded preponderant influence. In 1956, for example, Adenauer noted that Germany must come out in favor of atomic energy integration because world opinion distrusted a "pure national" arrangement—that is to say an independent, nuclear Germany.[174] Likewise, Etzel recognized that serious "psychological difficulties" in France continued to stand in the way of "political unity" in western Europe.[175] Even in the mid-1950s, notes one historian, "one cannot dispute . . . that Germany had to regain a degree of outside confidence by playing down the nationalist element in its foreign policy."[176] In short, the Germans knew that they were still mistrusted and that they would only fuel that mistrust if they were seen to be seeking a dominant role.

Recognizing that they could not ask for sole control, the Germans supported a joint control solution, which in practical terms meant that they endorsed integration. Hallstein, for example, believed that Germany could not allow the common market to fail since it would then be accused of moving toward a "new nationalism."[177] If the French were offering a system based on shared decision-making authority, then Germany had no choice but to agree or be suspected of having hegemonic ambitions. Adenauer agreed with the basic logic: "If integration failed because of our reluctance, the consequences would be unforeseeable. This means that . . . we have to carry out the Messina resolution resolutely and without qualification. . . . The integration of the Six is to be promoted by all conceivable methods."[178] In fact, it was only by agreeing to integration and the system of joint control it implied that the West Germans could achieve the "permanent settlement of our relationship with France."[179]

This commitment to joint control was so strong that it led the Germans to reject alternative arrangements. Thus in October 1956, Brentano informed

---

174. Quoted in Schwarz, *Adenauer*, 231.
175. Quoted in Mahant, "French," 232.
176. Ibid., 237–38.
177. Quoted in Vanke, "Europeanism," 59.
178. Quoted in Lee, "German," 54, n. 32.
179. Quoted in Vanke, "Europeanism," 66.

Adenauer that the Germans could not accept the British proposal for an intergovernmental free trade area lest they be blamed for the "rejection" of European integration, with dire consequences for their reputation.[180] Similarly, a Foreign Ministry briefing note addressed to the chancellor warned that if the Germans were to enter negotiations on a free trade area, then they would raise suspicions about their commitment to European integration.[181] These rejections of the FTA option were highly significant. As Erhard never tired of explaining, an FTA would be more beneficial to Germany economically than a common market of the Six, a fact that Adenauer acknowledged. In other words, the Germans supported integration despite knowing full well that it was economically inferior to available alternatives.[182]

The Germans assured the French of their benign intentions, eschewed a dominant role, and settled for joint control for two reasons. First, although its economy was growing at a breakneck rate and was more advanced than France's, the Federal Republic was slightly weaker than France until 1957. Using gross national product (GNP) as a rough proxy for the size of a state's economy, the West German economy was smaller than the French one between 1950 and 1956 and only achieved parity in 1957.[183] Accordingly, the Germans could not expect the others to allow them to dominate decision making. On the other hand, a system of joint control in which France and the Federal Republic had equal say reflected the prevailing within-coalition balance of power.

Second, German officials feared that their position in the western system continued to be precarious and resolved not to step out of line in case their allies responded by imposing further controls, seeking German neutralization, or altering the postwar settlement in some other way that harmed their interests. Adenauer was obsessed with the thought that the other western powers might opt to give up on the European experiment and neutralize Germany if it did not appear absolutely committed to integration.[184] Fears such as these were not unreasonable. Although the Paris Agreements had given Germany "the full authority of a sovereign state"

180. Ibid., 75.

181. Giauque, *Grand*, 25.

182. Küsters, "West," 63–64; Lee, "German," 43–44; and Mette Eilstrup-Sangiovanni and Daniel Verdier, "European Integration as a Solution to War," *European Journal of International Relations* 11, no. 1 (2005): 110.

183. The calculation is based on data from Susan B. Carter et al., *Historical Statistics of the United States: Earliest Times to the Present*, vol. 5, *Governance and International Relations* (Cambridge: Cambridge University Press, 2006), 567–72; and Brian R. Mitchell, *International Historical Statistics: Europe, 1750–1993*, 4th ed. (London: Macmillan, 1998), 905–28.

184. For Adenauer's fears of neutralization around the time of the Messina conference, see Giauque, *Grand*, 20–21; and Wolfram F. Hanrieder, "West German Foreign Policy, 1949–1979: Necessities and Choices," in *West German Foreign Policy: 1949–1979*, ed. Wolfram F. Hanrieder (Boulder, Colo.: Westview, 1980), 19–20.

over its domestic and foreign affairs, German sovereignty continued to be strictly limited in the diplomatic and military arenas. The Germans had agreed that they would not attempt to achieve unification or alter their boundaries by force and had given up the right to negotiate reunification. In addition, and more important, it was agreed that the western Allies would station large military forces on German soil and an American SACEUR would control all German units.[185] What this meant was that West Germany simply could not "pursue an independent or flexible foreign policy because the diplomatic-political, economic, and military instruments of policy were securely embedded within the Western alliance structure."[186] In other words, Germany was in a poor negotiating position.

Although these considerations meant that the Germans did not ask to dominate the coalition, they were equally determined to not allow the French to take charge. Germany's contribution to the overall enterprise meant that the Federal Republic deserved to be placed on an equal footing with France. It was widely accepted, according to Adenauer, that Europe could not survive "unless the German nation is a member with equal rights and equal obligations." Indeed, by becoming a member "with equal rights and equal obligations, in a federated Europe," Germany would ensure the "preservation of Western culture and the guardianship of peace."[187] Because integration promised to deliver that equality, the Germans judged it the best result they could get.

In addition to agreeing to joint control, the Germans made a number of concessions that leveled the economic playing field, thereby securing French support for the common market. In his meeting with Mollet in November 1956, for example, Adenauer agreed to some harmonization of social policies as well as a series of safeguards and exemptions for France once the common market deal went into effect.[188] As Maurice Faure explained to the National Assembly, "We demanded . . . substantial sacrifices on certain points. Although we did not get them without difficulty, they enabled us to move ahead." Indeed, Paris was forced to acknowledge "the spirit of European understanding shown by the partners of France."[189] Pineau acknowledged that much of the progress toward the common market could be attributed to the "favorable disposition of the Germans."[190] German officials were also forthcoming when it came to agriculture, and at meetings in Brussels in late January and early February 1957, they agreed

185. Trachtenberg, *Constructed*, 125–28.

186. Hanrieder, "West," 17.

187. Adenauer, *World*, 52–53.

188. Willis, *France*, 248; Gerbet, *Naissance*, 96–97; Svartvatn, "Quest," 98–102. For the details, see Pineau to French Diplomatic Representatives in the Five, the United Kingdom, and the United States, November 8, 1956, *DDF*, 1956, vol. 3, 249–51.

189. Quoted in Willis, *France*, 247.

190. Pineau to French Diplomatic Representatives in the Five, the United Kingdom, and the United States, November 8, 1956, *DDF*, 1956, vol. 3, 249.

to several measures whose net effect would be to promote the expansion of French agriculture at the expense of German farmers.[191] Then, later in February, Adenauer met Mollet again and agreed to French demands regarding their overseas territories. According to the terms of the agreement, Germany would subsidize France's possessions to the tune of two hundred million dollars over five years.[192] Given that "satisfactory solutions had been found to nearly every French demand," the French government heartily endorsed the Rome Treaties when it put them to the National Assembly later in the year.[193]

How can we explain the Federal Republic's decision to allow the French economy to be placed on the "same starting basis" as its own? The answer appears to be that the West Germans wanted economic integration at virtually any price because they believed it would ultimately lead to military integration, which in turn meant equality in military matters. Adenauer was devastated by the failure of the EDC. As one of his advisers noted, it "initially threatened to bring down the entire edifice of European unity and dealt Adenauer a hard personal blow."[194] A major reason for his disappointment was that the Federal Republic would have been an equal of France under an EDC agreement but was now the only subordinate member of NATO. As SPD politician Carlo Schmid observed at the time, Germany was not given full equality in the Atlantic alliance despite surface appearances: all German units would be under NATO control, something that was not true for the other states.[195] "The failure of the European Defense Community," notes Hanns-Jürgen Küsters, "was not only the decisive setback for the European idea but also for the politics of the Federal Republic to achieve sovereignty and integration into the Western alliance."[196] The Federal Republic had been "welcomed into the 'Western Club,'" but the "terms of membership were not (whatever the club might say) entirely equal."[197] West Germany was, in essence, a semisovereign state.

Given this state of affairs, and because they thought economic integration provided a route to political integration and hence political equality, the Germans were prepared to absorb substantial costs to bring it about. Adenauer endorsed a common market at Messina because he believed that it was something upon which a "stronger political form could be forged

191. Willis, *France*, 249; and Gerbet, *Naissance*, 97. For details of the meetings, see Bousquet to Pineau, January 28, 1957, and Pineau to Diplomatic Representatives in the Five, February 2, 1957, *DDF*, 1957, vol. 1, 160–63, 186–87.

192. Willis, *France*, 250; Gerbet, *Naissance*, 98; Vanke, "Europeanism," 82; Girault, "France," 375; and Guillen, "L'avenir," 111.

193. Mahant, "French," 74.

194. Quoted in Giauque, *Grand*, 19.

195. David Clay Large, *Germans to the Front: West German Rearmament in the Adenauer Era* (Chapel Hill: University of North Carolina Press, 1996), 224.

196. Küsters, "Federal," 495.

197. Large, *Germans*, 205.

later." Similarly, he supported supranational economic institutions in his *Integrationbefehl* because he believed they could be used to "further political developments."[198] His belief, he explained to Brentano, was that "over the long term, economic cooperation . . . cannot be realized without the development of political coordination as well."[199] He was more forceful in an exchange with Erhard: "European integration was the necessary springboard for us to participate in foreign affairs again."[200]

The chancellor was not alone in holding these views—most German officials saw economic integration as a prelude to political integration. Brentano, for example, drew parallels between the EEC and the *Zollverein*, a customs union that many believed laid the foundations for the creation of a German state.[201] This was also the view of CDU party member Renatus Weber: "Because of its possibilities of influencing many areas of life, economic integration . . . is especially suited to further general integration."[202] Meanwhile, Hallstein believed that "integration in the manner of the ECSC" could bring about the "political union of Europe."[203] As Edelgard Mahant notes in a summary of the relevant evidence, "Leading members of the CDU argued that for the sake of the eventual political unity of Europe, they were willing to accept economic sacrifices and a treaty which they might consider deficient in other respects."[204] In other words, because they believed that a political community and full equality would follow on the heels of an economic one, the West Germans were prepared to pay a steep price to secure the common market.

Britain: Refusing Integration, 1955–1957

The British reacted to the common market initiative in broadly the same way that they had responded to the coal and steel community proposal and the European army project. First, despite an early attempt to wreck the common market, they ultimately supported continental efforts to establish an integrated community capable of balancing against the Soviet Union. Their reason for doing so, as always, was that such a grouping would provide them with a bulwark against Soviet power and defense in depth on the continent. Second, they were determined to cooperate with the emerging

198. Quoted in Mahant, "French," 58, 232, 239.
199. Quoted in Giauque, *Grand*, 13.
200. Quoted in Küsters, "West," 55.
201. Mahant, "French," 232.
202. Quoted in ibid., 232.
203. Quoted in Vanke, "Europeanism," 58.
204. Mahant, "French," 231. On this point, see also ibid., 73, 238–39, 250; Giauque, *Grand*, 13, 25; Wolfram F. Hanrieder, *West German Foreign Policy, 1949–1963: International Pressure and Domestic Response* (Stanford: Stanford University Press, 1967), 23; and Küsters, "West," 69.

community as closely as possible and went to great lengths to associate with it. This decision was not, however, driven solely by balance of power considerations, as had been the case in the past. Instead, decision makers in London advocated close ties to the Six in large part because they feared the economic consequences of being shut out of the common market. Finally, their cooperative stance did not imply a desire for membership—sovereignty concerns ensured that top officials never entertained the possibility of joining the Six's latest endeavor.

Nonmembership

The British refused to consider membership in the common market because it would impinge on their sovereignty.[205] Even before the Messina meeting, Allan Edden, head of the Foreign Office's Mutual Aid Department (MAD), listed four principles that ought to guide British thinking, the second of which was that Britain must retain its freedom of action.[206] Two weeks later, the government elaborated its position in a telegram to all relevant diplomatic posts. Britain favored attempts to integrate Germany into Europe and wanted to cooperate closely with whatever community might emerge, but would not enter a supranational agreement itself.[207] This was an uncontroversial decision. Even historians who differentiate between Messina "optimists" and "pessimists" acknowledge that the difference between them was about the effect that entering the Spaak discussions would have on British autonomy and not about whether Britain ought to surrender its sovereignty.[208]

This remained the British position throughout the EEC negotiations. The Cabinet's instructions to Russell Bretherton, Britain's representative to the Spaak Committee, were clear on this point. He was to bear in mind that the United Kingdom "would find great difficulty in accepting limits on national sovereignty beyond those which would be essential to ensure the major benefits of a common market."[209] Similarly, in its final report on possible membership of the common market, the high-level Mutual Aid Committee (MAC) feared that "by joining a common market, we

205. See, for example, George C. Peden, "Economic Aspects of British Perceptions of Power," in *Power in Europe? II: Great Britain, France, Germany and Italy and the Origins of the EEC, 1952–1957*, ed. Ennio Di Nolfo (New York: W. de Gruyter, 1992), 156–58.

206. Simon Burgess and Geoffrey Edwards, "The Six Plus One: British Policy-Making and the Question of European Economic Integration, 1955," *International Affairs* 64, no. 3 (1988): 397.

207. John W. Young, "'The Parting of the Ways?' Britain, the Messina Conference and the Spaak Committee, June–December 1955," in *British Foreign Policy, 1945–56*, ed. Michael Dockrill and John W. Young (London: Macmillan, 1989), 200–201.

208. Roger Bullen, "Britain and 'Europe' 1950–1957," in *La relance européenne et les Traités de Rome*, ed. Enrico Serra (Brussels: Bruylant, 1989), 334.

209. Quoted in Richard Lamb, *The Failure of the Eden Government* (London: Sidgwick and Jackson, 1987), 72.

might be taken further than we should wish along the road of economic integration and eventual political federation, with Europe."[210]

In May 1956, Treasury officials balked at membership in the common market because the "end of the Messina road" was "political fusion of some kind."[211] A few months later, in response to a Treasury request to consider the political implications of close association with the community, the Foreign Office stressed the importance of sovereignty: "Great Britain must be regarded as a world power of the second rank and not merely as a unit in a federated Europe."[212] This communication is revealing: even though the British clearly believed that they had fallen from the ranks of the great powers, they refused to surrender sovereignty to a supranational community.

The Six understood that the British would cooperate with them but refuse to join the common market out of a concern for sovereignty. Dutch foreign minister Johan Willem Beyen informed British officials soon after the Messina meeting that he realized "the UK could not accept the supranational principle and could not therefore become a full member of any body of that nature."[213] Spaak made the same point in October, admitting that he saw little chance of Britain joining the common market, but adding that he hoped the British would associate with whatever arrangement the Six came up with for themselves.[214] Similarly, during the Spaak negotiations Bretherton reported that the French were willing to move quite quickly on a common market if "the United Kingdom was also taking part" or, as seemed much more likely, was "in some way closely associated with the operation."[215]

The Americans took the same position: top officials told the British they would like the United Kingdom to join the common market, but were not expecting it to do so.[216] The message was received clearly in London. The Six, noted John Coulson, an assistant under-secretary in the Foreign Office, were not expecting Britain to become a member of an eventual common market but hoped for "a similar sort of association with the United Kingdom as had been established for the ECSC."[217]

210. Quoted in Elizabeth J. Kane, "Tilting to Europe? British Responses to Developments in European Integration, 1955–1958," (PhD diss., University of Oxford, 1996), 33.

211. Quoted in ibid., 58.

212. Quoted in James R. V. Ellison, "Perfidious Albion? Britain, Plan G and European Integration, 1955–1956," *Contemporary British History* 10, no. 4 (1996): 20.

213. Quoted in Lamb, *Failure*, 70.

214. Young, "Parting," 210.

215. Quoted in Elizabeth J. Kane, "The Myth of Sabotage: British Policy towards European Integration (1955–1956)," in *Europe des élites? Europe des peuples? La construction de l'espace européen, 1945–1960*, ed. Elisabeth du Réau (Paris: Presses de la Sorbonne Nouvelle, 1998), 292.

216. Kane, "Tilting," 18.

217. Quoted in ibid., 18.

"With" But Not "of" the Economic Community

My other claims—that Britain supported continental efforts to integrate and sought to be closely associated with them—are more controversial because of the United Kingdom's efforts to sabotage the Messina project in the fall of 1955. The attempt was short-lived, however. By the beginning of the following year, the British returned to their traditional policy of supporting integration among the Six and developed Plan G—a wider European industrial free trade area with the common market of the Six at its core—in order to draw closer to them. Balance of power reasoning lay at the root of this support. As had been the case since the late 1940s, British officials concluded that an integrated continental coalition would serve as a viable counterweight to Soviet power in Europe. Their desire to associate closely with the emerging community, however, rested on economic considerations. Balance of power thinking pushed them toward a supportive stance, but it was primarily the economic consequences of being shut out of Europe that fueled their desire for closer association.

The Sabotage Attempt

The claim that the British sought to sabotage the common market negotiations is fairly commonplace. Based on their analysis of official papers, Simon Burgess and Geoffrey Edwards conclude that the British government "took the view that economic integration among the Six would be harmful to British interests and ought therefore to be actively discouraged."[218] Sean Greenwood concurs: "Behind the trappings of a modest conversion to 'Europeanism' lay nothing much more than a common British reflex urge to wreck the Spaak proposals."[219] Similarly, Richard Griffiths concludes that British policy was designed "to derail progress on the Rome Treaties."[220]

It is certainly true that Britain made a brief but nonetheless serious attempt to derail the common market negotiations in the fall of 1955. The origins of this effort lie in the Treasury, which dominated the decision-making process at this time.[221] Its control derived from two sources. First, the Treasury was the department best suited to work through the economic issues raised by the common market. Second, officials at the Foreign Office—the other department that could have played an important role—paid little attention to the common market in 1955, doubting that the Six would be able to achieve their stated objective. In June, Britain's ambassador to France, Gladwyn Jebb, concluded that "no very spectacular developments are to be

218. Burgess and Edwards, "Six," 412.

219. Greenwood, *Britain*, 78.

220. Richard T. Griffiths, "The United Kingdom and the Free Trade Area: A Post Mortem," in *Interdependence versus Integration: Denmark, Scandinavia and Western Europe, 1945–1960*, ed. Thorsten B. Olesen (Odense: Odense University Press, 1995), 170.

221. Burgess and Edwards, "Six," 393–94.

expected as a result of the Messina Conference."[222] This remained the view once the Spaak Committee began its deliberations. Macmillan, who was foreign secretary at the time, believed the "concept was doomed to failure."[223]

Treasury hostility to the Messina project was based on economic considerations. A European common market that did not include Britain would discriminate against British goods and damage exports, which were judged to be essential to the country's economic well-being. If the British were to join the common market, however, they might have to renegotiate the so-called Ottawa system and lose the preferential position that they held in Commonwealth markets. A common market would entail substantial economic costs whether Britain joined or not.[224]

In this context, Treasury officials concluded that they had to derail the common market talks. At a high-level departmental meeting on October 27, they agreed that "the establishment of a European Common Market would be bad for the United Kingdom and if possible should be frustrated," and sanctioned a proposal by Sir Leslie Rowan, the head of the Treasury's powerful Overseas Finance Division (OFD), that was explicitly designed to "wean the Six Powers away from the Common Market."[225] Two days later, a MAC document reflecting the Rowan view advised that Britain "must clearly try to prevent it [the common market] happening if we can."[226] The Cabinet endorsed the Treasury line on November 11.[227] As John Young observes, it was at this moment that Britain abandoned the policy it had pursued since 1950, namely "*benevolence* towards, but *non-involvement* in, supranational discussions."[228]

The United States and West Germany quickly put an end to the sabotage attempt. Having decided to try to kill the common market, the British approached the Americans, who had shown considerable enthusiasm for the Messina initiative, and the Germans, who they believed could be persuaded to abandon the common market in favor of an OEEC-based alternative. Both sets of exchanges were disappointing. The Americans, noted Prime Minister Anthony Eden, could not be dissuaded from their support for the common market. They "entertained for these projects an enthusiasm similar to that which they had shown towards the European Defence Community." The Germans, meanwhile, rejected London's claim that the common market would weaken the OEEC. As the Foreign Office put it,

222. Quoted in Kane, "Myth," 292.

223. Quoted in Martin Ceadel, "British Parties and the European Situation 1950–1957," in *Power in Europe? II: Great Britain, France, Germany and Italy and the Origins of the EEC, 1952–1957*, ed. Ennio Di Nolfo (New York: W. de Gruyter, 1992), 325.

224. On these points, see Kane, "Tilting," 21–24.

225. Quoted in Ellison, "Perfidious," 3, 6.

226. Quoted in Kane, "Tilting," 37.

227. Ellison, "Perfidious," 6.

228. Young, "Parting," 217. Emphasis in original.

"the German view is diametrically opposed to HMG [Her Majesty's Government]."[229] With that, British efforts to destroy the common market ceased. Sir Geoffrey Harrison, an assistant under-secretary in the Foreign Office, laid out the logic clearly: "In the interests of our relations with Europe and with the Americans ... let us push inter-governmental co-ordination rather than attack Western integration."[230]

A More Traditional Policy

In December 1955, Macmillan became chancellor of the exchequer and the Treasury returned to the more traditional British policy of supporting the common market and seeking close cooperation with the Six, while stopping short of actual membership. This shift began almost immediately. On January 23, Macmillan told Rowan that British policy was "too negative" and had to change.[231] What he wanted, he wrote a few days later, was a "constructive alternative" to the "merely negative attitude to European co-operation (as put forward by the Messina plan & the 6 powers)" and he quickly tasked Richard Clarke, a deputy under-secretary in the Treasury, with developing such an alternative.[232] Clarke understood the chancellor's intent and in a paper for his working party on February 26 he indicated that he wanted "a genuine plan, representing a significant and real tilting of our policy towards Europe."[233]

Clarke's committee considered six plans over the next few months. By the time it drafted its interim report in April, however, Clarke himself had concluded that only two of them offered the possibility of simultaneously strengthening western Europe and linking Britain to the continent: Plan E, which envisaged a partial free trade area in Europe; and Plan F, which called for a tariff scheme linking the Commonwealth and Europe. Senior Treasury officials concurred, and later in the month Clarke's committee was instructed to focus on E and F and determine which of the two was in Britain's best interests.[234] Before it could make any recommendations, however, Peter Thorneycroft, the president of the Board of Trade (BOT), suggested another plan, subsequently known as Plan G, for an industrial free trade area—agriculture and horticulture were to be excluded—comprising the seventeen OEEC states with the common market of the Six at its core. To the extent that both of them envisaged a free trade area around the com-

---

229. Quoted in Martin Schaad, "Plan G—A 'Counterblast'? British Policy towards the Messina Countries, 1956," *Contemporary European History* 7, no. 1 (1998): 45–46.

230. Quoted in James R. V. Ellison, "Accepting the Inevitable: Britain and European Integration," in *British Foreign Policy, 1955–64*, ed. Wolfram Kaiser and Gillian Staerck (London: Macmillan, 2000), 174.

231. Quoted in Ellison, "Perfidious," 9.

232. Quoted in James R. V. Ellison, *Threatening Europe: Britain and the Creation of the European Community, 1955–58* (New York: St. Martin's, 2000), 41.

233. Quoted in Kane, "Tilting," 47.

234. Ibid., 46–56.

mon market, E and G were essentially the same. As Macmillan noted, "I should be grateful for your comments on the B/T [Board of Trade] paper. But it is really E isn't it?"[235] Because it was deemed to be more acceptable to the Commonwealth, however, ministers instructed Clarke to examine Plan G on May 29.[236]

Plan G was, then, the culmination of Britain's attempts to support the work of the Six and draw closer to the emerging common market. To Thorneycroft, the proposal "would inevitably make the European Customs Union itself more probable and would have on France a psychological effect of great importance. Such an offer would considerably strengthen the French supporters of the Common Market." Most decision makers bristled at the insinuation that it had been designed to sabotage the common market. "Any suggestion that the free trade area proposal has been put forward with the object of killing the Messina Customs Union," noted a Treasury official in November 1956, "is untrue."[237] British policy certainly appears to have reflected a desire to support the common market. In October, the Foreign Office had instructed British representatives abroad that Plan G assumed the prior existence of a common market of the Six.[238] This fact was not lost on observers at the time. As one French official noted, the free trade area proposal marked an important change in British policy because it was the "first time that Great Britain seems disposed to participate in a preferential area other than the Commonwealth."[239]

Historians today tend to support this interpretation. The new policy, asserts Martin Schaad, "was not designed to undermine the common market. . . . Plan G itself was not a 'counterblast'." Similarly, Elizabeth Kane argues that in formulating Plan G "the United Kingdom had made an attempt to improve relations with Europe, not sabotage the work of the Six." Richard Ellison concurs and views it as broadly in line with prior policy regarding developments on the continent: "Sustaining the 'with but not of' policy towards Europe, the FTA was an attempt to find a *via media* between exclusion from and inclusion in the Treaty of Rome."[240]

The Balance of Power and Support for the Six

Much of Britain's support for the Messina project after January 1956 stemmed from balance of power considerations. Key players at the Treasury were convinced that British security depended more than ever on the establishment of a powerful continental combination that could stand up to the Soviet Union. They were well aware of "the growing importance of

235. Quoted in Ellison, "Perfidious," 15–16.
236. Schaad, "Plan G," 53.
237. Quoted in Kane, "Tilting," 71–72.
238. Schaad, "Plan G," 58.
239. Quoted in Warlouzet, "Quelle," 70.
240. Schaad, "Plan G," 54; Kane, "Myth," 300; and Ellison, "Perfidious," 28.

Europe to our defence." Indeed, "of the 'three circles,' Europe looks much more important than it did . . . in 1952." The common market was crucial in this context since it promised to solidify the emerging coalition and ensure that West Germany remained a part of it. Clarke's great fear, in fact, was that "the collapse of Messina will be a psychological setback to the West" and that "it might repel Germany from the West." This being the case, "if Messina looks like failing, we may want to move closer to Europe to keep it (and our defence) together."[241]

Treasury officials continued to think in balance of power terms as the Six worked through the details of the common market. Thus in March 1956, Clarke told his working party colleagues that rather than "find a negative strategy to kill the 'Messina' idea," he wanted them to "examine these various projects in order to see whether they could help to 'bind Germany to the West'." Similarly, the April interim report warned that unless Britain drew closer to the continent and encouraged the Messina project, the Federal Republic "would disassociate herself from the West."[242] Plan G, meanwhile, explicitly envisaged a cohesive continental grouping: the Six were expected to constitute a single unit within a wider free trade area.[243] Indeed, the emerging community's role in establishing a viable counterweight to Soviet power was so important that the British were prepared to sacrifice economic interests in order to see it come into being. Although recognizing that a customs union of the Six was economically less desirable than a broader European free trade area without a customs union, the Economic Steering Sub-Committee on Closer Association with Europe nonetheless supported it on the grounds that it would bring greater cohesion to western Europe.[244]

The Foreign Office also supported the common market in the belief that integration among the Six would establish a more favorable balance of power on the continent. As Coulson informed ambassador to Belgium Christopher Warner upon learning of the Messina initiative, "mainly with an eye on keeping Federal Germany in the Western camp, we have a general disposition to favour moves to integrate Western Europe." This kind of analysis became more popular as it became clear that the Six were, in fact, going to establish a common market. In February 1956, Clarke reported that some Foreign Office officials supported the project "in order to weld Germany to the West."[245] His reading of the situation appears to have been accurate. In May, an important memorandum warned that if the Messina initiative were to fail the Germans might become disillusioned with the West and gravitate toward the Soviet camp.[246]

241. Quoted in Kane, "Tilting," 48.
242. Quoted in ibid., 51–52, 54.
243. Ellison, "Perfidious," 1.
244. Schaad, "Plan G," 58.
245. Quoted in Kane, "Tilting," 18, 48.
246. Schaad, "Plan G," 50.

This is not to say that Foreign Office decision makers had no reservations about supporting the common market. The chief concern continued to be that if the continental states succeeded in establishing a viable "third force," the Americans would withdraw from the continent, thereby depriving the United Kingdom of one of the three pillars upon which its security rested. As Edden remarked in October 1955, Spaak "makes no secret that his own political aim is the third force, a concept which we regard as misguided."[247] Clearly, Foreign Office officials supported the Messina project with some hesitation.

The Economics of Association

Although the decision to support the common market project was driven by balance of power considerations, it seems that the British sought to cooperate closely with the community for mainly economic reasons. Plan G was clearly designed to mitigate the economic effects of nonmembership. As Thorneycroft explained in September 1956, "the proposals in Plan G had been devised to turn the developments in Europe to the advantage of the United Kingdom." That he was talking about commercial advantages was clear from what followed. The plan "would place the United Kingdom for the first time in a combination equal in scale to the other two great trading units of the world." Although they focused on the costs of not establishing a free trade area around the common market, officials made essentially the same point in their final report on Plan G to Thorneycroft and Macmillan in November 1956. It would be "economically to our disadvantage if a Customs Union were set up without a free trade area."[248]

Considerations such as these took on greater urgency after the Six signed the Rome Treaties. If the common market "came into being unaccompanied by a Free Trade Area," noted the Cabinet, "the United Kingdom would be confronted with a European economic bloc which would discriminate against our exports, and we should be liable to suffer severe damage as a result both of the loss of European markets and of the intensified competition from members of the Customs Union in markets overseas." Consequently, Macmillan believed that it was "more than ever necessary to press forward the negotiations for the free trade area." The Six had to be informed of "the danger they run if they do not bend their efforts to creating the free trade area."[249] In short, the British sought close association with the EEC through a wider free trade area for economic reasons.

Even in this case, however, balance of power calculations were not entirely absent. Clarke argued in February 1956 that because the Six were in-

---

247. Quoted in Kane, "Tilting," 20.
248. Quoted in Ellison, "Perfidious," 24, 27.
249. Conclusions of a Meeting of the Cabinet, May 2, 1957, CAB 128/31, and Harold Macmillan, The European Industrial Free Trade Area, April 30, 1957, CAB 129/87, Public Record Office (PRO), Kew, United Kingdom.

creasingly important to Britain's defense, the United Kingdom had to be closely associated with the common market. "We *must* be closely associated with Europe in defence," he explained, "and we can not do this and be separated in economic policy."[250] Power concerns meant that Britain had to pursue strong economic ties with the continental states. Later in the year, the government laid out another balance of power argument for association. Britain had to be closely connected to the common market because "if we stand entirely aloof, a movement calculated not only to benefit Europe economically but to revive it politically, may collapse." The feeling was that association increased the chances that the Six would establish a truly viable coalition.[251]

In sum, Britain continued to support continental integration in the mid-1950s and sought to cooperate closely with the emerging community while refusing to actually join it. Although decision makers initially tried to wreck the common market project for economic reasons, they quickly returned to their traditional policy of support and association when the Americans and Germans made it clear that they were committed to the Messina initiative. The reasoning behind this policy continuity had changed somewhat, however. Officials ultimately supported integration on the grounds that an integrated grouping would be a counterweight to Soviet power. But their desire for association, this time through the construction of a wider free trade area with the common market at its heart, was driven by economic concerns. Without an arrangement of this sort, British exports would decline and its economy would suffer.

Alternative Explanations

How do the domestic interest group and ideational entrepreneurship arguments fare in the EEC case? The answer, in brief, is that they fail to account for French and West German decision making in the two years leading up to the Treaties of Rome.

Interest Groups

There is scant evidence that German producers pressured the government to secure a customs union in the mid-1950s. In 1954, "the OEEC type of integration was praised by the BDI as the only possible way in the future." Then, during preparatory discussions for Messina, business groups "declared that the process of integration should not be continued by abandon-

---

250. Quoted in Kane, "Myth," 296–97. Emphasis in original.
251. Quoted in Kane, "Tilting," 70.

ing sovereign rights."[252] In other words, German producers wanted a wide European free trade area without supranational institutions. This became abundantly clear after the Messina conference, as the BDI warned against the dangers of "partial unions," a reference to its preference for an OEEC-type free trade area rather than a customs union of the Six.[253] As French ambassador to Germany André François-Poncet noted at the end of May, the "Federation of German Industry (BDI) . . . Mr. Erhard and the federal minister for agriculture . . . have already pronounced themselves against all new partial integration on the coal and steel pool model."[254]

Moravcsik's own analysis does not dispute this evidence. "A clear majority of continentally and globally competitive sectors," he admits, "favored a 'large Europe' FTA encompassing all OEEC countries." Indeed, supporters of a putative six-member customs union accounted for a mere 12 percent of German manufactured exports. Taken as a whole, German business had a "preference for an FTA" and "consistently if somewhat unenthusiastically endorsed Adenauer's efforts to secure a customs union." Agriculture, meanwhile, was "cautious and ambivalent, but not hostile."[255] In short, there is little evidence that economic producer groups were determined to secure a customs union and lobbied the government to that effect.

Because business pressure was clearly not the driver of West Germany's support for the Messina initiative, Moravcsik falls back on the claim that producers concluded that a "customs union was better than nothing and that it would probably be followed by the formation of an FTA in any case."[256] This is a curious assertion. If West German industry favored a free trade area, then why did the government not seek one from the start? This decision is especially puzzling given that the British were willing to establish a free trade area and that there was a robust debate in Paris about the relative economic merits of the two solutions.[257] Simply put, if the Germans had wanted to pursue a free trade area, there appears to have been an opportunity for them to do so. Even if I am wrong about this opportunity, however, Moravcsik has abandoned the argument that producer demands drove the German decision to integrate for the weaker claim that they did not stand in its way.

There are two further problems with the interest group argument as it pertains to the German case. The first is that the government pursued a

252. Werner Bührer, "German Industry and European Integration in the 1950s," in *Western Europe and Germany: The Beginnings of European Integration, 1945–1960*, ed. Clemens A. Wurm (Oxford: Berg, 1995), 104.

253. Alan S. Milward, *The European Rescue of the Nation-State* (London: Routledge, 1992), 200.

254. François-Poncet to Pinay, May 25, 1955, *DDF*, 1955, vol. 1, 683–84.

255. Moravcsik, *Choice*, 96–97, 99.

256. Ibid., 97.

257. Parsons, *Certain*, 99–100, 103, 107, 115.

supranational customs union solution even though it was clear that an intergovernmental free trade area would be more beneficial for German producers. Erhard repeatedly explained that, from a purely economic standpoint, a free trade area was superior to a supranational customs union limited to the Six.[258] His opposition to the supranational element rested on his belief that powerful institutions would reduce the amount of liberalization that could be achieved with negative consequences for the Federal Republic's exports. As early as December 1954 he publicly condemned "institutional integration" and "supranational authority" because he feared that powerful institutions might stifle liberalization.[259] As he told Etzel in November 1956, "A Europe manipulated by bureaucrats . . . would be more a danger than a benefit."[260] Erhard's aversion to a customs union derived from similar concerns. He feared that the proposed customs union would have a high common external tariff, comprise only a handful of other states, and exclude Britain, all of which would damage Germany's export trade. Thus, he rejected the Spaak negotiations on the grounds that they would create "new divisions within the free world." The customs union, he added for good measure, was an example of "European incest." It was "macroeconomic nonsense."[261] This logic was not lost on his colleagues.[262] Even Adenauer acknowledged that the Federal Republic's rejection of the British free trade area proposal came at great "cost to Germany's economic interests."[263]

The second problem is that what German business support there was for integration rested on political rather than economic calculations. As Gerhard Braunthal has noted in his analysis of the BDI, the association's support for Adenauer's policies rested on political reasoning, including a desire to reassure other states of Germany's good intentions and to tie the Federal Republic to the West.[264] Mahant, meanwhile, shows that business was willing to "make economic sacrifices to achieve . . . a united Europe."[265] Even Moravcsik admits that the source of business support for integration was its "backing for Adenauer's geopolitical agenda." He concludes that economic considerations alone cannot have driven West Germany to support the customs union: "Without geopolitical concerns, which business itself acknowledged, Germany would surely have supported a British-style

258. See, for example, Küsters, "West," 63–64; and Lee, "German," 43–44.

259. Quoted in Vanke, "Europeanism," 48. See also ibid., 56–57; and Mahant, *Birthmarks*, 85–87.

260. Quoted in Giauque, *Grand*, 25.

261. Quoted in Mahant, "French," 242; and Lee, "German," 43. See also Giauque, *Grand*, 13, 25.

262. Parsons, *Certain*, 101.

263. Quoted in Eilstrup-Sangiovanni and Verdier, "European," 110.

264. Gerhard Braunthal, *The Federation of German Industry in Politics* (Ithaca: Cornell University Press, 1965), 285, 288–89. See also Bührer, "German," 93–95.

265. Mahant, *Birthmarks*, 55.

FTA, and the shift would prove very significant for the outcome of the negotiations."[266]

In sum, the German decision to establish the EEC does not appear to have been driven by the demands of powerful economic interest groups. By Moravcsik's own admission, the major producer groups would have preferred a free trade area, and they showed only lukewarm support for a supranational common market. Moreover, the government negotiated the EEC even though officials knew that German producers would be better off in a wider free trade area. And, finally, those same producers went along with the government for primarily political rather than economic reasons.

The claim that the French government pursued integration in order to satisfy the preferences of powerful economic producers is equally difficult to sustain. For one thing, French business does not appear to have been enthusiastic about the Benelux proposal. Drawing on several detailed studies of French attitudes toward the economic community, Parsons finds that "the Common Market had almost no support in France." In 1955, "French businessmen . . . favored as little change as possible" and preferred to liberalize slowly through the OEEC. Similarly, Pineau's adviser Robert Marjolin noted *"the hostility of almost the whole of French opinion to the removal, even gradual, of the protection which French industry enjoyed."*[267] But liberalization was not the only problem. French producers also opposed the supranational component of the customs union, referring to it as "authoritarian" integration.[268] "All producers," noted the Quai in May 1955, were "hostile" to integration and the extension of integration beyond the ECSC would create "lively objections."[269]

Little had changed when Foreign Ministry officials became aware of the contents of the Spaak Report. They thought it "obvious that a consultation with the directly interested economic and syndical groups would lead very rapidly to a negative assessment . . . and crystallize the heretofore latent opposition to the Common Market."[270] They were right; producer reaction to the report was "essentially negative" and in July 1956 business representatives on the French Economic Council voted unanimously to reject it and relocate the talks to the OEEC where they hoped to delay liberalization "indefinitely."[271] A month later, "large parts of French industry" remained firmly against the common market.[272] Although he does not portray the evidence in this way, Moravcsik is forced to admit that French producers

266. Moravcsik, *Choice*, 97, 102.

267. Quoted in Desmond Dinan, *Ever Closer Union: An Introduction to European Integration*, 2nd ed. (Boulder, Colo.: Lynne Rienner, 1999), 31. Emphasis in original.

268. Parsons, *Certain*, 103.

269. Department Note, late April–early May 1955, *DDF*, 1955, vol. 1, 551.

270. Quoted in Parsons, *Certain*, 107.

271. Ibid.

272. Vanke, "Europeanism," 68.

were hostile to supranational institutions and were "no more than cautiously and conditionally supportive" of the customs union.[273]

Nevertheless, Moravcsik argues strongly for the importance of producer preferences in driving French support for integration. Specifically, he argues that the CNPF "moved cautiously toward support for the customs union even *before* the government formally did so." He dates this move to the spring of 1956: in April "most representatives of private industry opposed the customs union," but by July they supported it. In those months, he argues, business agreed to support the common market as long as a series of conditions were met. These included demands for safeguards, escape clauses, aid for the French colonies, and harmonization of social policies. When the French government wrote these "demands essentially verbatim into the French negotiating position," business came out in support of the customs union.[274]

There are several problems with this rendering of events. First, although the episode suggests that French producers came to endorse the customs union, albeit cautiously, it does not show that they pushed for integration as the interest group argument predicts. Second, as we have seen, the government had accepted the customs union in principle as early as the summer of 1955 and certainly by early 1956 when the Mollet administration came to power. Thus its commitment to integration preceded that of big business; it was not a response to it. Third, as the October 1955 memorandum to the Spaak Committee and Pineau's comments to the other five at the Venice meeting in May 1956 make clear, the business demands that Moravcsik identifies were all included in the French government's negotiating position well before July 1956.[275] If the demands were already included before business asked for them, then their inclusion in July cannot have persuaded business to support the customs union negotiations. Finally, it is not clear why business would rally to the customs union when the French government wrote their demands into its negotiating position in the summer. Surely business support would come only when the demands were actually met, and the evidence clearly suggests that they were not met until the series of high-level meetings beginning in November 1956. In short, the episode offers little support for the importance of producers in furthering integration.

Given the foregoing, the interest group case boils down to the claim that the French government pushed for integration because of pressure from

273. Moravcsik, *Choice*, 110, 112.

274. Ibid., 109, 114. Emphasis added.

275. Memorandum of the French Delegation to the Intergovernmental Committee Created by the Messina Conference, October 14, 1955, *DDF*, 1955, vol. 2, 660–63; and Memorandum of Conversation of the Conference of the ECSC Foreign Ministers, June 8, 1956, *DDF*, 1956, vol. 1, 917–30.

agriculture. Because of industry's tepid response, argues Moravcsik, it was the "strongly positive position of agriculture" that was "decisive."[276]

It is not clear, however, that pressure from French agriculture pushed France toward the customs union. For starters, as Alan Milward has pointed out, "agricultural exports were only a secondary, subordinate issue" for the French. Their importance was so limited that the claim that farmers drove France to the EEC is a "cliché ... [that] ought to be laid to rest."[277] Moreover, although French farmers undoubtedly wanted to develop their export markets, they did not conclude that this required a supranational customs union with a common agricultural policy. They had a preference for bilateral intergovernmental deals, opposed supranationality, and feared competition from all of the other five except Germany.[278] Indeed, even Moravcsik concedes that French farmers would have preferred "a long-term, bilateral arrangement with Germany that would assure them a larger share of specific German markets without opening France to stiffer competition from Italy or northern Europe" and that the peak farming group, the National Federation of Farmers' Unions (FNSEA), opposed "supranational institutions."[279] Finally, the evidence suggests that it was the government that lobbied farmers rather than vice versa. Beginning in the spring of 1956, officials worked hard to persuade farmers to support the common market deal in what Marjolin described as the "lengthiest ... and ... most difficult" discussions to date.[280]

Thus, interest group arguments cannot convincingly explain the construction of the common market. If government decisions are driven by producer preferences, then France and Germany would not have formed a supranational customs union: neither German nor French business demanded one in the mid-1950s. Indeed, this is a conclusion that Moravcsik is forced reluctantly to endorse: "Had economic interest been the sole motivation, European governments would probably have converged toward something like an FTA, not a customs union with quasi-constitutional institutions."[281]

Ideational Entrepreneurs

The ideational entrepreneurship explanation for the establishment of the common market rests on the claim that the major protagonists endorsed

276. Moravcsik, *Choice*, 110.

277. Milward, *European*, 283.

278. Craig Parsons, "Showing Ideas as Causes: The Origins of the European Union," *International Organization* 56, no. 1 (2002): 68; Parsons, *Certain*, 103; and Milward, *European*, 283–84.

279. Moravcsik, *Choice*, 112.

280. Robert Marjolin, *Architect of European Unity: Memoirs, 1911–1986*, trans. William Hall (London: Weidenfeld and Nicolson, 1989), 295.

281. Moravcsik, *Choice*, 90.

integration because it provided an organizational alternative to the nation-state. Believing that a nation-state system was prone to conflict, they sought to replace it with a supranational arrangement.

Parsons describes almost all of the key actors in France as being pro-integration. Mollet and French president René Coty "shared pro-community sympathies." Foreign Minister Pinay was "favorable to community plans," and his successor, Pineau, had been "pro-EDC." France's chief negotiators shared this basic outlook. Maurice Faure was an "ultra-Europeanist" and Marjolin was "entirely ready to direct European policy into new waters." The same was true of important functionaries, including Emile Nöel and Jacques Donnedieu de Vabres.[282]

Jeffrey Vanke suggests that a similar situation existed in West Germany. Adenauer, especially, had a "deep desire for creating a new Europe," one that was fundamentally different to the Europe of the "1920s and 1930s" where individuals "held no higher frame of reference for their loyalties . . . than the nation-state." Indeed, having examined the decisions that led to the establishment of the EEC, he concludes that "despite their countries' sometimes conflicting interests, and their own differing secondary motivations," the major protagonists in France and the Federal Republic "openly shared an impulse to unite their continent in an *unprecedented* way, a common spirit to integrate Europe."[283] It seems clear, then, that the actors most responsible for driving integration forward held "pro-community" ideas.

Proponents of the ideational argument do not, however, provide good evidence that the prime movers in the common market affair endorsed integration on the grounds that it would enable Europe to transcend the nation-state system. Indeed, Parsons is silent about the source of their pro-community ideas. Decision makers are designated as "Europeanist" or not depending on their attitude toward the common market: if they supported it, then they were pro-community; if they did not, then they were "traditionalists" or "confederalists." But Parsons does not investigate the reasoning behind their views—he does not ask *why* they supported integration.[284] Meanwhile, Vanke describes the development of a "European spirit" based on a rejection of the nation-state but does not offer compelling evidence that the major protagonists acted on the basis of this spirit.[285] Thus, he asserts that Mollet and Pineau were "among the most 'European' of Fourth Republic leaders" and that Adenauer was imbued with a "general 'Europe-

282. Parsons, *Certain*, 97, 108.

283. Vanke, "Europeanism," 15–16, 59, 93. Emphasis added.

284. Parsons describes the eight protagonists listed in the previous paragraph as holding pro-integration ideas several times in his book, but never addresses the source of their ideas. See Parsons, *Certain*, 56, 64, 74, 77, 79, 97, 108, 114–15.

285. Vanke, "Europeanism," 15–16, 31–35, 92–93.

anist' commitment," but he does not demonstrate that their "Europeanism" derived from dissatisfaction with the existing nation-state system.[286]

Worse still, an examination of the motivations of the major players suggests that they were patently not intent on transcending the nation-state system. The important actors in France saw integration as a means to establish a powerful coalition capable of balancing against the Soviet Union while maintaining a roughly even balance of power in the western half of the continent. Far from eliminating the French state, integration was meant to preserve it. Pinay appears to have advocated the centralization of western Europe as a means to defend France against the Soviet Union rather than surrender French sovereignty. The same kind of reasoning comes through clearly in Mollet's preelectoral *Le Monde* article, as well as Pineau's pronouncements about the simultaneous importance of centralization and material parity with West Germany. For both of them, integration was a means of enhancing French security. Marjolin placed less of an emphasis on integration as a balance of power tool, but this did not mean that he regarded it as a route to the abandonment of the nation-state. "I also thought," he wrote in his memoirs, "that the nation-state was not on the way out and that one could not expect the emergence of a European state in the foreseeable future." Indeed, he considered the "dismantlement" of the sovereign system to be an unachievable "mental construct."[287] The French did not, then, view the common market as a step toward eliminating the nation-state system.

This was also the basic attitude in Germany. Adenauer's support for integration derived from the belief that it would help secure rather than efface the German nation-state. The common market would help to establish a viable counterweight to Soviet power, thereby enhancing the security of all of western Europe including Germany. Moreover, because it offered the Federal Republic equal rights in the economic realm now and the possibility of military equality in the future, the chancellor and other important officials, including Brentano, Hallstein, and Ophüls, thought of it as a vehicle for restoring rather than surrendering sovereignty.

In sum, French and German decision makers did not endorse integration because they thought that it would lead to the elimination of the nation-state system. Proponents of the ideational entrepreneurship argument provide little evidence that "pro-community" or "Europeanist" elites supported the common market based on its potential to introduce an alternative to the Westphalian order. Indeed, a close examination of the historical record suggests that the key actors were as committed as ever to preserving their states, and that they viewed integration as the best means to that end given the prevailing distribution of power.

286. Ibid., 43–44.
287. Marjolin, *Memoirs*, 264, 267.

Conclusion

The evidence from the common market case supports my argument. The European and global distribution of power that existed at the end of World War II continued to obtain in the late 1950s. Faced with this power configuration, the French resolved to establish a centralized unit of power in the western half of the continent and embraced a particular variant of centralization—integration—in order to ensure that the West Germans could not outpace them. Indeed, they were so concerned about maintaining a roughly even balance of power at the heart of western Europe that they refused to accept the EEC until the Federal Republic agreed to a series of measures designed to put the French and German economies on an equal footing from the outset. Believing that a centralized coalition was essential for balancing against the Soviet Union if the United States withdrew from Europe and knowing that the most the French would allow them was equality within that coalition, the Germans acquiesced to France's demands. Meanwhile, the British continued to support continental integration because it promised to provide them with better defense in depth. But they saw no reason to surrender their sovereignty and actually join the emerging community. France, Germany, and the others were more endangered and should therefore be the ones paying autonomy costs for the common defense.

The alternative arguments do not fare as well as my own. There is scant evidence that powerful producers in France and West Germany demanded that their respective governments engage in integration. French businessmen had no enthusiasm for the common market and their German counterparts rejected supranational arrangements restricted to the Six. Indeed, German producers preferred a British-style free trade area to the deal they ultimately got. Similarly, officials in Paris and Bonn do not appear to have endorsed integration as a means to transcend the nation-state system. Mollet, Adenauer, and most of their subordinates continued to subscribe to a traditional view of the world.

So the evidence suggests that the origins of the common market lay in balance of power politics and specifically in French and German attempts to establish a favorable balance of power vis-à-vis the Soviet Union and one another. This finding has important implications. Most important, it means that contrary to received opinion, the construction of the EC is best understood not in terms of commercial interests or new political ideas but as the consequence of a particular distribution of power.

6. Beyond Postwar Europe

States balance against powerful competitors and in the context of the early cold war this drove France and the Federal Republic to establish the EC. Aware that they confronted an overwhelming opponent and that the Soviet Union derived its strength from a centralized organizational structure in addition to its formidable assets, the Europeans understood that they had to go beyond an alliance and establish a multistate coalition with a central governing authority in order to balance against it effectively.

There is substantial evidence that decision makers in Paris and Bonn recognized the imperative of building a centralized balancing coalition to ensure their security. Contrary to the common view that they wanted to keep Germany weak, French officials understood that they had to rebuild the Federal Republic and join forces with it. Moreover, they took it for granted that this could not be a coalition of the old sort. Instead, a viable third force had to have a central governing authority to compete with the Soviet Union without American help. Most Frenchmen in a position to influence national policy agreed. Indeed, it is striking how quickly the term "Europe" came to mean a centrally organized political-economic bloc built around a Franco-German axis.

German thinking developed along similar lines. Chancellor Konrad Adenauer was obsessed with the Soviet threat and worried constantly about the reliability of the American guarantee. As a result, he was committed early on to creating a "United States of Europe" or "European federation" capable of being a third global power. Despite the chancellor's exceptional influence, he did not simply impose his view on this matter on his subordinates. With the important exception of Economics Minister Ludwig Erhard, most high-ranking civilians and top military officials shared his basic outlook.

In short, there is good evidence for Edward Gibbon's two-hundred-year-old prediction: "If a savage conqueror should issue from the deserts of Tartary, he must repeatedly vanquish . . . the numerous armies of Germany, the gallant nobles of France, and the intrepid freemen of Britain; who, perhaps, might confederate for their common defense."[1]

Were it not for the prevailing regional and global distribution of power in the early postwar period, these plans might never have been proposed, and they would almost certainly not have seen the light of day. States confronting an overwhelming competitor face two impediments to building a viable countervailing coalition. First, they must possess enough aggregate power to compete with their opponent. If they do not, there is no point in joining forces. Second, they must have some reasonable expectation that they will not be destroyed the moment they begin to balance. Practically speaking, this means that there must be some reason that their adversary cannot use its power advantage against them.

Both conditions obtained in postwar Europe. For one thing, the Six had the means to balance against the Soviet Union should they want to—they were at less than a 2:1 power disadvantage to the USSR throughout the period under review. Equally important, the American offshore balancer gave them the opportunity to put their coalition into place. I am not the first person to stress the importance of the United States in the construction of the EC. Whereas most analysts claim that it was America's role as western Europe's pacifier that made integration possible, however, I argue that it was America's role as protector that moved the process forward. Simply put, the U.S. commitment to defend Europe gave France and Germany an opportunity to build the EC, an opportunity they took because they feared that the United States might not protect them indefinitely.

Of course, the French and the West Germans knew that constructing a centralized coalition meant surrendering sovereignty, something they were extremely reluctant to do. But they concluded that the geopolitical situation gave them no other option. Given the overwhelming power of the Soviet Union, they calculated that they could be secure over the long haul only if they established a centrally organized west European bloc. They traded away autonomy for security. France and West Germany could not compete in a superpower world, but maybe "Europe" could.

Why did the Europeans choose a specific form of centralization, namely integration? Again, the answer lies in balance of power politics. Even as they established their coalition, they were determined not to allow their partners to control it, believing that any state in command of the group might have the inclination and ability to shift the within-coalition distribution of power in its favor. They also knew that their partners would not al-

---

1. Edward Gibbon, *The Decline and Fall of the Roman Empire*, vol. 2 (New York: Modern Library, 1932), 95.

low them to take charge, and therefore agreed to a system of joint control and formed a community.

This was clearly the thought process behind French support for the EC project: key policymakers saw integration as a way to instantiate and perpetuate a roughly even balance of power west of the Elbe. The west Germans viewed matters much the same way. Unwilling to countenance French control, but cognizant that they could not seize command, they concluded that integration was the only viable option. In other words, France and the Federal Republic elected to integrate because neither could dominate the other and, at the same time, both feared being subjugated by the other.

Balance of power thinking also offers a plausible explanation of decisions not to integrate. Above all, it explains why the British refused to become involved. Viewed from London, any continental attempt to build a centralized unit of power was welcome since it would make Britain more secure. However, because an arrangement of this kind would stand a good chance of containing the Soviet Union, the British saw no reason actually to join it. By cooperating rather than participating, they would still be more secure against the Soviets without having to surrender their autonomy. France and Germany could bear the sovereignty costs of establishing a viable counterweight to Soviet power and the United Kingdom would free ride on their efforts.

These kinds of considerations also explain why the Europeans did not complement their economic community with a military one. France preferred an integrated European military to an independent German army. It would establish a bulwark against the Soviet Union and was at least designed to maintain an even Franco-German balance of power. But there was a more attractive alternative from a power perspective: a large U.S. force on the continent. As Lord Ismay famously put it, an American commitment to NATO would do more than any European solution to "keep the Russians out, [and] the Germans down."[2] Moreover, an arrangement of this kind had the added attraction of not requiring the French to surrender their sovereignty to a supranational institution. Still, the NATO option was not foolproof since the Americans might leave the continent at a later date. Therefore, the French proposed to supplement NATO with the WEU, an organization that would maintain a roughly even balance of power within western Europe and could be converted into a purely European force in the event of an American withdrawal. When the United States agreed to the NATO-WEU alternative, the European army project collapsed.

There is less evidence that the EC was the result of interest group pressure or a desire to transcend the nation-state. The French and German

2. Christopher Layne, "America as European Hegemon," *National Interest* no. 72 (2003): 19. To be clear, my argument is that the French wanted rough equality with the Germans. They did not want to keep them down.

governments do not appear to have pursued integration because powerful domestic groups demanded it. Most of the time they made decisions without consulting producers and with little regard for their interests. When producers did express an opinion, they were usually hostile to integration. Nor were decision makers driven by a desire to replace the nation-state system with an alternative form of political organization. Certainly, there is little direct evidence for this kind of thinking. Indeed, a close look reveals that France and Germany surrendered sovereignty reluctantly, believing that only a European community could compete with the USSR.

Likewise, there is scant support for the popular perception that the European order is the result of a conscious rejection of balance of power politics. Robert Kagan offers a neat summary of this view: "The Europeans, who invented power politics, turned themselves into born-again idealists by an act of will, leaving behind them . . . 'the old system of balance with its continued national orientation, constraints of coalition, traditional interest-led politics and the permanent danger of nationalist ideologies and confrontations'." Visionary leaders decided that "the integration of Europe was not to be based on . . . the balance of power. To the contrary, the miracle came from the rejection of military power and of its utility as an instrument of international affairs."[3] The facts flatly contradict this often self-congratulatory rendering of events: today's Europe is the direct product of traditional balance of power thinking.

Given my findings, it is worth asking why it is generally agreed that the construction of the EC can be attributed to the enlightened pursuit of economic self-interest, a desire to introduce a new political form in Europe, or both. Although I can only speculate, it seems that scholars and pundits alike have produced what Herbert Butterfield once referred to as a "whig interpretation" of history; that is, they have organized "history by reference to the present," and in doing so have produced a "gigantic optical illusion."[4] Noting that the Europeans have constructed an economic community to which they have surrendered a substantial portion of their sovereignty, observers have mistakenly concluded that economic gain and a desire to transcend the state system must have been what drove policymakers to build the EC in the first place. Such arguments may mesh neatly with our understanding of the community today, but they do not find a great deal of support in the historical record.

More generally, this book suggests that balance of power arguments can tell us a lot about international cooperation and institutions. This is likely to be a controversial claim since it is generally agreed that realism, which privileges balance of power explanations, has a hard time explaining either

3. Robert Kagan, *Of Paradise and Power: America and Europe in the New World Order* (New York: Alfred A. Knopf, 2003), 56, 59.
4. Herbert Butterfield, *The Whig Interpretation of History* (New York: W. W. Norton, 1965), 29.

phenomenon. Realists themselves concede this point. "Cooperation between states does occur," asserts John Mearsheimer before claiming that "it is sometimes difficult to achieve . . . and always difficult to sustain." Meanwhile, Joseph Grieco admits readily that realism "needs to develop a theory of international institutions."[5] One of my chief goals in writing this book is to rectify this situation. The result is a straightforward application of balance of power logic: states cooperate to balance against a common opponent; the form their cooperation takes depends on the power gap between them and that opponent, as well as the distribution of power within their coalition; and they establish institutions to facilitate their cooperative ventures.

I have tried to show that this argument accounts for perhaps the most important example of institutionalized interstate cooperation in modern times—the EC—and that it does so better than extant alternatives. Before I can claim to have laid the foundations for a balance of power theory of cooperation, however, I must show that the argument applies more broadly. Otherwise, I am vulnerable to the criticism that I have explained postwar European cooperation and little else.

How the Theories Travel

To determine how well my theory and its competitors travel beyond the EC case, I focus on two questions. First, can the theories explain why the EC is the only example of community building since 1815? Second, do they offer plausible explanations for the origins and form of other cooperative ventures that look at least somewhat similar to it?

Balance of Power Politics

My core claim is that states establish centralized coalitions, be they communities or unions, when they confront overwhelming competitors and have both the means and opportunity to balance against them. Recall that I distinguish between overwhelming and superior rivals based on whether the states being compared are great or minor powers. A great power can only confront a superior competitor. Even the mightiest great powers have not been so powerful as to render resistance by their peers useless. In contrast, a minor power confronting a great power faces an overwhelming opponent—its odds of survival in the event of a conflict are slim. That said,

5. John J. Mearsheimer, "The False Promise of International Institutions," *International Security* 19, no. 3 (1994–95): 12; and Joseph M. Grieco, "Understanding the Problem of International Cooperation: The Limits of Neoliberal Institutionalism and the Future of Realist Theory," in *Neorealism and Neoliberalism: The Contemporary Debate* (New York: Columbia University Press, 1993), 335.

a coalition of minor powers may have the combined means to contain a threatening great power. I assume that such groups have the capability to balance effectively as long as they are not on the wrong end of a gross mismatch, which is to say that they are at better than a 3:1 power disadvantage. Finally, I measure power ratios by comparing one state's military personnel, military expenditure, steel production, and energy consumption to another's.[6]

I code minor powers as constituting a plausible coalition if they inhabited the same geographic region and were members of the same alliance at any point between 1815 and 1980.[7] Of these, twenty-three were confronted by an overwhelming rival, which is to say that they were located in the same region of the world as a great power, or one of their members was geographically contiguous to a great power.[8]

Since 1815, only the post–World War II west European coalition, which was never at more than a 2:1 disadvantage to the Soviet Union, has had the means to balance against a rival great power. Twenty-one of the other candidates were at more than, often considerably more than, a 5:1 disadvantage to an adjoining great power rival. Another was at approximately a 4:1 disadvantage to not one but two adjacent great powers. Indeed, only one other coalition came close to avoiding a gross mismatch—it was briefly at a 3:1 disadvantage to its great power rival—but even in this case a closer

---

6. For a more detailed discussion of these points, see chapter 2 and table 1.

7. I coded all the states that were not great powers in the Correlates of War, State System Membership dataset (http://www.correlatesofwar.org) as minor powers, and assigned them to one of nine geographic regions using the United Nations, Macro Regions and Components list (http://www.un.org/depts/dhl/maplib/worldregions. htm). The United Nations lists twenty-one regional components that I aggregated into nine regions: Africa, Europe, East Asia, South Asia, West Asia, Central America, South America, North America, and Oceania. I used the Alliance Treaty Obligations and Provisions (ATOP) dataset (http://atop.rice.edu/publications) to establish whether minor powers were ever in the same alliance, but I excluded the periods of the two world wars (1914–1918, 1939–1945).

8. I assigned the great powers listed in chapter 2 to various regions using the United Nations dataset and coded them as being contiguous to minor powers if they shared a land border or were separated from them by less than 150 miles of water according to the Correlates of War, Direct Contiguity dataset (http://www.correlatesofwar.org). My analysis yielded the following twenty-three coalitions: *German* (eight German states); *Iberian* (Portugal, Spain); *Italian* (six Italian states); *North East European* (Estonia, Latvia, Lithuania); *North European* (Estonia, Latvia, Poland, Romania); *Central European One* (Austria, Czechoslovakia), *Two* (Czechoslovakia, Greece), *Three* (Czechoslovakia, Romania, Yugoslavia), *Four* (Austria, Hungary), *Five* (Bulgaria, Greece, Romania, Yugoslavia); *Central American* (twenty central American / Caribbean states); *East Asian One* (Korea, Japan), *Two* (China, North Korea); *West Asian One* (Iraq, Turkey), *Two* (twelve western Asian states); *South Asian One* (Iran, Afghanistan), *Two* (India, Philippines), *Three* (Pakistan, Philippines, Thailand), *Four* (Pakistan, Iran), *Five* (Myanmar, Cambodia, India, Thailand, Vietnams), *Six* (India, Pakistan), *Seven* (India, Bangladesh), *Eight* (Malaysia, Singapore, Indonesia, Philippines, Thailand, Brunei).

analysis reveals that its disadvantage was closer to 5:1.[9] In other words, apart from the Six, who comfortably avoided a gross mismatch, there are no historical examples of plausible coalitions with anywhere near the means to balance effectively against a great power opponent.

This finding is consistent with the general view that the EC is a unique development. If it is "unique" or "exceptional in international politics," as most observers claim, then the conditions that are supposed to have created it cannot have been present in other places or at other times.[10] Although the foregoing analysis is admittedly fairly crude, it suggests that this has indeed been the case. The power configuration that prompted the west Europeans to integrate after 1945 does not appear to have obtained at any other time or in any other place since 1815.

Although the EC is an unprecedented creation, several cases bear at least passing resemblance to it. After all, it is an example of interstate cooperation, albeit an extreme one, and cooperative agreements have been rife in international politics. States have established many alliances, including the German *Bund* (1815), the Triple Entente (1907), and the Baghdad Pact (1955). They have been almost as active in the economic realm, especially after 1945, with the formation of trade pacts such as the Association of Southeast Asian Nations (ASEAN), the Central American Common Market (CACM), and the North American Free Trade Agreement (NAFTA).[11] Upon careful inspection, none of these arrangements are exact analogues of the EC because they are examples of decentralized rather than centralized interstate cooperation.[12] To the extent that they involve cooperation among sovereign states, however, they fall into the same broad class of cases.

My theory provides a good first-cut explanation for the origins of several alliances. Specifically, states ally in order to create a favorable balance of power vis-à-vis a common rival.[13] Austria, Prussia, and the other German

9. The coalition was at only a 3:1 disadvantage to the Soviet Union in 1960 because it included China, which had a large military and economy. Note, however, that the Soviet Union spent five times more on its military and had a GNP per capita that was six times greater than China's. See Correlates of War, National Material Capabilities, 1816–2001, http://www.correlatesofwar.org; and Angus Maddison, Statistics on World Population, GDP and Per Capita GDP, 1–2008 AD, http://www.ggdc.net/maddison.

10. Andrew Moravcsik, *The Choice for Europe: Social Purpose and State Power from Messina to Maastricht* (Ithaca: Cornell University Press, 1998), 1; and Craig Parsons, *A Certain Idea of Europe* (Ithaca: Cornell University Press, 2003), 2.

11. For typical lists, see Melvin Small and J. David Singer, "Formal Alliances, 1816–1965: An Extension of the Basic Data," *Journal of Peace Research* 6, no. 3 (1969): 264–70, 276–79; and James McCall Smith, "The Politics of Dispute Settlement Design," *International Organization* 54, no. 1 (2000): 152–54.

12. Some of the trade pacts contain supranational dispute settlement mechanisms. These are examples of joint arbitration, not joint decision making.

13. For examples, see John J. Mearsheimer, *The Tragedy of Great Power Politics* (New York: W. W. Norton, 2001); and Stephen M. Walt, *The Origins of Alliances* (Ithaca: Cornell University Press, 1984).

states allied to overawe France after 1815; Britain, France, and Russia allied to contain Imperial Germany in 1907; and the United States and Britain joined forces with Iraq to deter Soviet expansion in 1955. Of course, this is not the only reason that states form alliances. Sometimes they want to restrain their partners or manage conflicts with them.[14] In many cases, however, alliances are built and maintained to balance against a third party.

Power considerations also explain why alliances are decentralized in form. In reviewing eighty-eight defensive pacts in a well-known dataset, I found only one that confronted an overwhelming opponent and three more that may have been directed against an overwhelming rival though the evidence on these is inconclusive.[15] In all of the other cases, the designated rival was superior, equal, or inferior to the most powerful member of the coalition that confronted it, but never overwhelmingly more powerful. This had crucial implications for the form their cooperation took. Simply by agreeing to act in concert, the allies stood a good chance of deterring or defeating their targets. To be sure, they could have generated even more power by establishing a central authority in each case. But this would have meant giving up sovereignty, which states are reluctant to do unless they have no choice. Therefore, they preferred decentralized alliances, knowing that these were enough to establish a favorable balance of power, while allowing them simultaneously to retain their sovereign prerogatives.

A similar argument accounts for the origins of several trade pacts. States that want to establish a favorable power position compared to a common opponent have good reason to supplement their alliances with trading agreements: they increase economic exchange among the allies, thereby building up a coalition's aggregate wealth and consequently its power. This kind of thinking has been fairly common historically: military allies have repeatedly formed trade pacts among themselves. "Even a casual glance at the customs unions that have formed since the conclusion of World War II," observes Edward Mansfield, "indicates that customs union partners tend to be political-military allies." In fact, he finds that all or many members of the following pacts were already allied when they were founded: the EC, the Council for Mutual Economic Assistance, the Andean Common Mar-

14. Paul W. Schroeder, "Alliances, 1815–1945: Weapons of Power and Tools of Management," in *Historical Dimensions of National Security Problems*, ed. Klaus Knorr (Lawrence: University Press of Kansas, 1976), 227–62.

15. For the list, see Singer and Small, "Formal," 264–70, 276–79. According to the ATOP dataset, only eighty-one of these were actually defensive pacts. Forty-two contained one or more great powers and therefore did not confront an overwhelming competitor by definition. A further thirty-five were directed against a minor power and therefore also did not confront an overwhelming competitor by definition. The only alliance that clearly faced an overwhelming opponent was the Bulgarian-Serbian minor power alliance of 1912, which was directed against Turkey, Romania, and great power Austria-Hungary.

ket, the Central American Common Market, the Latin American Free Trade Association, the Central African Customs and Economic Union, the Maghreb Group, the North American Free Trade Agreement, the US-Israeli Free Trade Area, the Common Afro-Mauritian Organization, the Association of Southeast Asian Nations, the European Free Trade Association, and the East African Common Market.[16] To be clear, not all trade pacts are the product of balance of power calculations. Nevertheless, as Jagdish Bhagwati has observed, "the incentives . . . need not be *economic* incentives. In fact, it is hard to imagine that the arbitrary groupings of countries that seek FTAs and CUs [customs unions] are dependent on economic arguments as their key determinants. Often, politics seems to drive these choices of partners . . . [and] also accounts for the occasional non-regionally proximate choices of partners in such blocs."[17]

Balance of power calculations also provide a simple explanation for why these trade pacts have been organized in a decentralized fashion. Because alliances do not confront overwhelming rivals, their members are content with the modest increments in power that come from decentralized economic cooperation. In addition, although alliance partners understand that they could generate even more power by centralizing decision-making authority, they prefer not to incur the associated sovereignty costs unless they have to. Thus, decentralized cooperation offers them the best of both worlds: it allows them to establish a favorable balance of power and to retain their sovereignty.

Enough said about decentralized cooperation. The historical record also yields a handful of centralized cooperative ventures that share similarities with the European case, notably the formation of the United States of America (1789), Italian unification (1859–60), and German unification (1871). None of these events are perfect comparables. In contrast to the European Six, the American colonies were not sovereign states when they integrated. Like the Europeans, the Italians and the Germans established a central governing authority over previously independent states, but in both cases a single state controlled it (Piedmont and Prussia, respectively). In other words, they engaged in unification instead of integration. There are other differences as well. Italy was created by conquest rather than interstate agreement, and the German Empire was a union of princes rather than states. Nevertheless, because all three cases involved centralization, they are at least minimally comparable to the EC.

16. Edward D. Mansfield, "Effects of International Politics on Regionalism in International Trade," in *Regional Integration and the Global Trading System*, ed. Kym Anderson and Richard Blackhurst (New York: St. Martin's, 1993), 210.

17. Jagdish Bhagwati, "Regionalism and Multilateralism: An Overview," in *New Dimensions in Regional Integration*, ed. Jaime de Melo and Arvind Panagariya (Cambridge: Cambridge University Press, 1993), 38. Emphasis in original.

The integration of Britain's former colonies to create the United States of America can be explained in balance of power terms. For one thing, the prevailing geopolitical situation gave them the motive, means, and opportunity to establish a coalition of some kind. The incentive to join forces was strong: Britain was an overwhelming opponent with a foothold in Canada and none of the colonies could hope to balance against it alone. But they did have the combined means to build a viable counterweight to British power. Even without accounting for the problems Britain would encounter in projecting power onto the continent, a putative coalition would be at only a 3:1 disadvantage in the late eighteenth century.[18] Moreover, the Americans had an opportunity to coalesce. Britain was unlikely to intervene because it had to devote most of its resources to fighting the Napoleonic Wars in Europe and understood that victory against France depended, at least in part, on maintaining good relations with the United States lest they choose to support the French in the American theater.[19]

The American response in 1789 was remarkably similar to the west European one in the 1950s. Given that Britain was considerably more powerful than the former colonies even if they formed an alliance, decision makers concluded that their coalition had to have a central governing authority. Only a centralized combination could compete with Britain effectively. A "union," argued John Jay in *Federalist* no. 4, could "apply the resources and power of the whole to . . . defense." On the other hand, if the former colonies retained their independence, "what armies could they raise and pay— what fleets could they ever hope to have?" Alexander Hamilton made a similar point with respect to economic power: a single economy would likely produce an "aggregate balance of . . . commerce . . . much more favorable than that of the thirteen states" and prevent enemies from "restrain[ing] our growth."[20]

Because there was no "colonial government capable of suppressing the others," the American states agreed to share control of the newly centralized entity—they were equally represented in the Congress where majorities were required for policymaking purposes, and no state had a veto.[21] In other words, they built a military-economic community. This arrangement was expected to have an important added advantage: it offered to preserve the existing distribution of power going forward. If a single jointly-determined policy was applied to all of the member states, then the "same degree of sound policy, prudence, and foresight would uniformly

18. I derived this power ratio by comparing the population of Britain with that of the United States in 1800. For the data, see Mearsheimer, *Tragedy*, 241, 282.

19. See, for example, Harry C. Allen, *Great Britain and the United States: A History of Anglo-American Relations (1783–1952)* (New York: St. Martin's, 1955), 301.

20. Alexander Hamilton, James Madison, and John Jay, *The Federalist Papers*, ed. Clinton Rossiter (New York: Mentor, 1999), 16, 55, 58.

21. Mancur Olson, "Dictatorship, Democracy, and Development," *American Political Science Review* 87, no. 3 (1993): 574.

be observed by each," thereby making it more likely that they would "remain . . . on an equal footing in point of strength."[22] In short, integration both reflected and promised to perpetuate the existing within-coalition distribution of power.

Balance of power politics can also at least partially explain Italian unification. Because none of the Italian states could balance against Austria alone—even Piedmont was at a 5:1 military disadvantage in 1859—they had a powerful incentive to establish some kind of coalition. It was clear that if they did join forces they would have the means to balance effectively. An Italian coalition would be at only a 2:1 military disadvantage to Austria and even a north Italian kingdom comprising just Piedmont and Lombardy would be at only a 3:1 disadvantage.[23] Of course, the Italians did not have the industrial might to compete, but at the time wars were still short and army strength was what mattered most. Moreover, by 1859 they had the opportunity to come together should they want to. By the terms of a secret treaty, Napoleon III of France pledged to support a Piedmontese bid to unify northern Italy against almost certain Austrian opposition.

Like the Europeans after 1945, the Piedmontese concluded that only a centralized coalition could balance effectively against their great power rival. Philosopher Vincenzo Gioberti laid out the logic as early as 1843. Centralization would "put the strength of each [state] at the disposal of all," and allow Italy to return to "the first rank of the Powers." It was only by "pooling the wealth and forces of our various states" that the Italians could ensure their security.[24] How Piedmont hoped to unify the peninsula is the subject of some debate, but it seems that it planned to use a war with Austria to unite northern Italy and then negotiate unification with the central states and perhaps the southern ones as well.[25]

There is also some evidence for these kinds of calculations in the other Italian states. To be sure, several state leaders, including Grand Duke Leopold of Tuscany and King Francis of Naples, opposed unification. But there was considerable popular support for some form of Italian union in

22. Hamilton, Madison, and Jay, *Federalist*, 19. On the issue of maintaining the within-coalition balance of power, see also Barry R. Weingast, "Political Stability and Civil War: Institutions, Commitment, and American Democracy," in *Analytic Narratives*, ed. Robert H. Bates, et al. (Princeton: Princeton University Press, 2001), 148–93.

23. For the data used to generate the military power ratios, see Correlates of War, National. My statement about a northern kingdom is based on Denis Mack Smith's claim that such an entity would have a population of eleven million (*Cavour* [New York: Alfred A. Knopf, 1985], 149). Note that the Correlates of War dataset does not include Lombardy.

24. Quoted in Denis Mack Smith, *The Making of Italy, 1796–1870* (London: Macmillan, 1968), 83.

25. Daniel Ziblatt, *Structuring the State: The Formation of Italy and Germany and the Puzzle of Federalism* (Princeton: Princeton University Press, 2006), 91, 94, 95, 96.

Lombardy, as well as in Modena, Parma, Tuscany, and the Papal States.[26] This attitude was at least in part based on balance of power thinking. As early as 1854, argues Denis Mack Smith, "in every other region of Italy there were some people who looked to Piedmont as their main hope in the struggle against Austrian dominance."[27] Similarly, Derek Beales observes that supporters of unification in the central Italian states "were influenced by the belief that in the international situation only Piedmont could protect them from intervention which would remove their liberty."[28]

As it happened, Italy came into being as a state rather than a union of states. Unlike the United States and Germany, Italy's constituent states were "erased from the political map as formal political units." This was not the result of conscious design. Instead, as Daniel Ziblatt argues, the states that fell into Piedmont's hands courtesy of the war with Austria and Giuseppe Garibaldi's unauthorized conquests in the south simply could not "do the basic work of modern governance."[29] If Italy was to be a great power, then the weaker Italian states could not be allowed to manage their own affairs and had to be absorbed into a unitary state.

The geopolitical situation also appears to have given the German states the motive, means, and opportunity to build a formidable coalition of their own in 1871. The incentive to join forces was provided by the fact that France was an overwhelming competitor. This claim may surprise some readers since Prussia is generally treated as a great power, but it is worth noting that it was at a 3:1 military disadvantage to France in 1865.[30] Given that military power was still the most important predictor of battlefield success, it was not clear *ex ante* that it would have been able to put up a good fight in a war with its western neighbor. There is no question about the others: Baden, Bavaria, the Hesses, Hanover, Mecklenburg, Saxony, and Württemberg were clearly minor powers.

Although there was reason to believe that none of the German states had the requisite capabilities to balance effectively against France on their own, they had the means to do so together. By 1865, a putative coalition would have been at only a 2:1 military disadvantage to France and Russia as well as being more powerful than Austria. Naturally, France was expected to oppose such a move: "It was . . . clear that any breach of the Main line [which would establish a German union] would be bitterly opposed by the French." Fortunately, however, an attempt at unification would have the support of Europe's flanking powers. As David Williamson observes,

26. Harry Hearder, *Italy: A Short History* (Cambridge: Cambridge University Press, 1990), 186, 189–90; Smith, *Cavour*, 178; Smith, *Making*, 282; and Ziblatt, *Structuring*, 92.

27. Smith, *Cavour*, 116.

28. Derek Beales, *The Risorgimento and the Unification of Italy* (New York: Longman, 1981), 88.

29. Ziblatt, *Structuring*, 79, 80.

30. For the data used to generate the military power ratios in this paragraph and the next, see Correlates of War, National.

"Both Britain and Russia were to welcome German unification as a potential check on France, and each regarded Germany as a possible ally against the other."[31]

The Prussians drew the same lessons from their situation as the west Europeans did from a similar one eight decades later: only a centralized coalition of German states would have the wherewithal to balance effectively against France. "From history," asserts Edgar Feuchtwanger, "these men drew the lesson that Germany required a strong cohesive state." This is also how John Breuilly interprets Prussian thinking. Chancellor Otto von Bismarck understood that the various German states could only compete with their neighbors if they established a "modern state," which is to say a "territorial unity in which sovereignty was asserted by specialised political institutions."[32]

Although it took them longer to embrace it, the other German states also recognized this logic. They were initially reluctant to centralize because they knew that the resulting union would be dominated by Prussia, and they would lose much of their sovereignty. But balance of power considerations ultimately prevailed. Specifically, they realized they were so weak that they could not survive unless they joined the Second Reich.[33] In doing so, they surrendered their military and economic sovereignty, but as Dennis Showalter reminds us, "states needing to be rescued from emergencies by their allies have their claims to autonomy correspondingly diminished."[34]

The German constitution was clearly a product of these power considerations. Its "basic purpose," argues Gordon Craig, "was to create the institutions for a national state that would be able to compete effectively with the most powerful of its neighbours." To that end, it provided for military and economic centralization. Because it was more powerful than the others, Prussia controlled this new centralized coalition. The king of Prussia was also emperor of Germany, the Prussian chancellor was the prime minister and foreign minister, and because Prussia had seventeen of the fifty-eight votes in the Federal Council, it could effectively block all constitutional amendments that it opposed. This is not to say that the smaller German states got nothing in return for joining the Reich. Bavaria and Württemberg were granted some independence in military affairs, and all of them retained control over matters such as education, health services, and the police.[35]

31. David G. Williamson, *Bismarck and Germany, 1862–1890*, 2nd ed. (London: Longman, 1998), 14, 32.

32. Edgar J. Feuchtwanger, *Prussia, Myth and Reality: The Role of Prussia in German History* (Chicago: Henry Regnery, 1970), 170; and John Breuilly, *The Formation of the First German Nation-State, 1800–1871* (New York: Palgrave Macmillan, 1996), 105.

33. Williamson, *Bismarck*, 41.

34. Dennis Showalter, *The Wars of German Unification* (London: Hodder Education, 2004), 9–10.

35. Gordon A. Craig, *Germany, 1866–1945* (Oxford: Oxford University Press, 1978), 39.

In conclusion, my theory appears to travel fairly well (see figure 2). Specifically, there is evidence for the following claims. First, states confronting a common opponent usually cooperate militarily and economically. Second, if their rival does not have an overwhelming power advantage, their cooperation is decentralized—they form alliances and trade pacts. Third, if their rival does have an overwhelming power advantage and they have the means and opportunity to balance against it effectively, they engage in centralized cooperation. On the other hand, if they do not have either the means or the opportunity in these situations, they eschew cooperation altogether. Finally, having chosen centralized cooperation, states unify if one of them has the capability to seize control of their coalition, and they integrate if none of them has an appreciable power advantage over its partners.

		Competitor		
		Superior	Overwhelming (Coalition viable)	Overwhelming (Not viable)
Within-coalition balance of power	Symmetric	Alliances and trade pacts	United States EC	No coalition building
	Asymmetric		Italy Germany	

Figure 2. Actual responses to powerful competitors

Interest Groups and Interdependence

Moravcsik's core claim is that states integrate when they are highly economically interdependent. It was elevated levels of interdependence that pushed domestic producer groups in France and Germany to demand integration and their respective governments to provide it. "If the motivations of postwar European leaders were distinctive," he argues in explaining why the Europeans have been alone in opting for integration, "it was because their countries were touched more intensely by economic trends common to all advanced industrial democracies, most notably the rapidly increasing potential for industrial trade." Later he "locates the source of European integration in the explosion of world trade after World War II."[36] And elsewhere he argues that the "most important motivation for integra-

---

36. Moravcsik, *Choice*, 5, 473.

tion was economic. The West European economies were then . . . extremely interdependent."[37]

Moravcsik uses exports as a percentage of GNP, or "export dependence," as a proxy for interdependence. All else being equal, the more export dependent a state is on its partners, the more interdependent it is with them, and the more likely it is to opt for integration. In fact, he makes exactly this argument in explaining why the Europeans integrated in the 1950s, but the states of North America and East Asia did not. The "EC members" were "by far the most export-dependent (as a percentage of GNP)." Then, turning his attention to the largest economies in each region, he claims that "Germany was between three and six times more dependent on its EC partners than the United States and Japan were on their regional partners."[38]

In order to test the argument, then, I must first determine interdependence levels in western Europe between 1950 and 1954. I focus on the five years prior to the beginning of the negotiations that ultimately led to the Rome Treaties because Moravcsik is explicit that high levels of interdependence precede integration. The trade boom began "very early in the postwar period, *before* significant trade liberalization had occurred." The expansion of trade *"predated* the EC and induced policy changes."[39] Like Moravcsik, I measure the export dependence of the largest economies in the region—West Germany and France—as well as coming up with an aggregate regional figure by summing the exports of all six founding members of the EC and dividing this figure by their combined GNP. My analysis yields the following interdependence figures for Europe in the early 1950s: West German exports to the other five were equivalent to between 3 and 4 percent of GNP; French exports to the other five were equivalent to approximately 2 percent of GNP; and, finally, regional interdependence was of the order of almost 4 percent (see table 2).

These benchmark figures allow for clear forecasts about what we should observe in other regions and time periods. The west Europeans did not integrate their economies before World War II. Thus, if Moravcsik is correct, they must have experienced comparatively low levels of interdependence before 1945, and they should certainly have been less dependent on one another for exports than they were between 1950 and 1954. Similarly, Moravcsik argues that there have been no examples of economic integration in other regions of the world since World War II. The EC is a "unique" set of institutions.[40] Therefore, it follows that groups of states in these regions should have been less interdependent than the Six were in the early 1950s.

37. Andrew Moravcsik, "European Integration: Looking Ahead," in *Great Decisions 2008*, ed. Karen Rohan (New York: Foreign Policy Association, 2008), 18.
38. Moravcsik, *Choice*, 494–95.
39. Ibid, 3, 40. Emphasis added.
40. Ibid., 1.

TABLE 2
Regional Interdependence

Western Europe	1950	1951	1952	1953	1954	Average
Germany	3	4	4	4	4	3.6
France	2	2	2	2	2	1.8
Region	4	4	3	4	4	3.7
Western Europe	1909	1910	1911	1912	1913	Average
Germany	3	4	4	4	5	4.0
France	5	5	5	5	5	4.9
Region	8	8	8	8	8	8.0
Western Europe	1926	1927	1928	1929	1930	Average
Germany	4	3	3	4	5	4.0
France	6	6	5	4	4	5.0
Region	5	5	5	5	5	5.2
Central America	2000	2001	2002	2003	2004	Average
Guatemala	5	6	6	6	6	5.7
Costa Rica	4	4	4	6	6	4.9
Region	3	4	4	4	4	3.7
Southeast Asia	1993	1994	1995	1996	1997	Average
Indonesia	3	3	3	3	4	3.3
Thailand	5	6	6	6	7	6.0
Region	9	11	12	11	12	11.0

Sources: Marc Flandreau and Frédéric Zumer, *The Making of Global Finance, 1880–1913* (Paris: OECD, 2004); Susan B. Carter, et al., *Historical Statistics of the United States: Earliest Times to the Present*, vol. 5, *Governance and International Relations* (Cambridge: Cambridge University Press, 2006); Brian R. Mitchell, *International Historical Statistics: Europe, 1750–1993*, 4th ed. (London: Macmillan, 1998); *Annuario statistico italiano* (Rome: Tipografia Elzeviriana, 1878–); *Annuaire statistique de la France* (Paris: Statistique général, 1878–); International Monetary Fund, *Direction of Trade Statistics* (Washington, D.C.: IMF, 1981–); and World Bank, World Development Indicators, http://worldbank.org/.
Note: In order to generate each state's interdependence (export-dependence) figures, I summed its exports to the other states in its trade area and divided this figure by its GDP. For each trade area, I list the two states with the largest economies. I generated interdependence figures for each region by summing intra-area exports and dividing this figure by the area's combined GDP. Western Europe refers to the Six; Central America refers to the eight members of CACM; and Southeast Asia refers to the five members of ASEAN. Figures report relevant state or trade area exports as a percentage of GDP.

In stark contrast to these predictions, the six founding members of the EC were more, not less, interdependent in the first half of the twentieth century than they were in the 1950s. Germany was more export dependent on the other five in 1909–13 and in 1926–30 than it was between 1950 and 1954. The difference should not be overstated—its exports in all three periods equaled approximately 4 percent of its GNP—but it would be difficult to claim that Germany's situation after the war was historically unprecedented. Meanwhile, France was between two and three times more export dependent in the earlier periods than it was in the early 1950s. Finally, regional interdependence was considerably higher before World War II than after it. Early postwar Europe does not appear to have exhibited unusually high levels of interdependence. Indeed, Moravcsik appears to recognize this, noting that it was only in 1988 that "the level of trade in manufactured goods . . . had almost returned to its historic high prior to World War I."[41]

An analysis of the non-European world after World War II casts further doubt on the economic interest argument. Take Southeast Asia, a region Moravcsik considers explicitly. The five members of ASEAN were highly interdependent by his standards between 1993 and 1997, but they did not integrate. Indonesia, which had the largest economy in the group, was almost as export dependent on its four partners as Germany was on its five partners in the early 1950s. Thailand—the second largest economy—was three times more export dependent on its four partners than France was on its five partners in the early 1950s. As a whole, the group was approximately three times more interdependent than Europe between 1950 and 1954. Yet the signatories chose not to surrender their sovereignty in authoritative international institutions.

Other regional comparisons yield similar results. The eight members of CACM were considerably more dependent on one another for export markets between 2000 and 2004 than the Six were in the early 1950s. Guatemala, which had the largest economy in the group, exported goods whose value was equivalent to almost 6 percent of its GNP to the other seven members of the group. The figure for Costa Rica was almost 5 percent. As a whole, the group was as interdependent as the Six were between 1950 and 1954. But the CACM members chose to cooperate rather than integrate.

In sum, there are good reasons to doubt the economic interest argument. It does not seem to be the case that the Six were unusually dependent on one another for export markets in the early 1950s. Therefore, it is hard to argue that economic integration is the product of high levels of interdependence. If it is, there should be many more "Europes."

Ideational Entrepreneurship

The ideational entrepreneurship argument does not travel beyond postwar Europe for two reasons. First, the different ideas that French and German elites embraced after the war were the product of unique historical events, namely the Depression, World War II, and the onset of the cold war. It was a combination of this particular economic crisis, this particular war, and this particular global struggle that prompted decision makers to reconsider "the appropriate 'constitutive rules' linking the . . . nation-state itself and its European environment." The Depression and the Second World War unsettled the existing consensus, which nonetheless prevailed until 1947 when the prosecution of the cold war made it difficult to continue with

41. Ibid., 41.

traditional policies. At that point, key policymakers reconsidered their positions and filed into opposing traditional, confederal, and community camps. This argument cannot be generalized, and Parsons does not try to do so. There is no attempt to describe systematically the kinds of events likely to trigger debates about legitimate forms of political organization and those that are not. Thus, it is impossible to develop a list of other epochal moments and determine whether or not they led to a major reevaluation of existing political structures. It seems that we can only know whether an event was epochal after the fact. If it prompted a reconsideration of traditional ideas, then it was; if it did not, then it was not.[42]

The second reason that the ideational account cannot be generalized beyond the EC case is that community ideas prevailed by accident. Parsons does not argue that there was something intrinsic to the community model that caused it to win out in the 1950s. It was not more logical, better presented, more appropriate to the situation, or inherently more appealing than the alternatives. Instead, community ideas affected policy when leaders who held them happened to come to power for reasons unrelated to their views on Europe. Parsons is clear on this point: "Major steps toward today's EU all resulted when pro-community leaders *achieved power on other issues* and then stepped beyond the demands of their allies and supporters with European initiatives." We would still be able to test the theory in other cases if Parsons had a theory about why certain leaders come to power, but he does not. Indeed, the role of contingency is so powerful that the EC would look quite different today "given a heart attack or two and some plausible coalitional reshuffling."[43]

Because he recognizes that his argument does not travel, Parsons claims "we must revise the prevailing standards for social science" that privilege "general theorizing above all." He rejects the common view that "undocumented generality" is preferable to empirically corroborated but contingent accounts like his own. Instead, what matters is "documentation" in the form of "process-tracing evidence . . . [and] correlation of explanatory logics and outcomes." This being the case, he argues, "documented particularity deserves the same respect . . . [as] documented generality." The "ultimate criterion" for determining a theory's value ought to be its "ability to explain the widest range of potential variation in important outcomes, whether that variation occurs for general or particular reasons."[44]

Europe's Future

The theory presented in this book yields several predictions about Europe's future. Specifically, it suggests answers to the following questions:

42. Parsons, *Certain*, 23.
43. Ibid., 25, 235. Emphasis added.
44. Ibid., 28, 30.

What are the chances that the Europeans will establish a "United States of Europe"? How likely are they to create an integrated military? And what does the future hold for the single market and the euro?

The key to understanding the EC's future is the collapse of the Soviet Union in 1991, which fundamentally altered the European power structure. In 1984, the USSR was an overwhelming adversary, as it had been throughout the cold war. It held a greater than 14:1 military advantage and 3:1 economic advantage over both France and Germany. A decade later, as its last troops were being removed from the former East Germany, Russia was barely the most powerful state on the continent. Although it still held more than a 3:1 military advantage over France and a reunified Germany, it was economically weaker than both of them.[45]

The main consequence of this shift in the balance of power is that the Europeans no longer have a compelling geostrategic reason either to pursue further integration or to preserve their existing community. During the cold war, the Soviet threat provided a powerful incentive to integrate, and they responded by constructing the EC. Its demise has removed that incentive. The Europeans are therefore unlikely to embark on political or military integration and further economic integration is improbable. Indeed, the economic community could well unravel over time to the point where it will bear little resemblance to its current form.

There is no chance that Europe's new power architecture will fuel political integration. Because it involves surrendering sovereignty, states will only consider political integration if they are faced with an overwhelming adversary that threatens their survival. In the early 1950s, the scale and proximity of the Soviet threat led the Six to countenance creating the European Political Community, which would have sat above the heavy-industry and defense communities and, some hoped, lay the foundation for a viable European state.[46] Today, the EC faces no major threats, and certainly none as dangerous as the Soviet Union during the cold war. Its members are unlikely to even consider political integration, let alone pursue it.

Events since 1991 support this perspective: political integration has not even made it onto the agenda over the past two decades. This might seem like a controversial claim. After all, Charles Kupchan believes that the Europeans are "building a political union," while Jeremy Rifkin suggests that those skeptical of the Europeans' ability to create a "United States of Europe" will likely be "proved wrong." A few years ago, European Commission president Romano Prodi declared that the single currency was "just an antipasto," a purely "political step . . . beyond which there will be others."

---

45. I use GDP instead of steel production and energy consumption here as an indicator of economic power. For the argument that this is the appropriate measure of economic power after 1970, see Mearsheimer, *Tragedy*, 60–67, and for the data, see *The Military Balance* (London: Institute for Strategic Studies, 1963–).

46. On the European Political Community, see Edward Fursdon, *The European Defence Community: A History* (New York: St. Martin's, 1980), 156, 212–17.

Yet the EC has made no move toward political integration in the interim. Member states still retain absolute authority over key issues that would fall under Community control if they were to engage in political integration, especially defense, foreign policy, and taxes, but also education, health, pensions, and immigration.[47] Tony Judt puts the point well: "The European Union . . . is not a state. It does not raise taxes and it has no capacity for making war."[48]

Some claim that the European Constitution, which was signed by the twenty-five EC member states in Rome in 2004, contradicts my view. But they are wrong. For one thing, the constitution never came into effect because the French and the Dutch refused to ratify it. Moreover, a close reading reveals that it was not an attempt at political integration, despite all of the lofty rhetoric to the contrary. In fact, there is substantial agreement on this point. According to international legal scholar Joseph Weiler, the biggest "deception was to pretend that the legal mongrel . . . was a Constitution," when it was merely a reform treaty that included "a far from radical amendment of the institutional architecture and decision-making processes . . . non-radical nods towards further democratization . . . and some sensible cleaning up of language." Judt concurs: "After two years of deliberations, the Convention emitted something more than a draft but decidedly less than a constitution. Shorn of its portentous . . . preamble . . . [the] document offered little by the way of classic constitutional proposals." Moravcsik agreed at the time, describing it as "a conservative text containing incremental improvements."[49]

A similar verdict applies to the Treaty of Lisbon that was designed to replace the rejected constitution. Ratified in 2009, it looked a lot like its predecessor and contained nothing that could be called a serious move toward political integration. Indeed, most commentators agree that the "official self-congratulation" that accompanied its ratification masked the reality that it was little more than a "slimmed down" constitution. As one scholar put it, what remained after a series of "cosmetic alterations" was "probably the least significant treaty the EU has ever signed."[50] Not even its one real institutional innovation—the position of EU president—is evidence that

47. Charles Kupchan, "The Travails of Union: The American Experience and Its Implications for Europe," *Survival* 46, no. 4 (2004–05): 109; Jeremy Rifkin, *The European Dream: How Europe's Vision of the Future Is Quietly Eclipsing the American Dream* (New York: Tarcher, 2005), 84; and Christopher Booker and Richard North, *The Great Deception: Can the European Union Survive?* (London: Continuum, 2005), 597.

48. Tony Judt, *Postwar: A History of Europe since 1945* (New York: Penguin, 2005), 797.

49. Joseph H. H. Weiler, "Editorial: The Irish No and the Lisbon Treaty," *European Journal of International Law* 19, no. 4 (2008): 650–51; Judt, *Postwar*, 729; and Andrew Moravcsik, "A Too Perfect Union? Why Europe Said 'No'," *Current History* 104, no. 685 (2005): 356.

50. Andrew Glencross, "The Grand Illusion Continues: What the Lisbon Treaty Means for the European Union and Its Global Role," February 5, 2010, http://www.fpri.org/enotes/201002.glencross.grandillusion.html; Perry Anderson, *The New Old*

political integration is in the offing. "The job," notes the *Economist*, "is not 'President of Europe,' as some call it, but president of the European Council, the bit of the EU controlled by national governments."[51]

In sum, there has been no meaningful political integration in Europe over the past two decades. At best, the EC has gained some symbolic powers but nothing more. Given that there is no threat on the horizon that comes close to resembling the Soviet Union during the cold war, this is likely to remain the case.

What about military integration? The current distribution of power also means that the Europeans will not establish a military community in the foreseeable future. States go down this road only when faced with an overwhelmingly powerful adversary. It was fear of Soviet power that drove the Six to flirt with the idea of creating an integrated defense community in the early 1950s. But even then they backed away from the EDC project. Today, not only is there no Soviet Union; there is no serious military threat to Europe. Thus, it follows that the Europeans are even less likely to build an integrated European army.

At first glance, the events of the past two decades might appear to invalidate this prediction. Following the U.S. invasion of Iraq, the Europeans talked openly about "a political and military counterweight to the US," and French president Jacques Chirac went so far as to assert that Europe wanted to live in a "multipolar world." Some observers have taken such statements seriously and argued that a European military community may be just around the corner. A decade ago, Samuel Huntington suggested that a "truly multipolar" world in which Europe would be one of the great powers was a mere ten to twenty years away. Meanwhile, Jeffrey Cimbalo viewed the 2004 constitutional treaty as a prelude to the creation of a "powerful federal national security apparatus." Indeed, American defense planners were sufficiently worried about developments in Europe to announce their commitment to "prevent[ing] the creation of . . . a separate 'EU' army."[52]

Upon closer inspection, however, there is scant evidence that the Europeans either intend to, or have taken concrete measures to, establish a viable defense community. To be sure, they have cooperated with one another, but cooperation does not equal integration. The creation of a single military entity that could act as another great power in the world has not been up

World (Cambridge: Verso, 2009), 59; and Simon Hix, *What's Wrong with the European Union and How to Fix It* (Cambridge: Polity, 2008), 183.

51. "Unwelcome, President Blair," *Economist*, August 1, 2009.

52. Wolfgang Münchau, "Time to Abandon the 'Core Europe' Fantasy," *Financial Times*, November 3, 2003; "Europe Should Bolster Powers in Face of US: Chirac," *Agence France Presse*, November 5, 2004; Samuel P. Huntington, "The Lonely Superpower," *Foreign Affairs* 78, no. 2 (1999): 37; Jeffrey Cimbalo, "Saving NATO From Europe," *Foreign Affairs* 83, no. 6 (2004): 113; and Seth G. Jones, *The Rise of European Security Cooperation* (Cambridge: Cambridge University Press, 2007), 5.

for serious discussion. The 1992 Maastricht Treaty, which stipulated that a common foreign and security policy (CFSP) was one of the three pillars of the European Union, merely urged the members to define "common positions" and implement "joint actions" if and when they had shared interests. Maastricht was a recipe for intergovernmental cooperation, not supranational integration. The same is true of the European security and defense policy (ESDP) that was launched by Britain and France at St. Malo in 1998 with the intention of giving Europe "the capacity for autonomous action, backed up by credible military forces." The rapid reaction force (RRF) that it created is not a standing force, but rather a pool of national units, which the EC can draw on only if member states unanimously agree to use force. Moreover, the intergovernmental European Council sits above the political-military structure that authorizes and oversees operations conducted by the RRF. Thus, ultimate authority rests not with the EC, but with the member states—all of whom have a veto. Even the creation of a high representative for foreign affairs and security policy, known as Europe's "foreign minister," has not altered the situation in any meaningful way. Foreign policy and defense decisions are still subject to unanimity, which means that the member states are in charge.[53]

Many foreign policy and defense experts agree that there has been no meaningful military integration in Europe since the cold war ended. Robert Art notes that "there is as yet no single entity called Europe that speaks with one voice on foreign, security, and defense matters." In a careful analysis of military developments in Europe since the cold war, Seth Jones finds abundant evidence of cooperation, but admits that "major foreign policy and defense decisions are still made in European capitals. The European Union is not on the verge of becoming a supranational state, nor is a European army imminent." Similarly, John McCormick is convinced that Europe is unlikely to "match the United States in military power," not because it does not have the assets to do so, but because "it lacks a common security policy and a unified command and control structure."[54] None of this is to deny that the European states cooperate with each other in military affairs, but they are no closer today to having an integrated military than they were in 1991. Nor is there good reason to believe they will move in that direction anytime soon. If anything, the current balance of power predicts that the opposite will happen.

What about Europe's economic community? It is likely to unravel slowly over time to the point where it becomes a shadow of its former self. As we

53. Glencross, "Grand"; Jones, *Rise*, 81–85, 197–202; "The Ins and Outs," *Economist*, March 17, 2007; and Andrew Moravcsik, "Don't Know? Vote No!" *Prospect*, June 26, 2008.

54. Robert J. Art, "Europe Hedges Its Security Bets," in *Balance of Power: Theory and Practice in the 21st Century*, ed. T. V. Paul, James J. Wirtz, and Michael Fortmann (Stanford: Stanford University Press, 2004): 183; Jones, *Rise*, 5; and John McCormick, *The European Superpower* (New York: Palgrave, 2007), 81.

have seen, the EC is a product of the cold war: it was the fear that they might have to balance against the Soviet Union without American help that impelled the Europeans to integrate. In the post–cold war world, however, there is no compelling geostrategic reason to maintain the Community. This is not to say that it will unravel completely in the next few years or that the Europeans will eventually jettison every one of its features. Member states derive several nonsecurity benefits from the Community and large institutions do not willingly or quickly go out of business. NATO, for example, has survived by transforming itself from an alliance designed to contain the Soviet Union into a vehicle for maintaining American influence in Europe.[55] Still, the collapse of the Soviet Union has deprived the EC of its fundamental purpose. As a result, narrow national self-interest is likely to trump commitment to the Community and condemn it to a slow demise. Like NATO, this does not necessarily mean that the EC will cease to exist, but also like the Atlantic alliance, the Community will probably look quite different in the future, especially regarding the important matters of trade and money. The most plausible scenario, in fact, is that it will eventually be a community in name only.

The events of the 1990s—especially the Maastricht Treaty and the introduction of the euro—might appear to contradict my economic prediction. One might argue that, far from coming apart, the EC took a giant leap forward in the first post–cold war decade. A closer look at the situation, however, reveals that this conclusion would be wrong. For starters, the USSR did not break apart until 1991 and Russian forces did not fully withdraw from Germany until 1994. Thus, the change in the balance of power brought on by the end of the cold war did not manifest itself clearly or immediately. Moreover, structural changes rarely have an immediate impact on state behavior. Given that it took almost fifteen years for the Community to form at a time when the Europeans feared for their survival, we should expect it to take even longer to unravel since what is at stake now is the relatively less important issue of reclaiming economic sovereignty. Finally, it is important to bear in mind that the negotiations that led to Maastricht and the euro began in the 1980s.[56] This being the case, the appropriate question is not why Europe embarked on deeper integration in the 1990s, but why it maintained the momentum generated before then. Why did Europe keep moving toward monetary union despite the end of the cold war?

The answer is that progress toward economic integration continued in the 1990s because of prosperous economic conditions. With their economies humming along during that first decade after the cold war, the Europeans had no incentive to kill the goose that appeared to be laying golden eggs. Between 1987 and 1991, while the Maastricht Treaty was being

55. Kenneth N. Waltz, "Structural Realism after the Cold War," *International Security* 25, no. 1 (2000): 19–21.

56. Moravcsik, *Choice*, 381, 386.

negotiated, Germany's economy grew at 4 percent per year while France's grew at 3 percent per year.[57] By comparison, the American economy grew at 2.5 percent annually. European leaders were enthusiastic about the euro, because they believed that it would perfect the single market and boost intra-European trade, making everyone even wealthier. Although conditions worsened somewhat in the middle of the decade, they improved markedly between 1997 and 2000, which was just when the Europeans were scheduled to lock their currencies and introduce the euro. During this period, France's economy grew by more than 3 percent per year and German growth picked up from less than 2 percent in 1997 to more than 3 percent in 2000, which was its best year since 1991. Thus, although economic motivations are not a fundamental cause of integration, prosperity can sustain it, at least in the short term.

Since the turn of the millennium it has become clear that the EC is no longer delivering prosperity. Consider that between 2001 and 2007, France's economy grew at less than 2 percent annually while Germany fared even worse with annual growth hovering around 1 percent. Both countries experienced 10 percent unemployment for most of this period, compared to 5 percent in the United States. On top of that, per capita growth slowed considerably and productivity growth halved between 1999 and 2008. Even its supporters acknowledge that the euro, which was supposed to boost Europe's economy, has had a "very small effect on the area's growth rate." And the so-called Lisbon Agenda "has singularly failed in its aim of making the EU 'the most dynamic . . . economy in the world, capable of sustainable economic growth with more and better jobs . . . by 2010'." And almost all analysts expect matters to get worse. According to one estimate, Europe's economy will be growing at 1 percent per year by midcentury—half the rate of the United States and China—largely because of a shrinking and rapidly aging population.[58]

As soon as conditions started to worsen after 2000, France and Germany began breaking EC rules. Beginning in 2001, both states repeatedly violated the Community's competition policy, which is designed to promote a single European market by prohibiting states from aiding their own industries. This is no small matter as this policy is "at the core of the Rome treaty." In fact, the French government's bailouts and other assistance to companies such as Groupe Bull, Alstom, and Aventis were so egregious that a special French parliamentary committee felt compelled to note France's "refusal to abide by community rules." Economic experts agreed, noting France's willingness "to bend EU rules" and engage in "protectionism." But

---

57. For the data on economic growth and unemployment in this paragraph and the next, see World Bank, *World Development Indicators*, http://www.worldbank.org/.

58. Anderson, *New*, 508; Andrea Boltho and Barry Eichengreen, "The Economic Impact of European Integration," *CEPR Discussion Paper* no. 6820 (2008): 38; Glencross, "Grand"; and "Europe's Population Implosion," *Economist*, July 19, 2003.

Germany was even worse than France; Berlin's bailouts of coal mines and provincial banks consistently made it the number one provider of state aid in Europe. Then, in 2006, France and Germany moved to protect their national oil and gas companies from foreign takeover. "It was," notes Walter Laqueur, "as if the Common Market no longer existed."[59]

The major players have also consistently broken the rules underpinning the single currency. In 1997, states that wanted to adopt the euro promised to run budget deficits of no more than 3 percent of GDP and to hold their public debt to no more than 60 percent of GDP. It was only if states abided by the terms of this "stability and growth pact," so the argument went, that they would be able to ensure the stability of the common currency. Despite the pact's purported importance and the fact that France and Germany had been primarily responsible for putting it into place, they violated the rules with impunity, running up deficits and accumulating debt well in excess of the agreed levels for every year between 2002 and 2005.[60] Then, rather than trying to fulfill their obligations, they forced their partners to change the terms of the pact. As John Gillingham notes, "If the survival of the EMU depends on the existence of sound and binding rules, it is in fact already dead—done in by the chronic violation of the growth and stability pact."[61]

The reemergence of economic nationalism became especially clear as the financial crisis took hold in 2008 and 2009. France and Germany led the way, feuding about how to address the emergency. French president Nicolas Sarkozy favored a large stimulus and called for the European Central Bank to take an active role in reviving lending across the euro zone. German chancellor Angela Merkel, in contrast, resisted an EC stimulus, criticized the ECB for reducing interest rates, and vetoed a common fund to bail out banks. At the same time, both France and Germany rushed to protect their own industries and workers, often at the expense of those elsewhere. Perry Anderson describes the situation well: "Each national government took its own steps to deal with the emergency, with ad hoc measures to bail out banks, feed auto industries or prop up the labour market." Former French president Valéry Giscard d'Estaing, a staunch supporter of the Community, was appalled, condemning this selfish and contentious

59. John Gillingham, *Design for a New Europe* (Cambridge: Cambridge University Press, 2006), 19; John Rossant, "The Pernicious Rise of Core Europe," *Business Week*, May 10, 2004; "Rescuing Alstom," *Economist*, September 27, 2003; Kim Willsher, "France in the Dock as Bad Boy of Europe, *Guardian*, May 31, 2004; Tobias Buck, "Decline in EU State Subsidies Grinds to a Halt," *Financial Times*, April 19, 2005; Carl Mortished, "EU States Renege on Promises to Reduce State Aid," *Times*, April 21, 2005; and Walter Laqueur, *The Last Days of Europe: Epitaph for an Old Continent* (New York: Thomas Dunne, 2007), 200.

60. For details of the breaches, see http://ec.europa.eu/economy_finance/publications/.

61. Gillingham, *Design*, 69.

behavior as "retrograde," and vainly urging governments to "see the European market as a whole" or risk putting the single market at risk.[62]

Not surprisingly, European publics have supported their governments' efforts to protect the home front at the expense of the larger Community. They have done so partly because of their dissatisfaction with the EC. According to polls conducted by the Commission, two thirds of German and French citizens polled between 1980 and 1991 thought their country's membership in the EC was a "good thing." Between 1992 and 2004, only half felt this way, and in some years the figure fell to one third.[63] Voters have repeatedly registered their discontent with the Community, voting against governments "committed to ratifying the proposed constitution" in the 2004 elections for the European Parliament (EP) and, in the French and Dutch cases, rejecting the constitution itself. In 2009, turnout for the EP elections was barely 40 percent in France and Germany, 20 to 30 percentage points lower than in the national elections that immediately preceded them.[64]

But the public's opposition to the EC is not based solely on its failure to deliver prosperity. Europeans have also backed their governments because many of them have become more nationalistic since 1991. They invariably think in terms of what is good for their country rather than for Europe as a whole. When asked, shortly after the cold war ended, how often they thought of themselves not only in national terms but also as Europeans, 47 percent of French respondents and 59 percent of German respondents answered "never." According to a different poll conducted in 2004, almost 90 percent of French respondents saw themselves as French "only" or primarily French. The figure for German respondents was the same. In short, should governments want to roll back the EC, they are unlikely to meet strong resistance from their publics.

Given that member states are now willing to put national interests ahead of those of the Community, the slow fraying of the EC, which has been evident for almost a decade, will probably continue. There is actually a clear consensus among experts that the single market is not delivering prosperity in its current form and that something needs to be done to fix it. Not surprisingly, many suggest that further integration is the best solution. Among other things, they argue that the member states need to liberalize and integrate their services sector, which accounts for about two thirds of the region's GDP. The same applies to the energy sector, and an internal market for financial services needs to be created. The European Commission

62. Charlemagne, "Those Selfish Germans," *Economist*, May 2, 2009; Anderson, *New*, 507; and Steven Erlanger, "Economy Shows Cracks in European Union," *New York Times*, June 9, 2009.

63. All the poll numbers in this paragraph are from the Eurobarometer, Interactive Search System, http://ec.europa.eu/public_opinion/cf/subquestion_en.cfm.

64. Gillingham, *Design*, 43; and "Swing Low, Swing Right," *Economist*, June 13, 2009.

warns that, above all, states must "resist protectionist temptations and reject measures that promote national interests at the expense of the single European market."[65]

In the current environment, however, the single market is more likely to fracture than consolidate. Political scientist Simon Hix notes that any initiatives to push the integration process forward are liable to create winners and losers, and those who expect to lose out will doubtless oppose them.[66] France and Germany have already killed the Services Directive, which aimed to establish a single market in services but "threatened entrenched interests across the board."[67] What is more probable, then, is a move—fueled by nationalism and dissatisfaction with the Community's performance—to scale back existing institutions. After all, there is good evidence that a simpler setup, one that involves fewer rules and impinges less on state sovereignty, may well yield similar economic results, and perhaps better ones.[68] As Anderson observes, the "standard objectives of inter-capitalist state cooperation" can be achieved with "free trade agreements of a conventional kind, [and] without creation of any complex of supranational institutions or derogations of national sovereignty."[69] The Europeans may eventually come to the same conclusion, at which point the EC will look a lot more like a regular free trade area and a lot less like it does now.

The single currency, whose impact even the European Commission admits is an "open question," could encounter a similar fate.[70] As many predicted, the Europeans have been feeling the strain of membership since the euro's inception in 1999.[71] Its one-size-fits-all monetary policy has at various times proved too tight for some and too loose for others. Not surprisingly, fiscal policy has been another source of friction, pitting members that want to run greater deficits against proponents of tighter fiscal discipline. More recently, and again as predicted, it has become clear that given the rules constraining monetary and fiscal autonomy, member states that get into trouble can only be rescued by transfers from their more fortunate partners who may not want to bail them out. In other words, there are several good monetary, fiscal, and redistributive reasons for member states to at least consider abandoning the euro.

For many economists, these very real problems can only be mitigated through political integration. If Europe becomes a single state rather than a

65. Hix, *What's*, 31; Gillingham, *Design*, 70; and Tony Barber, "Europe Expected to Suffer Long-Term Loss of Potential Economic Output," *Financial Times*, July 3, 2009.

66. Hix, *What's*, 48.

67. "Not at Your Service," *Economist*, March 12, 2005; and Gillingham, *Design*, 23.

68. Gillingham, *Design*, 76, 225–27.

69. Anderson, *New*, 86.

70. Ambrose Evans-Pritchard, "EU Economists Look in Vain for Benefits of Euro," *Daily Telegraph*, October 9, 2004.

71. See, for example, Josef Joffe, "The Euro: The Engine That Couldn't," *New York Review of Books* 44, no. 19 (1997): 26–31.

collection of separate states with a single currency, these troubles will simply not arise. Paul de Grauwe, an adviser to European Commission president José Manuel Barroso, makes the point clearly: "Without a political union, in the long run the euro zone cannot last." Nobel Prize–winning economist Paul Krugman agrees, arguing that "to make the euro work, Europe needs to move much further toward political union, so that European nations start to function more like American states." As Wolfgang Münchau observes, "Historical experience has shown that all large-country monetary unions that did not turn into political unions eventually collapsed."[72]

The collapse of the euro zone is a more likely outcome than political integration. For one thing, there is no good economic reason to keep it together. Measured in terms of economic growth, Europe now has one of the worst performing economies in the world. Moreover, nationalism, which remains the most powerful political ideology in the world, is alive and well in all the member states. As Anatole Kaletsky notes, there is a "refusal [on the part] of national politicians (and presumably their voters) to treat economic policy on a continental scale, instead of viewing it in a narrowly national perspective." Much to the dismay of euro enthusiasts, the French and German governments have repeatedly attacked the ECB for adopting monetary policies they oppose and have chosen to eviscerate the original stability pact rather than incur the costs of compliance. Meanwhile, as other states have run into trouble, the Germans have made it abundantly clear that they are "tired of supporting countries that do not, to their mind, try hard enough." All of this selfish behavior has taken place amid a growing "sense that decisions were being taken 'there' with unfavorable consequences for us 'here' and over which 'we' had no say: a prejudice fuelled by irresponsible mainstream politicians but fanned by nationalist demagogues."[73]

It is not hard to imagine that continued economic woes could turn these frequent but relatively low intensity disputes into outright threats and crises. At that point, it would not be a great surprise if Germany abandoned the euro and returned to the deutschmark. "A German exit from the euro zone, in a huff," note economists Simon Johnson and Peter Boone, "cannot be ruled out." Only a few years ago, bankers even suggested that Italy "might benefit" from going back to the lira despite claims that weak economies cannot risk leaving the euro. This would be costly for any country, but not prohibitively so. Member states continue to have their own central banks

72. Landon Thomas Jr., "Is Debt Trashing the Euro? *New York Times*, February 7, 2010; Paul Krugman, "The Making of a Euromess," *New York Times*, February 15, 2010; and Wolfgang Münchau, "Is the Euro Forever?" *Financial Times*, June 8, 2005.

73. Anatole Kaletsky, "Stability Pact's Ghost Will Return to Haunt EU," and "Stability Pact Reform Stirs New Misgivings," *Times*, July 20 and September 7, 2004; Mark Landler, "Rate Rise Opposed in Europe," *New York Times*, November 25, 2005; Simon Johnson and Peter Boone, "The Greek Tragedy That Changed Europe," *Wall Street Journal*, February 13, 2010; and Judt, *Postwar*, 731.

that are responsible for issuing their own euro notes and coins and which hold most of their foreign reserves. Nothing would have to be built from scratch. Moreover, complete abandonment of the euro is not the only option. As Gillingham points out, it would not be difficult for the euro to continue circulating alongside reissued national currencies.[74]

In sum, the European Community's best days are probably behind it. This is not to say that the European states will stop cooperating with each other. Indeed, there are plenty of reasons for them to continue working together. But the current distribution of power in Europe means that it is unlikely that the EC will continue to survive in its current form. As time passes, it is likely to look more like other international institutions and less like the exceptional case it seemed to be for so long.

---

74. Simon Johnson and Peter Boone, "The Greek Tragedy that Changed Europe," *Wall Street Journal*, February 13, 2010; Ambrose Evans-Pritchard, "Eurozone May Have a Reverse Gear," and "Ditching Euro Could 'Benefit Italy'," *Daily Telegraph*, February 7, 2004 and July 12, 2005; and Gillingham, *Design*, 67, 69.

Index

Note: Italic page numbers refer to figures and tables.